In Years to Come

Joyce A. Ford

Published by:
Starmartin Publishing, LLC
PO Box 49266
Denver, CO 80249
www.starmartinpublishing.com

Ford, Joyce A.
In Years to Come/ Joyce A. Ford – 1st Ed.

Library of Congress Control Number: 2006910787

ISBN: 0-9786594-0-6

First American Edition: December 2006

A letter from Joyce...

I've heard the saying that everyone has a book in them. I knew that I definitely had a book inside of me when I began writing my memoirs at age sixteen. It has taken thirty-five years for me to complete this book. There were times when I felt that I couldn't write another word because of memories that I had to experience all over again.

It is my desire that the readers of this book will find inspiration in my story rather than sorrow or pity. Please understand that I define myself as a survivor and not a victim. I achieve victory everyday because I have overcome many adversities that occurred in my life. I am telling my story to give hope to others who may be or have been in similar situations.

According to the statistics I should be on drugs, in jail, or at least living an unstable life. I am proud to say that I have beaten the odds. I did not allow uncontrolled circumstances to dictate my life.

I am writing a true and honest account of my life story to the best of my knowledge and I make no apologies to anyone who may be offended by the truth.

This book is dedicated to my brothers:
Roy jr., Henry, Khalid, (Robert) Stephen, Frank, Joe,
and Ralph.
To my sister, Sara.
To my four sons:
Doniel, Jamal, Jamaine and Marcus.
And In loving memory of:
Roy Ford Sr.
Maryann Ford
Ben Ford Sr.
Sarah Ford
Jerry Ford
Louis (Ford)Bonner
Michael Ford

ACKNOWLEDGMENTS

There were several times when I had to fall on my knees to get through another chapter in this book. I want to thank my higher power for pulling me through. Thank you, God.

I thank my brothers and my sister for their support and encouragement.

I thank my children for believing in their mother and encouraging me to finish this book.

I am grateful to my dear friend, Nancy Mabry. She didn't give me a break with her constant reminders that I had a book to complete. She also served as a proofreader and critic

I thank my editor, Holly Armstrong, who took on the tedious task of editing this book. Thank- you for your patience and the great job you did.

I thank Kelly for a great cover design.

And last but not least I thank family and friends who were instrumental in helping me complete this book. Thanks to those of you who read my sample chapters and supplied me with feedback.

Introduction

Maryann

Maryann Ford was admitted into the County Hospital on a cold dreary afternoon shortly after the New Year in 1959.

"This will be a better year," she whispered to her best friend, Mrs. Simms, who sat nearby watching her being tucked inside dingy hospital sheets. Mrs. Simms forced a smile and nodded in agreement. Maryann was so exhausted that she fell asleep easily allowing Mrs. Simms to slip quietly out of the room. Tears dripped down her face as she braced herself for the long ride home on the icy roads.

Maryann awoke during the night to a burning sensation as a hot fever seeped through her body. Her throat felt as if it were on fire. And when she swallowed her saliva was like boiling water inside of her mouth. Sharp stabbing pains pierced her upper body like little needles. The pressure in her chest felt as if it were going to burst open. The raspy breathing coming from her sounded like the howling of a wounded animal.

"You are seriously ill," the doctor had informed her when she went to the clinic hoping to get something to relieve the pain.

"I am admitting you into the hospital," he said after listening to the harsh sounds in her lungs. Maryann was too weak to protest and relieved when they pumped pain medication into her body. When she mercifully drifted off to sleep she dreamed about her past.

The childhood that Maryann cherished with the family she loved haunted her long after she woke up. The dreams were so vivid that when she opened her eyes she expected to be surrounded by the grandparents who loved her.

Being quarantined seemed foolish to Maryann, but the doctors insisted that she be put into a separate room from the other patients because they weren't sure what was wrong with her when she arrived in the hospital.

"You have pneumonia," the doctor told her the day after she was admitted. "Both of your lungs are infected so we will be giving you lots of medications." The machine hooked up to her made Maryann cough and sometimes she felt as if she wasn't going to catch her breath again. It hurt to cough, but it helped bring up the nasty yellow and green stuff the doctors told her was infection.

Maryann hated the hospital room she was put in because it didn't have any windows. The overhead florescent lights were too bright and hurt her eyes. The room was so small that it made her feel closed off from the rest of the world. If she could look out of a window Maryann was sure the room would be better. Looking out of a window was something Maryann enjoyed. Sometimes at home when the house was quiet she would stare out the large window in the living room. During the day she watched people walking or cars driving by. At night she stared at the moon or the stars. She drifted into her own world with thoughts that took her away from everyday problems.

Maryann lay on her back staring at cracks in the ceiling that seemed to stare back down at her. The longer she stared at the cracks the closer they seemed to be. Sometimes the overhead light flickered on and off emitting a yellowish tint that dimly lit the room. Ice-cold air seeped into the room through open cracks in the floors, walls and ceilings. Maryann's body shivered unintentionally as cold devoured her flesh. The faint beating of her heart was the only reminder that she was still alive.

It was early in the morning when she drifted back to sleep. Her determination to live was inspired mainly by her children. They were all she had and she was all they had. Despite the pain, Maryann used her strength to keep sucking air into her infected lungs. She had to keep breathing to live. On her third day in the hospital Maryann began experiencing a different type of pain; she went into labor and gave birth to a premature baby. The baby was born alive, but died later in the day. Giving birth took a toll on her body and made her weaker. She hadn't told anyone except Mrs. Simms about the pregnancy. No one noticed she was pregnant because it was hard to see on her thin body.

"The baby didn't have a chance for survival," the doctor told her as tears flowed from her eyes. "God knew what was best," she whispered.

***

Maryann grew up in Aberdeen, a small town in Mississippi that was populated with poor minority families. The people of Aberdeen were caring and supportive. They did whatever work they could to feed their families. Maryann's grandparents were Jack Andy and True, and they owned a small farm where Maryann spent her childhood romping through the fields. True was a woman of Indian heritage who practiced some of the Indian ways she had been taught as a little girl by her mother, who was a full blooded Indian that had married True's father, a poor black man. True was full of wisdom and love and she generously helped others in the small community. Most people overlooked the strange things that True did such as burying her food in the ground because she wouldn't eat it fresh.

Jack Andy and True were married for many years and Jack Andy was well liked by everyone who knew him. He sold peanuts by the side of the road and was nicknamed "the peanut man." The love Maryann received growing up with her grandparents nurtured her and shielded her from harmful truths.

Irene was True's and Jack's only daughter. She was a teenager when she fell in love with Frank Strong, a handsome dark skinned man who lived nearby. They were young and inexperienced so their relationship deteriorated shortly after their daughter was born.

Maryann was born on a cool October morning surrounded by True and the midwife. True immediately took over the responsibility of raising her grandchild. Irene was in Maryann's life, but their relationship was more like sisters than mother and daughter. Maryann knew her father, Frank, and kept in touch with him even after he moved to Chicago. The bond between Irene and Maryann was weak, but she respected and loved her mother. Maryann was a young teenager when Irene remarried and had two sons, Jessie and Jerry.

As a young child Maryann was taught how to cook and did household chores at an early age, which was a blessing to her grandparents. True was a woman with beliefs well beyond her time. Being illiterate herself she understood that education was important and made sure that Maryann received the typical schoolhouse education offered to people of color. Irene had attended the one room schoolhouse and True was proud to have a daughter who knew how to read and write. Maryann was smart so learning was easy for her and she did well.

At eighteen she married a tall and handsome man named Roy Ford. It was love at first sight for both of them. Roy's older brother, Ben, introduced them. The men in the Ford family had reputations for being womanizers, but Roy was different. He was quiet, shy and sweet in ways that warmed Maryann's heart and she loved him. People teased them because Roy stood over six feet tall, dwarfing Maryann's five-foot-one frame.

Times were hard in the south especially for people of color. In the 1940's Mississippi was oozing with prejudice and hatred against people of color. It was overflowing with Jim Crow laws and the lynching of young black men was a common occurrence. Although Aberdeen was a close community there was also a lot of poverty. People lived in shacks and some barely made enough to survive.

After they married, Maryann and Roy moved into a small place with Roy's brother Ben and his wife Lea. It wasn't uncommon for multiple families to share a home because there were benefits. Besides family closeness it was often cheaper to live together. Families shared everything so money went a long way and most jobs didn't pay enough to take care of larger families in the poor areas. Roy easily found work as a laborer because he was blessed with a muscular and healthy body.

Maryann and Lea were both expecting their first child only a few months apart. The sister-in-laws shared a closeness that surprised even them. They had more in common than just marrying brothers. Neither of them had sisters so they decided to become each other's sister.

Ben told everyone he fell in love with Lea when he first noticed her in a field with her mother picking cotton. He said the first thing he saw was the large thick ponytail hanging down her back. "She was too beautiful to be getting her hands all messed up picking cotton", he chuckled when he told the story. They married in a small church after a short courtship.

Roy Lee Ford jr., Maryann and Roy's firstborn came into the world on a gusty morning in the early part of March. "I want more!" Roy shouted when he held his son for the first time. The baby was the oldest grandchild on both sides of the family. Lea and Ben's son, Little Ben, as they nicknamed him, was born a few months later.

The babies came fast and neither Roy nor Maryann was prepared for their rapidly growing family. It wasn't long before their family swelled to four sons, Roy jr., Jerry, Henry, and Robert.

Ben was the first to leave Mississippi. He moved north to Milwaukee, Wisconsin seeking a new life for his family. Settling down in Milwaukee was a dream come true for him. It took a lot of courage for Ben to leave his parents and siblings behind but he knew the only way for his children to have a chance at a decent life was to move away from Mississippi where there was so much hopelessness. He was sure a better life existed beyond Mississippi and was determined to find out.

Ben arrived in Milwaukee, a city alive with industry where factories and foundries posted "Help Wanted" signs. It didn't take him long to find a job. He was used to the prejudices of white people, but it didn't seem as bad in Milwaukee because a white man offered him a good job.

The good news about Ben's fortune spread throughout the Ford family and one by one-Ford family members migrated to Milwaukee, including Roy and Maryann. They left Mississippi with mixed feelings of excitement and apprehension, vowing to return to Mississippi one day to buy land and raise their children there.

True held tightly to Maryann's four crying sons as they waved goodbye to their parents. The children were left behind because they needed to find jobs and a place for the family to live. They would send for them later.

Living conditions in Milwaukee were much better than either Roy or Maryann had imagined. Roy was hypnotized by the flashing neon lights that glowed over several businesses throughout the city. The powerful odor of yeast from nearby beer breweries filled the air.

Maryann found a job as a waitress and cook in a downtown cafeteria while Roy went to work as a laborer in one of the large foundries. Working conditions in the foundry wasn't the best and presented some serious dangers, but the pay was better than any he had ever earned.

When Maryann became pregnant with her fifth child she quit working and was reunited with the sons she left in Mississippi. By that time Roy's parents, Ben Sr. and Sarah (whom most people affectionately called Hon and Papa) were also moving to

Milwaukee so they brought the boys with them. The two families merged and set up household together. Papa went to work in a boiler room of a factory while Hon helped with the grandchildren. Several relatives left Mississippi that year; so many families in Milwaukee had relatives living with them.

Stephen was the first to be born in Milwaukee. The weather was hot and humid in the middle of July when he made his entrance. The first girl, Sara, was born two years later, next came Frank, Joe, and finally another girl they named Joyce. The last of Roy's children was a boy named Ralph born on August 6, 1956.

***

Maryann opened her eyes wincing from the bright light that someone had switched on. The intense smell of antiseptic reminded her that she was in the hospital. She felt an urge to scream for help because the pain in her chest had not eased. When she opened her mouth to scream a small sound came out that was barely above a whisper. Visions of her children filled her mind. She missed them.

The children had been taken to a place called "The Children's Home", an orphanage that wasn't far from the hospital. Ten-month-old Louie, the youngest of her children, was being taken care of by Mrs. Simms.

None of Roy's relatives had come to the hospital to visit her yet. She wondered about Lea and didn't understand what happened to the friendship they once shared. When had they drifted apart? After Roy's death his family only came around the first year, and then they stopped. Sometimes Ben dropped in to check on her and the kids. She appreciated when he came because he usually brought food or gave her a few dollars that she badly needed.

She was aware of the gossip that was going on in the Ford family. The nosey ones were trying to figure out who Louie's father was. Most people believed that Bro Tot, Cousin Liza's husband was the father of Louie. Maryann didn't confirm or deny it because it wasn't anyone's business who the father of her child was.

In Years To Come

Roy jr., Jerry, and Henry were old enough to visit her in the hospital. Where were they? They hadn't come to see her either. She asked Mrs. Simms about them, but she didn't know where they were.

"Roy jr., Jerry, and Henry are probably with Hon and Mr. Ford," Maryann told her. She heard that Joyce hadn't been taken to the orphanage with the others because Hon and Papa took her to stay with them.

***

It was hard raising the older boys after Roy's death. Jerry, Henry and Robert were always getting into some type of trouble. Roy jr. didn't give her trouble with the police, but he had an attitude that made her wonder what was wrong with him. Roy jr. fussed when she asked him to help her with the younger ones. He knew she had to work to supplement the check she received, but he always made threats to move out of the house. She heard him say that he didn't want to be bothered with the younger kids. She excused his behavior as being immature. Roy jr. was a bit spoiled by others in the family because he was the first grandchild. He should have been at the hospital everyday visiting her. She is his mother. Hon and papa moved into a nice single-family house on 13th street where Roy jr. went to hide from her.

She once found out that Roy jr. was in Indianapolis with her sister-in-law, Sister. They were stupid for not telling her where he was. She got along okay with Sister, but that woman was different from any that she had ever known. After her husband, Robert shot her in the leg it was Maryann who gave Sister the money for therapy and a blood transfusion the doctors said she needed. That was when she had money from Roy's insurance policy. It was good that they treated him well, but she prayed that one day Roy jr. would at least act like he cared about his mother and siblings. It bothered her that Roy jr. preferred to be around his extended family.

Maryann remembered how devastating it was for the

children after Roy died. Roy jr. was only sixteen so she gave him more excuses for not visiting her now.

Maryann opened her eyes from a restless sleep. Her entire body was writhing in pain. She looked around the room and saw an image sitting in a chair near the door. Mrs. Simms? She attempted to lift her head to get a better look, but was too weak. The person moved closer and when Maryann could finally focus her eyes she saw that it was Hon.

"Hi May Ran," Hon said, almost whispering her name.

Maryann tried to talk, but the breathing took all the air and she couldn't speak.

"Don't be trying to talk now. You need to rest your voice and from what I hear your body could use the rest too so I won't stay long."

Maryann smiled at her. Hon was always good to her.

Hon took Maryann's hand and held it while she talked to her. Maryann loved the sound of her soothing voice and felt the tension ease as she relaxed.

There was so much Maryann wanted to say to her mother-in-law who had been so kind to her over the years, but the words couldn't come out. Hon had helped her with the kids when they lived together in the two-story house on Eighth Street. Roy adored his mother and loved his father.

"Don't worry about the children. They are doing fine in that place in Wawatosa. They miss you so you have to get better so you can go home."

Maryann loved her mother-in-law as much as any daughter in law could. It had been awhile since she had seen Hon and a part of her felt guilty for not visiting her.

"You have to take better care of yourself," Hon was saying. Maryann wanted to laugh because Hon always fussed at her when they lived together.

Maryann nodded to let Hon know she understood. Hon was grateful when the nurse gave Maryann a dose of pain medication.

Maryann wasn't a complainer, but Hon could see she was in pain.

When Maryann drifted off to sleep Hon left the room. She was disturbed by the way May Ran looked and prayed silently for God to heal her. She made a mental note to talk to Pastor Ward so he could go to the hospital to see about May Ran.

***

Maryann remembered the hard times in her marriage and was thankful that God always pulled them through. When Roy was diagnosed with tuberculosis it was severe enough for him to be hospitalized. Hon, Ike and some cousins joined Roy at the Merdale Sanitarium for treatment because they also had TB. Maryann had her hands full at home with the children but still commuted back and forth to visit Roy. Eventually Roy recovered and was back home, but Ike; his youngest brother wasn't as lucky and had to have a full lung and part of the other lung removed.

Most marriages face challenges, but the most difficult time came for Roy and Maryann when Stephen, Frank and Sara were all critically ill at the same time. Maryann watched helplessly while Roy paced the floor of the children's ward at the county hospital. The doctors gave them little hope of their children recovering from the respiratory infection that had turned into pneumonia. When Sara developed meningitis things got worse.

The doctor treating the children talked about a new drug that was still in the experimental stages. The drug had side effects that were still unknown but doctors believed the children would have a better chance of survival if given the drug. Reluctantly, Maryann and Roy agreed to have the drug administered to their children.

Stephen improved after a few small doses of the drug. Frank was given smaller doses than Sara but more than Stephen. He too began to improve. Sara was given the largest doses because she was the most critically ill.

Maryann and Roy waited for any news to relieve the

mounting tension they felt. Sara fought bravely while her frail body lay still and listless in the hospital crib.

The side- effects from the drugs began to surface as soon as Frank could talk again. The drug had affected his hearing and speech.

"He needs to wear a hearing aid," the doctors explained to Maryann and Roy. The doctor's main concern was for Sara, who was given massive doses of the drug. Stephen didn't suffer any side effects.

It took awhile for Sara to come around. Sara's hearing and speech were permanently damaged. Before the illness Sara was a happy-go-lucky five-year-old who screamed, yelled, laughed and talked constantly. Sara's grave condition had improved more than the doctors had hoped, but her life would never be the same.

The day after Sara was out of medical danger Maryann was looking down at her daughter when their eyes met. Sara always had beautiful bright eyes. Today she noticed the confusion behind them. "I love you," Maryann said softly to her. Sara watched as her mother's lips moved. She saw the action, but heard no voice. She heard nothing, not even the sound of her own breathing.

"She is deaf and dumb," the doctors said after examining her. The news of Sara's deafness was shattering, but they were thankful that she was alive.

"Sara will have to attend a special school for the deaf and dumb where she can be taught how to communicate," the doctors suggested.

The only school in Wisconsin was several miles away in Delevan. It was an on-campus school where children lived in a dorm-like setting.

"She will be home for summer vacation and holidays," the administrator told the still grieving parents, who were reluctant to leave her there.

Sara's loud screams filled the hall when they walked away. Roy wanted to run back and grab his daughter, but he knew she had to stay because she needed to learn how to communicate and he couldn't teach her.

***

It was early morning when Maryann opened her eyes again to see Mrs. Simms standing by her bed looking down at her with a pleasant smile. Maryann always appreciated the smile that seemed to be plastered on her friend's face.

"I had another dream last night," Maryann whispered to Mrs. Simms who strained to hear what she was saying. Maryann described her dream while Mrs. Simms listened; concerned that she was talking about her dead husband again.

"The dreams feel so real that I'm disappointed after I open my eyes and discover that I'm still in this room."

Mrs. Simms handed Maryann her social security check that had arrived that morning.

"Thank you, Mrs. Simms" Maryann said as she took the envelope and placed it on the nightstand with her other private things.

"If only Roy were here", she whispered more to herself than to Mrs. Simms.

"I will only be a moment," the nurse said who had come in to check Maryann's vital signs.

"How are you feeling Mrs. Ford?"

Maryann could only nod and smile.

The nurse spied the social security check on the nightstand. She felt sorry for Maryann. They had discussed her earlier in the nurse's lounge. Someone mentioned that she had at least ten children.

"We have to hurry up and get you better so you can get home to those children. I know you miss them and they miss you too." Maryann smiled at the nurse and nodded again.

"This should ease the pain," the nurse said poking Maryann in the arm with a needle. Maryann closed her eyes and made a face when the needle entered under her skin.

It wasn't long before Maryann drifted off to sleep, much to Mrs. Simms relief. She was concerned about Maryann talking too much and lately her conversation had been focused on her dead husband, Roy. Maryann talked about him as if he were going to walk through the door. She hardly ever referred to him as being deceased. Mrs. Simms questioned the nurse about the medication she was giving Maryann.

"Does it make you say crazy things?"

The nurse laughed, "It is only pain medicine and antibiotics. I don't believe either would make a person say crazy things."

***

Maryann was thinking more about Roy and still wondered why he had to die. She had uncertainties about his death because it didn't make sense to her. She refused to accept what the detectives told her and hoped one day to afford to hire a private detective who would investigate his death and find out what really happened to him. Her desire was to know the truth.

Maryann would never forget what happened that day. It was Friday, December fifteenth, ten days before Christmas when Roy picked up the check at the credit union. He had borrowed money to buy Christmas gifts for the children. The combination of his paycheck and the loan totaled over five hundred dollars, a lot of money in 1956. Things had changed in their lives. Roy was making more money and they were finally living in a place of their own. For years they had lived with Hon and Papa and now having their own place was a luxury.

Maryann went with Roy to the house of Roy's cousin, Marilee, who lived with John Wilson. Maryann and Roy had known John when he lived in Mississippi. For a while they had even lived in the same duplex in Milwaukee. Marilee and John lived downstairs while Roy and Maryann lived upstairs with Hon and Papa. He came from Mississippi with Marilee. Maryann liked

Marilee and the two of them got along well. Because she had to work the next morning, Maryann left after a few hours.

"You go ahead and drive home," Roy said giving her keys to the car. He had started playing coon can with John. Coon can was a card game that was popular among the men. They always played the game for money and often didn't stop until the wee hours of the morning. Roy loved playing coon can and was good at it. Maryann left Roy there and drove home.

Late Friday night when Maryann climbed into bed Roy still had not come home. She knew that Roy could walk to his parent's house, which wasn't far from where he was and sleep on the couch.

"He's probably with Ben or Ike," she reasoned as she laid her head on the pillow and fell asleep.

It was a restless night, and she tossed and turned trying to ignore the gnawing feeling in the pit of her stomach. When Roy wasn't home by the time Maryann left for work the next morning she was sure he was at Hon and Papa's house. When they had first arrived in Milwaukee Roy was caught up in the city life. Mississippi didn't have open taverns where people drank beer nor were there many entertaining places. Roy enjoyed drinking beer and that was okay with her. He gambled but always gave his paychecks to Maryann, leaving him very little monies to gamble with. Maryann was concerned that she had left him with the Christmas money in his pockets.

Saturday morning was a cold day with a blistering wind that dropped the chill factor to below zero. Piles of snow from the last blizzard still lined the streets. It was late in the afternoon when Maryann got off work. Her feet were tired after standing all day in the café. Each step she took felt like she had lead in her shoes. She wanted to get home so she could rest. Her mind turned to Roy as she walked up the block from where she had parked the car on the street. She had a few words to say to him.

As she moved closer to the house she noticed curtains being pulled aside. Someone was peeking out of the window. She smiled

14

to herself, thinking it was one of the smaller kids, probably Joe or Frank who were always excited to see her come home. After preparing them something to eat she would rest and Roy could watch the children. He was probably in bed now with Joyce lying across his chest fast asleep. That was her favorite place to lie down and suck her thumb. He had that girl spoiled rotten. She chuckled while thinking about the crazy nickname he gave her, *Woman*. What kind of name was that for a little girl who wasn't even two years old yet? Maryann smiled knowing how much Roy loved his children, but those girls, Joyce and Sara, seemed to have stolen the man's heart. Sometimes Maryann wondered if he had room for her.

Although she wasn't concerned about Roy being with another woman she wasn't so naive as to believe it wasn't possible either. He would definitely have to explain what kept him out all night.

Roy jr. and Jerry were not happy about babysitting when she left for work that morning. She made them share the responsibility of watching the kids until Roy came home. Roy jr. and Jerry did a good job of watching the older kids, but she was concerned about leaving the younger ones, Joe, Joyce and the baby, Ralph, with them. They hardly ever changed his diaper although she taught them how to do this and fix his bottles.

She was surprised when the door to the house flung open and Jerry began running towards her. Roy jr. came outside too, but he stood on the porch watching.

"I am going to get that boy about running out here without a coat on," she mumbled to herself.

"What is wrong with him?" she said aloud noticing that Roy jr. had left the front door open. He is letting the heat out of the house. Jerry was close and Maryann was about to say something to him when he blurted the words out.

"Daddy is dead!"

Maryann felt her head spin as the words sank in. Jerry's voice was cracking as he repeated the words again. She didn't remember anything that happened after that. Jerry told her later that he had to chase her down the middle of the snow packed streets as she screamed frantically at the top of her lungs. He caught up with her three blocks away where she finally collapsed.

Maryann didn't want to identify the body because she couldn't face seeing her husband lying in the morgue cold and lifeless. Roy was thirty-seven years old; too young, and too strong to even think of as being dead. Ben identified his brother's remains and broke down when he had to tell his parents. Hon screamed before fainting into Papa's arms.

Detectives investigating Roy's death claimed they retraced his steps the night of his death and concluded that he committed suicide. Refusing to accept this account of his death, Maryann withdrew into a world of depression believing he would never do that to her. Roy would never deliberately leave her and the children. He loved them too much.

"Roy would never cause this much pain and hurt," she told everyone. Yet the evidence presented suicide as a great possibility.

The sixteen-year-old boy who found his body was with a father and son team who had come early that morning to demolish the property. They were walking inside the house going from room to room when the boy discovered a man hanging from a window in the room of the upstairs apartment. It was the lifeless body of Roy Ford. The police noticed his own belt tied around his neck like a noose. He was over six feet tall so he wasn't hanging from the window. He was fully dressed and in a kneeling position. Detectives determined later that the knot used to tie the belt was unique and only a few people knew how to do it, Roy was one of them. Also, the place where his life ended wasn't random; it was the first house Roy and Maryann lived with Hon and Papa when they moved to Milwaukee. It was also the same house where Marilee and John lived in the downstairs apartment. The house had been condemned a few years earlier and was to be torn down that day. It was speculation by the detectives that Roy chose that house because he felt comfortable enough in there to go through with the suicide. Relatives took the children to stay with them for a few days while Maryann retreated to a rocking chair near the living room window, where she sat for hours everyday until after the funeral.

Conflicting stories by several witnesses raised doubts and anger in the minds of the Ford family. Some witnesses claimed Roy won a large sum of money while gambling. Others said he lost all the money he had. One man claimed he saw a man identified later as John Wilson follow Roy out of the tavern that night. Most people believed John Wilson robbed and murdered Roy. The last known person to see Roy alive was John Wilson. The police questioned him the day after Roy's funeral and although his story was suspicious they had no evidence proving that he was responsible for Roy's death. When Roy's pockets were searched there was only a handful of change. Regardless of the inconsistent stories the detectives and coroner decided that the cause of Roy's death was suicide and that is what was put on his death certificate.

For months following Roy's death Maryann struggled with it. Sleep did not come easy, especially lying in the bed they once shared. Maryann remembered the heartfelt talks, the tears, the laughter and the hope they once shared. She lived on a diet of cigarettes and coffee and lost a lot of weight, leaving her a thin frail woman. She continued to function and care for her children, but her body felt the strain.

***

Maryann opened her eyes to the quietness of the hospital room and noticed Mrs. Simms was gone. She shivered as the cold devoured her. "If only Roy was here," she mumbled. Tears streamed down her face as memories of Roy filled her mind. She imagined him being with her, saying funny things to make her laugh and kissing away her tears.

Maryann worked in a restaurant part time, but most of her income was from the social security check. It was difficult for her to work because she had a hard time finding someone to watch the children. The older boys were not dependable. They were always getting into trouble and Henry and Robert spent a year in the Children's Home. Maryann had her hands full with the younger children and couldn't keep up with the older boys.

Physically she was weak and fragile, often neglecting herself for the sake of the children. Many times she went without dinner so her children could eat. There just wasn't enough money to take care of eleven children.

When she first felt sick she ignored the pain and coughing, believing that whatever was wrong would go away. She had been sick many times before and always bounced back. This felt different and when she began spitting up blood it scared her. After some persuasion from Mrs. Simms she went to the clinic and the doctor admitted her into the hospital. The conversation that eventually sent her to the doctor was fresh on her mind.

"You need to go to the doctor." Mrs. Simms's round face was full of concern when she spoke. "You cannot get better without some medicine."

"It's just a bad cold; I'll be okay in a few days." Even as she said the words Maryann wondered why the cold hadn't gotten better already. It had been awhile. She laughed nervously.

"You're always trying to play mother with me," Maryann said.

"If you're not better in a few days I'm taking you to the doctor myself." Mrs. Simms didn't dismiss the worn look on her friend's face or the weight loss. Maryann nodded in agreement, not wanting to get her started on one of her lectures. She didn't bother to tell her about the blood she was spitting up.

***

Mrs. Simms was different from most people Maryann had met since moving to Milwaukee. She was always lively and happy-go-lucky. From the beginning she was a good friend to

Maryann. After Roy's death the only ones that had shared Maryann's life were her children. They were her companions. Having a friend brought purpose and laughter back into Maryann's otherwise dull life. It gave her someone to talk to and helped her work through feelings that surrounded Roy's death.

***

Maryann fought back tears when Mrs. Simms walked into her hospital room that evening. It was obvious that Mrs. Simms was tired. Maryann knew she worked all day and drove all the way to the County Hospital to visit her. She cherished Mrs. Simms and thanked God for bringing this friend into her life. Maryann told her about seeing Roy standing in the middle of the room the night before.

"He was right there," Maryann pointed to an empty spot.

***

Her first encounter with Mrs. Simms was after Maryann moved into a house she purchased with the insurance money from Roy's death. It was a nice single-family house located on a narrow street called Eleventh Lane. When Maryann got the insurance check she already knew what to do with it. After buying the house, longer periods of time passed between visits from family until they finally quit coming. She pondered with the thought of moving back to Mississippi to be near her mother. It seemed like the right thing to do, but she was held back by the thought of leaving Roy. What would she do in Mississippi anyway? Grandma True and Jack Andy were gone so she decided to stay in Milwaukee. Maryann felt like the world stopped the day her grandmother passed away. Maryann had moved away so True couldn't visit as often as she would have liked, but the few times she did come were enjoyable for both of them. Jack Andy didn't live much longer after True died.

Mr. and Mrs. Simms adopted a boy named Henry, who was the same age as one of Maryann's sons. Henry became friends with the Ford boys so they were always around each other. Mrs. Simms noticed the woman living across the street had a house full of children. She asked Henry about her.

"She's my friend's mother," he said.

Mrs. Simms was curious about the woman, especially after seeing someone in that house peeping through the curtains at her when she walked to her car.

Maryann always enjoyed looking out the window and began watching her neighbor when she found out that she was Henry's mother. Henry was a nice kid, friendly and very helpful. Henry's parents drove nice cars and always seemed to have money according to what her boys told her. They said their house had beautiful furniture in it. Mrs. Simms owned a small restaurant somewhere near downtown and Mr. Simms had a good-paying job in a factory.

One day while peeking through the window Maryann saw the woman look up at her and tried to move back, but didn't move quick enough. She was sure the woman saw her.

Mr. Simms was a rough-looking man who wasn't attractive at all. Maryann laughed about how odd they looked together. It started out as curiosity, but soon Maryann was looking out the window like a nosey neighbor spying on the couple. Having no social life with ten children made a person do strange things. She felt the stab of loneliness every time she saw any couple. It was easy to daydream about how wonderful life would have been if Roy were still alive.

One day while Maryann was doing chores the doorbell rang. She peeped out to see Henry's mother standing on her porch. Her heart almost leaped from her body. The woman stood there with a big smile on her face. Maryann opened the door and came face to face with the woman she had been spying on.

"Are you going to invite me in?" the woman asked with a soft soothing voice. Maryann nodded, unsure of how to respond. Her eyes were glued to the woman as she walked through the door wearing a freshly ironed white uniform that reminded Maryann of her cafeteria days.

"My name is Simola Bonner, the woman said. I'm Henry's mother; I live across the alley in the gold house.

Maryann shook the outstretched hand.

"I'm Maryann Ford," she said.

"It's just you and the children living here?"

Maryann nodded.

"Your sons come over my house sometimes."

Maryann knew they went over to her house and prayed they didn't beg for food.

"Can I offer you something to drink?" Maryann only had a little coffee, but she was willing to share.

She declined the offer.

It had been a long time since Maryann had a visitor and she still couldn't believe the woman was sitting in her living room.

Frank and Joe were chasing each other and ran into the room. They stared at the visitor and held tightly to Maryann's dress. It was a good feeling having someone to talk to other than the children.

"Your children are adorable," she remarked, smiling back at them. Frank's tiny eyes looked like black beads staring right at her. Simola observed the warmth in Maryann and felt sorry for the young mother, especially after learning that she was a widow. Maryann was painfully shy and now Simola understood why she was peeking out of the window. At first it had made her angry because she was sure the woman was spying on her, but as time went on she began to notice that there weren't any adults visiting her. She sensed that things were hard for Maryann.

The boys who played with Henry had told him that something happened to their father and he was dead. Now looking at her, Simola detected something else in this woman-- she needed a friend.

During that first awkward visit they were both reserved, but in time they became close. Maryann didn't want to call her Simola so she began calling her Mrs. Simms by shortening her first name, and she referred to her husband as Mr. Simms. It wasn't long before the two women began sharing everything from their most intimate secrets to family problems.

It took awhile for Maryann to withdraw from the seclusion she went into after Roy's death but eventually she did. She enjoyed and took advantage of the quiet times spent at Mrs. Simms house without the children. The two of them could sit for hours sipping coffee and talking. Mrs. Simms proved to be more than a friend: there were times when Maryann considered her a savior.

Maryann was grateful to have someone who would listen to her. Since the death of her grandmother she didn't have anyone she could talk to. Some of the Ford family members thought of her as a crazy widow because she never stopped grieving Roy's death. After Maryann broke down and cried Mrs. Simms assured her everything was going to be okay.

***

When Mrs. Simms left the hospital that evening Maryann was sleeping like a baby.

Maryann opened her eyes to darkness that engulfed the room causing her to strain at the image she saw.

"Roy?" Was she losing her mind? It was Roy standing there.

She rested her head back onto the pillow reflecting on the first time she met Roy.

***

Ben introduced them. Roy had a crush on her but was too shy to approach her. Ben had already claimed Lea, a light-skinned girl with long hair and freckles. The rumor was that Lea had fair skin because her father was a white man. No one knew for sure except Lea's mother, who everyone called Mama Nora. She was a short thin woman with a mean look and a loud voice. They said she had a mean streak in her but loved her children, Lea and Nathaniel. Lea wasn't petite like her mother but rather big boned. Her brother Nathaniel had the color of his mother and was a man who loved to drink and have fun.

Roy's funeral was a ritual. Maryann sat in the front row staring at the casket. He didn't look like himself. His head was huge. She was told it was swelling from the pressure around his neck from the belt. How would she go on without him? Her heart seemed to scream out.

The children kept her from breaking down. Somehow she found the strength to go on for the sake of her children. Gifts poured in from people who had heard about the widow with ten children and no money to buy Christmas gifts for them. There were plenty of toys, fruit, and clothing donated by strangers that Maryann would never meet. Many of Roy's co-workers and even his boss were shaken by his death. Maryann felt honored when Roy's boss asked to be a pallbearer at his funeral.

***

"Mrs. Ford"? Someone was calling her name. Maryann opened her eyes. The doctor was standing over her.

"Your fever keeps going up. We are going to give you something to help bring it down."

Maryann nodded to let him know she understood. She was so tired all she wanted to do was rest. She closed her eyes while the doctor's hands probed her body. She winced when he pushed on one side.

Mrs. Simms was watching. She was the one who asked for the doctor out of concern for her friend whose body burned with a heat Mrs. Simms had never felt before. The doctor assured Mrs. Simms that they were doing all they could to bring down the fever, but the infection was still in Maryann's lungs.

After the doctor left the room Maryann smiled at Mrs.

Simms. Her voice was barely audible and Mrs. Simms struggled to hear.

"I saw Roy again last night. He was in the room with me."

Mrs. Simms nodded.

"He was smiling at me," she pointed to the spot. "He wanted to tell me something. He was there and then he was gone."

Mrs. Simms turned away when tears began streaming down Maryann's face.

"This room is too cold. Can you tell them to put me in another room? I want a room with a window."

Mrs. Simms nodded again.

"And the doctors and nurses haven't checked in on me."

Mrs. Simms wanted to remind her that the doctor had just left, but she didn't say anything.

"Did they forget that I am in here?"

"I'll make sure everything is taken care of," Mrs. Simms assured her, fighting her own urge to cry. She usually left after Maryann went to sleep, but she seemed restless tonight. When it was time to leave Maryann grabbed her arm.

"Please don't leave me. They'll forget about me."

"No they won't. I'll make sure they won't. I'll be back to see you tomorrow."

"Louie isn't Roy's child so if something happens to me please take care of him. I'm not worried about the other children because I believe Roy's family will take them."

"Of course I'll take Louie. You know I love that baby."

Maryann remembered Mrs. Simms offer to adopt Louie when he was first born. Louie was her lovechild. Maryann was still young and craved the companionship of a man, but what she didn't need or want was another baby. Louie's father was a handsome, charming man who gave her the affection she craved. When she got pregnant again with his second child she was devastated. Before Maryann went into the hospital Mrs. Simms was concerned about her being pregnant and depressed because she didn't want another baby.

It was the worst winter Maryann had ever experienced. Large piles of snow covered the streets. Mrs. Simms fussed at Maryann about walking through all that snow with no boots or gloves and only a thin scarf wrapped around her neck. The coat she wore didn't have buttons and was torn in several places. Mrs. Simms wished she could afford to give her friend more.

The heating oil ran out during a bad snow leaving Maryann's house cold as the temperatures outside dropped. It was a few days before her social security check would arrive. Mrs. Simms didn't have any extra oil or money to give her so she pleaded with Maryann to send her kids to stay with relatives for a few days where they would be warm. Maryann was stubborn because she didn't want them knowing how bad things were for her. She lit the gas stove and had the children huddle around it covering themselves with blankets and clothes. Mrs. Simms was upset about this so she did what she felt was right and called the police.

The policemen showed up at Maryann's door and immediately felt the cold chill inside of the house. It was predicted that temperatures would drop below zero that night. They convinced Maryann to allow her children to be taken to the homes of relatives. Maryann reluctantly asked Roy's family for help. It was heartbreaking to watch the police cars drive away with her children. Maryann and Louie went to Mrs. Simms's house where they slept in one of her bedrooms.

After the social security check arrived Maryann went back to her house. She was horrified by what she saw. Icicles frozen solid hung from the ceilings of the house. Layers of ice had formed on the furniture, walls, and linoleum floors. Maryann realized that if she and the children had stayed in the house they would have froze to death.

***

Mrs. Simms was standing over her bed when Maryann

opened her eyes.

"Hey, sleepy head," Mrs. Simms said.

Mrs. Simms had been in the room watching Maryann sleep for a short time. She looked peaceful and from the expression on her face was probably dreaming again.

"Has anyone checked on the children?"

"The kids are fine," Mrs. Simms assured her.

"I'm so cold, please tell them I'm cold," Maryann pleaded with her. Her large eyes were glassy with a far away look in them. Her frail body looked thinner and weaker and she was shaking as if she were freezing.

"I'll go talk to them now," Mrs. Simms said, needing a reason to leave the room. Mrs. Simms went to the nurse's station and talked with them.

"I'm worried about Maryann," she told them.

The nurses looked at her sympathetically.

"She is shivering because she is cold."

The tears came without warning and Mrs. Simms had to lean on the counter for support.

"I will check on her," one of the nurses offered.

When Mrs. Simms returned to the room Maryann was propped up with pillows and more blankets were piled on the bed.

"I am still cold."

"You have a ton of blankets on you!" Mrs. Simms laughed. The two of them talked even though it was still hard for her to understand Maryann, whose voice was still barely above a whisper.

"I'll be here tomorrow to check on you."

She kissed Maryann on her forehead. The heat of her body caused Mrs. Simms to leap back. Maryann was hot again from the fever yet she shook as if she was submerged in ice. .

The next day Mrs. Sims stood in the room staring at the vacant bed where Maryann spent the last twenty-eight days of her life. She dabbed at her eyes while tears flowed. No one said she was going to die. She felt a stab of guilt about leaving her last night. She shouldn't have died alone.

Mrs. Simms toyed with the letter in her hand. It was from Maryann and addressed to her. The first paragraph opened with, *I'll tell you just how sick I was when I get out of here.* Mrs. Simms folded the paper. She would read the rest of the letter later. At least Maryann's suffering was over, but what about her children? Mrs. Simms thought about the baby, Louie, who was at home with Henry. She was going to find a way to adopt the baby that she had grown so fond of.

I would like to thank Mrs. Simms for supplying so much information about my mother. I would not have been able to share her last days if it had not been for the one person who was there.

Chapter One

The Ninth Child

My name is Joyce and I am the ninth child of Roy and Maryann. I saw the grownups coming back from the funeral. I didn't know what a funeral was because they didn't allow children to attend. I stood in front of the large window in my grandparent's living room staring at the falling snow. Tiny flakes were falling and sprinkling everything with a layer of whiteness. The sound of the wind whipping around the outside of the house was like a loud whistling noise. I couldn't pull myself away from the window because the snow was hypnotic. Piles of snow kept getting bigger on the outside window ledge.

"Your mama is in heaven with your daddy." The words burned in my brain as I thought about them. I knew heaven was a good place to go, but I didn't want mama there. I searched my memory for some recollection of my daddy: he was a man without a face. I was almost two years old when he died. Many unanswered questions rambled through my young brain. What did my daddy look like? I got frustrated trying to sort everything out. Then an anger I couldn't explain rose up inside of me. Why did mama leave us to go to heaven to be with my daddy?

In the depths of my mind nothing made sense. They said mama was sick and had to stay in the hospital for a while. They told me she was coming home as soon as she was better. Now they are telling me she's in heaven with my daddy. The only thing I understood was the emptiness I felt. I looked up in the sky because that is where they say heaven is, but all I saw was snow. Where is heaven? Hon said heaven is way beyond the clouds. I wondered if mama could look down and see me. I waved anyway.

Last night they took us to a place with people all around us. They called it a wake. It was in a funeral home. There were people crying and strangers staring at me. The place smelled funny like the rubbing alcohol that Hon uses. The smell was making me sick to my stomach and I felt like throwing up. My butt was numb from sitting on the hard wooden bench. When I scanned the room I recognized a few people from the church Hon attended. Mama used to go to that church too and even sang in the choir.

An older woman was standing over a large box that was in the corner of the room. She was crying and her loud sobs filled the room. I saw several people go to comfort the woman. Who was she? I didn't know her, but I recognized Mrs. Simms who was sitting in the back of the room. She was crying too.

Uncle Ben walked through the door followed closely by Aunt Lea. I wanted to run to him but I was told to stay on the bench. Ralph and Joe were on the bench with me but they wouldn't be still. I smiled when I saw Uncle Ben coming towards us. He looked like a tall tree when I glanced up at him. He picked me up lifting me high in the air. I squealed with delight because Uncle Ben was the tallest person in the whole wide world. People were looking up at me now as I held tightly onto him.

That is when I again noticed the large box in the corner. I clung to Uncle Ben and he walked towards the box. As we neared it I felt panic coming over me. I could see there was something in it. I turned away not wanting to look. Finally we were standing over it. When I looked into the box I saw a woman who looked like mama.

She had on a pretty light blue dress. Her hair was brushed back except for a few curls cascading down her forehead. Both hands were clasped across her chest and a slight smile was on her face. She looked as if she was asleep. Mama looked so beautiful with lipstick on. I wanted to shake her and wake her up. Why was she in there? I looked at Uncle Ben for an explanation.

Wasn't she supposed to be in heaven? What was going on?

"She can't hear you," Uncle Ben's soft voice whispered to me. Did I say something? Without warning I felt my body leap forward. Strong arms held me as I struggled to get inside the box with Mama. I could feel Uncle Ben's heart beating when he held me close to his chest. It was beating fast like mine. It was Uncle Ben who kept me from jumping into the casket with mama, but not before I touched her hard cold flesh. I screamed as loud as I could, but no sound passed my lips. The silent scream came from somewhere deep inside.

I was tired and unable to struggle anymore. My body went limp when Uncle Ben handed me to Hon. When I was placed into Hon's soft bosom I was still shaking. My arms and legs felt weird and everything was fuzzy. I could see and hear people but I couldn't respond.

Today is the funeral, February twenty third. The snow is falling while people are gathering at Hon's house. Most are bringing food. When the lady who cried so loud the night before appeared at Hon's house I was curious about her. She was a thin short woman who wore cat-eyed glasses. Her hair was tucked beneath a hat, but I could see gray strands sticking out. I saw Hon embrace her before they disappeared inside Hon and Papa's bedroom. When they came out later the woman kissed and hugged all of us. When she bent down to kiss me I wanted to pull away from her because I didn't want her to kiss me. It was her hot tears that fell on my face and the look on Hon's face that stopped me from doing it.

"You're a big girl now, four years old today," she whispered to me. My birthday? I'm four years old today? I watched her hug and kiss the rest of my siblings and wanted to ask how she knew it was my birthday. No one told me it was my birthday. I didn't want to believe it. There were no balloons, no party, and no birthday cake. I looked around the room at the sad faces and no one in the house was happy. Everyone was crying--it couldn't be my birthday. I ran out of the room back into the living room to watch the snow again. A voice from behind startled me. I turned to see Hon.

"That was your other grandmother," she said. "Her name is Irene, and she is from Mississippi."

I was confused. How could I have two grandmothers? Hon was my grandmother.

"She is your mother's mother."

I didn't know my mother had a mother.

I was still looking out the window when the other grandmother walked past moving slowly. A man was holding onto her so she wouldn't fall. I watched as she got into a car and the man drove away. I tried to sort out all the information stored in my young mind. The snow was blowing hard against the window so I couldn't see anything anymore. Without warning a loud scream erupted, filling the entire room. I heard the noise, but didn't realize it came from me until Hon grabbed me and held me close. She rocked me while I sucked my thumb and quietly cried myself to sleep.

Chapter Two

Hon and Papa

My fondest childhood memories take me back to the white frame house on Thirteenth Street, the home of my grandparents, Hon and Papa. I was told that Papa was born in a shack in the backwoods of Mississippi to parents whose memories of slavery were still fresh. Papa didn't know his real age because he had no birth certificate. He could have claimed to be much younger than the sixty-five years he assumed he was.

Papa was a big man, good-looking, with strapping African features. He had a large head that matched his massive body, and very little gray hair to give away his age. Standing over six feet tall and wearing a size 15 triple E shoe he looked like fierceness itself. Papa's baritone voice and hearty laugh softened everyone's hearts and we all loved him.

Hon was a petite, thin woman with silver gray hair and small watery eyes. She was born March 5, 1895, in Aberdeen Mississippi where she grew up in a close family with her parents, Sarah and Monroe McMillan, and five siblings. Her face looked tired; unlike Papa she had aged into her senior years.

When Papa and Hon married she was in her twenties. She bore six children--five sons, Ben Jr., Roy, Henry, Guy, and Ike, and a daughter, Letha, whom they called Sister. In between Hon gave birth to premature twin boys who didn't get an opportunity to take their first breath. The boys were so small both of them fit into a shoebox and were buried behind the old barn.

I loved the feel of Hon's bony hands that were rough and wrinkled from years of scrubbing other people's floors. I felt strength in her touch and it had a calming effect on me. Hon was held in high esteem by all family members and was the one who kept the family together.

After Mama's death my brothers, sister and I became hot commodities in the family. I clung to Hon's dress while listening to family members discuss which one of us they wanted to take to live with them.

"You're too old to take care of all these children," Ike, Sister, Ben, and Guy told them. Hon and Papa didn't want to split us up, but they faced a hard battle against their own sons and daughter.

"Roy's crazy kids are going to drive both of you to your graves," I heard someone remark.

"I want Joyce," Aunt Lea demanded while Uncle Ben nodded in agreement. I watched Aunt Lea and turned away when she smiled at me. I didn't know her because she never came to our house. She seemed like a nice lady, but I didn't want to leave Hon and Papa. Aunt Lea was what people called a high yellow woman. She had very light skin with an oval face and sharp features that reminded me of a white person. Her dark brown hair was thick and hung on her shoulders. Uncle Ben bragged that when she was younger her hair fell down her back. She wasn't a beautiful woman, but she wasn't unattractive either. She was full figured with big legs and large breasts. The freckles on her face were hardly noticeable from a distance.

I was silent in the backseat of Uncle Ben's Cadillac the entire trip to their house. Aunt Lea had given me a quick hug when we were at Hon's house. I could smell the faint scent of perfume on her, which reminded me of mama. Hon told me I had to go with them.

"Are you okay back there?" Uncle Ben asked turning around briefly to smile at me.

I nodded my head and smiled back at him. I remembered Uncle Ben coming to our house and giving mama food. He sometimes gave us pennies or a nickel to buy candy.

"She's just a little shy," he assured Aunt Lea who was sitting in the front seat next to him.

I liked the cozy feel of their small house and adored my cousin, Annie Mae. She was a Hershey-brown-skinned girl with slightly slanted eyes and thick black lashes. Her hair was long and hung down her back the way aunt Lea's must have when she was a girl. Her perfectly straight teeth were a bright white and when she smiled she lit up the whole room. She had a small voice that was soft and soothing. Everything about Annie Mae reminded me of her parents. She had the tallness of her father and the feminine grace of her mother. Annie Mae was the same age as my brother Henry. I hadn't even started school and she was already entering high school. When I compared her to all my other girl cousins she was by far the prettiest.

Nathaniel was Annie Mae's little brother and the youngest of Uncle Ben and Aunt Lea's three children. Some called him Maine, but I called him Nate. They said he was named after his Uncle Nathaniel. He was big for his age even at that time. Nate was dark like his father with short wavy hair. The oldest son, Little Ben, had left home and enlisted into the Army. He looked important in his army uniform when he came home on leave to visit. Little Ben reminded me of Papa; they had similar features and identical heads and body types. When he laughed I could have sworn it was Papa.

Aunt Lea was nice to me but I didn't warm up to her for a while. She was a great cook and I enjoyed the times when all of us ate dinner together.

Uncle Ben and Aunt Lea were always arguing about

something. I didn't like it when they argued. I would hide somewhere in the house until they quit. One day I saw Uncle Ben hit her. I screamed when I saw blood dripping from Aunt Lea's lip. I felt my body shaking and I heard myself crying.

I woke up later in Hon and Papa's house remembering the terrible fight between Uncle Ben and Aunt Lea. I was glad Uncle Ben brought me back to Hon and Papa's house where I was reunited with Joe and Ralph. I didn't realize how much I missed them until we romped through the house playing the way we always used to. When I saw Uncle Ben again he looked sad and Hon was still fussing at him.

"Ben, you cannot keep beating your wife."

Uncle Ben hung his head as if he were truly sorry.

"I am not going to hit her again," he promised.

When he saw us standing nearby he waved his hands.

"Come over here and get your money," he said to us.

The three of us rushed over with our hands out. He gave each of us a shiny nickel.

"Thank you Uncle Ben", we all said together. The gold tooth in the front of his mouth glinted in the sunshine when he grinned. We challenged each other to a race as we ran to the corner store. I knew Hon had more to fuss about with Uncle Ben.

Mr. and Mrs. Simms adopted Louie. Roy jr. was eighteen and old enough to be on his own so he moved somewhere. Jerry went to live with Cousin Liza. Henry, Robert, Stephen, Frank, Joe, Ralph, Sara and I were placed with Hon and Papa. Although we lived with Hon and Papa, we were still wards of the State. Miss Gregg, a young social worker in her twenties, made frequent home visits. When I came back to live with them Hon promised I would never have to leave her again. From the beginning Joe, Ralph and I were grouped together because we were the youngest.

Gossip was a pastime for the women in our family. They would gather at Hon and Papa's house for an evening of gossip. The group included both of my aunts, Sister and Lucille, plus

Cousins Liza, Lorean and Rosie. They were all attractive women who were meticulous about their appearance. They always had their hair, makeup and clothes almost perfect.

If the walls in Hon's living room could talk there would have been a lot to tell. I would sit nearby so I could listen to their conversations. Much of what they talked about I didn't understand, but I gleaned what I could. Sister always talked about men and said things that had the other women reeling with laughter.

Sister was my father's youngest sibling. There are several ways to describe Sister; she was average height with golden brown skin and thick black hair. Her oval face had features that seemed chiseled on her. She had unusual slanted eyes that squinted when she laughed and full lips that looked as if she was pouting. Sister reeked of sex appeal and didn't mind flirting when then opportunity presented itself.

She was married to a quiet man we called Uncle Robert. I always thought he looked smart because of the black-rimmed glasses he wore. I noticed the way he looked at Sister and knew he loved her. I also listened to Sister talk about him and believed that she was sometimes mean to him.

Uncle Robert and Sister courted in Mississippi and got married when she was a teenager. Their first child, a boy, was named after his father. Uncle Robert and Sister moved to Milwaukee from Mississippi but eventually moved again to Indiana where Uncle Robert got a job in one of the factories.

Sister had children, but she also had a fiery spirit, so there was very little that kept her settled down. As soon as her oldest daughter, Alice Jean, was old enough she took on the responsibility of raising her mother's children.

We all called Lucille by her first name even though I knew her as my aunt. Lucille was a tall thin woman with pretty brown skin. Her cute round face had a set of deep dimples in each cheek. She had dark eyes and naturally arched brows. The dimples deepened when she smiled. There was talk that she wasn't really my aunt, but Papa's niece whom he and Hon adopted when she was a toddler. Lucille was a few years younger than Sister, but the two of them were raised together. Lucille was young when she had her first three children by three different men. She and her children lived with us in Hon and Papa's house. Even after having three children she maintained a figure that continued to turn heads in her direction.

Lucille shared a large bedroom at the top of the stairs with her children. Her oldest son, James, whom we called Football, was my age, her daughter, Tallandra was a couple of years younger and Terry was the baby. All of us played, ate and enjoyed good times together in Hon and Papa's house.

Cousins, Liza, Lorean, and Rosie were sisters and my father's first cousins. They came often to visit their Aunt Hon. Liza was the oldest of the trio; she was a tall light skinned woman with beautiful thick curly hair. Her trademark was the black-rimmed cat-eyed glasses that she wore. Liza was married to a man everyone called Bro Tot. He was a handsome man, tall and thin with a sly smile. He didn't come with Liza when she visited, but she talked about him with the others.

I enjoyed playing with Cousin Liza's grandchildren that she sometimes brought with her. But there was something about Cousin Liza that made me feel uncomfortable. I couldn't describe it because I didn't understand being disliked for no reason. Cousin Liza always hugged my brothers and gave them kisses, but she only stared at me. Sometimes she spoke to me and sometimes she didn't. I don't remember ever being hugged or kissed by her the way my brothers were. They were always excited to see her. Cousin Liza had a loud voice too, and she was a finger-popping woman who loved to dance. She was always the first one on the floor when the music started.

Lorean lived in Milwaukee with her husband, John, and two children, Leslie Mae and Johnny. I remember Lorean visiting more than the others. Sometimes she brought Leslie Mae and

Johnny with her. Leslie Mae was a few years older than me. She was cute and wore her hair in braids with ribbons tied around them. I would admire the ruffled dresses she always wore. Johnny was my age. He was a rough boy who liked to climb trees and play in the dirt. I had more fun with him than Leslie Mae. There was an endless supply of cousins to play with.

Rosie lived in Chicago Heights with her husband, Willie T. They didn't have any children and Rosie seemed to have plenty of money. I listened to all the talk about how beautiful her house was in Chicago Heights. They said that Willie T. gave her everything that she wanted. Rosie seemed to have a little more than the rest of them and always wore prettier clothes. She was a short woman, barely five feet tall, but walked with her head up as if she was seven feet tall. She had large eyes like Betty Boop and a round face with skin that looked flawless.

I learned how to eavesdrop without being noticed. My attention span was short so I filtered out most of what they said, but when I heard my brothers, sister, mama or daddy's name mentioned it piqued my interest. I learned a lot about the family while listening to the women gossip. They were always talking about someone in the family including my mama and daddy. They referred to us as "Roy's crazy kids." I didn't know anything about my father except his name and the word crazy had no meaning to me. The women ignored my presence and acted as if I were invisible, making it easier for me to listen while I played with my toys.

Down in Mississippi my mother's name was pronounced May Ran instead of Maryann.

"May Ran was pregnant when she went into the hospital," Lucille was saying.

"She was?"

"Yes she was; I believe she tried to get rid of that baby and that's probably what killed her."

"Hush your mouth"

"That woman she was hanging around with probably gave

her something to try to get rid of it."

"Mrs. Simms?"

"She's the one who adopted May Ran's baby".

"Uh huh."

"Someone said that the dead baby came out of her in little chunks."

"Say what!"

"Yes Lord, a friend of mine working at the hospital witnessed that."

"I wonder who the daddy was," Liza said dryly.

Rosie shot her sister a look of caution.

"It don't really matter who the daddy was," she remarked. "The baby never made it into this world alive."

Cousin Liza stared in another direction as if she was thinking. The others knew that Liza's husband, Bro Tot, was accused of fathering May Ran's baby, Louie. If that was true they were sure that he was also the father of the baby May Ran lost. Folks claimed to have seen his car parked in front of her house many times and some said that Louie looked like Bro Tot.

Bro Tot was a known womanizer and why Liza put up with it was nobody else's business. A few years earlier Bro Tot brought a group of children home to Liza and announced that they were his biological children by another woman. Cousin Liza was shocked at first, but after learning the woman had died she agreed to take in his four or five children. Instantly, her family grew from the two daughters they had together to about six or seven. Liza's only explanation was that she loved her husband.

"I didn't know May Ran was that sick." Rosie's eyes showed surprise.

Lucille was shaking her head. "I didn't know either," she confessed.

"I would have gone up there and seen her had I known she was that sick. I liked May Ran and she was a good sister-in-law," Sister said.

"You hardly knew the woman," Lucille told her, laughing.

"I knew she was a good woman and my brother loved her," Sister said.

"He must have loved her because they were having babies every year."

"Yea he sure kept her barefoot and pregnant."

Laughter filled the room as they continued talking.

"It was May Ran who gave me the money to buy blood after that low down man shot me". Sister's expression had changed like it always did when she talked about Uncle Robert.

"Those children are worrying my mama and daddy," Sister said changing the subject. "I told them they are too old to be raising them. They're already tearing up the house, next they are going to kill them just like they killed their own mama and daddy."

I cringed when she said we were going to kill Hon and Papa. The words felt like a knife cutting through me.

"I had to put Jerry out of my house because he wouldn't get a job." Liza looked at the others as if she was waiting for some confirmation.

"Jerry is damn near grown anyway," Rosie said.

"I heard he moved in with Mag", Liza said.

"Why did she let him move in with her? She has enough children of her own without having to take in another one."

They laughed again.

"How many children she got now?"

"Last I heard, Mag had about nine," Liza was shaking her head.

"Mag is something else." Sister was laughing. "She couldn't even wait until my brother came back from the war before she was lying up with another man."

"Uh huh"

"She must have known that Guy wasn't going to stay with her after she had another man's baby."

"The woman didn't have *one*, but *two* babies while he was

away. He divorced her butt when he got back." More laughter followed.

"Mag was a hot little thing when she was living in Mississippi," Rosie said.

"Humph." Liza shook her head.

"My brother damn near went crazy behind that woman. Now he is married to a white woman."

"He better be careful," Lorean said shaking her head.

"He lives in Denver, Colorado. He told me that in Denver people don't mess with colored people the way they do here. He is going to send me a ticket so I can ride the train down there to see him one day."

"Henry is living down there with Guy isn't he?"

Sister nodded. "Yeah, he moved down there because he was getting in a lot of trouble wanting to fight everyone."

"Henry is one crazy man," Rosie added. "I heard he busted up a tavern and whipped two or three men."

"Guy took him to Denver so he could help him. Last I heard Henry was in a hospital for people who can't control themselves."

"That's good because I'm scared that one day he will end up hurting somebody really bad."

"He's not getting in trouble down there though. Guy is taking good care of him," Sister answered.

"I sure do miss Cousin Henry" Liza said laughing. "He is a hell raiser."

The subject turned back to us.

"I don't understand why my mama and daddy want to be bothered with all these children. I know they don't have a mama or daddy, but I don't want them worrying my mama and daddy."

"Girl, did you know that Roy jr. is running after that big fat woman who is working at the restaurant?"

Rosie joined in the laughter. "What big woman"?

"She has to weigh at least four hundred pounds."

"What? What is wrong with that boy?" Lucille laughed.

"She gives him the keys to her car and is probably giving him money too."

"I wonder how they do it." Sister's laughter was floating through the house. She was laughing so hard she could hardly get the words out.

Lorean hit her playfully. "Only you would think of something like that."

"She is supposed to be the best cook this side of the Mississippi."

"You can look at her and tell that."

"Roy jr. needs to leave that woman alone and help take care of his brothers and sisters."

I sat in corner of the room playing on the floor and thinking about what I heard. They said that Roy jr. could have kept us together in mama's house.

"The county welfare offered that boy a cook and a housekeeper so he could keep all his brothers and sisters together in the house that May Ran bought."

"He didn't want to do it?"

"Roy jr. told those people that he was not going to take care of all those children. He told them they could do whatever they wanted with the children because he didn't want the responsibility."

"That boy ought to be ashamed of himself for not caring about his own brothers and sisters."

They nodded in agreement.

"May Ran wasn't ever the same after Roy died. I thought for sure she wasn't going to make it through the funeral. Did you see the way she was sitting there all in a daze?"

"Yea, before Roy's funeral she sat in a rocking chair near the window for three or four days drinking coffee and smoking cigarettes," Lorean said.

"It's a shame that they both died and left all these children behind."

"I still don't believe my brother killed himself," Sister

added.

"You damn right Roy didn't kill himself," Liza added.

"My brothers are going to find out the truth. Ike said he isn't going to rest until he finds out what happened to Roy."

"They didn't really investigate what happened anyway," Lucille said.

"All I know is that my mama and daddy are stuck raising May Ran and Roy's children."

I couldn't pretend their words didn't affect me. When the conversation became too complicated I moved away from my spot, but their words lingered on in my mind. I couldn't help seeing an image of mama lying in a hospital bed spitting up chunks of the baby that was in her stomach. They said the baby came out in chunks. I was plagued with nightmares about my mother and sometimes my throat would constrict thinking about it.

I was mad at Roy jr. for not keeping us together. Maybe Cousin Liza was right about him not caring about us. Roy jr. comes to visit at least once a week. When he drives up in front of the house we are excited to see him and proud that he is our big brother. He drives a nice car and sometimes has money that he shows to us but Roy jr. is stingy and never gives us anything. He talks to Hon and Papa and ignores us. One time Ralph jumped on the back of Roy jr.'s car as he was driving away and fell. The entire right side of his face was scraped. Ralph looked like a monster so I was glad when the skin came back.

Hon and Papa's house was located near the end of the block on a one-way street. Each house on the block was unique in shape and size. When I lived there it seemed like Hon and Papa had the largest house in the world. The two-story house was as tall as the oak tree in the front yard whose branches hung over the rooftop. There was nothing fancy about the house. It was painted a bright white with the darkest green trim I had ever seen. The front porch wasn't very big, but it provided shade from the sun. The wooden steps of the porch creaked when we ran up and down them. I sometimes envisioned Hon and Papa sitting in the wooden chairs on the porch when it was too hot to be inside of the house. They would be out there along with all the other neighbors watching us kids play in the street.

Papa and Hon had only one neighbor because on the left side of the house was a business. Large green trucks filled with linen from hospitals and institutions drove in and out of the driveway that was next to our house into what looked like a garage with windows. The neighbor on our right had three teenage daughters who hardly ever came outside. Hon would talk to the person who lived next door and I could hear them laughing and taking while we played hide-and-seek. The back of the house had a bigger porch where Frank created his own profitable business.

The backyard was like the Garden of Eden to me. It was lined with fruit trees and grape vines. During the summer we filled our bellies with plums, berries, and grapes. Rhubarb grew wild and we would pull long green or red stalks from the ground and snack on them all day.

When I looked in the back yard all I saw was the beauty of the trees and anticipation of when the fruit would ripen. I didn't see the old wrecked car that had rusted out and was a haven for rats. I didn't notice litter, debris, broken glass or any of the things that cluttered the yard. What I saw were beautiful flowers, fruit trees and all the room in the world to play.

There were two playgrounds in the neighborhood. One was to the left about a half of a block in Franklin Square. All of us spent time at Franklin Square playing during the summer and ice-skating during the winter. To the right was Juneau playground; it was a small playground with a couple of swings, slides, and a monkey bar. The ice cream parlor was around the corner and a couple spaces down from there was a movie theater. Yes, it was fun being a kid when I lived with Hon and Papa.

At their house the first room you step into is a small den. We spent most of our time in the den when we weren't playing outside.

Torn plastic curtains with large red and white flowers hung from two rectangular windows matching the red and white flowered pattern linoleum floor. The den was also my bedroom at night. I slept on one couch and Henry slept on the other one. When Sara came home from the deaf school she slept on the couch with me. The other furniture in the room was a black and white TV and Papa's overstuffed chair.

Papa warned us not to sit in his chair but none of us wanted to sit in it anyway because we knew about the snuff smeared underneath it. Papa's habit of dipping snuff was nasty and I hated the spit can he kept nearby where he would spit out globs of brown stuff. I thought it was disgusting watching Papa pour snuff into his bottom lip.

I was upset with Papa when he put some of the nasty snuff on my thumb. I was a thumb sucker and that was his way of trying to get me to stop sucking my thumb. I remember crying and waving my hand in the air trying to get it off. Papa had warned me that he was going to do it. I was devastated when he actually wiped the stuff on it. I enjoyed sucking my thumb and rolling my dress up as far as it would go. I kept hearing people telling me to put my dress down. I would roll it up to my neck showing my panties. My brothers sometimes imitated me by rolling their shirts up to their necks. I didn't care because my thumb had become my security blanket. At first I would cry and beg Papa not to put snuff on my precious thumb, but later I learned it washed off easily with soap and water.

Papa and Hon's bedroom was directly across from where I slept. Their room was darkened by green walls and pulled down shades. A double bed was shoved so close to the wall that Papa climbed in and out of bed from the bottom because he slept near the wall. A small dresser with a large round mirror completed the furniture in the bedroom leaving hardly any space to move around in there. The faint smell of ben gay or alcohol lingered in the air.

The living room was in the front of the house where sunlight filtered into the room through a large window in the center. A set of nice plastic curtains hung on the window in there. A few throw rugs covered the worn areas of the linoleum floor. It was the best room in the entire house and off-limits to all children. The couch, chair, coffee table, and end tables with lamps were all in great condition. Hon entertained guests in the living room. Most of the people were from Hon's church, including the preacher, Rev. Ward, who always came to pray for us. The social worker, Miss Gregg, was also a regular visitor in the living room.

The kitchen was huge with a large gray metal table in the middle of the floor. A gas stove and small refrigerator took up very little space. We didn't have chairs to the table so we ate our meals standing. It never bothered us that we ate the same thing everyday for dinner: beans and cornbread. Hon did mix up the beans because one day we would have pinto beans and the next day northern beans or lima beans, but it was always beans. Meat was rare in our house. We ate off of tin pie pans and drank from washed out vegetable cans. Utensils were scarce so we ate in shifts.

A staircase leading from the kitchen went to the attic part of the house. The attic is where most of the family slept. The first bedroom at the top of the stairs was a large pink room that Lucille shared with her children. The bedroom had a sun porch on the back that ran the length of the house. Sometimes I would walk out to the porch and look over the entire backyard. We played on the porch when it wasn't too hot and sometimes we just liked to climb down from it.

The next room was the unfinished part of the attic where all my brothers slept. It was a huge room with no windows or walls so it was always hot, stuffy and dark. Large wooden beams hung down and the only source of light was a single light bulb turned on by an overhead cord. I didn't like the room because of the eerie feeling it gave me. For some reason I believed that dead people could come in through the walls.

My brothers were paired off and that is how they slept,

Stephen with Frank and Joe with Ralph. Robert had his own bed because Jerry was living with another relative. Most of my brothers peed in the bed so the potent odor of urine filled the room.

The other bedroom past the opening was facing the front of the house. Like Lucille's bedroom this room was finished with walls and floors. My teenage cousins Jean and Claire Jean shared this bedroom. During the summer Jean and Claire Jean leaned out of the window and talked to people on the street below.

Jean had a boyfriend named Warren who came to the house almost every day. He was a good friend of Robert and Henry. I never knew why Jean liked him because he was ugly. He was dark skinned with budging eyes and thick pink lips.

Jean was Ike's daughter and looked a lot like him. She was short with a cute face and a smile similar to her father's. I don't know where Jean's mother was living but I knew she was still alive. Claire Jean was Lucille's biological sister, but they looked nothing alike. It was hard to see anything familiar connecting them. Claire Jean was tall and dark skinned with short hair.

It didn't bother me that I didn't have a real bedroom. I never had one anyway. I enjoyed sleeping on the couch because it was close to the bathroom and to Hon and Papa's bedroom. At night when everyone was asleep I could hear the scrambling of something moving across the kitchen floor. My brothers told me it was the mice.

Papa and Hon didn't mind keeping other grandchildren besides us. Sister's children stayed with us during the summer. John was Sister's third child who spent more time living with us than he did at home. At times as many as twenty people lived in Hon and Papa's house. I never thought that our living conditions were odd or unusual. It seemed normal to have that many people in the house. In the summertime we all sat in the den watching TV after a long day of playing and during the winter months it became our favorite meeting place. Papa would sit in his chair in the middle of the room and watch TV with us. Hon sat on the couch while most of us sat on the floor.

Papa ate anything that was an animal. I remember several times seeing a squirrel in a pan after Papa skinned it. I knew it was a squirrel because the bushy tail would be hanging over the side of the pan. Papa prepared the squirrel meat with yams or sometimes he cooked rice, we didn't care what it was as long as it was meat. The rarity of meat left us craving for it. I remember when Papa brought home a live goose that lived with us like a pet. I was afraid of the goose because it chased me through the house, one day it pecked me on the hand. A couple of weeks later we saw it hanging on the outside clotheslines upside down with its feathers plucked. I was glad Papa cooked it.

Papa bought food from the grocery store around the corner once a month. When it was shopping day Papa took as many of us that wanted to go. We walked with Papa to the store where he bought food on credit. Frank always brought along his wagon to load the food into. Papa bought a few rolls of pork sausage or bacon. It never lasted more than a week, but at least we savored the taste. Hon or Papa cooked the sausage or bacon on Sunday mornings with a pot of rice. Long after the meat was gone we dipped white bread into the sausage or bacon grease and ate grease sandwiches.

There were two taverns around the corner from us that Papa went to buy his pint of VSQ. He went to Poor Charley's most of the time because he had credit there. We would follow Papa to the tavern because he would buy each of us a bag of potato chips, cheese popcorn or peanuts. "Put it on my bill" Papa would tell the man behind the bar. He would stuff the half pint of liquor in his back pant pocket. When Papa got home he would open the bottle and hold it up to say his favorite verse.

"Up to my head and down to my toes this is where poor man money goes." We would laugh at Papa who would quickly gulp down a couple of swallows of the liquor and put the bottle back into his pocket.

The house was always busy with the rapid flow of relatives who flocked around Hon. I learned from eavesdropping that Hon was the advisor in the family. Everybody came to her to discuss his or her problems.

Hon had two sisters and three brothers. The three sisters were always visiting each other. Hon took me with her when she caught the Greyhound bus to Chicago to visit them. I had a whole new network of cousins in Chicago, so I always enjoyed those trips.

Sometimes when relatives gathered at Hon and Papa's house it would turn into a party. The teenagers had records and there was a record player in the living room. We watched as Cousin Liza, Rosie and Sister would dance around the room. Cousin Liza would pull her dress up and gyrate to the music. We would laugh because the other women would do things too. Lucille loved to bend over and stick her butt out and she would move it around making everyone clap and laugh. They did dances called The Dog and Punch the Bull.

They loved Ray Charles's songs and would stack as many as they could on the record player creating their own party while songs like *What I'd Say* and *Hit the Road Jack* belted from the record player. The children would join in trying to imitate them. We would sometimes lift our dresses showing our legs, and prance around the house singing, "Oooh, aah, oooh aah, tell me what I'd say."

Relatives rarely came to see any of us so sometimes I felt as if I was in their way. Uncle Ben and Ike were the only two who acted like we existed. Besides giving us hugs or playing with us they gave us money. Ralph was a chubby boy who ate all of his food and any leftovers he could get. Uncle Ben brought leftover food from his house to give to Ralph.

"Hog head," Uncle Ben would shout out when he entered the house. That was Ralph's signal that Uncle Ben was bringing

49

food for him. Ralph would rush in with his head down and run towards him like a bull. We would laugh at Ralph and hope that he would share the food.

Sara came home for major holidays and all summer. I didn't understand why she couldn't talk or hear. She could laugh and scream really loud. When she cried she sounded just like us, but she couldn't speak any words. It was confusing to me because it seemed like she should be able to say words too. I tested her all the time and she really couldn't hear. I would scream at her while her back was turned or make funny noises, but she never turned around. I don't know how we communicated with her, but she always seemed to understand what we were saying and for some reason we understood her too. Everyone said that Sara looked like Mama. I wasn't sure anymore because as time went on I was starting to forget what Mama looked like.

Sara was treated special because she was deaf. She always got an extra nickel from the uncles. Lorean really liked her and would hug her longer than she did the rest of us. I was always sad when Sara had to go back to the school.

I cried so hard one time that Ike let me stay with him for about two weeks. He lived with his girlfriend, Gloria in a two-bedroom duplex. She was a nice lady who always wore her hair pulled back into a long ponytail. I met new friends on the block and enjoyed the time I was there. That was the summer when root beer became my favorite flavored Popsicle.

Hon gave me as much attention as she could, but at her age she didn't have much energy or patience. The few occasions when I accompanied Hon we rode the city bus. She took me shopping at the Goodwill. We always had nice clothes even though they were used. Hon bought me dresses with candy cane slips that made them stick out at the bottom, and I had a nice pair of patent leather shoes that shined like new money to wear to church.

The bus ride to the County Hospital was long because it was several miles out of town. We got up early in the morning to get ready. Hon always packed lunches and snacks because we were there all day. It would be hours before the doctor would see her. I noticed that the waiting room was always full of black people who were also waiting to see a doctor. The County Hospital was for poor people, so mostly black people went there for their medical care.

Papa worked in the boiler room at his job but his job-title was a fireman. Papa always packed a lunch to take to work. All of us eyed the black metal lunch box he carried. Papa would deliberately leave something in his lunchbox and would give it to one of us to finish off. Papa gave everyone a turn to eat the leftovers and it was always exciting when it was my turn because I never knew what Papa had left. Sometimes it was a piece of lunchmeat sandwich with an apple or another piece of fruit. Sometimes it was cookies and some soda or coffee in his thermos.

There was another sad day at our house and Hon was in distress. The tears flowed and the prayers were endless. Many church people came over to comfort Hon. I didn't know my Uncle Henry and had only heard his name mentioned during the gossip sessions or when Hon spoke of him. I knew he was living in a place called Denver. There was something wrong with Uncle Henry so he was in a hospital to help him get better. They said that Uncle Henry was a very strong man with a mean attitude so it was hard for people to restrain him. Somehow Uncle Henry jumped out of the hospital window, breaking his legs. They wanted to fix his legs, but Uncle Henry wouldn't let them so gangrene settled into his legs and he died. Hon and Papa grieved for Uncle Henry. When I saw tears in her eyes I knew she was thinking about my daddy or Uncle Henry.

The first day of school felt like the first day of a death sentence. I didn't want to go to school so I cried and begged Hon not to take me. The thought of having to stay with a room full of kids I didn't know frightened me. Other kids in the kindergarten class also kicked and screamed when their parents left them. Hon stared at me through teary eyes so I knew she really didn't want to leave me either.

"You have to go to school," she told me. Hon had talked to me several times about going to school. I had assured her that I was ready for school, but deep down I didn't know how I was going to feel on that day.

After Hon left the classroom I settled down and it wasn't so bad. We sang songs, ate graham crackers, and drank milk. We took naps on blue padded mats. Hon was waiting for me when I walked out of class my first day of school. I never cried again.

I became best friends with twins named Linda and Brenda. I hadn't seen twins before and was really drawn to the identical-looking girls. Both girls were dark skinned with hair that was always combed the same. They wore the same clothes, had the same smile and even had identical voices. My new friends amazed me. I wasn't the best ice skater so when the skating rink opened up Brenda and Linda would stand on opposite sides of me and help me along. By the end of the semester I loved kindergarten.

Stephen graduated from the sixth grade that year. I remember how proud Hon was that evening when we were getting dressed for Stephen's continuation. He was handsome in his black slacks, white shirt and red blazer. Stephen was a good-looking boy anyway, but now he looked more like a young man than a boy. When his name was called Hon nudged me and we both smiled when Stephen walked across the stage.

That summer Stephen's interest in girls peaked. A girl named Charlene lived down the street from us. Stephen was always hanging out down there talking to her. Stephen's best friends were our cousins, Nate and John, who were the same age as he. They apparently had more in common besides being cousins. Nate didn't seem to have any friends except for Stephen and John. He was over our house almost every day that summer because John was living in the house with us.

I was in the first grade when I first noticed something different about Hon. In kindergarten she had walked me to school and usually picked me up. Hon said she didn't have the energy to take me to school anymore when I went into first grade, so Joe was given the responsibility of walking me to and from school. I gained another friend in first grade named, Valerie Taylor. By my second year of school Hon could barely move around the house.

Frank didn't attend Public school with us. He went to a school for handicapped kids along with two other kids on our block, Ricky and Daryl, who were crippled from polio. I didn't understand why Frank had to go to school with them because he wasn't wearing braces on his legs nor did he need crutches. We were aware that Frank was hard of hearing because sometimes we had to shout at him so he could hear what we were saying. Hon said he was supposed to be wearing a hearing-aide but Frank didn't like to wear it. It was also hard to understand his words because they sounded different.

A bright yellow school bus stopped on our block every morning to pick up Ricky, Daryl and Frank.

Ricky was Frank's best friend. Papa and Hon bought Frank a bright red wagon and he went everywhere in his wagon, one foot inside the other out scooting along the sidewalk, sometimes with Ricky inside the wagon. The two of them searched the alleys for bottles that Frank cashed in for money. Frank also had a con game: he would stand on the street corners with Ricky, begging people who were passing by for money. Sometimes people gave him money especially when he had Ricky with him. Frank invested the money in candy so after the corner store closed he opened his own store on the back porch. His store was a wooden crate with the candy underneath and a can with a lid on it that held the money. Frank charged neighborhood kids twice the price for his candy. If it was a penny in the store he charged two pennies. Frank didn't give anyone any candy free and that included us. His store would close down when there were no more kids outside.

At night when all was quiet I could hear Frank's high-pitched voice singing until he fell asleep. It was actually funny to hear him singing.

My older brothers, Henry, Robert, and Jerry, were supposed to be in high school, but they didn't go. Henry did strange things, which gave the gossiping women another reason to call us crazy. Everyone said Henry looked like the uncle he was named after. His complexion was the color of peanut butter and he was built like a fighter with large biceps and muscles that rippled through his body. Henry was a natural fighter who terrorized most people that came in contact with him. When he was around Hon and Papa he was gentle, but on the streets Henry was close to dangerous. He stole things along with Robert. He liked to smoke cigarettes, gamble, and drink too.

Robert stole anything he could get his hands on, including cars. He would ride past the house waving at us while we stood in the yard looking in awe as he drove by in a new Cadillac. Robert also gambled, drank wine, smoked cigarettes, and stayed out late most nights. He would get a game of cards or craps together so he could gamble. Robert was good-looking with a mixture of mama and daddy's features. He spent a lot of time at Mrs. Johnson's house around the corner where his girlfriend, Brenda, lived. Mrs. Johnson was a gambler too so they sometimes stayed up all night gambling.

Jerry moved in with Aunt Mag after Cousin Liza told him to leave. Aunt Mag was our cousins, Guy jr., Ida and Lonnie's mother. Jerry's skin was dark but he had eyes that sometimes looked greenish. He wore his hair in what people called a "process." His hair was straightened by lye and he kept it laid down by wearing a scarf around his head. Jerry didn't mind working, but he had a hard time finding a job so he and Guy jr. started working with Uncle Ben cleaning out people's basements. Jerry was smart in school and got good grades, but his interest in school fizzled so he dropped out.

Jerry was a gambler too, but his main vices were smoking and drinking. Just like his brothers he wasn't at the legal age to drink, but he did it anyway. The more that Guy jr. and Jerry hung out the more trouble they got into. Although barely teenagers, they smoked cigarettes and drank cheap wine.

Sundays were reserved for going to church. Hon attended Antioch Baptist church, a big church with many members. Mama attended Antioch and sang in the choir when she was alive. Cousins Liza and Lorean and many other family members also went there. If Papa went to church I don't remember it. I went to church with Hon sometimes and was impressed by the large building with many pews and colorful stained glass windows. Images of Jesus were all over the building and a cross that was taller than me hung on a wall.

The church had a large choir with a mixture of men and women. A separate children's choir was also large. Hon sat with a group of older women called "Mothers of the Church." All of them sat in the front pew opposite of the Deacons. They wore all white clothes including their gloves.

I was proud to see Hon among this elite group of gray haired women in the church. A nurse dressed in her crisp white uniform and matching cap sat near the back of the church. Hon told me she was there just in case someone got sick. I felt as if I were important in that church because everyone dressed up.

I remember the beautiful two-piece green suit that Cousin Liza wore one Sunday. It had a real fox-fur collar on it and she looked like a movie star when she stepped inside the church.

I didn't always go to Hon's church. We discovered a small storefront church at the end of our block. The church was mostly made up of neighborhood kids. I liked going there because in Sunday school we were taught about Jesus. I learned how to sing church songs like "Jesus Loves Me" and "He's got the Whole World in His Hands," and it was easy walking the half a block to church.

When Hon had money we went to the movies a few blocks away. It was the only theater in our neighborhood and was usually crowded on Sunday. The line was always long. After finally getting into the movie I was usually disappointed because it was either Godzilla or King Kong fighting another creature or each other. I hated both of these beasts and hoped each time they would show a different movie. I got my wish one Sunday when the feature movie was about black singers. I was out of my seat when Gene Chandler sang "Duke of Earl." It was great because he had a cape, walking stick, and top hat on. Everyone went wild when Chubby Checker sang "The Twist."

We probably didn't live in the cleanest house because there were so many people living in it, but it was neat. There wasn't any trash in the house or piles of dirty dishes in the sink. The floors were clean and so were our clothes. I'm sure it must have been a challenge to keep everything clean, especially after Hon became ill. We did have roaches and I hated when they crawled on me while I slept

Most of the kids in the neighborhood avoided us like we had the plague. It didn't matter because I had so many cousins and brothers to play with, so we never needed outside friends. I did make friends with a girl named Pudding who lived around the corner. I could get to her house by going through the neighbor's broken fence across the street. She was a small medium-brown-skinned girl with large braids and a head full of ribbons and bows. Pudding lived with her mother and father in a big two-story house. She was my age and an only child. I felt sorry for her when she told me that she didn't have brothers or sisters because I couldn't imagine life without brothers, sisters, or cousins.

The first time I visited Pudding at her house I remember how beautiful everything looked. Several rugs covered the floor and the windows had cloth curtains covering them. Pudding had her own bedroom filled with a large collection of dolls.

"Your family must be rich," I told her.

"Your family is just poor," she replied.

She was right that we were poor. Hon and Papa wouldn't ever be able to afford the things Pudding had in her house. All Pudding's tops matched her shorts. I wore dresses most of the time and when I wore shorts it was with one of my brothers' t-shirts. It was nice playing with her dolls, but I didn't like going to her house because I didn't feel comfortable.

Pudding's mother was a mean-looking woman who made me wait on the porch. Her father was a tall man who always wore a suit to work. I overheard her mother talking to Pudding one day. It was summertime and the screen door was open.

"I don't want that girl in this house," she said almost screaming at Pudding.

"Mama, we want to play with the dolls in my bedroom," Pudding protested.

I waited on the porch even though I wanted to leave. I didn't like Pudding's mother.

"That little girl is dirty," her mother said.

What did she mean I was dirty? Hon made sure that I washed my body and changed my clothes everyday. Hon told me that it was important that I change my panties even if I wore the same clothes. Hon always washed my clothes so I would have clean clothes to wear. I didn't have a lot of clothes like Pudding, but they were clean.

Pudding's bottom lip was stuck out when she came outside.

"She told me we couldn't play in the house."

"I heard your mother fussing at you," I told her.

She nodded her head.

"We can go to my house."

"My mama told me if I ever went into your house she'd beat my butt."

I stared at Pudding who was half smiling at me.

"There is nothing wrong with my house." I was on the verge of tears.

"Yes there is." Pudding nodded. "Your house is nasty. That raggedy car in your front yard has all kinds of trash in it. Mama and Daddy said that there are too many people living in your house and all of you are nasty."

I had the urge to punch Pudding for what she said, but

57

instead I threw her doll to the ground and walked away.

"I don't ever want to play with you again," I told her.

I decided that despite her great doll collection I didn't like her. I quit going over her house, but I could see her peeping through the fence like she did the first time I met her. She didn't have anyone to play with now. Her mother was probably happy that she didn't have to open the door and see me sitting on their doorstep anymore.

Margo Johnson lived on the same block as Pudding. She was Brenda's little sister and became my new best friend. She never teased me or talked about my house. I visited Margo when Robert went to visit Brenda. If I went with him I could stay as long as he did. Joe and Ralph went there too to play with her brother. She didn't have a lot of dolls like Pudding, but we had a lot of fun together.

I loved summer time because I had fun playing outside. The summers in Milwaukee were hot and humid but it didn't bother me. I went out to play early in the morning and only came inside to eat or use the bathroom. Even when it rained I didn't go inside like most kids. I stayed outside playing in the water that filled gutters. I loved the feel of the rain on my face and sometimes I held my head back with my mouth open so rain could fall inside. I took my shoes off so I could walk in the rain. I wouldn't go inside until Hon hollered for me, but not before my clothes were soaked.

One day while playing barefoot in the rain I felt a sharp pain on the bottom of my foot. I screamed in pain and hopped over to the curb where I inspected my foot and saw a nail sticking halfway into my foot. Joe helped me into the house and we removed the nail. There wasn't much blood but the throbbing pain was awful.

When I woke up the next morning my foot throbbed in pain and I didn't dare move off of the couch except to hop to the bathroom. The next day when I awoke the right side of my face was swollen. It felt like my entire body was in pain. I was crying for Hon. the expression on her face scared me even more.

"Your face is swollen," she said.

"My foot hurts and I can't walk."

Hon examined my foot while I cried out in pain. "Henry!" Hon screamed for my brother. Henry rushed over to us. Everything happened quickly. Henry picked me up from the couch and carried me to the waiting car and Uncle Ben drove us to the hospital.

I could hear what the doctors were discussing with Hon while I laid on a small bed in a silent room.

"The nail she stepped on was probably rusty," he told her.

Then they said something about lockjaw and infection. I was admitted into the hospital in the children's ward. I cried and screamed every time they gave me a shot. I slept a lot the first couple of days. Hon was there when I opened my eyes I saw her. The room was huge and there were other kids in nearby beds that looked like big cribs. When I started feeling better I stayed up longer and was able to talk to my grandmother who visited me everyday and forced me to eat my dinner.

"You have to eat your food so you can get better."

I ate as much as I could, even though my appetite was gone.

I don't remember how long I was in the hospital, I just remember being happy when I was well enough to go home.

That summer Stephen stepped on a nail and had to go to the hospital and Frank almost drowned at the Boy's Club.

"He jumped in twelve feet of water after the pool was closed and everyone had left," the man told Hon. He was lucky that the lifeguard went back in and noticed something in the bottom of the pool. He jumped in to find out what it was and discovered Frank down there.

We crowded around Frank when he came home from the hospital. "I thought I could swim," he told us. "They wouldn't let me swim in the deep end of the pool so when they weren't looking I jumped in." We all laughed about it. Frank described how he couldn't breathe and how they had to pump water from his lungs. We didn't know any better and laughed about that too. He said he would never do it again.

By the time I turned eight Hon was going to see the doctor all the time. Because she didn't have a private doctor she took that long bus ride to the county hospital where she waited hours to be seen by a doctor.

During the bus ride to the hospital I would look out of the bus window at large brick homes with beautiful lawns that looked like they should have been in a picture book. We didn't have houses like that where we lived so I wondered what kind of people lived in them. When we finally arrived at the hospital the wait began.

We were shuffled to a large room with several others who were waiting to see the doctor too. I played on the cold linoleum floors with other children while Hon talked with the people. We ate our lunch at noon without ever leaving the room. It was late afternoon when Hon finally saw the doctor. The office visit would only last about thirty minutes and then we were on our way back home. When we made it to our house it was evening. During the school year Hon was either in bed or at the clinic. Papa was doing most things around the house like cooking and watching us. I didn't know what was wrong with Hon except she needed to rest. I sometimes sat on her bed staring at her while she slept. I watched her take slow deliberate breaths. Although she never complained, I knew she was sick. Hon didn't go to church anymore because she had a hard time getting out of bed, so church people came over to pray with her. At first Hon would get out of bed and go into the living room, but after a while she accepted visitors in her bedroom.

The first time she went into the hospital to stay overnight I cried and was relived when she came home. Nothing had changed though, she went to bed and that is where she remained most of the time. At night while lying on the couch I could hear her moaning in pain. Papa would get up in the middle of the night to get her water so she could take her medicine. He helped her to the bathroom and fed her. It bothered me to see Hon like that. When she did get out of bed, she always tired quickly. Hon went back into the hospital and everyone was upset. I saw relatives were crying and knew it had to be bad.

The one thing that my grandparents didn't want to see happen to us came at a time when they were powerless to do anything about it. Hon was in the hospital and Papa couldn't take care of me so I went to live with Uncle Ben and Aunt Lea. We would stay split up "until Hon gets better," we were told.

Uncle Ben lived in a small house near an alley. It was an older house made of materials that were often found on roofs. The house wasn't visible from the street because a larger house blocked it. It was easier to access the house from the alley. The house had an enclosed front porch off of the living room and the den was converted into a bedroom for Uncle Ben and Aunt Lea.

On the wall above the den was a picture of a small child. I didn't like the picture because the eyes of the child seemed to follow me around the room. I found out later that it was their daughter who died when she was a toddler. Aunt Lea blamed Papa for her death.

"He took her for a ride in his car with the windows open and she got pneumonia and died."

I didn't want her blaming Papa because the child died.

The kitchen was a bright yellow and when the sunshine reflected off the kitchen walls it was brighter. Yellow was my favorite color. In the kitchen was a table with matching chairs so we sat down and ate our meals. The bathroom was on the main floor and the two bedrooms were upstairs.

Annie Mae got pregnant by her high school boyfriend and Uncle Ben made them get married. Aunt Lea and Uncle Ben spoiled Annie Mae's baby girl.

Nate was now in Junior high school. He was tall like Uncle Ben and heavy like his mother. He had nice teeth like his sister, but his laugh was crazy and eerie. He made faces that scared me and I would always look away from him.

It was hard to know what was going on with Aunt Lea. She didn't talk much to me and I tried to stay out of her way.

In Years To Come

One day when I came home after school she made me take a bath and put on the clothes that I usually wore to church. I stood before her in my pink chiffon dress and white leather shoes. Aunt Lea started crying. She wiped her tear-streaked face and took my hand. I climbed into the front seat of the car and watched her out the corner of my eyes. I was too short to see over the dashboard so I had didn't know where she was taking me.

The drive was long and silent. I played with the sash on my dress and kicked my feet nervously. I wanted to talk to her but the words wouldn't come out. I didn't have enough nerve. Finally the car stopped and a feeling of relief rushed over me. I looked up at the large building we were parked in front of and a familiar feeling came over me. I knew this building. It was the County Hospital. I was sure my heart skipped a beat.

Aunt Lea finally spoke. "Hon asked too see you." She took my hand and squeezed it tightly. The smell of chlorine and anesthetic quickly filled my nostrils when we walked through the revolving door. Aunt Lea's grip hurt my hand. She walked fast, almost dragging me behind her. We got into an elevator going up. People were getting on and off between floors so the ride seemed to take forever. Finally we got off the elevator. My white shoes clicked loudly on the linoleum floor as she dragged me along beside her.

"Where are you going with that child?" The voice coming from behind us made me jump. Aunt Lea stopped to turn and face an angry nurse.

"Please let me take her in to see her grandmother," she pleaded.

"Children are not allowed up here!"

Aunt Lea looked down at my confused face. "Her grandmother is terminally ill and...."

"No children allowed!"

The nurse stood with her hands on her hips. Aunt Lea had no choice. She reluctantly took me back to the elevator. She sobbed aloud in the elevator ignoring the people who were staring at her.

"All she wanted to do was see you."

Then I began crying. I wanted to see her too. I missed her so much.

"I want to see Hon," I cried out as Aunt Lea led me into the child nursery in the hospital lobby.

"You have to stay here until I come back," she said. "I am going back upstairs to see Hon."

The other kids who were left in the child nursery were busy playing with the toys. I stood at the door watching Aunt Lea disappear into the elevator. I put my head on the back of the chair I sat down in and cried softly into the cushion. That is where I was when she came back later for me.

"I tried," she whispered, more to herself than to me.

We never talked about my attempted visit to see Hon. I learned from whispers among relatives that Hon was not doing well. I didn't want to accept the possibility that Hon might not come back home.

It was springtime in Milwaukee. Flowers were blooming and the trees were waking up from their winter sleep. Birds were chirping and there was warmth in the spring air. It was a time to be alive, not dead.

Hon didn't come home from the hospital. When news of her death reached me it felt like I was thrown into another dimension. I sat on the couch in Uncle Ben's house staring in disbelief. What would happen to us now? I didn't like living with Uncle Ben and Aunt Lea because Cousin Nate was mean to me. I had waited patiently for Hon to get better so I could go back home.

"Can I go back to live with Papa?" I asked Aunt Lea.

She shook her head.

I reminded her that my brothers were still there.

"We will be going to court about all of you," she said.

Joe, Ralph and I ended up living with Uncle Ben and Aunt Lea. Stephen and Frank moved in with Ike. They placed Henry into a mental institution called Southern Colony. Jerry and Robert caught the bus to Indiana and moved in with Sister and her family. Sara was still living at the school for the deaf. Lucille moved into her own house with her three children. John, Jean and the rest of the cousins moved back to live with their parents. The family came together to mourn the loss of Hon. Nate and another older cousin was supposed to be watching us while the adults went somewhere. They became restless waiting for the adults to return so Nate began scaring us. He made it look like Hon's dresses that were hanging in the hall closet were flying around by themselves. We couldn't see a face as the dress wavered over the stairs. We were scared and started crying. We wanted to leave. Nate walked us over to where Lucille was living. We told her about the flying dresses and one cousin said he saw Hon at the top of the stairs looking down at us. Lucille let us stay at her house until the adults came to pick us up.

When I saw Hon lying in the casket I wasn't scared or sad. I remembered how much pain she was in and now everyone said she wasn't feeling any more pain. She was beautiful as she slept in the casket. All I could do was look down at the woman I loved.

I wished that I could have talked to her one last time before she died and went to heaven. Even though Hon was in heaven, a piece of her was inside of my heart because I could feel her presence. People wanting to look at her interrupted my thoughts. I wouldn't leave my spot and I couldn't talk to her with them around.

I still didn't understand how people got to heaven. Everyone was crying and Sister was practically screaming on the other side of the room.

"That's my mama," she screamed out.

I felt a sting of sadness creeping over me. Papa was restless and began pacing back and forth. Suddenly a loud cry exploded from the back of the room. It was Papa. He cried out Hon's name before rushing out of the door. I missed Hon and wondered why people had to die.

Chapter Three

Uncle Ben

Uncle Ben's house looked like a square box with an enclosed porch. I enjoyed playing on the porch when I couldn't play outside although I still preferred the openness of Hon and Papa's porch. Looking out of the porch windows all I could see was a large yellow house that was a lot bigger than ours sitting in front of us blocking the view to the street. I thought it was a dumb place to put a house. It was hard to sleep on those hot summer nights because no one had air-conditioning or a fan to cool us down. We could hear cars going down the alley where the back of the house was. If it was a big truck the house actually shook. I wondered why they moved into a house that didn't even have a yard. We played on the paved concrete in front of the house. I made friends with the little girl next door and we sometimes played hopscotch. We never became really good friends though.

Aunt Lea was a good housekeeper so everything was always neat and clean. The house was furnished with modern furniture that looked practically new. The living room was carpeted and I loved taking my shoes off so my feet could sink into the softness of the carpet. I was amazed when I watched Aunt Lea maneuver the vacuum machine around the living room. It was like magic watching it suck up dirt from the carpet. The loud noise bothered me, but I couldn't help watching the machine work because I had never seen anything like it.

Moving in with Uncle Ben and Aunt Lea was supposed to be temporary but things changed after Hon passed away. I believed Uncle Ben didn't mind us living with him, but I wasn't sure of Aunt Lea's feelings.

Aunt Lea began acting strange towards us. It wasn't anything she said, but her attitude was unmistakable. When she spoke her voice was filled with anger that matched the frustration on her face. She complained about us to Uncle Ben almost daily. She complained about having to comb my hair. I would sometimes cry when I sat between her legs getting my hair combed because she kept on talking about how much she hated to do it. She complained about having to cook more food and do more laundry. The worse complaint was about us wetting the bed every night. The look on her face every morning told us how she felt.

I knew she didn't like having to wash so many sheets and I felt bad about wetting the bed. Joe, Ralph and I wet the bed every night. Joe and Ralph were peeing in the bed when we lived with Hon and Papa, but I don't remember when I started. I think it was after Hon passed away and I began having night terrors. I felt humiliated and ashamed, especially after Nate began teasing us. I quit drinking water at night, but that didn't help either. Aunt's Lea's anger led to us being whipped for peeing in the bed, but that didn't help either. The more she lashed out at us the more I withdrew. I missed Hon and Papa and cried myself to sleep at night. I could hear Joe and Ralph whimpering too and knew they missed Hon and Papa too.

Uncle Ben was more patient with us. He tried to make us feel wanted and at the same time tried to please Aunt Lea. When he walked through the door in the evenings we were always excited to see him. He stood taller than the doorway with his thin frame. It felt good to put my arms around his neck and give him hugs. Sometimes he gave me a peck on the cheek causing me to giggle.

Being the hard worker that he was Uncle Ben was tired when he came home yet he still took a few minutes to play around with us. It was the only attention that we received so all of us lapped it up. Aunt Lea complained so much about us that Uncle Ben whipped us or yelled at us. He always looked sorry after spanking us and sometimes he dug deep into his pockets to give us a dime or nickel so we could run to the store.

Nate was the biggest terror in our lives. I'm not sure why he hated us so much, but from the moment all of us came to live with them Nate started picking on us. He never hid the contempt that he obviously felt against us. He did mean things to us when Uncle Ben and Aunt Lea weren't around and we were scared of him. He knew we were afraid and used it to his advantage.

Nate was tall like Uncle Ben except he had a larger frame and looked like a grown man. He hit, slapped, and pinched us every time he got the opportunity. Sometimes just the way he looked at us was frightening. He dared us to tell someone what he was doing to us. We didn't tell anyone. I don't think Aunt Lea would have believed us anyway because she was still pampering him like he was a little kid. He never got whippings or in trouble for anything. He always got whatever he wanted from them.

I resented the closeness between Aunt Lea and Nate because it reminded me of when I lived with Hon and Papa. Although there were as many as fourteen children living in that house Hon and Papa made all of us feel special.

I prayed to God to help Papa find a way to take us back to live with him again. I missed my siblings as well as the cousins who lived with us. I wanted to go back to the only home I had known. I missed Franklin Square and Juneau playground. I missed the backyard paradise and the church down the street. Most of all I missed the feeling of safety I felt while living with Hon and Papa. We were never beaten up, pushed down stairs, or subjected to the torture that Nate put us through. Nate wasn't satisfied until he had us screaming in pain and begging him to stop. He laughed the entire time he was twisting our arms or punching us. But we had no other place to go, so we had to endure his abuse.

Sara came to live with us after her school closed for summer break. She slept on the couch in the living room because she didn't pee in the bed. Sara taught us how to form words using the deaf alphabet to talk to her. We had a card with all the hand signs on it so we talked to Sara using the card to spell out words. We developed our own way of communicating though because we couldn't catch on to the sign language she was trying to teach us.

Because there was no yard we went to the park a half of a block away to play. It was a nice park with a swimming pool, and a toy library. We could check out a toy to take home to play with and return it a week. We didn't have any toys to play with so it was nice to go to the toy library. I was careful not to break any of the toys because then we would have to pay for it.

I loved to go swimming even though I never learned how to swim. I would walk to the park with Sara and we would go to the swimming pool and spend the entire day splashing around in the water.

Lots of neighborhood kids played softball in the park. Sara liked to play softball so she joined them. Sonny was a tall thin boy about eighteen years old who lived in the yellow house in front of ours. He was supposed to be throwing the ball to Sara, but hit her with it instead. We knew that Sonny hit Sara deliberately because he started laughing and teasing her. Sara was still crying when we got home. I told Uncle Ben what happened and he left the house.

Uncle Ben returned a short time later with Henry and Robert. I hadn't seen them since we left Hon and Papa's. It was Robert who jumped out of the car and ran to where Sonny was standing on his porch. Everything happened so fast that it was like watching a movie. Robert punched Sonny and the two of them began fighting. We cheered Robert on. At least twelve children lived in that house and Sonny was the oldest. The other children came out of the house and I began fighting with a girl about my age.

When it was over Sonny was beat up. Robert warned Sonny to keep his hands off of all of us before he left. He didn't know that Sonny wasn't the biggest problem in our life.

Nate hadn't bothered us that summer, but we knew it was only because he was busy doing other things and wasn't home much. I clung to Sara because I felt secure with her. We walked to the ice cream parlor, the grocery store and the park together. She was my best friend.

Bruce, the neighborhood bully, was a couple of years older than me. He threw rocks at us and chased us if we passed by his house on the next block. We had to pass his house on our way to the store so we usually checked the alley before running to the store.

We didn't see where Bruce came from, but suddenly he was behind us. Sara ran faster than I did and while trying to keep up with her I fell on a rock. I began screaming because of a sharp pain in my leg. Bruce ran in the other direction and Sara came back to help me. She pulled on my hand, trying to help me off the rock. Each time she pulled the pain shooting down my leg caused me to scream. I didn't care whether Bruce was nearby anymore. I checked my leg and saw that it was stuck on a nail that was being driven deeper into my leg every time I moved. Sara was screaming now because of the blood. After freeing my leg, Sara helped me back to the house. I was limping and the large gaping hole in my leg showed nothing but white meat. When Aunt Lea saw my leg she wrapped it with a towel and rushed me to the hospital. I cried the whole time they stitched up my leg. That summer I also got stitches in my arm from falling on a pointed fence while swinging from a tree like Tarzan.

I was sad to see Sara leave at the end of the summer and go back to the deaf school.

We didn't see much of Papa, but Uncle Ben told us that he moved out of the house on Thirteenth Street and was living above a tavern that Ike owned.

"The house was condemned and torn down by the city," I

In Years To Come

heard Uncle Ben tell Aunt Lea.

I heard other stories about Papa going to see Sister in Indiana with his new girlfriend. I didn't like Papa having a girlfriend and refused to believe it.

Everyone was asleep when Uncle Ben came home one dreadful night. We woke up because Uncle Ben started wailing like a sick animal. I couldn't understand the words he was shouting. I thought at first he was having another argument with Aunt Lea, until I heard him call our names. I pulled the covers over my head and waited.

"Get up! Everybody get up!"

I followed the others downstairs. My legs felt weak and I was sleepy when I sat down on the couch. All of us looked at each other. Uncle Ben was out of control. He was pacing the floor, mumbling and crying. I didn't look at Nate who was sitting in a chair across from me. Aunt Lea was crying too so I knew something was wrong. I hadn't heard them fighting, so what was going on? Uncle Ben stopped pacing long enough to look at us. I saw tears streaming down his face; his eyes were red and puffy. The only other time I saw him cry was when Hon died.

"Pal's gone," he said in a voice that sounded like an echo.

My heart began racing. Pal is the name Uncle Ben called Papa. He was the only one who called Papa that. Where did Papa go?

"Pal is gone," Uncle Ben repeated. "He's dead."

The words hit me like a brick wall and I wanted him to take them back. Papa wasn't dead. Papa couldn't be dead. He was never sick; he was never in the hospital. How could he be dead?

Uncle Ben lips trembled as he told us what happened to Papa. "Pal was standing near an open window putting on his pants and he fell out of the window." Uncle Ben's red eyes glared at us. "He fell three stories down and the back of his head hit a parking meter crushing his skull. I believe that woman pushed him out!"

What woman pushed Papa out the window?

70

"I know she killed him," Uncle Ben mumbled.

"Ben, please try to calm down," Aunt Lea's voice was shaky. "They said it was an accident."

"It wasn't an accident! She killed him!" he yelled.

I began crying for Hon and Papa. I also cried for Joe, Ralph, and me. What would happen to us now? With Papa gone my hopes were gone too. I always believed in the back of my mind that someday Papa would come back and get us. Now he was dead too.

Our household was tense in the days preceding Papa's funeral. Relatives came from out of state. Uncle Guy lee took the train from Colorado with his wife and children. He called her "Pudding," so we did too. She was a petite woman who spoke broken English. I laughed at the way she pronounced some words. Her three children, Viola, Gil, and Ruthie had brown hair and pretty tan skin. They could have been the Copper Tone kids on the TV commercials. I loved Ruthie's curly hair and wished mine were like hers. They all had large eyes and broad smiles like their father.

Everyone was shocked by Papa's death. It had only been six months since Hon died. We repeated the same rituals and went through the same motions. Children didn't go to funerals, but we always went to the wake and viewed the body. O'Bee's funeral home had that same smell that made me want to throw up. I didn't remember going to my father's wake, and barely remembered my mother's. I remembered everything about going to Hon's wake and now Papa was at the same funeral home. It didn't feel like six months had passed since Hon's death. It seemed like I was just there looking into Hon's casket and now I was looking down at Papa. I wasn't afraid when I looked at Papa. He looked handsome in his brown suit. Papa wasn't much of a suit wearer, but it looked good on him. The beautiful smile I loved was plastered on his face. I was happy to see Papa again, although it would have been better if I could have talked to him. His head didn't look busted up the way uncle Ben had described it. Papa was now in heaven with Hon so I imagined the two of them having a good time. The thought of them being together helped me get through the wake without shedding a tear.

It took awhile after Papa's death for things to get back to normal at Uncle Ben's house. The woman that Uncle Ben accused of killing Papa had left town after being threatened. She said she didn't kill Papa and that he fell after losing his balance while putting on his pants. The woman was gone a couple of weeks before her body was found in St. Louis. They said she had been murdered.

Papa died in November, and a few weeks later I was in school when the news came that President Kennedy had been shot in Dallas. The principal closed the school and sent all of us home. When I walked out of the school most of the teachers were weeping and clinging to each other. I rushed home to find Aunt Lea sitting in front of the TV crying.

"He was a good man," she repeated over and over as we watched the anchorman on TV describing what had happened. A picture of President Kennedy's smiling face flashed across the TV.

"He cared about people," Aunt Lea said.

I looked into the face of the man that everyone was upset over. I wasn't thinking about the stranger as much as I was thinking about Papa. He cared about us and now he was dead. I began crying. Nate was sent home from school too and even he looked upset. When Uncle Ben came home we spent the entire evening in front of the TV listening and watching what happened. President Kennedy died.

Sometimes when we were in the living room sitting around Uncle Ben talked about Hon, Papa, and my daddy. I listened when he told stories about his life in Mississippi. He would laugh at the memories as if he could see them in his mind. Uncle Ben talked about my daddy and the childhood they shared together. According to him, the two of them had been very close.

"Your daddy was a shy man," Uncle Ben said when he described him. "I introduced him to your mama. Your daddy loved your mama more than any man could love a woman. Roy and I were a year apart so we were like two peas in a pod. Because I was the oldest Roy looked up to me."

I watch the smile develop on his face.

"We played on the dirt roads and among the trees. Sometimes we went to the river where we swam butt-naked in the water. We stayed away all day and took food with us. We didn't go to school because we had to help in the fields. That's what the boys did back then."

My mind was trying to imagine what it must have been like. "Didn't my daddy kill himself?" I blurted the words out before I realized it.

"Who told you that?"

I hunched my shoulders. I couldn't remember who said it because I heard it during one of the gossip session. I heard it plenty of times.

"Your daddy didn't kill himself," Uncle Ben said, raising his voice. "Those investigators didn't check everything so they never found out who killed him. Somebody killed him; he would never kill himself."

I was sitting on the floor near the chair where Uncle Ben was sitting. I looked up in time to see a tear falling down his face. "Roy would never have killed himself," he said softly.

Nate treated us worse than he ever had before. I dreaded coming home after school. Aunt Lea worked downtown so she got home later than we did. Nate was left in charge of us. He got out of school earlier than we did and was eagerly waiting when we walked through the door.

In the beginning he would punch us in the stomach and pinch and twist our arms. He teased us unmercifully and called us terrible names. I don't remember when it all escalated to the point that he began doing even worse things to us. Nate liked to smash our faces into the wet spot where one of us peed in the bed the night before. At first he held us down for just a few seconds to smell the urine but then he started holding us down longer. He seemed to get a kick out of watching us fight for air because we couldn't breathe. Nate was more powerful than all of us put together. We were just children and he was already in high school, so our efforts to get him off of us were useless. When he smashed our faces into the mattress he held us down by sitting on us. I could feel his weight on my neck and it felt like he was crushing me. The smell of urine filled my nose and I would immediately start fighting for air. I could hear his laughter fading away as I felt myself slipping. When he finally let me up I would slide to the floor gasping for air. I couldn't cry because I had to get air into my lungs. I believed that Nate wanted to kill us. He made me watch him do the same thing to Ralph and Joe. It didn't matter how much we begged or pleaded. Nate showed us no mercy. He preyed on us because we were younger, weaker, and smaller than him.

My attention span in school was short. I couldn't concentrate on my schoolwork because most of the time I was thinking about Nate and what he was going to do to us. I never knew what he was going to do from day to day. Nate was very careful to cover his tracks to make sure Uncle Ben and Aunt Lea didn't find out.

After having his fun with us he made us wash our faces so that evidence of tears couldn't be seen. He made us pick up anything that was knocked over. Whatever object he threw at us we had to pick up too. He was also careful not to leave visible bruises on us. His constant reminder that he would do us bodily harm if we ever told on him was backed up by the evil looks he gave us when Uncle Ben and Aunt Lea weren't looking.

The walk home from school was too short. I cried most of the way home just thinking about what we were going to have to endure. Needless to say my grades deteriorated and I didn't pass the third grade that semester.

Christmas came quickly and I looked forward to it. Uncle Ben teased us about not getting us anything, but he usually gave himself away by the big smile that followed. On Christmas Eve I stared out the window watching for Santa Clause.

When we woke up Christmas morning there were a lot of toys under the tree.

"We were good. That is why we got all these toys," I reminded Joe and Ralph. "Santa Clause brought us a lot of stuff."

I had been hoping for one toy. I didn't know if we had been good or not. Nate told us that we were bad, and the way Aunt Lea treated us sometimes made me feel like I was a bad kid.

But I got the nurse doll that I wanted. She wasn't a fancy doll. She was a white doll with a nurse's uniform and hat on. I named her Nora. The other doll was also white but she couldn't close her eyes and the hair was part of her head so I couldn't comb it. I named that doll Nancy. I also got a tea set and dishes. Ralph and Joe ran around the house shooting at each other with their shiny silver play guns. They also got trucks, cars and a whole lot of Indians and green army men.

When Aunt Lea had taken us to visit Santa Clause in the department store I remember being eager to talk to him. I loudly told him about the doll I wanted, and then I whispered in his ear to make Cousin Nate disappear. Santa smiled at me and told me to be good. I knew if anyone could get him to disappear Santa could.

When I woke up Christmas morning I almost expected Nate to be gone. Nate stood in the living watching us open our gifts. I could feel his eyes looking and was afraid to look up at him. Sara came to Uncle Ben's and stayed with us during the Christmas break. The two weeks flew by quickly and I was sad again when she left.

We were all excited when Uncle Ben announced that we would be moving to a new house.

"They are building a highway right through this house," he said. "The city is buying our property."

The smile and excitement on his face showed that he was happy. "We are going to get a bigger and better house."

I was anxious to move.

The new house was a two-story on Hadley Street. The color

of the house was pink with a mixture of turquoise and black trimming. Uncle Ben and Aunt Lea must have loved pink because the Cadillac they bought was also pink. It was a big house just like Uncle Ben described.

The main floor had a living room, dining room, den, bathroom and a big kitchen with a walk-in pantry. Upstairs were four bedrooms. The basement was big with a room that could also be a bedroom. I could look out the living room window and see the street just like at my grandparent's house. The porch was larger than the one Papa and Hon had. We had a front and back yard too. It wasn't very big, but at least it had grass and trees.

We were back at Twelfth Street School now, but it had changed in the short time I was away. Some of my friends had moved away including the twins, Linda and Brenda. My friend Valerie was still there so we walked to school together.

I felt disconnected from the school I had started Kindergarten in. Sometimes I walked to the edge of the school grounds and looked down Thirteenth Street, reminiscing about the days we lived with Hon and Papa. The house was no longer there because the city had torn it down. The empty lot looked small without the house on it. Uncle Ben's new house was better, but nothing changed with Nate who abused us even more.

We were in our new house about a month when Aunt Lea announced that Ralph wasn't going to school that morning. Ralph's round chubby face flashed a broad smile. It made him feel special because he didn't have to go to school. I wanted to ask why Ralph was staying home, but the look on Aunt Lea's face told me she didn't want to be asked any questions. Ralph stood at the back door waving at us while we walked down the alley.

"Why did Ralph get to stay home?" Joe asked me.

"I don't know. Maybe he has to go to the doctor," I said.
I could think of no other reason for Ralph to stay home from school. We joined other kids who were walking to school and soon forgot about Ralph.

"I bet Ralph had fun today," Joe said to me as we walked home. It was after school and I had forgotten about Ralph not being in school until he failed to meet us at our designated spot. I hunched my shoulders, still puzzled about it.

I could smell food cooking when I entered through the back door. Aunt Lea was in the kitchen and I was glad to see her.

"Hi," she said smiling at us.

"Hi," I said. Joe stopped to talk with her while I whisked through the house in search of Ralph. I was surprised he wasn't in the den watching TV. Nate was in there so I left. I went from room to room looking for him, but he wasn't anywhere. I finally went into the basement.

When Joe came upstairs I told him that Ralph wasn't anywhere in the house.

"Maybe he is outside playing."

I shook my head. It was too cold outside and Ralph was a crybaby when he got cold. Joe couldn't understand why I was upset.

"Aunt Lea did something to him, I know she did," I kept repeating to him.

"He's probably somewhere hiding." Joe tried to calm me down. I shook my head. I looked around again for Ralph before we were called us down to dinner.

My worst fears were confirmed when Ralph wasn't there. He was always the first one at the dinner table. Uncle Ben was home by now too. He didn't say much and didn't seem to be his usual happy self. I could sense that something was wrong. I kept looking at the empty seat where Ralph should be sitting. Aunt Lea hadn't even bothered putting a plate there.

I sipped on kool-aid, because my throat felt dry. I fought the urge to ask about Ralph. My heart pounded wildly in my chest as my imagination ran away. I imagined him being left somewhere alone and cold. I was sure Aunt Lea was capable of doing that to him. I picked at my food. Near the end of dinner Uncle Ben finally spoke.

"Ralph is gone to a home."

I stared into his eyes as the shock went through my body.

"Lea couldn't handle him anymore."

I couldn't believe what I was hearing. He was making excuses for her. Why didn't he just acknowledge the truth? She didn't really want Ralph. In fact she didn't want any of us. I didn't respond because I couldn't. How could she send Ralph to a home? I remembered that morning when he was smiling and waving goodbye to us. He didn't know that she was going to send him to a home.

Uncle Ben hung his head down. My eyes filled with tears. I looked directly at Aunt Lea who was pretending to be upset and on the verge of crying. How dare she fake it! Who did she think she was fooling? I felt nothing but contempt for her.

"Where did he go?" I was relieved to hear Joe ask.

"Mr. Burgner picked him up this morning and took him to a home."

Mr. Burgner was the social worker that came to visit us. The little food in my mouth lost its taste. I fought back tears because I didn't want to cry in front of them. I had the urge to run out the door and never come back. But I sat rigidly in my seat, listening.

"Ralph is okay," Uncle Ben said more to himself than to us. "He had to go. Lea was washing sheets everyday and the bedroom is starting to smell."

Aunt Lea threw her hands up. "Lord knows I tried." I rolled my eyes at her. Her tears didn't move me. I believed that deep in her heart she never wanted Ralph and she didn't want me either. Nate was the only one who seemed to enjoy his meal. He acted as if nothing was happening as he slurped his food down. The smirk on his face showed signs of victory. I bet he knew about it. He was probably part of the plan to get rid of Ralph.

I was watching him across the table sneering and making faces at us when no one was looking. He made me sick. If only I was strong enough to beat him up. At least Ralph didn't have to worry about getting beat up by Nate anymore. It was times like this when I began wondering why my parents had to die. Why did Hon and Papa have to die? Why did my brothers and I have to be separated from each other? All I had were questions and no answers.

Later while sitting on my bed I held up the only thing that was left behind. It was a red and blue sweater that Ralph wore all the time. I decided to keep his sweater until I saw him again. It was the only thing I had left of him. I knew now that people could easily get rid of kids. I didn't know what a home was, but it didn't sound like a place where I wanted to go. I didn't want to think about Ralph being there all by himself. A home must be a place where they kept children no one wanted. Maybe they locked them in rooms and fed them bread and water like in jail. If I knew where Mr. Burgner took him we could rescue him.

"I think I'll be the next one to go," I told Joe. He stared at me with frightened eyes.

"No, we won't be sent to a home."

We were both still peeing in the bed. I woke up every morning wondering if it was the day I would be leaving.

There was a lot of tension between Aunt Lea and Uncle Ben over the next couple of weeks. They had always argued, but now it seemed like they were arguing more. I overheard angry words and accusations, and our names being mentioned. I also noticed how Nate watched Uncle Ben. I felt guilty about the arguments because I thought they were about us. One day Uncle Ben was walking downstairs behind Aunt Lea. They were exchanging heated words when I heard Aunt Lea scream. I didn't see what happened, but Aunt Lea ran down the stairs crying. She said Uncle Ben had hit her.

We came home from school to an empty house. That was unusual because Nate was always home. It was an eerie quietness that made me feel uncomfortable. We heard the key in the door a few hours later. Uncle Ben entered the house dressed in his bellman uniform. He was happier than I had seen him in days. The expression on his face changed when he saw that Aunt Lea and Nate weren't there. We stayed downstairs in the den while he went through the house looking for any sign of them.

"What do you think happened?" Joe whispered.

I shrugged my shoulders.

"If she left he'll probably be glad she's gone." But even as I said the words I knew they weren't true.

As the evening turned into night it was obvious they were gone. Uncle Ben heated up leftover food for us to eat that evening.

"I'm bringing Ralph back here." Uncle Ben told us.

Joe and I looked at each other with a feeling of triumphant.

I knew Uncle Ben would do it. We missed Ralph so much.

"We are just going to have to do without your Aunt Lea."

I let his words fall on deaf ears as I imagined living with just my brothers and Uncle Ben. For the first time since Hon and Papa died, I felt happy.

We managed to get through the next few days without Aunt Lea. Uncle Ben cooked dinner in the evenings and retreated to the living room. One evening Uncle Ben was sitting in the dark.

"He's playing the blues," Joe whispered in my ear.

I nodded my head. I didn't understand why people liked the blues so much. I liked music, but not the blues. The words to the song he was listening to tell about how bad the man felt after his woman left him. I didn't want Uncle Ben to listen to that record because he was starting to get emotional. I saw the tears in his eyes and couldn't help feeling sorry for him. We left him crying alone in the dark.

We got ourselves ready for school the next morning. Uncle Ben made sure we ate a bowl of cold cereal before he left for work. I wanted to assure him that we didn't need Aunt Lea, but I couldn't say that to him.

When Uncle Ben came home he fixed dinner for us, but he didn't eat much. He went through the same routine as the night before, listening to his blues records in the dark. The more he listened to the records the more emotional he seemed to get. I wanted to ask him if he had contacted Mr. Burger about Ralph yet, but I decided to wait.

The next morning while we were eating in the kitchen Uncle Ben started talking to us.

"Aunt Lea and Maine are in Ohio with Annie Mae." They had been gone about a week and it didn't surprise me that they went to Ohio. After Annie Mae got married she and her husband moved there. It seemed every time she visited she was pregnant again. I seldom saw her smile anymore and wondered why she was so sad.

Uncle Ben interrupted my thoughts.

"I'm going to Ohio to get them. Lea's doing her best to help raise you."

I nodded my head. I should have known he was going to change his mind. He was going there to get her.

"I'll be gone for a short time so I want you to stay in the house, lock all the doors and don't let anyone in."

"Yes sir," Joe answered.

Uncle Ben left that evening. We watched from the back window as the long, pink Cadillac disappeared down the alley. When the car was out of sight Joe and I began playing in the house. We couldn't believe we had the house to ourselves. We ran through the house, jumped off of furniture, and started dragging each other over the carpet by our legs. Later we watched TV until our eyes wouldn't stay open anymore. We didn't have anyone to tell us when to go to bed. The next morning we ate cereal and spent the day playing. Uncle Ben didn't want us to go to school either. We didn't know how far Ohio was from Milwaukee except that Uncle Ben told us it wasn't far.

We expected them back anytime. Within a few days the cereal was gone and the food was low, that's when we began looking at every car that passed through the alley hoping it was Uncle Ben. The food wouldn't last much longer. We had no sense of time--days were quickly turning into nights.

"Maybe Uncle Ben's coming home today", I said eating dry Jell-O that made me sick and left my lips feeling funny. As the day turned into night again I started crying because of the stabbing hunger pains in my stomach.

"Don't cry. We'll get some food." Joe tried to comfort me. He had tears in his eyes too.

The next morning we woke up to an empty house again. We were hungry, cold and scared. I knew Joe had an idea or plan when he suddenly ran out of the den. He returned carrying an armload of bottles. "All we have to do is cash these in," he said grinning.

The smile on my face must have made him feel better. The bottles were worth two cents each. We took them to the corner store and cashed them in for something to eat. That night we hardly watched TV because we kept running to the window every time a car passed by. We didn't bother sleeping in our beds anymore. We slept on covers on the floor in the den. Another thing that was strange is that neither of us peed on the floor or couch.

There was still no sign of them the next morning when we woke up. We cashed in the remaining bottles so we could eat that day. Time was spent either watching TV or staring out of the window. The next day Joe said all the bottles in the house were gone so we had to go through other people's trash bins to find more bottles.

I was hesitant the first time I looked inside the dirty trash bins they called "ash pits." They were made of cinder blocks with metal tops on them. The first time I climbed in one the smell was so foul I thought I was going to throw up. It wasn't just the smell that bothered me: rats ran in and out of them all the time. I was scared, but the hunger pains pushed me. We shouted at the other whenever we found a bottle.

After putting our bottles together we had enough to buy another day's worth of food. Neither of us knew how to cook so we ate cupcakes, chips, and soda. Sometimes we bought baloney and bread to make sandwiches.

We didn't know how to use the washing machine so all our clothes were dirty. We did buy some bar soap to wash our bodies, but we had to put back on dirty clothes. I tried to wash my hair but I didn't do a good job so it itched and smelled like the trash bins we climbed in and out of. Sometimes I felt bugs or something crawling on me and did my best to be brave because we needed the bottles for food.

The nights were colder and even under layers of covers I didn't feel warm. Curled up on the floor of the den I cried myself to sleep every night. Joe kept assuring me that Uncle Ben would be back soon. The realization that we were alone in a big house was now frightening.

Another day passed and still no Uncle Ben. Most of my dresses were torn from climbing in and out of the ash cans. Some of the clothes had bloodstains on them from the cuts we got because of broken glass or something sharp that was in the ash cans.

We had to be careful because the neighbors were spying on us. I saw them peeking from windows and doors while we went through their trash. I even suspected a few neighbors deliberately left bottles for us to find. Mrs. Nelson who lived next door knocked on our door, but we refused to answer it because of Uncle Ben's warning not to open the door for anyone.

The house was getting colder and we didn't know how to turn up the heat. It was too cold to even stand in front of the gas stove so I stayed underneath the blankets. I tried not to cry even when my hands were numb from going through the trash bins. My body shivered and my teeth shattered for a long time after we were back inside the house.

We were in the den watching TV when a knock on the door sent us running to the window to see who was there. A tall white man in a white trench coat stood on the porch. He had large thick black glasses and something that looked like a suitcase in one hand. I looked at Joe who shook his head. The man continued to knock on the door. We knew it was Mr. Bergner the social worker who came by to visit with us.

"Shouldn't we at least ask him about Ralph?" I whispered.

"No, we can't open the door for anyone! You know what uncle Ben told us."

"Joe? Joyce?" He was calling our names. "I know you're in there; it's okay to open the door. I've talked to your uncle. He sent me here. Come on and open the door."

"I'm not going to a home!" I shouted to Joe, backing away from the door.

"Me neither," he agreed.

Mr. Burgner kept talking to us through the door.

"I know you're in there. I'm here because your uncle called and wanted me to check on you so it's okay to open the door and let me in."

"We don't want to go to a home!" I shouted.

"Open the door and we'll discuss it." Mr. Bergner's voice was calm.

"When is Uncle Ben coming home?"

"If you open the door we can talk."

My shoulders slumped. I was tired. My head itched, my body was bruised and I smelled bad. All I wanted to know was when Uncle Ben was coming home. I didn't want to think about going back in the trash bins. A rat ran over my foot the last time I crawled in one and I screamed so loud that Joe came to see what was going on. I was tired of eating cupcakes, chips and drinking sodas. The house was cold and worse at night.

Mr. Bergner was smiling when Joe swung the door open. He walked inside of the house and sat on the couch. I was embarrassed about my torn dress and dirty hair.

"Hi children."

"Hi Mr. Bergner," we both said at the same time.

"How are you?" his eyes shifted between the two of us.

"Okay," Joe mumbled.

I didn't say anything. I wasn't okay because I wanted to know when Uncle Ben was coming back.

"When was the last time you ate something?" Mr. Bergner's facial expression changed.

"We ate this morning."

Mr. Burgner took out a pad and started writing on it.

"What did you eat?"

"Cupcakes and chocolate milk," Joe said.

"Have you had anything else to eat?"

We shook our heads. We didn't want to tell him about the money we had because it was for dinner.

"Where is Ralph?" I blurted out.

"Ralph is doing fine."

"Will you take us to see him?"

Mr. Burger stopped writing and looked at me.

"Yes, I can arrange for you to see him."

Joe and I smiled at each other.

"Right now my main concern is the two of you. I know you want to stay here and wait until your uncle returns, but I cannot leave you here alone."

"When is he coming back?"

"I don't know when your uncle will return".

"What are we suppose to do?" I was confused now.

"Please don't get upset, but I have to take you with me."

"Uncle Ben told us to wait for him," I protested.

Mr. Bergner cleared his throat. "Your uncle and aunt are in another state, a long ways from here. I don't know when or if they will be coming back." He stared at us. "I can't leave you here alone."

Mr. Bergner's voice was stern as he continued talking.

"It is clear that you have been neglected." He actually looked upset. Why would he be upset?

"Your uncle wants you to leave with me."

"He's not coming back?"

"I don't know if he is coming back or not."

"I want to wait here for Uncle Ben," I told him.

Mr. Burger ignored me. "When is the last time you attended school?"

The question caught us off guard. I hunched my shoulders, watching him scribble on the pad.

"Go put some clothes in a bag." We knew he was serious so it was useless to keep insisting that uncle Ben was coming back. I followed Joe downstairs to the basement where the pile of dirty clothes was. We grabbed some clothes and began stuffing them in our paper bags.

Mr. Bergner was waiting for us by the door when we came back upstairs.

"Wait," I said before walking out the door. "I have to get something from upstairs."

"Hurry up." Mr. Burger watched while I ran upstairs.

I grabbed the red and blue sweater off of the clothes hanger and stuffed it in the bag.

Mr. Bergner allowed us to walk out of the house first and locked the doors behind us. Everyone knew Mr. Bergner's car with the big emblem and "City and County" scrawled on the doors. Uncle Ben called it the welfare car. I noticed neighbors peeping at us and some were on their porches watching as we climbed into the car. Joe jumped in the front seat, which was fine with me. I sat by the right window in the back.

It was cold outside and a fresh layer of snow had fallen overnight. When he pulled away from the curb I didn't bother asking where we were going. It didn't matter anymore. Uncle Ben had not come back so maybe he didn't want us either.

Except for an occasional question from Joe we rode in silence. I stared out the window trying to keep my mind off of what was about to happen. Uncle Ben told Mr. Burgner to come get us because Aunt Lea didn't want us. Nobody wanted us.

Mr. Burger finally pulled over to the curb in front of a large white house.

"Where are we?" Joe asked him.

"You're in front of your foster home."

"What's a foster home?"

I was alert in the back seat waiting for Mr. Burger's explanation.

"A foster home is a house you live in with parents who want children like you and your sister. They are nice people who will treat you like you are their own children."

"Really?"

I felt excited while Mr. Bergner gave us an overview of a foster home.

"Is this the same as being in a home?" I asked him.

Mr. Bergner looked at us, puzzled.

"Uncle Ben told us about a place called a home where people went when nobody wanted them. I think they lock you up and feed you bread and water."

Mr. Bergner shook his head and laughed at my description. "This is a foster home where people do want you. Mr. and Mrs. Watson live here. They are two very fine people."

I got out of the car and stared at the house in front of me. It was best looking house on the block, surrounded by a white picket fence. It even had a two-car garage. I had never lived in a house that had a garage before. I looked at Joe, who smiled back at me. We both felt a sense of relief and followed behind Mr. Bergner through the gate and up the walkway to our foster home.

I stood behind Mr. Burger shivering in the cold air while he rang the doorbell. I could see the doorknob twisting as if someone was trying to open the door but couldn't, finally the door swung open and Ralph stood there, smiling. I let out a yell of delight when I saw him. Joe, Ralph and I spent the next few moments wrapped up together.

We held onto each other until Mr. Burgner convinced us to let go. He promised that we would all stay together and never be separated again. A large man was standing behind Ralph when he opened the door. Although the man was friendly I couldn't help laughing at how funny he looked. His head was too small for his extra large body, and his protruding stomach made him look like Santa Clause. He wore large black glasses that covered his small beady eyes. Mr. Burger introduced him as Mr. Watson, our foster father. I decided the fat man with the friendly smile was okay.

Mr. Watson led us through a kitchen into the living room. I took in the beauty of the house as we passed through each room. The place was like a palace in comparison to any house I had ever lived in.

Each room was carefully decorated and once we entered the living room I was in for the biggest surprise of all. Sitting in an overstuffed chair near the window was a woman. She wasn't a young woman, but she had all the ingredients of a beautiful woman. Her skin was light tan, and her hair was jet black and straight. Short bangs hung over her forehead above dark slanted eyes and thin eyebrows. She was a beautiful woman. Was she really married to the fat man who greeted us at the door? Mr. Burger sat across from her while we were motioned to a nearby couch.

"This is Mrs. Watson," Mr. Burgner said.

"Hello," we mumbled.

She gasped. "What did they do to these babies?" she asked Mr. Burgner.

We listened while Mr. Burger explained what had happened to us.

"A neighbor called and said she thought the children were alone in the house."

He tricked us. He said Uncle Ben had called him. It surprised me when tears began streaming down her face. This lady we hardly knew was crying for us. I had never felt so touched. I wanted to run to the woman and comfort her. Mr. Burgner must have noticed the puzzled look on my face so he asked us to leave the room so they could talk alone. I knew then that he hadn't talked to

Uncle Ben.

Ralph was already anxious to talk with us anyway. We still couldn't believe we were together again.

"I'm glad you came here!" His voice was filled with excitement as he told us how nice Mr. and Mrs. Watson were to him. He described how they took him shopping and bought him all new clothes. They even gave him another name.

"My new name is Billy," he said.

Joe and I started laughing. "Your name is Ralph," we said.

"You don't look like a Billy to me," Joe told him.

Ralph was offended by our laughter. "They call me Billy," he said.

"Why Billy?"

Ralph started whispering to us.

"Dad's name is Willie," so I guess Billy rhymes with Willie.

Joe and I were laughing so hard we were almost rolling on the floor.

"Sometimes Mother calls me Junior"

Despite Ralph's serious expression we laughed again.

"I get to do a lot of fun things too. I go to church with Mother every Sunday."

We hadn't been to church since leaving Hon and Papa's house. Ralph did look happy. He told us that Mr. Burgner picked him up after we left for school that day. We told Ralph about Aunt Lea and Nate leaving and how we waited a long time for Uncle Ben to come back home.

Mr. Bergner left after a couple of hours. He told us he would be back in a few days to see how we were doing. Mrs. Watson came into the kitchen where we were sitting at the table. She looked at me. "You are taking a bath and getting that hair washed."

They had two bathrooms so Joe took a bath upstairs while I bathed in the downstairs bathroom. The water got dirty quickly so Mrs. Watson let it out and ran more water. I went through three tubs of bath water before I was clean. When she washed my hair I went through several more. Mrs. Watson rubbed a strange smelling ointment on my body that made my cuts sting.

We ate our first home-cooked meal in a long time that evening. I couldn't eat much because I was still sick to my stomach. Joe and I followed Ralph's routine of kissing Mr. and Mrs. Watson good night.

"Goodnight Mrs. Watson," I said.

"Call me Mother."

I stared in disbelief at the woman who said those words. She was smiling at me.

"Goodnight Mother," I said, kissing her on the cheek.

Chapter Four

The Watsons

I felt like a princess in a fairytale living in the beautiful house located at 3022 North Tenth Lane. It was a two-story house with a kitchen in the basement. I spent the first couple of days going though the house looking at all Mother's crystal and glassware that she had all over the house. There weren't any other houses on the block with a two-car garage. I was sure Mother and Dad must be rich people, especially when I saw they had two cars. Dad drove a big white Pontiac Bonneville that was as long as a Cadillac and Mother drove a white Ford.

The main floor of the house had two bedrooms, a bathroom, kitchen, den and living room. Mother and Dad had their own bedrooms. Mother's bedroom was furnished with beautiful off white French provincial furniture. Beautiful porcelain dolls decorated her satin covered bed; the top of her dresser was lined with sweet smelling colognes, perfumes, and talc powders. The long closet the length of the room was full of suits, dresses, coats, furs and hats.

The large walk-in pantry in the kitchen had been converted into storage for mother's shoes and purses. I loved mother's bedroom and the smell of her perfumes.

In Years To Come

It was odd that my new parents slept in separate bedrooms. This was different from what I had been exposed to. I thought married people were supposed to sleep in the same bedroom together. How were they supposed to protect each other if one slept in a different room? I remembered Hon and Papa sharing a bedroom and so did Uncle Ben and Aunt Lea even though they fought sometimes. I saw on TV that married people slept in the same bedroom even if they slept in separate beds, but not Mother and Dad.

Dad's bedroom was across from the bathroom. It was a light colored room without pictures or personal effects. Dad slept in a dark wood, full-size bed that sat in the middle of the room. A matching chest stood in the corner with his aftershave, hairbrush and cologne. An odd odor hit me when I walked into his bedroom one day to dust the furniture. It was the aftershave that scented his bedroom. His bedroom was always neat and clean so I didn't have to do much in there except dust, Sweep, and mop. Every morning when he got up, Dad made his bed. His t-shirts, socks and underwear were always folded and neatly stored inside the dresser drawers. His clothes were always lined up in his closet, clean and pressed.

In the kitchen was a white refrigerator with a matching gas stove that looked new. Mother seldom used the upstairs kitchen and did the cooking in the basement kitchen. The main floor bathroom was smaller than the one upstairs. Mother kept a portable whirlpool inside of the downstairs tub that took up too much space. That first night mother put me in the tub and turned on the whirlpool. It scared me at first when the bubbles popped up around me, but after awhile I liked the way they tickled my skin and made me laugh.

The living room, dining room, and den were carpeted and divided by an archway. There were earth tone colors in both rooms. Beautiful beige furniture highlighted the living room. Mother had good taste, so everything in the house looked like it belonged there.

Mother had many crystal pieces that sparkled and some

92

were filled with assorted candy on the coffee table and end tables. Accent pillows covered the couches. A large TV with a maple cabinet stood in the corner of the living room.

In the den was a fireplace trimmed in gold. It was shiny and glinted in the light. Mother's pride and joy was the large ebony piano situated just between the living room and den. I stared at the ivory keys and sometimes ran my fingers over them just to hear a small sound. I yearned to play the piano like mother.

There were three bedrooms upstairs where we slept. My bedroom was at the top of the stairs and had a window overlooking the yard. Ralph and Joe shared a bedroom near the front of the house. It had pale blue painted walls and was only a few steps from the upstairs bathroom.

Between our bedrooms was the third bedroom where Mother's grandson, Freddy, slept. He was a handsome twenty-one-year-old that lived with us. He left the house early every morning and didn't return until late at night so we didn't see much of him. And when we did come face to face with him he didn't say anything to us.

Just as Ralph had told us, the first thing Mother did was take Joe and I shopping. I can't describe the feeling of holding her hand as we dashed in and out of the downtown department stores. Mother always dressed to impress, which made her look important. Sales people rushed over to help us in every store we walked into. Mother bought dresses that she said would look good on me. I had never been downtown before so it was an amazing experience seeing all the stores and tall buildings. The only places I had ever gone shopping were the Goodwill or discount stores. These stores were different and the experience that day with Mother would be with me forever.

I believed that Mother and Dad were rich. How could they afford to buy us new clothes if they weren't? Mother didn't bother looking through the sack of clothes we brought with us from Uncle Ben's house. She took the sack from me and dumped it in the trashcan. I was able to retrieve Ralph's sweater, which was now too small for him.

Everything was perfect as we settled into our new home. I had pretty clothes to wear, a beautiful house to live in, and a new school to go to. I made new friends and was beginning to overcome some of my shyness. I looked forward to coming home after school because I knew that Nate wouldn't be there to hurt me. I was more focused in school and attacked my schoolwork with a renewed interest.

It seemed strange for Mother and Dad to attend separate churches. Dad was an usher at a church I never attended. Mother ventured out to several churches, but never his. Every Sunday Dad put on a black suit, white shirt and white gloves. His fat belly would stick out, making him look like a penguin.

The first Sunday we went to church with Mother I remember seeing her walk out of the bedroom and gasping because she looked so beautiful. The clothes she had on were the prettiest I had ever seen. Her two-piece suit was lovely and the accessories matched perfectly. The jewelry mother wore in her ears and around her neck sparkled like glass. Mother draped a silky mink coat around her shoulders. I rubbed my hands over the coat and felt how soft it was.

Mother wore her hair short and curled it by using hairpins. When she took the hairpins out of her hair it left small ripples of shiny black curls. The bangs were straight and cut to fit Mother's forehead. She looked like a movie star. When we walked through the doors of a small storefront Church I could feel every eye upon us. Mother's mink coat swayed around her body when she walked. People stopped talking as if they were in some kind of trance.

I felt pretty in my new dress. Joe and Ralph wore the nice suits mother had bought them with bright white shirts. Everyone respected "Sister Watson" as they called her.

The preacher motioned for her to come to the pulpit. My eyes followed her as she walked gracefully across the floor, taking a seat at the piano. When she began playing the piano the church came alive. Her voice floated through the church like an angel. That explained the beautiful ebony piano in the living room at the house. I felt the emotion from the music and started singing too.

Everyone in the church was soon stomping their feet and clapping their hands while praising the Lord. Mother closed her eyes and continued singing. Her voice vibrated through the church in perfect harmony. I felt moved as her words about joy, love, and Jesus fell on my ears. I had missed going to church so it felt good to be back.

I was surprised when Ralph stood up and walked to the front of the church. When he turned to face us his round face had a smile that seemed to go all the way around his head. Mother began to play and Ralph's voice filled the church as he sang "At the Cross, at the cross." When did he learn how to sing? Joe and I looked at each other as if we were both thinking the same thing. The people in the church clapped endlessly when Ralph finished. I stood up to clap with the crowd, proud that my brother had sung a song all by himself.

The preacher was sweating as he pranced back and forth in a way I'd never seen before. "The blood...was streaming...down the cross...." I closed my eyes to block out his facial expression but could still hear the quivering of his voice. His description of how they crucified Jesus was so vivid I wanted to cry. How could they do that to Jesus? People in the church began shouting a few Amen's. Women around me were fainting. Mother had come down to sit in the congregation so she was sitting next to me. Without warning she jumped up and began to shout and lift her hands towards the heavens. She fell over and the ushers rushed over and started fanning her with paper fans. Mother recovered, much to my relief.

At the end of the service the preacher called Joe, Ralph, and me to the front of the church. They had already placed three chairs facing the congregation. My legs felt wobbly as I made my way to the front. I could feel the people staring at us as we faced them.

Mother had requested a special prayer for us. We sat in the chairs while the preacher began shouting again as he prayed for God to help us and heal our broken hearts. Emotions in the church were high and I felt tears running down my face.

A woman they called Sister Greenlee was standing behind us when we opened our eyes after the prayer. I watched as the offering plate was passed around to help mother provide for us. The sound of coins clinking in the plate could be heard. I saw several people put folded money into the plate while the preacher begged them to give generously. Sister Green Lee was announced as our new Godmother who promised to help watch over us. I smiled at the woman with the large eyes and soft voice. We never saw Sister Greenlee after that day.

We visited several other churches and learned this was Mother's routine. Her voice and piano playing always affected people in the church. A special collection for mother was always taken.

After church Mother let us go to the neighborhood movie theater. The most popular were Elvis Presley movies. I fell in love with Elvis Presley from the first movie I saw him in. I could sit through his movies over and over and never get bored. There were always two movies playing so Mother timed it to pick us up after the last movie. Mother also fixed ice cream with fudge or caramel toppings for dessert. We didn't eat much junk food so having ice cream was a treat. Mother was a health-conscious person who kept things like wheat germ and artificial sweetener around.

Mother was an excellent cook and canned her own jelly, jam, and applesauce. The jars of food were stored in the small room in the basement that she called a cellar. There were mostly tools in the cellar.

A wall in the hallway leading into the living room had a lot of awards and certificates bearing Mother's name. I was impressed with Mother's achievements. Mother had an unusual name and when I first heard it I couldn't help repeating it. *Abyssinia Watson*

96

sounded enchanting so I said it over and over just so I could hear it. Mother had a certificate that was signed by President Kennedy. I stared at it and knew she must be an important person be getting something from the President.

Mother had one child, a daughter named Ruby. I met Ruby a few weeks after we moved in. I remember looking at her flawless skin and wondering how old she was. Ruby had skin the color of honey and thick flaming red hair. She had long eyelashes, thin lips, and wore a pale-pink shade of lipstick. It was hard to believe that Freddy was her son. She also had two teenage children named Bobby and Vicky. I met them when Ruby brought them with her during one visit. Bobby ignored us like his brother Freddy always did. Vicky looked different from her mother and grandmother. Unlike them she had thick lips and large eyes. She was a quiet girl who didn't talk much. Dad wasn't Ruby's biological father either. Mother had been married before to another man before she met him.

Rudolph was the first foster kid to live with us. He was a tall, thin boy with dark skin and a crooked smile. He made us laugh because he always told jokes. He complained about being in foster homes, but tried to fit in. He didn't stay long and Mother never talked about him after he was gone.

Linda was my first foster sister. She was a short sixteen-year-old girl who came from a broken home. Although she was a little on the heavy side she had a pretty face. When mother introduced her as our new foster sister I clung to Linda as if I'd known her all my life. She was helpful, friendly and nice to us. She helped me with my homework and we talked about our families.

Linda told me about her family. Her mother was a white woman who married Linda's black father. That explained Linda's light skin, brown hair, and hazel eyes. She told me that problems erupted between her parents, leading to the abandonment of her and her two brothers.

"I am going to get my brothers out of the foster home as

soon as I turn eighteen and get married," she told me.

Linda's determination gave me hope that maybe my own family was also thinking about coming back for us. Among Linda's possessions was a portable record player. When we weren't watching TV we listened to records. Linda had all the latest Motown records. I loved to listen to the Temptations, Smokey Robinson and the Miracles, The Four Tops, and my favorite group, The Supremes. My favorite song at that time was "I Hear a Symphony." I knew the words to that song because I listened to it on the radio that mother kept on in the basement. I was always walking around the house singing songs I heard on the radio.

"Those are white songs," Linda told me when I began singing the ones I knew the words to. I didn't care if they were white songs. I liked them anyway.

"I can't get no satisfaction, I can't get no satisfaction, and I tried. And I tried and I tried," I would scream the words loud trying to imitate the singer of the song. Linda laughed at me.

"I guess you like the Beatles too?"

I nodded my head. "It's been a hard day's night, and I've been working like a dog," I sang shaking my head like I had seen the Beatles do on the Ed Sullivan Show.

Linda walked the few blocks to North Division High School in the mornings. She was always home when we got out of school in the afternoon. One day a cute guy walked her home after school. He was tall, dark-skinned, and handsome. Linda had already told me about him. She invited him in and they were sitting on the small couch in the TV room when I walked in.

"This is my foster sister, Joyce," she said, introducing us.

He smiled at me.

"Joyce, this is my boyfriend, Donald." I smiled back at Donald. Then I joined Ralph and Joe in their bedroom where they were playing on the floor.

"Linda's got a boyfriend," Ralph whispered to me.

"I bet they're kissing," Joe said. We all laughed.

"Let's peek at them."

I don't know why I went along with Ralph and Joe, but I looked out the door to see what they were doing. Donald had his arm around Linda and they were watching TV.

"They're watching TV," I whispered to them.

"You can come out here," Linda said after seeing me peek out the door at them. I felt myself blush when I sat down on the floor to watch TV with them. Donald left before Mother called us downstairs to eat dinner.

Linda left for overnight family visits on the weekend. I missed her and sometimes envied her for having a family to go home to. The most memorable time I spent with Linda was the Sunday she took us to the movies. I was looking forward to seeing an Elvis Presley movie. When I saw *Imitation of Life* scrawled across the front of the movie theater I was disappointed.

I couldn't say the words and didn't understand what an Imitation of Life movie was. I understood the movie *GIRLS! GIRLS! GIRLS!* Pretty girls always surrounded Elvis Presley in his movies. Linda was excited about the *Imitation of life* movie so I pretended that I was too.

When the movie started it captured my attention and held it all the way to the end. How could a child be so mean to her own mother? I cried so hard at the end that Linda held me. She was crying too. It was so sad and especially when Mahalia Jackson started singing that song. I could hear other people in the movie theater crying too. We sat through the movie again and cried some more.

Things were starting to change at home with Mother. I didn't know what was wrong except mother was starting to hit us. Most of the time I had no clue what I had done. Mother's mood swings were getting worse and I told Linda about them. She yelled at us and often it was followed by a physical reaction. She would slap, pinch or throw something at us. I didn't understand what was happening. Linda told me that Mother's attitude towards her was cool too. She said Mother didn't want her having a boyfriend and they had already exchanged words about Donald. The first time I heard her accuse Linda of doing nasty things with Donald I didn't know what the words she used meant. Linda's constant denial didn't change Mother's mind.

"I don't want that boy over here anymore," Mother told Linda one evening after Donald had left.

Linda looked up at mother who was standing with her hands on her hips.

"Donald is my boyfriend Mrs. Watson," she answered.

"I don't want him over here again," Mother said through clenched teeth. She walked back down the steps. Linda sat on the bed shaking her head.

The arguments between Mother and Linda escalated into a fistfight between them. I was horrified when I saw Mother smash Linda's face against the wall. Linda gasped because mother was choking her. I wanted to pull her away from Linda or do something to help, but my feet wouldn't move. It felt as if they were glued to the floor. When Mother finally let go of Linda she slid down the wall sucking in air and coughing. She curled in a fetal position on the floor crying. I saw ugly bruises on her arms.

The most frightening part was looking into Mother's dark, angry eyes that glared at me when she passed by. She looked wild and crazy, and I believed at that moment that she could have killed Linda. I jumped when Mother walked by me. That night I lay in bed wondering what happened to the woman I met in the living room that first day. I didn't know how to console Linda and I was powerless to stop Mother.

"I'm getting out of here," Linda told me after we had crawled into bed that night. I didn't want her to go, but it was obvious that she and Mother weren't getting along. When I came home from school the next day Linda had moved her things out. I didn't get a chance to say goodbye to her.

A new foster sister was unpacking her clothes when I

discovered her in my bedroom.

"Hi," she said without looking up.

She was an attractive girl with skin the color of caramel candy. Her small Afro fit around her face like it was made for it. Large hoop earrings hung from both ears. She flashed a smile at me and I saw her teeth were almost perfect.

"My name is Nita," she said extending a hand.

"Joyce," I mumbled.

Ralph and Joe were whispering about how pretty Nita was when I walked into their bedroom. Nita was wearing a hot pink mini-skirt that clung to her body, showing off her curves and lots of leg.

We adored Nita. She got along well with all of us including Mother and Dad. She and Mother seemed to have a lot to talk about because I could hear the two of them in the kitchen laughing and talking.

When Nita walked to the store around the corner she took me with her. She caught the attention of men who whistled at her, but Nita kept walking like she never heard anything.

Nita was seventeen and didn't like going to high school. She told me that she thought it was senseless and was thinking of dropping out. She was upbeat most of the time unless she was thinking about her three younger brothers who were in foster homes somewhere in the city.

Until Nita came to live with us we hardly ever saw Freddy, but now he was always around in the evenings. I thought it was strange that he was spending more time at home. It didn't take long to figure out that Nita was the reason.

By now Mother was hitting us, throwing things at us and criticizing everything we did. She was careful not to do it in front of Freddy or Nita. I told Nita about Mother's abuse and showed her my bruises. But although Nita sympathized with me I'm not sure she was convinced that Mother was out of control.

Nita didn't stay with us very long. I suspected that it had

something to do with her sneaking into Freddy's room at night. I never told Mother about it because I didn't want to get Nita in trouble.

We were the only foster children living there for about four or five months when Michael came. His skin was so light he looked white. At first I thought he was white until Mother explained that he was a black boy with light skin. He was of mixed race; his mother was white and his father was black.

He didn't have nice skin at all. His face was covered with ugly red pimples. I didn't like looking at him because he had crusted scabs on his face. He would bust the pimples and they turned into dark red spots. His hair was jet black and straight like white people. He used grease or something to make it slick.

In the beginning he was moody and stayed to himself. I didn't care because I didn't like looking at his red pimples and his funny, colored eyes gave me the creeps. Michael became friendlier towards us after a while. I still avoided looking at his eyes or face.

I was moved into the basement after Nita left. Sometimes Mother allowed me to go upstairs to watch TV in the family room with Ralph and Joe.

One day Michael lured me into the bathroom when I went upstairs to watch TV. When I heard the click of the lock I knew something was wrong. It happened so quickly that I didn't have a chance to react. He stared at me with those eyes and I backed away from him and wanted to scream.

It didn't take long for me to find out what he wanted. He opened his pants and pulled it out. I couldn't move. I stood there staring at it. I had never seen one like that before. My little cousins always ran around without their diapers, but this was different. In the next instance he grabbed my hand, forcing me to touch it. I tried to pull back, but he was too strong. He put his hand over mine forcing me to pull back and forth on it.

"Play with it," he said, his eyes piercing mine. He was so close I could smell the sweat of his body.

I shook my head and tried to pull my hand away.

"I said play with it!"

"Please let me go," I pleaded with him.

He ignored my cries and responded only with heavy breathing. I cried in agony because my arm ached as he forced me to pull on his penis. Finally something warm dripped on my fingers. I was horrified. He didn't give me time to see what was making my hand feel funny. Instead he rushed me to the sink and washed my hands with soap and water. He also washed my tear-streaked face with a washcloth.

"If you tell anyone something bad will happen to you." The words rolled off his lips slowly.

I nodded. I just wanted to get out of that bathroom. Michael then nonchalantly washed his hands, zipped up his pants, and opened the door.

My body was trembling when I sat back down in front of the TV with Ralph and Joe. Neither of them had noticed I was gone. They were absorbed in the cartoons. Michael was soon laughing with them as if nothing had happened. I didn't understand what had taken place in the bathroom. I just had a terrible feeling inside of me because I knew it was wrong. I wanted so badly to tell Mother, but Michael's warning stopped me.

Mother was still acting strange so I decided not to tell anyone. I wanted to forget it. Sleep didn't come easy that night. I kept checking my hand to make sure nothing was on it. I didn't know that that would be the first of many trips to the bathroom. Every time I tried to watch TV he was there waiting to take me into the bathroom. It didn't matter how much I resisted or begged him not to. Sometimes he picked me up and carried me in. Once inside his threats quieted me down and I would pull on his penis until the stuff came out. Ralph and Joe never noticed anything wrong. Every incident left me feeling queasier. I hated Michael. I began spending more time in the basement to avoid him.

I would sit on the bottom stair and listen to the TV shows

they were watching. When Ralph and Joe laughed at something I tried to imagine what was funny. Sometimes Michael stood at the top of the stairs looking down at me. He would smile and try to get me to come up. I looked away so he couldn't see me cry. I felt safer downstairs.

I suffered another attack when Michael lured me upstairs with promises of not touching me. I felt stupid for believing him. As if to punish me he twisted my arm and laughed at my tears. This time Michael tried to shove his thing in my mouth, but I wouldn't open it. I gritted my teeth, determined that he would not put that thing in my mouth. He finally got tired of trying and made me use my hand to get his satisfaction. I never went upstairs again until after Michael left.

Mother was upset and very emotional when she explained to us why Michael had to leave so suddenly. Michael turned eighteen and was drafted into the Army. I didn't know what a draft was, nor did I care about the war in Vietnam. The only thing I cared about was that he was gone. Mother rambled on about how young he was, how horrible the war was, and how he could get killed. I secretly crossed my fingers hoping for the latter to happen to him. I didn't want to ever see his pimply face again.

I didn't want Mother to bring any more foster children into the house. The thought of someone taking Michael's place frightened me. Mother thought I was jealous of Michael because the mention of his name made me frown. I wanted to tell her about him, but his threats were still fresh on my mind. I wondered even then if Mother would believe me because she loved Michael so much. I decided that I would never tell anyone.

We used the kitchen in the basement to eat in but the other side of the basement was unfinished. That was the where mother made me sleep. My new bedroom consisted of concrete floors and walls. I slept on a small cot in a corner of the room. There was no place to put dolls, stuffed animals, or pictures. I had no dresser and there was no closet to hang clothes in.

My first night sleeping in the basement was the scariest. I tried to pull the covers over my face because the dancing shadows on the wall looked like ghosts. I found out later that a tree outside of the window created the funny images when it mixed with the moonlight.

After Michael left, Mother's behavior became even worse. I didn't know what had changed Mother and Dad, I only knew that whatever was going on was terrifying. Mother made me do chores that left my body sore and aching. It was painful scrubbing floors on my hands and knees. My fantasy of the princess in a castle had lost its attraction. I now felt more like Cinderella living in a dark, spooky dungeon.

I had been sleeping in the basement for about a month when Dad started coming downstairs to wake me up at five o'clock in the morning. I was lying in bed when I felt strange hands on my body. The smell of dad's cigar filled the air.

"I'm checking to see if you wet the bed," he said calmly. I could only lie there while his thick hands probed my body, mostly between my legs.

"Get out of bed!"

I watched him pat a few places on my bed. I was nervous about the way he had touched me.

"It's time for you to start on your chores," he said before leaving. I felt the same creepy feeling of humiliation I had always felt when Michael took me into the bathroom.

I began peeing in the bed again, even though I had stopped when I first came. Dad immediately felt the wetness on my pajamas, but still subjected me to a body search that was mainly focused between my legs. I couldn't do anything but let him do it.

I began listening for his footsteps on the stairs because I didn't want to wake up with his hands between my legs. At least if I heard him I knew what to expect. Hearing Dad's heavy footsteps descending into the basement made me cringe. The smell from his cigar always preceded him into the room. Sometimes I stared at the smoke rising to the ceiling rather than at him.

There was no bathroom in the basement and mother didn't allow me to come upstairs at night so I was forced to squat over the drain to pee. Later, Mother later gave me a large pail with a lid on it and told me that it was my bathroom. I crawled out of bed at night to use the pail. It was usually pitch black in the basement except for the light coming in through the window so sometimes I couldn't find the pail and used the floor. In the mornings I would get a bucket of water and clean the concrete just in case.

My imagination went wild when I thought about spiders and other insects crawling around in the basement. I tried to hold myself until the morning but it didn't work.

Because we were peeing in the bed it gave them the best excuse to keep beating us. Dad took his belt off and whipped me while I stood naked in front of him. He always made me strip and he held me down against the cold concrete floor and beat me. He acted as if he enjoyed watching me tremble in pain. He made panting noises that sounded like he couldn't breathe, but that didn't stop him from hitting me until he was tired. After he finished beating me he made me take the wet sheets off the bed and hand-wash them on a scrub board with mother's homemade lye soap that left my hands cracked and bleeding.

The weekends were worse because I had more chores to do. I couldn't even think about going outside to play during the summer. I washed every floor in the house on my hands and knees. I scrubbed the bathrooms and washed the windows. I dusted all the furniture in the house and when that was completed mother made me clean and shine every pair of her shoes and purses that filled the pantry from top to bottom.

I no longer walked to school with Ralph and Joe because I never finished my chores in time. At school tension was mounting with my teachers and classmates. I was late for school everyday anywhere from thirty minutes to an hour and a half. The school secretary gave me a grim look every time I asked for a late slip to get into class. When I brought home the tardy slips to be signed by Mother it became another excuse for her to beat me.

I was embarrassed walking into class late. I felt the stares boring a hole in me as I slipped into my seat. The teacher's obvious irritation was evident in her voice and my classmates began acting indifferent towards me.

Things were changing so rapidly around the house that I didn't know what to expect on a daily basis. Mother and Dad were becoming more and more abusive. Ralph and Joe were getting whippings from Mother for wetting the bed. Ralph would scream in the middle of the night from bad dreams. One night he jumped to the bottom of the stairs trying to get away from what he described as the devil. He was lucky that he didn't hurt or kill himself by falling down the fifteen stairs. He only suffered a few scrapes and bruises.

"That dream is coming from the depths of your own evil mind," Mother told him.

Dad would listen to Mother's complaints about us that were endless and usually untrue. We never bothered defending ourselves because it was obvious the two of them were against us. They hated us, especially me. If I even looked as if I wanted to protest something Mother said I got slapped across my face. I became so nervous that if Dad or Mother reached across the dinner table for anything I jumped or put my hands up. I cried easily, and the slightest movement caused me to react. I backed into things because I was afraid to turn my back on them. The whippings increased to two or three times a day depending on the mood they were in.

My life was a living hell. I began thinking about my real family. Where were my brothers, Roy jr., Jerry, and Henry? What about Uncle Ben? Did he ever come back? Did they think about us? Maybe they didn't know how to get in touch with us. I was sure that must be the reason why they hadn't contacted us. At night I was usually stiff and sore from either a beating or doing chores. I wanted to believe that one day my real family would come back and get us.

Mr. Bergner visited us about twice a month. Mother had us

practice what to say and how to act around him. I wanted so badly to tell him about what was really going on, but I didn't have the courage. Mr. Bergner was impressed by all Mother's goodness that telling him would not have mattered anyway. Sometimes I wondered whom he really came to visit. He spent more time with Mother sipping tea and laughing. On the days that mother knew he was coming of course we didn't get beaten, at least not until after he left. It was sickening to watch the way Mother manipulated him.

She was a great actress, and I understood that we were no match for her. She was too good.

"How is everything going?" Mr. Bergner would ask me with a funny grin on his face.

"Fine," I would mumble, forcing a smile. Ralph and Joe would answer the same way. We had to make it seem as if we couldn't be happier. "Please take me out of here!" I wanted to scream at him. I never did because of the look on mother's face. When Mr. Bergner walked out the door I had the urge to run after him. I never did that either.

When school let out my classmates were looking forward to the summer break while I was hoping that by some miracle school wouldn't let out. Weekends and holidays were already dreadful for me. School had become a refuge for me, even though I had lost my friends. I was socially withdrawn and quiet all of the time. I didn't want to be anyone's friend and I didn't want anyone to be my friend while I struggled to hide my unhappiness. I continually watched the clock as minutes ticked away dreading the end of the school day.

School let out in early June with the usual burst of happiness from the children and teachers. I overheard many of my classmates telling of plans to visit other states, staying with grandparents in nearby cities, or just having a fun going swimming or playing in the park. The only thing on my mind was how, or if, I would survive the summer.

The heat of summer was a welcome change from the bitter cold winter and rainy spring. I especially remembered the cold days when the wind seemed ready to rip me apart. Some days I had to climb over tall snow banks on my way to school. It was painful to breathe when it was really cold outside especially if I had to run to avoid getting to school any later.

I was surprised to see Mr. Bergner's county car parked in front of our house when I got home from school. I rushed through the door and was surprised to see Sara standing in the living room. With a squeal of delight we hugged each other. Sara was now a teenager and beginning to show curves like a woman. Her skin was a clear brown color and her hair was long and thick. She wore it pulled back into a ponytail. Sara was nodding her head as she looked around the room. I was sure she was giving her approval. If only she knew the sadness we were feeling.

Sara moved into the vacant bedroom upstairs. I sat on the bed while she unpacked her things. I still had not learned sign language, but we still managed to communicate. She showed me pictures of her friends and teachers at school. In every picture she was smiling. I laughed because Sara was the only black face in most of the pictures. I wondered what it felt like to live around all white people. Sara didn't seem to mind. Sometimes I believe she forgot the color of her own skin. Her collection of pictures, letters, cards and stuffed animals gave the bedroom a personal touch.

She had letters wishing her a good summer vacation. That's when jealousy overtook me. Why couldn't I be the one who was deaf? Sara proved that you didn't need to hear or talk to function. She seemed to be doing fine without hearing or talking. Sara didn't have to do anything around the house. She was able to spend time outside. Sometimes she visited with the neighbors next-door, went for walks or sat on the front porch. I was always inside the house looking out of the windows and wishing I could join the other kids who were playing. I watched the girls playing double dutch in the streets or jacks on their porches.

Mother allowed Joe and Ralph to play outside. I tried my best to understand why Mother treated me so bad. A couple of times that summer she did allow me to go outside, but it was in the late evening just before dusk so all I could do was sit on the porch. If it were a hot night the other kids would be outside playing so I would sneak over across the street where Raleigh and his sister Carol lived to play with them.

Some nights Mother would play the piano and sing while the neighbors gathered on their porches to hear Mother as her voice drifted down the block. Sometimes I even forgot how evil she had become and enjoyed the music too. The neighbors loved and respected mother. Most regarded her as a God-fearing, loving woman. What everyone else saw was just her outer shell. None of them knew that while the summer was alive with music and fun in the sun, I was doing backbreaking chores or recovering from the last beating.

Sara wasn't aware of the beatings at first. I secretly hoped her presence in the house would help us. I thought maybe Mother wouldn't hit us while she was living there. I was wrong. It didn't occur to me that Sara's handicap was a benefit for Mother. While Sara stared at the television upstairs, Mother beat me in the basement. My screams went unheard. I prayed for Sara to walk in and see what she was doing to me. It never happened.

I began resenting Sara and wanted her to leave and never come back. Mother didn't beat Sara nor did Ralph or Joe get as many whippings as I did. My resentment towards my sister was so bad that when she tried to talk to me I turned away from her. Sara didn't understand what was going on so it was easy to take my frustrations out on her.

I dreaded washday. On Saturdays I stripped the beds and sorted all the clothes by color. I had to remember that white clothes needed special preparations such as bleach for the wash and bluing for the rinse. I had to make sure that I didn't wash any clothes with colors that could run onto the other clothes and ruin them. Mother was very particular about the way clothes were washed.

The pressure I felt on washday was overwhelming. The old

wringer washer had to be pulled from a corner in the basement and placed directly over the drain. The rollers on the bottom made it easier for me to move, but it was still heavy. I had to fill the washer using a hose that was connected to the water taps on the basin. This took a long time because I had to fill two washbasins and the washing machine. White clothes required hot water, and my hands felt like they were on fire when I had to dip them into the water to put the clothes through the wringer. If too many clothes went through the wringer would lock up. When that happened I had to pop it open and pull the clothes out to reset it. I stood directly over the washing machine on a stool Mother provided for me. My legs ached from standing so long. My hands were dry and cracked by the end of the day. I still had to do other chores between washing, rinsing, and hanging the clothes on the line. After taking the wash off the line I had to fold everything into separate piles according to which it belonged. Sheets, towels, and pillowcases were stacked into a pile of their own.

Mother taught me how to iron clothes. She wanted everything to be starched and she certainly believed in ironing everything from pillowcases to her silk underclothes. It was difficult to do the ironing because she hated wrinkles or *cat faces* as she called the small creases. Often I had to redo things because of one wrinkle. I spent at least a couple of days ironing every week. By the time I finished it was time to repeat the cycle again.

It was a bright, warm, July morning. Washday was two days behind me with another coming up too soon. I was trying to finish the basket of ironing left to do. I had been up since five when Dad woke me that morning by rubbing his hands over my body. It was one of my lucky days because I hadn't peed in the bed. I was still sleepy from a restless night. The whipping mother gave me the day before was still causing me pain so every movement hurt. I didn't bother looking at the ugly bruise that covered my right side. I felt hungry and realized that I didn't get enough to eat the night before. Mother was limiting the amount of food we ate. My first mission

111

was to check to see if the freezer was unlocked. It was usually stocked with jellyrolls and doughnuts, so if the freezer was accidentally left open I could help myself to the pastry.

It wasn't easy eating frozen food but anything tasted good when hunger pains were stabbing at my stomach. The freezer was open. I didn't see any jellyrolls so I took out a slice of frozen bread and rubbed some butter on it. It tasted good even though it was cold and hard.

I put the ironing board up, plugged in the iron and tackled the bundle of wrinkled clothes. Mother's white silk slip was on top of the pile so I grabbed it first. The moment I put the iron on it I knew I had made a big mistake. I gasped at the material clinging to the iron. An ugly brown imprint stared back at me. My hands began shaking as I held up the slip to inspect the damage.

My mind was spinning as I envisioned Mother's anger. My first thought was to hide the slip somewhere, but the burnt smell was in the air and the iron looked hopelessly damaged with the material clinging to it. I unplugged the iron and tried to reason with myself. I knew that I was in for it so I had two choices: I could stay and wait until Mother got up, or I could leave the house. I had thought many times how nice it would be to just leave; now I wanted to do it.

Mother had graduated from beating us with a belt to using a homemade whip that felt like it was taking my skin off with each lick. Dad made it using cable wire. I was sore and didn't want to go through another beating. I was tired of the pain and the humiliation. I was ready to leave.

I stood at the back door moments later staring at the knob. There were bolt locks on the door that wouldn't open without a key. I was about to give up when I saw that the door was not completely closed. The lock had not gone in all the way. I pulled on the door and it opened easily.

The bright sun hit me like a blinding flashlight. I was aware of my legs moving because I was running as fast as I could. I never looked back and ran until my chest began hurting. When I couldn't take another step I fell on the grass and struggled to catch my breath. I didn't know how far I had run and still expected Mother to come around the corner in her car. When enough time passed without her showing up I began to relax.

I continued walking down the street, glancing over my shoulder constantly. The further I walked the more confident I became. I smiled and said hello to everyone who passed me on the sidewalk. I skipped, jumped and ran like the nine-year-old child I was. I wanted to believe that I was in another world. I would run somewhere far away and they would never see me again. The only thing that really mattered was that I was free.

A beautiful park with bright green grass was in my path. I ran into the park soaking in all its beauty. There were swings, slides, and monkey bars that I rushed to play on. It had been a long time since I played on any of them. Kids were already playing so I joined in the fun.

I soon forgot about Mother as I laughed and screamed with my new friends. The trees, the grass, the crystal blue sky, even the birds chirping made me feel alive again. As the day wore on and the sun got hotter I left the park to venture on.

I walked down a street that had a lot of businesses lined up on both sides. It was fun peeping through store windows. I was fascinated with the people who hurried about with packages stuffed under their arms and children being pulled along. When I looked into one store window I was surprised at what I saw. It looked as if people were washing clothes. I decided to go through the open door. The place was very hot with a smell of bleach. I sat on a hard chair watching with fascination as women pulled loads of clothes from the machines or threw clothes in other machines to dry. I had never seen an automatic washer or dryer before. I didn't know they existed. I wondered why Mother with all her modern appliances didn't have one. I laughed when the machines began shaking. A lady who noticed that I was captivated by the action explained to me about the cycles the machine went through.

Before long I was helping the women with their washing. It was so easy to throw clothes into the machine and take them out when the machine stopped. I helped the mothers by watching their kids and even ran to the store to buy more soap for them.

Time passed by quickly as women came and left with loads of laundry and soon it was dark. Reluctantly I left the laundromat when it closed. The women were generous with their nickels, quarters and dimes. The change in my pocket made me feel better as I walked to the grocery store to buy something to eat. I hadn't expected the ladies to pay me for helping them. I counted over two dollars.

After sleeping in the basement the darkness didn't scare me anymore. I walked a few more blocks before sitting down on some steep steps beneath a flashing neon light. A few people walked past me into the place. A man's voice startled me and when I looked up to the top of the steps he was pointing at me.

"Why are you sitting on these stairs?" His voice sounded angry, yet his face was kind.

"I was resting, sir."

His voices softened. "You can't sit on these stairs; I'm running a business here." I looked up at the flashing light and recognized the beer sign.

"I'm sorry, sir."

To my surprise, he reached in his pocket and handed me some money. "Here. Go buy yourself a candy bar and go home."

"Thank you," I mumbled as I walked away. I counted the seventy-five cents over and over again, mixing it with the other money I had.

As I continued down the street I saw the bright lights of a grocery store. I hurried into the store and bought a soda, a bag of potato chips and a candy bar. In the back of the store near the trash bins were large boxes. I grabbed one and began dragging it behind me. I had something to sleep in.

I went through the neighborhood in search of the perfect spot to put it. A large white house with tall trees appealed to me. I towed my box into the yard and knew the spot the moment I saw it.

I put my box on the lawn behind two large trees. I crawled inside and felt safe there. I stared into the night sky watching the twinkling stars. The air was warm and comforting.

"Thank You, God," I whispered before falling into a restful sleep.

I awoke the next morning well rested and alert waking up when the sun was rising. I climbed out of the box. It felt so good awaking to the sounds of birds chirping and bees buzzing, and the feeling of freedom.

I rushed to the grocery store to buy a breakfast of soda, cupcakes, and candy. Then I slowly walked back to the laundromat. I washed up in the bathroom with the bar of soap I had purchased.

The entire day was spent helping women with their laundry. Like the day before, they rewarded me with nickels and dimes. When darkness fell again I was exhausted. I walked back to my box hidden beneath the bushes. Another warm night helped me to drift into an undisturbed sleep.

The next morning I awoke abruptly to the sound of a slamming door. I peeked out my box in time to see an old man walking out the gate. I waited until he was out of sight and quickly got up. My body was craving some real food so I bought some lunchmeat, bread, soda, and potato chips at the store.

I walked down the street, proud to claim this as my neighborhood. I passed the same people as the day before who were sitting on their porches or playing in their yards.

I hated that my dress was dirty and wrinkled. Maybe I could ask one of the women to help me wash it today. When I arrived at the laundromat I was disappointed to find it closed. I was too early. I walked around the neighborhood looking at the beautiful houses while I waited.

When I returned to the laundromat it was open and there

was a woman in there preparing to wash. The lady looked at me funny and I didn't feel comfortable asking her if she needed help, so I sat on the chair. I knew other women would be coming later.

I was still sitting there when two policemen walked through the door. They were talking to the man who took the money out of the machines. He pointed in my direction. Did he think I stole something? I was scared because the policemen kept looking over at me. I wanted to run out, but they were blocking the door as if they wanted to keep me in. I looked at the woman who was washing clothes but she looked away. I pretended I couldn't see them when they began walking towards me. I swung my legs back and forth nervously. I would tell them I didn't steal anything.

The tall policeman was the first to speak. "What's your name?"

I blurted out the first name that came to mind. "Rosie."

"Rosie?"

I nodded.

"Where do you live, Rosie?"

I tried not to appear afraid. My head was spinning because they looked mean. I fought the urge to cry and answered with a quick, "around the corner."

They exchanged glances.

"What's your address?"

"I don't know. I live in a yellow house."

"Come with us."

"Am I going to jail?" The frightened feeling was beginning to creep up on me.

"No, we just want you to show us where you live."

"Then you will let me go?"

"That's right," the shorter police officer answered, smiling at me.

It felt strange sitting in the back of a police car. It reminded me of riding in the county car. I closed my eyes and prayed there would be a yellow house around the corner.

When we turned the corner it was there. The biggest house on the street was a canary yellow with white shutters. I smiled with triumph.

"That's it! That's it!" I shouted.

"It's a yellow house all right". He pulled over to the curve and the tall policeman got out and opened the rear door for me.

"Thank you," I said, hopping out as fast as I could. I expected them to leave, but they started walking up to the house and pulling me along with them.

"No," I said, reluctant to go with them.

Then the door opened and a man and woman walked out. They were surprised to see us walking up to their house.

I didn't wait for them to question the couple.

"This isn't my house," I mumbled.

The short policeman took me back to the police car while the tall one told the startled couple that they had made a mistake.

"Why did you lie to us?"

I didn't answer him.

The shorter police officer turned around. "We were called to the laundromat by the owner. He said you've been hanging around there for the last couple of days. He said that some of the customers were concerned about you."

I hung my head in silence.

"We need to know who you are and where you live."

"I live around here."

He shook his head.

"Look around, little girl. All you see around here are white people. You are a colored girl. I know for a fact that there are no colored families living in this area."

His words brought on a reality that I hadn't thought about. That explained a lot of things. I hadn't seen a black face in the last couple of days either. I was on the predominately white side of the city. Papa had told us about the beautiful homes on the other side of town. Papa was right! White folks had everything. Even Mother's house, as nice as it was, couldn't compare to the beautiful homes here.

I still refused to talk. The tall policeman had climbed in and was talking on the police radio.

"We have a colored girl approximately nine to eleven years old who is a possible runaway."

Why did this have to happen? The last couple of days had been so perfect.

I listened as information about me came back on the car radio.

The police officer behind the wheel was looking at me.

Without warning the tears came.

"Want to tell us about it?"

I nodded my head.

"Is your name Joyce Ford?"

I nodded my head again.

"Why are you so far from home, Joyce?"

"I...I burnt a hole in Mother's slip by accident when I was ironing it."

"So why did you run away?"

The other policeman was talking to me now. I didn't like the way he looked at me.

"Because I was scared that Mother was going to beat me."

"You're telling us that your mother was going to beat you because you burnt a hole in her slip while ironing it?"

"Yes," I mumbled. I knew by the look on their faces that they didn't believe me.

My biggest mistake was running to an all white neighborhood. I should have walked in the other direction.

The next time he spoke his voice was softer.

"We can't help you if you don't tell us the truth."

I don't know why I felt compelled to tell them everything. I wanted to trust these policemen. I told them how I burnt the slip and was afraid. I told them how mother was beating us almost every day.

118

I felt relief rush over me as I emptied my soul. They seemed to be listening to me. Maybe they would help me. I told them how I survived the last couple of days. I even showed them the house where my box was carefully hidden in the bushes.

I knew I had made a mistake when one of them laughed at me. I tried to resort to being silent again.

"I think you've really hurt your foster parents by what you've done; you're a very selfish little girl. That story you told us about the slip is plain ridiculous. Your real parents are dead so complete strangers take you into their home, give you a place to sleep, give you something to eat and you want us to believe that they beat and hurt you for no reason?"

Their words cut through my heart like a knife leaving me numb.

"If it wasn't for them taking you into their home, you wouldn't have anywhere to go."

I sat with my hands folded listening while they took turns telling me how great and wonderful Mother was. Apparently the shorter police officer knew her.

I stared out of the car window. I wanted to fade away. The police car was moving but I didn't know where we were going until I began to recognize the streets. They were taking me back home. My heart thumped and my palms felt sweaty. I imagined Mother being angry and upset with me.

"If you ever do this again to your mother I will personally spank you," the short policeman promised.

I said nothing.

"I don't believe this story any more than the first story you told us when we picked you up at the laundromat. You've done nothing but tell us a bunch of lies. Mrs. Watson is a respected woman in the community. Do you really expect us to believe that she hurts you? If you got a spanking it was well deserved. Instead of being grateful to these people who took you and your brothers into their home you tell us a bunch of lies about them. My understanding is that you came to their home filthy, hungry, and abandoned by your own uncle and aunt."

Each word he said brought back painful memories and the tears flowed. I had no way to respond to what he was saying. Mother did do a lot for us when we first came to live with her. Now I realized it was long ago. The angry look on his face told me what I needed to know; he didn't believe me nor would he believe what was going on behind the closed doors on Tenth Lane.

It was just like Mother to convince the police that she was a wonderful, caring, devoted, and loving mother. If only they knew the truth I wondered what they would do.

"Don't ever do this again ". The short policeman narrowed his eyes when he talked.

I nodded my head in response, too choked up to speak.

"Do you hear me? He was almost yelling at me.

"Yes," I mumbled.

The tall policeman didn't say anything, but I noticed him looking at me through the rearview mirror. I didn't care if he saw me crying.

The drive home felt longer than the walk I had made a few days earlier. The sun was still blazing when we pulled up in front of the house. Several neighbors were sitting on their porches enjoying the warm summer evening.

My head jerked up when I heard the slamming of a door. I looked out in time to see Mother rushing out of the front door of the house. I could hear her high-pitched voice screaming. She ran to the police car.

I shrank back, afraid of what she would do to me.

She opened the car door and began shouting, "My baby! My baby!" I was totally in shock. And when I looked into her face I was horrified. Her eyes and nose were red and puffy, and her face was tear-streaked. She grabbed me and hugged me with a force I had never felt before. I couldn't believe this was happening. I clung to Mother mixing my tears with hers as they dripped on my dirty dress.

I didn't know how to react to these emotional feelings she was displaying. I was so overwhelmed I was sobbing out loud.

"Thank you, Jesus," Mother yelled between sobs. Mother's display of genuine concern affected everyone that witnessed the scene. The policeman who had lectured me was ready to say something when Mother interrupted him. "She's home safe and that's all that matters."

I began thinking that I was terrible to put Mother though so much grief. I wasn't sure if this was an act or if Mother really did care. My mind kept flashing back through the painful past as I held onto her. I couldn't let go. I wondered if tomorrow I would wake up and she would be like the woman I met that first day in the living room.

Neighbors who came outside to witness our reunion frowned at me. I felt the angry vibrations and knew what they must be thinking. The tall policemen separated us so they could talk to Mother, who was still sobbing. The tears were real; the scene seemed genuine enough to convince everyone that she had suffered while I was missing for two days.

The police car left within an hour and all the neighbors went back in their houses. I stood in the kitchen waiting for the worst to happen. Ralph, Joe, and Sara stared at me, unsure if they should talk to me or avoid me. We stood in the kitchen staring at each other and waiting.

Surprisingly, Mother didn't hit or curse at me. She told me she was so worried about me that she hadn't been able to sleep or eat. Thoughts had plagued her mind that something bad had happened to me.

"Why did you do this to me?" she asked, interrupting her own story.

I could only shake my head. I was confused about everything that was happening. I had prepared myself for the worse and now she was acting as differently. Nothing she was saying or doing was consistent with the way she had been acting before I left.

Was this the beginning of something new? Was it possible that Mother and dad were sorry for all the things they had done to me? Would things change? It seemed possible.

That night mother celebrated my homecoming by cooking large, juicy hamburgers and French fries. We were all stunned by Mother and Dad's behavior. Joe and Ralph later told me that Mother cried the whole time I was gone.

I sat in the tub washing off three days of dirt. I was feeling better than I could remember in a long time. I was showered with so much attention from Mother that I was starting to believe things would be different. Dad hadn't been in the basement to bother me for a few days either.

Joe and Ralph were eager to hear where I had been the last couple of days. Mother told me not to talk about where I had been or what I had done. I repeated what the policeman had told me.

"There's no better place than being home with people who love and care about you."

I didn't even tell Mother about my adventure. I said a prayer before I crawled into bed that night. Maybe this was the start of something better.

The next few days were filled with excitement while Mother and Dad continued to give all four of us more affection than I could remember having.

It didn't take long for things to return to the way they were. The beatings and molestation started again by the end of the next week.

One day I was trying to get away from the broom Mother was swinging at me and when I put my arm up to protect myself the broom handle cracked and broke. I felt a sickening thud and pain shot up my arm. I fell to the floor holding my arm and moaning in pain. Mother's only concern was to see if it was broken. When she saw that I could still move it she tried to hit me again. This time she missed and I ran downstairs as fast as I could. I felt stupid to have thought that she was changing. She gained all that admiration and pity from the neighbors and policemen by her display. She had fooled all of us.

Ralph came down into the basement while I was filling my bucket with water to clean the floors. He was dragging sheets behind him.

"I peed in the bed," he said. We both knew it meant he would get it when Mother got up.

"I'm running away, he announced with a grin on his face.

"You can't run away!" I was angry with him for thinking about it.

"You did it." His young innocent face looked up at me.

"That was different."

"No it's not. I'm tired of getting whippings all the time."

He had been getting his share lately.

"But you can't run away," I scolded him. "For one thing, there's a deadbolt on the door and you need a key to open it. Another thing is you're too young to go anywhere alone."

"Will you come with me?" his voice was pleading. I couldn't do it again. I already knew what the result would be. I wished that I could take him and run somewhere safe.

"Don't go," was all I could reply."

"Sara said she'll go with me," he said with determination. "We can climb out of the basement window."

When I looked up again Sara was in the room. She had a stupid smile on her face as if they were simply going to walk to the corner store. I was angry with both of them because they didn't understand what they were doing. The two of them together wouldn't make it out there very long. I asked Sara if she was going to run away with Ralph. With a look of excitement, she nodded yes.

I watched them crawl out through the basement window. I was sure they would be home before the night was over. Mother and Dad had put extra locks on the back door after I ran away. Mother was furious when she woke up that morning and found Sara and Ralph gone.

"It's your fault," she screamed at me. "If you hadn't been so hot between the legs all of this wouldn't have happened."

What did she mean about me being hot between the legs? The day wore on with more angry accusations and threats.

"You ran away to meet your boyfriend," she said. I know what you really did out there for two days."

I tried to keep out of her way while she stormed through the house.

"It was probably one of those men you've been messing around with who raped that little girl last week. He was probably out there looking for you." I didn't have a clue what she was talking about. Mother didn't bother calling the police because she knew, like I knew, that they wouldn't be gone for long.

A police car pulled up late that evening after the sun had gone down. Sara and Ralph were sitting in the back seat. Mother denied knowing they had runaway. I found out later that Ralph had borrowed a dime to call the police so they could bring them home. He said they were tired and hungry after playing all day in a park.

Ralph was crying and telling Mother how sorry he was in front of the policemen. Mother never shed a tear nor did she seem to be upset. It was hard to know what Mother felt. We found out after the policemen left.

The policeman didn't write in his report that Sara and Ralph ran away, instead he wrote that they were playing outside and simply got lost. This time there was no tears, hugs, or neighbors to witness anything.

Mother contained her anger until after the policemen left. Her rage flared and she hit Ralph with such a force he fell hard to the floor. I watched as she raised the belt, hitting him again and again and again until she was out of breath. Ralph screamed and squirmed on the floor, trying to get away.

Dad was standing nearby yelling and threatening to whip all of us. I felt sorry for Ralph. He had expected the same treatment I got when I returned home, but instead of a celebration with hamburgers and fries, he got beaten.

I held my breath waiting for mother to do something to me. Sara was sitting on a chair with tears rolling down her face. To my surprise, Mother grabbed Sara. It was like watching her with Linda all over again. Sara didn't allow Mother to hit her and the two of them began to struggle. Sara was screaming as she wrestled with mother. I watched my sister fight back with everything she had. Mother was physically powerful too and threw Sara into the wall. As if guided by an unseen force Sara grabbed the phone from the wall and hit mother in the head with it. Mother was out of breath and as if she was jerked back to reality, she gave Sara a final look and walked away.

Dad was still angry and I saw him kick Sara, causing her to double over and moan in pain. Sara sounded like an ambulance as her high-pitched screams filled the house. I felt sorry for her because she didn't understand what was going on. She had tried furiously to explain why she went with Ralph. I'm convinced that Sara was the reason Mother didn't come after me that night. Mother warned all of us to not even think about running away from her house again.

After that night Sara went to live with Mother's daughter. Mother wanted to separate her from us. We were allowed to walk to Ruby's house a few times over the summer to visit Sara. She was happier living with Ruby and James. She said they were nice to her. They allowed her to catch the bus and go visit with her friends from the deaf school. The only problem Sara had was from Ruby's son, Bobby who apparently tried to touch her. I wished Mother had sent me to live with Ruby. Mother had me where she wanted me. The only reason Sara was with Ruby was because she had gotten in the way.

It was another bright summer morning. The sun was out, the birds were singing, a perfect day. I was dusting the furniture in the living room while watching Mother pacing from the kitchen to the bathroom. I knew when she was in a bad mood. I went through carefully dusting everything even though there was little or no dust on anything.

I was looking at a small picture that had recently been placed on one of the end tables when I felt her presence. I looked over to see her with her hands stuffed in the pockets of her housecoat. I knew immediately by the look on her face that I was in for it. When she walked over and grabbed me I was expecting to be hit or thrown into the wall. Instead, she put me in a chokehold.

"What are you doing?"

I couldn't speak so I shook my head.

"Are you spying?"

What was she talking about? I didn't know what she was talking about but I couldn't tell her because she was choking me. Mother finally released me. I saw that her eyes were wild with anger and her lips were curled under. I didn't know what was coming next.

She pulled something shiny out of her housecoat. It looked like something silver or blue. Then I recognized that it was a gun. Mother was going to shoot me. Suddenly I didn't want to die. I saw my life flashing before me as we stared at each other. I didn't resist when she grabbed my hair and pulled my head back. I was now staring into her face. The gun was pointed a few inches from my nose. I could feel the coldness of it on my face.

"I'm going to kill you." The words were said slow and deliberate as if she was making sure they sank into my brain. I don't know if I was still breathing at that point. I was sure any movement would make the gun go off. I saw her finger on the trigger. I heard it being pulled back.

Just about the time I was sure she would let go she stuck the gun in my opened mouth. I tasted the cold metal against my tongue.

"I'm going to blow your damn head off!" The gun was gagging me.

"Don't you know I will kill you?"

I couldn't respond. I felt hot tears streaming down my face. Why was I crying now? What difference did it make? I wanted to beg for my life, but it was hard to do with a pistol in my throat. If I died at least I would see Hon and Papa again. I would see everyone in heaven including my real mama and daddy. It seemed like a lifetime passed before the ordeal was over. Mother let go of me and I fell to the floor. I waited until I no longer heard footsteps before I moved. My hands were trembling. It was the first time I'd ever seen a real gun. I realized that Mother had the power to kill me whenever she wanted to, and there wasn't anything I could do or say to stop her. I had no doubts that she hated me enough to do it. I didn't know what stopped her from shooting me that day. I never saw the gun again.

After Labor Day, school was back in session. I was happy for the few hours I would be away from home. I would miss the summer's warmth because fall was creeping up on us but I looked forward to being back in school. It had been a hard summer.

A few weeks into the school year, Mother bought me a pair of shoes. I almost gagged from the smell of them. Joe and Ralph looked away to keep from laughing as she held them up for everyone to see. It was obvious they weren't new. I stared at the ugly red and beige shoes, horrified that she expected me to wear them to school. I couldn't wear those shoes to school! The kids would laugh and tease me.

I hung my head so she wouldn't have the satisfaction of seeing me cry. I saw the smirk on her face and knew she was laughing inside. I tried to get out of the house without wearing those shoes, but Mother made sure I wore them and even allowed me to leave early that day for school. Ralph and Joe were kind enough not to talk about the shoes as I walked slowly behind them.

No one seemed to notice my shoes as we played the few minutes before the bell rang. I had almost forgotten about them when I stood in line with my class until someone started laughing. I turned around to see almost every kid on the playground pointing and laughing at my shoes.

"Look at that number on the back," one of the kids yelled.

I turned my shoe over and saw a number five on the back of it. I hadn't noticed it before. The kids continued teasing me in the classroom.

"Those are bowling shoes," one kid yelled.

I was teased all day about the ugly bowling shoes. I knew mother did it on purpose; she wanted everyone to hate me as much as she hated me.

I was walking home with my brothers when a group of kids started following us.

"Your sister's got on bowling shoes."

Joe and Ralph tried not to laugh at me. I kept walking, looking straight ahead and trying to shut out the words from the kids. Mother made me wear the shoes two more times before throwing them away, but the memories of the kids teasing me remained in my mind.

Mother and Dad were making life miserable for all of us, but I felt they directly targeted me. When I completed my morning chores, Mother would comb my hair. She hot combed it every morning. The very thought of her combing my hair would make me shake because she always burned me. If I moved too much she hit me in the head with the hot comb. My scalp was always sore so I bit my lip to keep from screaming when hot oil dripped on my scalp. The heat caused painful blisters and sores on my scalp and my hair fell out. Soon there were only a few strands left on my head. Mother showed no sympathy when she combed my hair, mixing blood, pus, and hair together. My head felt as if every strand of hair was being plucked out with a hot poker. The trail of burns Mother left on my neck ears and back eventually healed.

Mother was frustrated and she couldn't do much with my hair after it fell out. She told everyone I burned my own hair out trying to press it. The back of my head was completely bald.

One morning while mother was trying to do something with

my hair she left the room and came back with a hairpiece. I stared at it. Was she going to put that on my head? I begged her not to make me wear it. I knew the kids at school would tease me. I would rather have a baldhead than wear a wig piece.

But my pleas for her not to put it on my head prompted Mother to hit me. The worst part of all was that it didn't even match my hair color. My hair was black and the hairpiece was brownish with gray streaks in it.

The first time I walked into my classroom with the hairpiece pinned on the back of my head I heard kids giggling. I didn't look up.

"She's got a wig on!" Anthony Williams shouted.

"Ugh," another kid responded.

"Hey, wig girl!"

I kept my head down as the laughter floated around the room.

"I'm going to pull off your wig at recess," one boy said. Everyone in the room joined in the laughter. The teacher finally got the kids to quiet down, but I still heard the remarks from my classmates. How could Mother do this to me? Everyone knew I was wearing fake hair.

I got into two fights on the way home after school because kids wanted to pull off the hairpiece that Mother had pinned on. I knew it would be hard to get off because it felt like she put a million hairpins in it. When they yanked it I only felt a burst of pain.

The few girls who had been kind enough to play with me even gave up. I spent recess alone watching from a distance while my former friends jumped rope or stood around in groups giggling about the silly things girls talked about. I accepted being a loner. I didn't have to pretend if there was no one to pretend with. I daydreamed about being in another world where everyone liked me. These fantasies helped me get through the hard times.

Dad made me strip before every beating. He would sit and watch me take off each piece of clothing. I usually hesitated before taking off my panties, hoping that he would tell me I didn't have to take them off. Dad only looked harder and urged me to continue. When he hit me with the belt it always landed between my legs. I tried to keep my legs closed but Dad would hit me in areas that made me open them.

At night when I was alone in the basement I would check the welts that ran between my legs from my thighs to my knees. The beating not only left these ugly welts, but also made it very painful for me to use the bathroom. I would grit my teeth because of the stinging pain. After beating me Dad would nonchalantly smoke a cigar.

When Mr. Bergner visited us one day I repeated the story that Mother had told me about my brother, Roy jr. I told him that Roy jr. did bad things to Sara and me and watched while Mr. Burgner wrote it down.

Another girl was raped in the neighborhood and Mother told me that it should have been me. She said it was my fault that something bad had happened to the little girl. I cried for the little girl because I didn't mean for anything to happen to her. I was sorry and I told Mother.

I stopped participating in class even though I knew answers to the questions that the teacher asked. I chose to turn my mind off and I didn't want any attention drawn towards me.

At home I did my chores and accepted things the way they were because I felt hopeless.

Mother started getting creative with the things she did to us. She began locking us in the small cellar in the basement. The room was about two or three feet wide and six feet tall. It was located at the bottom of the stairs. Dad stored tools and Mother put her homemade canned fruits in there. It wasn't much room in that small space because of the shelves on both walls. I begged and pleaded with Mother the first time she put me into the cellar because I was afraid and I thought I was going to die in there. Mother threw me inside and closed the door. I heard the lock click. I screamed and pounded on the door while my heart was racing. I felt as if I couldn't breathe. There weren't any widows in there and just an area under the door where air could circulate.

"Please, Mother! I won't do it anymore," I begged. I finally stopped banging on the door. The place was so dark I couldn't see my hand in front of me. There was nowhere to sit down and standing caused my legs to ache. I leaned against the shelf and was poked by dad's tools. My heart felt as if it was going to blow up. I calmed myself down by closing my eyes and began imagining myself being in heaven with my real mama. The time always passed slowly when I was inside of the cellar.

When Mother opened the door to let me out I took a long deep breath of fresh air that hit me in the face like a dash of cold water. My legs were numb and the ache in my back reminded me of how cramped the space was. I welcomed the bright lights, although it was blinding at first. I crawled on my hands and knees out of the cellar because I couldn't feel my legs. Mother stood watching me crawl. The look on her face confirmed that this wouldn't be the last time.

I wasn't the only one being put inside the cellar room. Ralph and Joe took their turns. Mother put a padlock on the door so that we couldn't open it from the outside. She put the key in her pocket. Once when she opened the door Ralph had passed out.

Mother cooked every day and had dinner ready when Dad got home from work. There was a big table where we ate dinner in the downstairs kitchen. She was an excellent cook, but there were a few things I hated. One of those was Mother's homemade crackling bread. The very smell of it made me want to throw up. Crackling bread was basically fat meat that was cooked in the cornbread. To me it tasted horrible. I would choke trying to swallow the pieces of fat meat. One day I left some of the crackling bread on my plate.

"Eat the rest of that bread," Mother said to me.

She stood over my chair, watching me. I took small bites of the bread, hoping it would help me get it down.

"I said eat the damn bread."

I broke off more pieces and forced myself to eat it. My stomach felt as if it were gurgling. I finished the bread while Mother stood next to me.

I started to get up from the table.

"Sit your ass back down," Mother said.

She brought a large pan of crackling bread and put it in front of me. I felt sick just looking at it.

"Eat it," she said. I couldn't believe she wanted me to eat an entire pan of the one thing I hated most. I reached for a piece of the bread.

A few minutes had passed and I had only eaten a few bites of the bread.

Mother slapped me in the face, catching me off guard.

"I said eat!" She spat at me through clenched teeth.

The feeling in my stomach alerted me that the bread wasn't going to stay down. I ran from the table and made it to the bathroom just in time. Everything came up. When I returned to the table Mother was waiting.

"Eat," she said.

I stuffed the bread in my mouth. I had to rush to the bathroom a few more times before the whole pan was gone. I can't describe the sickening feeling in the pit of my stomach. I could barely move when Mother finally allowed me to leave the table. One time I didn't make it to the bathroom so Mother made me clean up the mess on the floor.

All of us learned how to fight against each other thanks to Mother. We tattled on each other and told her things so that she wouldn't be mad at us. Sometimes we made up things just to keep her off of us. It was a survival game between us.

Joe and Ralph knew that Mother hated me the most so they told her things about me to keep Mother and Dad off of them. If I said something wrong or ran across the street when a car was coming they told on me even though they were doing the same thing. Mother and Dad continued to beat and verbally abuse me. Sometimes they involved Ralph and Joe. I didn't care anymore about what was happening to me. I was almost completely withdrawn from reality. When Joe and Ralph told on me I didn't react. It hurt me, yet I believed in my heart that my brothers loved me. I believed they were doing it because of Mother.

I was upstairs taking a bath one day when I heard voices downstairs. I could tell something was going on so I strained my ears to hear the voices, but they were too low. I thought I heard someone say my name so I got out of the tub. I wrapped a towel around me and tiptoed to top of the stairs where I listened to the conversation. I got excited when I recognized the voice of my brother, Stephen. He was talking to Ralph and Joe.

"How are things going?"

"Okay," Joe answered. I wanted to run downstairs to see Stephen. I rushed back to the bathroom and retrieved my clothes. I would be all dressed when Mother called me downstairs. There were long pauses between sentences and I couldn't hear who was talking anymore.

"Where is Joyce?" Stephen asked.

I smiled to myself. Mother was going to call me down to see him.

"She's upstairs taking a bath," Mother's voice sounded angry. "Why? Do you want to join her?"

Stephen said something to Mother and the next thing I heard was a lot of shouting, cursing, and screaming. I heard both Mother and Dad's voices yelling at Stephen. It was over almost as quickly as it started.

I stood with my back against the wall and my eyes closed until I heard a door slam. Mother was screaming about killing someone.

"Joyce, get your ass down here," her voice echoed upstairs.

"Okay, Mother," I answered, regretting the confrontation awaiting me. I pretended to still be in the tub so it took me awhile before I walked downstairs.

Mother was in the kitchen pacing back and forth. Ralph and Joe stood on the stairs leading into the basement. They both looked scared. Dad was in the kitchen talking to Mother and trying to keep her calm.

"You shouldn't have pulled the knife on him," Dad said to her.

"I will cut his ass from A to Z," Mother spat out.

I walked into the kitchen.

"One of your brother's was here," she said to me.

I tried to look surprised because I didn't want her to know I had heard what was going on.

"He tried to jump on me because I wouldn't let him go upstairs where you were. I don't know what nasty things you did with them before you came here, but I'm not having that kind of mess going on in my house."

Dad ignored me. "Calm down," he was saying to mother. I watched as her chest heaved in and out.

"I was going to kill the bastard," she said, a snarl covering her face. Ralph and Joe never moved from the spot where they stood. Mother continued her verbal assault about my brother.

"He better not ever come back here," she warned.

Later when talking with Joe and Ralph I learned what had really happened. Stephen had come over with our cousin John. From the moment they stepped into the house, Mother watched them. She didn't allow Stephen to talk with Ralph and Joe alone, nor did she invite them all the way into the house. They stood on the landing between the kitchen and the basement talking with Joe and Ralph. When Stephen asked them how they were doing and if they liked their foster home they told him everything was good because she was making it difficult for them to talk with him. When Stephen asked about me she went crazy.

Before either of them could say anything she told him I was upstairs taking a bath and asked him if he wanted to join me.

Stephen couldn't contain his anger and began cursing at her. Mother cursed back at him and the next thing they saw was the butcher knife in her hand.

"She swung the knife at him," Joe said, still upset.

"She was going to cut him, but Dad grabbed her hand before she could stab Stephen."

I was horrified that Stephen almost got stabbed.

"Dad told them to get out," Joe finished.

"Stephen promised Mother he was coming back," Ralph added with a broad smile. I knew Stephen would come back and bring all our other brothers with him. The thought made me smile too. They wouldn't leave us here.

We waited for Stephen to come back and rescue us, but he never showed up again. I was beginning to lose faith in my family as the torture from Mother and Dad escalated.

Mr. Bergner confirmed to Mother that Stephen lived down the street from us. I was surprised about this. Why hadn't Mr. Bergner told us? He was Stephen's social worker too. Now it was too late, because Stephen moved away.

Mother was curled up on the couch when I came home one day. I could hear her sobs when I walked through the door. I didn't want to go into the living room, but Mother wanted us to let her know when we were home from school. Still dressed in her housecoat, Mother looked up at us and I saw that her eyes were red. She dabbed at them and blew her nose with a tissue.

"Michael was killed in Vietnam," Mother told us. I was sure my heart skipped a beat. Michael was dead? I looked at Joe and Ralph and saw that they were saddened by the news, but I felt nothing but relief.

I had a nightmare that night about Michael dying. I saw him lying on his back with blood streaming down his bumpy face. I also saw Mother lying next to him with her heart cut out and Dad's head chopped off from his body. I could feel myself peeing in the bed, but I couldn't wake up.

Mother and dad began doing other things to us. We were already being beaten, slapped, punched, and locked in that dark cellar.

I was in the basement when they came down and made me strip down to my slip and panties. She tied both of my hands together in front of me with clothesline rope. Then she took the other part of the rope and threw it over a large pipe in the basement and they began pulling on it. I felt my arms lifting my body up. When I was suspended from the pipe, Mother tied the end of the rope and left me swinging. The heaviness on my arms was the most horrible part of it. It felt like they were being pulled out of their sockets. I started begging Mother to please let me down. I kept moving, but the more I moved the tighter the rope got around my wrist. I hung there while Mother beat me with the cable cord. I swung back and forth against the slapping of the cord. I screamed with each lick and the pain rushed through my body like bolts of lightning. It seemed like I was hanging there for hours before Mother finally let me down. There was no feeling in my hands or arms. My entire body was in pain as layers of welts appeared on me. Dad always helped Mother hang us on that pipe in the basement, allowing them to beat us with ease.

One time while I was hanging on the pipe Mother ordered Joe to hit me. Joe gave me a couple of lashes with the whip but I knew he didn't want to do it. Dad seemed to enjoy seeing us hang from the pipe. Sometimes he watched me struggle against the rope.

I was getting beat from either Mother or Dad for being late to school everyday. Both of them knew it was impossible for me to get to school on time because I wasn't allowed to go to school until my chores were completed. There were times I didn't even leave the house until an hour after school had started. The routine was the same when I made it to school. I went to the office and the secretary would give me a pass and a pink tardy slip so I could get into class. I had to bring the tardy slip home so a parent could sign it. When I brought the tardy slips home to mother it was just another excuse to beat me. After awhile I decided not to give any more tardy slips to Mother. I got an idea that if I signed the tardy slips Mother would never have to know about them. I watched Mother sign the tardy slips and practiced her signature until I was satisfied my forgery was good enough to pass. I copied every loop and curve she made. I wanted the signature to look genuine. I felt confident I could write her name as well as she did. When I handed my first forged tardy slip to the secretary she looked satisfied that it was Mother's handwriting. Every day I signed the tardy slips and turned them in to the office. Meanwhile, Mother waited for me to bring them home.

"Were you on time this morning?" she asked me one day.

"They let me go to my class anyway," I lied.

Mother looked at me as if she was trying to figure it out, but she didn't say anything. The more slips I signed the better I became. I even began writing correspondence on them.

Everything was going fine until one morning when I handed in a slip. The secretary gave it back to me.

"The principle wants to talk to you."

I sat across from Mr. Krause in the large office he had. I dared not look at him because I thought they had found out about what I was doing.

"I'm concerned about your tardiness."

I nodded.

"But I'm even more concerned about your parent's willingness to allow this to happen."

I swallowed hard. I didn't want him to involve Mother.

"I promise I'll be on time tomorrow," I said, knowing it was a lie.

"We need to do something about it," he said to me.

I sat there silently, waiting for something to happen.

"Go to your class."

I hurried out the door, relieved that I had at least stalled him for the time being.

In Years To Come

When I got home that afternoon, Mother was waiting.

"Have you been signing my name on tardy slips?"

They had called her anyway even after I promised to be on time tomorrow.

"Huh?"

I looked away. Mother hit me hard and I fell backwards over the coffee table.

"I can't believe you are signing my name to tardy slips!" she yelled at me. You've got to have the devil in you to even think of doing such a thing. Do you know what that's called? Do you? Well I'll tell you what it is. It's called forgery. People go to jail for signing other people's name to things. I should send your ass to jail."

I sat on the floor while she continued. I never wanted to sign her name; I only wanted the beatings to stop.

"Get out of here!" she screamed at me.

I scrambled to my feet and ran down the stairs to the basement. I waited for her to come down and finish what she started. She never mentioned it to me again that evening.

The next morning I was in for a big surprise. Mother was already up and dressed.

"I'm going to go to school with you today."

That was why Mother didn't beat me the night before. She didn't want me to have any fresh bruises. Of course I made it to school on time that day because Mother drove us and parked in front of the school where the kids were playing on the playground. I could feel all eyes on us when we climbed out of the car. Mother walked in front of us with her head covered with a beautiful fur hat and matching coat. I kept my pace close behind her. I heard the whispers.

"Look at that lady."

"Is that their mother?"

"That lady sure is pretty. Wow!"

It was a good feeling that Mother was so impressive to the kids. When we walked into the office I was ready to confess to what

I'd done and apologize for it. When we settled into the principal's office I could see that he was impressed with Mother too. He pulled out the stack of tardy slips and handed them to mother.

"I must admit that she did a pretty good job," Mr. Krause said.

That must have been her cue because Mother started crying like something disastrous was happening. Mr. Krause attempted to calm her down while I tried not to notice the angry looks he was giving me.

"How could you do this to a woman as wonderful as Mrs. Watson?" he asked me.

I looked at the floor. I didn't bother saying anything. I listened while Mother told him how she took us in after we were abandoned by our own family.

"I gave these children a home. I bought them clothes with my own money."

I looked up in time to see the principal glaring at me and shaking his head.

Mother described our life like it was full of luxuries and happiness. She finished her story by saying, "...and she did this to me."

The Principal was clearly on Mother's side now.

"I don't understand why she comes to school late everyday," he said.

Mother was sobbing and shaking her head.

"She does this to defy me. She is deliberately coming to school late to make me look bad. I don't know what she does between home and here. Her brothers get here on time. I don't have near as much trouble with them as I do with her."

"What do you do between the time you leave home and the time you get to school?" He looked directly at me.

I shrugged my shoulders. I didn't dare look up because tears were threatening to fall.

"Don't tell me you don't know." the principal had raised his voice.

I said nothing.

"We can take care of this situation right here," he told Mother. "I'm going to start punishing her every time she comes in late." He showed Mother the paddle he kept in his desk.

Looking at me, he said, "Have Mrs. Martin fill out a slip so you can go to class."

I stood up without looking at Mother. When I walked into the classroom all eyes were on me.

"I saw her come in with her mother," I heard one of the girls say.

I handed the teacher the pass and slid into my seat. I could feel the kids staring, so I looked straight ahead.

Just about the time I was beginning to get comfortable in class, Mother walked in. I was surprised to see her. Why was she coming to my classroom?

"That's her mother," I heard someone whisper.

"Is that your mother?" A boy in front of me asked.

I nodded.

The teacher excused herself from the class and began talking with Mother. I glanced at them every chance I got. I did my class work and didn't bother anyone.

"Class!"

Everyone's attention was on the teacher.

"This is Mrs. Watson. She wants to say a few words to you and I want you to pay attention to her.

I wondered what Mother had to say to my class. They looked at me for a moment then back at Mother. I had to smile in spite of everything. Mother looked gorgeous standing next to the teacher, who always wore drab clothes.

I wasn't prepared for the heartbreaking speech Mother delivered that day. I'm sure my mouth hung open as the words dripped off her lips like hot sauce. She not only told the class that I was a foster child, but also went on to tell them that I forged the tardy slips, and that I was a bad child at home who did nothing but give her trouble. Some kids laughed at me while others gave me cold stares. Mother degraded me more by telling them that I didn't have a mother or father. I felt ashamed that I had no parents even though it wasn't my fault. It seemed unnatural for children not to have at least one parent so I had never told anyone. I wanted the floor to open up and swallow me. She could have beaten me rather that humiliate me the way she did. School was the only place I'd had any peace, but now she had ruined that too. The kids would never treat me the same.

I was right. Mother scarred me that day without having to use the whip. No only were the kids teasing me about being a foster child, but Joe and Ralph were being teased too. They threw rocks at us and chased us home, threatening to beat us up. They acted as if we had some kind of disease because we were foster children.

"Foster child, foster child," they would chant at us.

"How come you don't have a mama or daddy?"

"Why do you treat that nice lady so bad?"

The questions were endless, and I didn't have any real answers.

"My mama said that foster children are messed up and she wants me to stay away from you."

I watched Cynthia walk away with the small crowd of girls who had gathered around us. I held my silence, allowing the teasing, hitting, and rock throwing.

When I walked into school late the next day, the principle had permission to paddle me. My teacher could also slap my hands with the pointer and I was not allowed to go outside during recess.

Thanksgiving, Christmas, and the New Year came and went. My birthday was in February and I turned ten.

I bathed on the main floor most of the time but I didn't like the bathtub because it was crowded with mother's portable whirlpool in it.

I don't know when my body hair started growing. I just

remember when Mother made me aware of it. I was drying myself off one day when she walked into the bathroom.

"Oh, my God!"

I jumped because I didn't know what was going on. She was staring at me with her mouth open. When she walked up to me I expected her to hit me, but instead she lifted up my arms.

"Remove the towel," she said.

I stood there naked while she looked me up and down.

"I knew it! I knew it!"

I had learned to shut up and wait for an explanation.

"I knew you were a child of the devil."

"Look!" She was pointing to my privates.

I looked down. I didn't see anything.

"Look closer."

I felt stupid looking for something I couldn't see.

"Don't you see something growing?"

"Yes," I whispered.

"It's growing under your arms too."

"What is it?"

"It's the mark of the devil," she said.

When I inspected my underarm, she was right. There was a thin layer of hair that was barely noticeable.

I asked mother what I could do to get rid of it.

"You can't do anything, it's already there. It's growing on your arms too and will soon be all over your body"

I didn't want to be the devil's child. I felt ashamed of myself and tried to cover myself up.

In desperation I began scrubbing myself with mother's homemade lye soap, but all it did was take the skin off and make me bleed. Once the skin healed, the thin layer of hair grew back. One time I even tried to burn it off using matches but ended up with severe burns. I endured a lot of pain before finally giving up because nothing stopped it from growing back.

It was cold in the basement during the winter because the

concrete walls and floors held the cold. The furnace was an incinerator that required a fire to heat the house. Dad made fires when he was home. He made the first one in the mornings that kept the house warm all day and another at night that kept the house warm until the morning. My bed was near the furnace so when Dad made a fire the room was bright with a glowing light. I would watch the flames dance on the walls all the way up to the ceiling as the fire burned intensely in the incinerator. It didn't take long for the heat to warm my body. I was hypnotized by the flames and stared at them until I fell asleep. Sometimes I felt as if invisible hands were lifting me from my bed. I thought it must be the hands of God. He was holding me in his big powerful hands and rocking me back and forth.

"You're with me now," he was saying. I looked into the face of God who smiled back at me.

I felt safe in his powerful arms. Angels were all around my bed singing me to sleep, "He's got the whole world in his hands..." It was very peaceful when I was with God.

The fire was almost completely out when Dad woke me up in the mornings so I would be shivering underneath the covers and sometimes my teeth would chatter. Dad immediately went to work examining me while I sucked in my breath and waited. He would drool and lick his lips.

"Get up!" His voice always sounded like a lion's roar.

Each day I went through it and it never got any better.

Sometimes if my bladder was screaming for relief I would be squirming. I tried bravely to pretend everything was okay so he would leave and I could use the drain or the pail. He purposely stayed until I had no choice but to relieve myself in front of him. The last thing I wanted was for him to see me squatting over the hole on the floor. Yet if I didn't do it I would pee on myself and that was almost as bad as peeing in the bed. I could feel those tiny eyes staring and watching while I squatted over the drain. He left only after I was finished. A short time later the sound of the key in the back door could be heard.

Dad made a fire in the furnace before he left for work. The fire limped along until it started getting hot. I stood next to the incinerator to warm my body. It didn't take long before the fire was going full blast. By the time the rest of the household woke up there was plenty of heat.

Joe and Ralph didn't have to get up as early as me, so they didn't know what it felt like to get up in a cold house. The basement was the coldest part of the house. My feet were so cold that it felt like I was standing outside in the snow without shoes. I kept them near the fire so they wouldn't freeze. The concrete floors were painful to stand on barefoot so I always kept my shoes close to the bed.

There was never any warning of what kind of mood Mother was in, so I tiptoed through the house dreading the moment she woke up. Many times I fought sleepiness, fatigue, and sometimes sickness to get my chores completed. One morning mother woke up humming. I heard her voice before the footsteps came. My heart was pounding inside of my chest. I looked down at the stairs left to wash with the urge to throw the rag in the bucket and tell her I wasn't going to do it anymore, but I knew the consequences.

I was well past the first set of stairs when mother's voice yelled upstairs.

"Joe! Ralph!"

I heard feet hitting the floor.

"Yes, Mother?"

"Get up!"

I'd finished the last step when she called me.

"Joyce!"

"Yes, Ma'am?"

I rushed to face her. The sneer on her face hinted that she wasn't in the best mood.

"Have you finished those stairs?"

"Yes, Ma'am."

"Did you piss in the bed?"

"No, Ma'am."

She turned away, leaving me standing there. I heard her feet creaking going upstairs. I stood still, not sure if she expected me wait for her to return.

"I'm tired of you pissing in my bed!" I heard her yell.

Screaming drifted down the stairs. I felt my body jump out of habit.

The sounds of a scuffle could be heard, followed by a stifled cry. I wanted to know what she was doing up there. It was Ralph's squeaky voice that screamed.

More yelling from Mother followed more movements.

The next sound was her coming down the stairs. I stared as she appeared in the kitchen dragging Ralph behind her. Joe was walking behind them.

Mother threw Ralph to the floor as if he were just a rag. He was bare from the waste down, wearing only a t-shirt. Tears were running down his fat cheeks. Mother disappeared into her bedroom and came hurrying back with the whip in her hand. I turned my head, not wanting to witness it.

Joe was breathing so hard I could hear it across the kitchen. His eyes were downcast. The sound of the belt hitting against Ralph's bare skin made me flinch. Ralph's screams filled the kitchen and he sounded like he was getting louder with each lick.

"I'll stop! I'll stop!" he screamed as the whip lashed down on him.

I closed my eyes, trying to shut out his screams.

I was surprised when Joe's cries replaced Ralph's.

"I won't do it anymore!" Joe said before the whip slammed down on him. I blinked back tears knowing I was next.
Ralph was still on the floor squirming and trying to get away. I saw the ugly red marks that covered his backside.
Joe's long legs kicked back at her as she brought the whip down on him again and again. His screams were louder with each hit.

Out of breath, Mother stood glaring at them as they nursed their painful bodies.

"I'm sick of you pissing in my bed!"

Ralph was still on the floor but much quieter now. I felt rigid and unable to move. None of us anticipated her next move. I heard a drawer being yanked open and saw mother pull out the longest butcher knife in the house. My heart was beating erratically now. What was she doing? Was she going to kill us? She dropped to her knees and grabbed Ralph's private part.

"I'm going to cut it off and flush it down the toilet!"

"Please, Mother, I'll quit! I'll quit!"

"I know you're going to quit because you are not going to have nothing to piss with."

Joe's eyes were as large as saucers as he watched the scene in front of him. I was convinced at that moment that she was going to cut it off.

She had Ralph's private in one hand and the knife in the other.

"Be still," she ordered, but Ralph squirmed and kicked on the floor.

"Please don't!"

"Shut up!"

Although it probably lasted a couple of minutes it seemed like hours passed before Mother let go of him. Tears rolled down my face. I was relived that she didn't cut off my brother's private part. There were many more times when mother stood over both Joe and Ralph with the butcher knife vowing to cut off their penises. Each time I held my breath.

There was only one time that Mother and Dad attacked me together. I don't remember the reason. It never mattered because all the beatings were brutal and unjustified. Mother called me to the main floor bathroom where the two of them were waiting. The bathroom was small so dad's massive body took up most of the space. I wasn't sure why they chose the bathroom. The attack began almost immediately. I was hit over and over. After awhile I couldn't hear myself scream anymore although my mind seemed to shriek each time the whip cut into my bare flesh. Each strike came quickly in a constant rhythm, leaving very little time for recovery. I tried to brace myself and use my arms as a shield. Numbness swept over my hands and arms as they were slapped away. I tried in vain to defend myself. Dad's raspy breathing was close. I could feel the hotness of his breath on my neck. Suddenly his large hands grabbed me and I was shoved into something hard. My face felt as if it exploded with pain. My head was spinning and I saw stars and bright colors dance before me. It was an effort for me to open my eyes because the pain was so intense. I sat on the floor and waited for the next blow to come. My body involuntarily tensed, but the blow never came.

As I struggled to open my eyes a stinging sensation in my right eye caused me to quickly close them. I heard the click of the doorknob and my body was rudely pushed aside as footsteps walked out. The hard sound of Dad's shoes squeaked on the floors, but I knew Mother was still in there with me. I kept expecting her to hit me. To my surprise she opened the door and I felt cool air filtering in. It was then that I realized I was holding my breath.

"Get dressed," she spat at me, throwing my clothes in my face. They had made me strip before they took turns beating on me. I waited until the door closed again before attempting to get up off the floor. My right eye bothered me every time I tried to open it. I stood in front of the mirror to see what was wrong with it. The face that stared back was scary. The right side of my face was red and my right eye was swollen. Blood ran down the side of my mouth from a large cut on my puffy lips. Hot salty tears stung as they ran down my bruised face. I gasped at the welts that covered my body.

"Please help me," I mumbled to the person in the mirror.

Dinner was quiet that night. I noticed Joe and Ralph staring at me. Although they felt sorry for me they couldn't acknowledge my injuries. We all had to pretend everything was okay.

Dad didn't look at me as he piled his plate with food. I

struggled to eat because my swollen lips made it difficult for me to get the food into my mouth. I tasted my own blood with every bite. They didn't make me eat all of my food that night and it was hard scrapping the food into the trash can while my stomach still growled from hunger.

Sleep came quickly easing the throbbing pain I felt. Dad woke me up at five o'clock the next morning. I winced as his hands probed my body. The pain was unbearable so I screamed.

Dad stopped touching me. That's when he really looked at me. His mouth was open as he stared.

"You can go back to sleep," he told me. "You won't be going to school today anyway."

I quietly slipped upstairs to the bathroom where I looked in the mirror. I was shocked at how worse my face was now. My right eye was huge and completely closed with a purplish tint to it. It stuck out like it wasn't part of my face. On the left side a large bruise appeared on my cheek. My lips were so swollen I could barely talk and red welts were all over my legs, arms and thighs.

I kept imagining the look on my teacher's face if I showed up for school. I decided I was going to sneak out of the house and go to school. It was my only chance to convince someone of what was going on in mother's house. After putting on my clothes, I crept around the house trying not to wake up Mother while figuring out how to get out of the house. Mother and Dad put double bolt locks on the doors and windows after we ran away that summer.

I tugged at the door, and to my surprise, it opened. I couldn't believe my luck; somehow Dad had forgotten to pull the door completely shut again. It was still dark outside and the cold winter air made me shiver. Dad was probably running late for work and rushed out the door without locking it. It was only six in the morning, but I didn't care. I was willing to sit on the school steps if necessary. Just as I was about to turn the knob again I heard Mother's voice.

"What are you doing?" I looked up to see Mother standing

there.

I knew she was surprised to see how bad my face looked.

"Get up here," she said.

"Yes," I said, relieved that she didn't question me further.

I knew she wasn't going to allow me go to school. Mother always kept us home to heal up if she went overboard beating us.

It was amazing how Mother tended to me that week I stayed home from school. That morning she allowed me to take my time doing my chores. She didn't even yell at me. I was almost beginning to feel human as my wounds continued to heal. Mother used ointments, lotions and ice packs on my body to help me heal. Dad didn't touch me that week either. My scars healed and my eye went down. The scars on the inside were still there and there would be more scars to replace those on the outside too.

The next week I returned to school with a note full of lies about me having the flu. I was disappointed about how little attention anyone paid to my now semi-black eye. No one questioned me about it, so I didn't volunteer any information. The beatings started all over again within two weeks, but Mother and Dad never ganged up on me again.

Mother didn't have to go to clinics and wait in long lines like Hon had. She called Dr. Dunlap to come to the house if she or one of us became ill.

Dr. Dunlap was an older white man who carried a medium sized black bag. He was cold and impersonal so I never said anything to him. I wondered why he never questioned the bruises on our bodies. I was sure he could see them, but he acted as if there was nothing there.

Once he came to give us shots, but he forgot to bring alcohol so he used some of mother's perfume. I hated shots but I loved the way I smelled that day. Dr. Dunlap gave us little orange pills that were supposed to stop us from peeing in the bed.

"Have them take one of these every night before going to bed," he told mother. We faithfully took our orange pills, but it didn't stop us from peeing in the bed.

I didn't know what type of illness Mother suffered from, I only knew she had to have an operation. I don't know why it bothered me when she told us she would be in the hospital for a while.

The first time I met Helen Travis she was sitting in the basement kitchen talking to Mother when I came home from school. Mother had lots of friends that she talked to on the phone, but few came to the house. Seeing Miss Helen in our house was a surprise. Mother's friends were well-known people in organizations that she belonged to. Miss Helen didn't look like any of these people. She was a short, frail-looking woman with large discolored eyes.

"This is Joyce," Mother said.

Where did this lady come from? Mother told us that Miss Helen was moving into the house to help take care of us.

"She's going to be taking care of you while I'm in the hospital."

I noticed the cigarette hanging from Miss Helen's mouth. At least she didn't look mean.

Miss Helen cooked a good dinner that evening. I was going to wash dishes, but she kindly shoved me aside and took over. That's when I decided she must be okay. Maybe she was the person we needed in the house to help us. Over the next few days Mother did very little as she prepared to go to the hospital. Miss Helen took over the responsibilities around the house. She made sure that we stayed away from Mother while she rested. If only Miss Helen knew how welcomed it was to be away from Mother.

We stood on the sidewalk while dad backed the long Bonneville out of the garage. Mother was sitting near him in the front seat. Her face was tearful when they drove away. We continued waving good-bye until the car disappeared down the street.

For the first time in months I was able to go to sleep right away. That night I dreamed about Hon and Papa. They reached out for me, but then Mother's face came between us. I woke up shaking, remembering the last time I saw Hon before she went into the hospital. I felt a sense of guilt when I thought about how nice it would be if Mother didn't come back home. People didn't always come out of the hospital, but I felt that Mother would return.

Miss Helen seemed to care about us. Everything around the house changed and even Dad treated us better. It had been so long since I'd gone a day without being hit that I had come to expect it. If Miss Helen raised her hand to do something I immediately took a defensive position. The first few times I was embarrassed, but as time passed I learned to adjust.

My chores were less because Miss Helen was helping me do them. She was taking good care of us. I wished she would stay forever with us. It was the beginning of summer and we were able to go to the park and play outside with the other kids. We weren't afraid to talk to each other.

Miss Helen scolded us at times, but she never lifted her hand to hit us. We were too young to go to the hospital to visit Mother so Miss Helen and Dad kept us informed on her condition. The operation was successful and she was improving daily. I didn't want to think of her coming home yet, but I had to accept that she would be back one day.

I still slept in the basement while Miss Helen was in the bedroom upstairs. Dad was still checking me every morning, but I only got a few whippings. Miss Helen talked a lot and I thought she was funny. One day she kept laughing at everything we said or did. I noticed the glossy look in her red eyes. It didn't bother me how she looked because I liked her.

"I had no place to go when your mother offered to let me come here to live for awhile. She said all I had to do was help her with the three of you. Mrs. Watson is the most loving and caring woman I know. She is a God-fearing woman."

I knew then that it would do no good to tell Miss Helen about Mother because she was brainwashed like the others.

In Years To Come

Mother had been gone about a week. I was supposed to be asleep when I heard Miss Helen in the other part of the basement. I peeped in just as she was putting a bottle up to her lips. It reminded me of the whiskey bottle Papa use to drink from. She wiped her mouth with the back of her hand before putting the cap on the bottle and tucking it safely in the pocket of her apron. I realized then that the thing sticking out of Miss Helen's apron was a whiskey bottle. She wore the apron all day and I had seen something sticking out.

Laughter floated out of the living room where Dad and Miss Helen were entertaining some of Miss Helen's friends. I saw them drinking whiskey from glasses. I was shocked to see Dad drinking along with them.

We took advantage of the situation by having as much fun as we could. Miss Helen finally told us to go to bed. Mother would be angry if she knew what was going on in her house. She had talked about how much she hated liquor. It was obvious Miss Helen was drunk; she was swaying when she walked. I went to bed but not to sleep, because Dad's drunken voice was loud when he talked. Their voices grew louder as music drifted from the radio.

Over the next week Miss Helen's drinking buddies kept coming over. They drank, cursed, and danced to music on the radio. Dad was part of the party and so were Ruby and her boyfriend, James.

A few nights later I awoke to the sound of music and laughter. Someone was in the other part of the basement. I climbed out of bed to see who was there. I froze. A man was standing over the drain, peeing. He turned around and saw me and began talking. I didn't understand anything he said because his words were slurred. He zipped up his pants and looked at me. I wanted to run, but my legs felt heavy.

Just as he began walking towards me a bright light came on. Miss Helen stood in the doorway looking from him to me.

"What the hell are you doing?" she asked him.

"I came in here to relieve myself when this girl came from

somewhere to look at me."

"Go back to bed;" Miss Helen's voice was angry. I could tell from the way she talked that she had been drinking. I heard them whispering about me.

"That girl has a problem with men," she told him. "Mrs. Watson said that she did some bad things with her brothers before she came here."

"Yeah, something is wrong with that girl," the man agreed.

Mother came home after a few weeks in the hospital. We celebrated by cooking a special meal. Miss Helen helped me make potato salad and I added candied cherries on top.

Mother was walking very slowly after Dad helped her out of the car. Dad and Miss Helen stood on both sides of her and helped her walk to the house. Walking up the steps was especially hard for her and she moaned in pain each time she lifted her feet.

It took awhile for her to walk up a few stairs. I was relieved that it was going to be some time before she completely recovered. Knowing she couldn't climb the stairs meant I was safe for the moment.

Everyone in the house waited on Mother during her recovery. She needed help with everything: bathing, dressing, and using the bathroom. Miss Helen helped her do every single one. She was with Mother all day.

The whiskey that Miss Helen kept tucked in her apron never seemed to run out. I saw her several times turn the bottle up and drink from it when she thought no one was looking.

We went through another change once Mother recovered. At first it was verbal abuse. Mother began telling Miss Helen bad things about us, especially me. It wasn't long before Miss Helen's attitude changed towards us. Mother was soon out of bed and that is when I felt the full impact of her rage. Mother told Miss Helen not to help me with my chores anymore. Miss Helen lost interest in us and devoted her time and attention only to Mother. When Mother began beating us again Miss Helen didn't seem to care and left the room when trouble began. Miss Helen watched us beg her to stop beating us but she never interfered with anything that Mother did. After awhile Miss Helen started screaming at us too.

The potatoes that Dad brought home were usually in large burlap sacks. Mother had a stack of these sacks stored away. They were brown with a musty smell to them.

"I'm going to put you in one of these burlap sacks and throw you into Lake Michigan" she told me. I didn't know how to swim so I started having bad dreams about drowning. Mother also told Ralph the same thing. We both watched the pile of burlap sacks get larger. One day Mother was sitting at the table with Miss Helen when I walked past them.

"Stop," she said.

I stopped. Without looking at me she said to Miss Helen, "What do you think, should we put her in the sack tonight?"

I trembled at the thought.

"Why not?" Miss Helen's voice was shaky so I knew she must have been drinking whiskey. "Let's do it," she urged with a drunken laugh.

I waited while they discussed how I was going to be packed in the sack and thrown into the Lake. How could Miss Helen do this to us? She had completely turned her back on us. I once believed she was going to be our source of help to get away from Mother. I waited all evening for them to come get me and finally drifted off into a restless sleep.

It felt strange around the house after Miss Helen left. I don't know the reason why she left so quickly One day we came home from school and she was gone. Mother didn't offer any explanation. Despite Miss Helen turning against us, she was a distraction and her presence in the house made a difference.

I was still frustrated about the change that my body was going through. The hair never stopped growing and the shame I felt went deeper than anything else going on in my life.

Brother Randolph was the next person to come into our

lives. He was a deacon at one of the churches we visited on Sundays. He started coming to our house in the morning before we went to school. He was a tall, loud man with a wide smile. He wore dark suits with matching hats. He wasn't exactly a handsome man, but he had a lot of charm and a good sense of humor.

I liked Brother Randolph because he was nice to us. He was nice to everyone and at church he shook everyone's hand. He looked important sitting on the front pew in the church. I can't recall when he began visiting our house. I just remember one day going into the kitchen and he was sitting in a chair sipping coffee and talking to Mother. When Brother Randolph visited, Mother would hurry me off to school even if I didn't finish my chores because she was preoccupied with him.

Mother had beautiful gowns. She wore a silk housecoat over her gowns. Brother Randolph would be sitting at the table with the Bible open discussing something from it. His deep voice echoed when he talked. Mother was always smiling and laughing when he was around.

I began regarding Brother Randolph as a Godsend because he was distracting Mother's attention from us. She continued to hit us even with him there, but it was nothing like the beatings we got when he wasn't around.

Brother Randolph quizzed us about the Bible after giving us Bible verses to remember. A few times I witnessed some touching between them, but I never believed it to be anything more than friendly gestures. I hadn't been exposed to anything to identify what I was seeing. Brother Randolph was a respectable married man with children.

Several times we came home after school or during lunch to find Brother Randolph still in our house. It was always the same greeting.

"Hi Brother Randolph," we would say, glad that he was still there.

"Hi children," he would respond with a big smile.

155

Usually Brother Randolph and Mother would be in the living room or kitchen. Mother would be fully dressed and seated at the piano playing church songs. Mother said that she and Brother Randolph had to practice songs for church. I found it amusing that Brother Randolph practiced one song all the time. He didn't have a good singing voice so we laughed until we were in tears listening to his tuneless voice. Sometimes we even mocked him.

"Jesus, Jesus is with me...."

Brother Randolph always left the house before Dad got home from work. Dad never saw what we saw or knew that Brother Randolph had been at our house all day. Mother told us not to say a word and we never did.

"Do you think he has a job?" Joe asked one day.

"I think his job is to go around healing people," I said. I really didn't know if he worked. Brother Randolph always wore suits so he didn't look like a man who worked.

I was convinced that Mother and Dad hated me. Ralph fared better than I did and Joe was treated the best overall. Mother liked Joe better so he didn't get as many beatings. Mother never threatened to put him in burlap sacks and throw him into Lake Michigan either.

Ralph was the one that Dad was most fond of so he seldom got beatings from him.

And then there was me. I never knew what was going to happen to me.

Once Mother turned her anger towards Joe and it lasted for weeks. It all started when we were walking home from school one day. Joe saw something shiny lying in the middle of the street. It was during the spring after the snow had melted. We found all kinds of things in the streets after the snow melted. Joe rushed over to the object and picked it up before another car could run over it. He held up what was left of the bracelet so that we could see it.

"It's all beat up," I told Joe who put it in his coat pocket.

He took it out later and examined it again. "What does this

bracelet look like to you?"

I stared at it and saw that it was silver and had small round silver things hanging from it

"It looks like a beat up bracelet," I said laughing.

Joe shook his head. "The round things look like money."

I looked again at it.

The round things were about the size of a dime. No one would be fooled by it.

"I know exactly what I'm going to do," Joe said.

I didn't think about the bracelet again until the next day when Joe picked up a brick off the side of the road.

"What are you going to do?"

"Watch this." Joe began slamming the brick down on the round things that he had broken off from the bracelet. When he finished beating on the round pieces they were smooth. I still wondered how he planned to use it.

Joe only smiled while he worked on smoothing out the round pieces.

A few days later Joe opened his hands to show me how well he had smoothed out the pieces to make them look like dimes.

"I am going to put one in the soda machine at church."

We had started going to a church around the corner from the house. I suspected that we weren't visiting churches anymore because of Brother Randolph spending so much time at our house.

On Sunday we walked around the corner to the church. It was down the street from Mrs. Simms' house. A few times we sneaked over to visit with Mrs. Simms and see our brother, Louie. He was such a cute kid and said things that made us laugh. We got a kick out of him. He was losing his front teeth and still had a baby face. When Louie talked he stuttered his words making him even more comical. A few times Mrs. Simms let Louie walk down the street with us. One day we were walking down the street with Louie when he saw a bottle lying in the gutter.

"It's wine!" he shouted.

In Years To Come

The three of us had heard about wine, but I had never seen a bottle of it.

Louie held the bottle up. "There is still some left in it," he said. I was horrified when Louie screwed off the cap and turned the bottle up to finish off the wine.

"That's nasty," I shouted at him.

Louie only smiled and rubbed his belly. He told us that his brother, Henry always shared wine with him. We didn't tell Mrs. Simms what Louie had done, although I was tempted to.

The church we were going to was across from the house my mama had bought. I didn't know that we were living around the corner from Mrs. Simms or the house my mother had bought until we started going to the church. We saw Mrs. Simms one day and she showed us where she lived. When we told Mother that we once lived in a house around the corner she claimed she had known our mama and took food to her when we lived there. Mrs. Simms told us that it was a lie. I stood in front of Mama's house trying to recall a memory of living there, but there was nothing.

That Sunday Joe gave each of us one of his homemade dimes. We were restless all through church because we were eager to try our coins in the soda machine. The church service seemed to go on forever. Finally it was over and we rushed to the soda machine. Joe slid his coin into the slot first. We all squealed when a soda slid out. I slurped on the orange soda I bought all the way home. Ralph and I praised Joe for what he had done.

Two months passed before Mother found out about it. She found what was left of the beat up bracelet when she was looking through the boys' bedroom. We had used all the pieces, so all that was left was the other part.

Mother made threats to beat all of us unless we told her about the bracelet.

Ralph spoke up first.

"Joe found it in the street when we were walking home from school."

I didn't want to tell on Joe, but I had to say something because Mother was giving me that look.

"Joe found it in the street," I told her.

The expression on her face changed and she turned to Joe, grabbing him and slamming him against the wall.

"Why did you steal my bracelet?" She screamed at him.

I was confused. Why did she say he stole her bracelet? I was with him when he found it. All of us saw it lying in the street. We had never seen Mother wear a bracelet even similar to it. Ralph and I knew what Mother was trying to do. Joe knew too. All of us knew the truth about the bracelet, but Mother's version was the one we would go along with.

When we told mother how Joe used the homemade coins to get soda from the machine at church Mother was enraged.

That evening when Dad came home from work he got an earful from Mother. She told Dad that Joe stole the bracelet out of her jewelry box in her bedroom. We knew she was lying, but there wasn't anything we could do.

"I bought that bracelet in another county," mother said, wiping tears from her eyes. "It was worth a lot of money," she told Dad. "The bracelet was made especially for me and it had coins from many countries on it." Mother hung her head. It was amazing to see how well she could act.

She told such a convincing story complete with real tears that I began doubting what really happened, even though I had seen the beat up piece of jewelry in the street that day. Dad tried to comfort her, and his anger towards Joe swelled.

Dad really didn't know if Mother owned this bracelet because she had so many pieces of jewelry. He obviously believed her. Because of Mother, Dad smacked Joe hard across the face. I wanted to run and hide somewhere because I knew a beating would soon follow. Dad took Joe to the basement where I could hear his screams a few minutes later. The sound of the whip against Joe's bare flesh could be heard between the screaming.

I bit down hard on my lip, praying that it would be over soon. I could hear Joe swearing that he found the bracelet in the street. His words only fueled Dad's rage.

When Dad emerged from the basement he was breathing hard with sweat pouring from his face. He cursed under his breath. I slowly made my way downstairs to see if Joe was okay. He was sitting in a corner of the basement crying. Bloody welts and bruises covered his bare backside. He winced as he slowly put his shirt back on. He eyes looked at mine for a moment and I felt a tinge of guilt wash over me. I knew Mother was lying. And Joe was the victim she chose to hurt this time.

A few days later Ralph told dad he saw Joe take the bracelet from Mother's jewelry box. A short white man came to the house to talk to Mother about the jewelry that Joe was supposed to have stolen. Mother again put on an act of sorrow for the man. He said something to her about insurance and left.

Mother wanted to keep Ralph and me on her side so she gave us special treats so we would verify the lie she told us over and over again. Although I grieved for my brother's anguish I was glad it wasn't me.

Mother told many people about her foster son stealing a priceless piece of jewelry and turning it into a heap of junk. Mother gained sympathy from that story. As the summer wore on, the bracelet story died down. Joe was soon back in Mother's good graces again, and I was fearful of what awaited me.

Mother was in a bad mood one day, constantly hollering and cursing at us. We walked around the house waiting for her to explode.

It was raining hard outside so I huddled in the basement. There was an eerie silence in the house and the sound of the rain pounding on the roof could be heard all the way downstairs in the basement.

"Come here!" Mother screamed. She didn't call any names so all of us rushed upstairs to the kitchen.

"Get out!" she shouted at us.

We looked at each other. Did she mean for us to leave the room or the house?

"I said get out of my house!"

This time we didn't wait for an explanation. Her eyes were burning with anger. The back door was unlocked and I opened it with shaky hands. The three of us stepped out into the cold rain. We heard the door slam behind so we began walking towards the gate.

I had on shorts, a sleeveless blouse, and no shoes. Joe and Ralph were also barefoot. The cold rain pounded us as we walked. We finally ran down the street seeking some shelter from the rain. We found it two blocks away inside the doorway of a business. The overhang protected us from the rain so we stood there until the rain eased up.

"What's wrong with Mother?" Ralph asked.

"Let's get out of town," Joe suggested, looking up at the sky.

"How are we going to do that?"

Joe looked at me. "I know where the bus station is."

"What town can we go to?"

"Chicago."

It seemed like a good idea to go to Chicago. I could still remember the bus rides to Chicago with Hon. We walked and talked about all the things we were going to do when we got to Chicago. Joe mentioned how we survived getting bottles from trashcans. The thought of going through trashcans was awful, but going back to Mother was worse. We were careful where we walked because we were all barefoot. It took us awhile to get downtown. I saw the greyhound dog on the neon sign long before we got there.

"That's the bus station!" Joe pointed to the place with the dog on it.

We walked into the bus station glad to be out of the rain again. My clothes were wet and my hair was now frizzy.

"What do we do now?"

Joe shrugged his shoulders, "we can't get a ticket unless we have money."

"Let's beg people," I suggested.

We looked at the crowd of people and changed our minds. Most of them looked mean.

"We'll go to the tavern; it's not too far from here."

"What tavern?"

"Ike's tavern," Joe said.

"How do you know where Ike's tavern is?"

"I've been there before," Joe answered.

We followed Joe down the street as he led the way to the tavern.

"There it is," he shouted when we turned the corner. I looked where he was pointing.

We ran the rest of the way to the tavern and pushed the heavy door open. The smell of liquor mixed with cigarette smoke filled my nostrils. It was dark so our eyes had to adjust. We immediately saw Ike sitting at the end of the bar. With water dripping from our clothes and barefoot, we ran to greet our uncle.

"Ike!" we shouted, eager to embrace him.

"I'll be damned," Ike said, a smile crossing his face. "Where are the three of you coming from?"

We all started talking at once.

Cousin Liza's daughter Carol, who we called Baby sister, walked into the bar from the upstairs apartment. She recognized us and gave us a hug.

"Come on upstairs," she suggested. We went with her to the apartment over the tavern where Cousin Liza and Bro Tot lived. Baby sister was the mother of our cousins, Squeaky, Shirley and Jan who I played with over Hon and Papa's house. She gave us potato chips and listened while we told her about Mrs. Watson.

""Mrs. Watson told us to get out of her house," We told her.

We were still talking when the knock on the door alerted us. Baby Sister opened the door and two men walked in. I looked up at them.

"Are these the children?"

"I'm sorry," Baby sister told us. "I had to call the police."

I knew at that moment she hadn't listened to anything we were telling her. She couldn't have been listening and still be willing to send us back there.

The detectives drove us back home. Mother denied ever telling us to get out of her house. We didn't deny anything that Mother was saying to them because it didn't matter anyway. No one believed us. At least we got a chance to tell our family where we lived so they could visit us.

We went through another summer without anyone coming to visit us. Sara was busy visiting her deaf friends so we only got a chance to see her couple of times that summer. Sara told me that Bobby asked her to have sex with him. I didn't understand what she was saying but it made her mad. Sara told me that it was a bad thing and she told him no.

I learned after listening to their conversations that Ruby's daughter was pregnant. Vicky was only sixteen at the time.

"She's too young to have a baby," Mother told Ruby. "Have her put the baby up for adoption."

When I saw Vicky later that summer I noticed her belly was big. Vicky's eyes were sad and she didn't talk much. I didn't want Vicky to give her baby up, but I never saw the baby after she had it so I assumed she gave her baby up for adoption.

I made it through another summer and was glad when school was back in session. Things weren't much better at school, but at least I was away from Mother. The Principal and teachers decided that I was a problem child and gave up trying to reform me. The teacher started ignoring me when I walked into class late. The office quit giving me tardy slips and the Principal stopped spanking me with the paddle. I went to the office every morning to get a pass so the teacher would let me in class. The kids ignored me and I ignored them preferring to be by myself.

The holidays came and went, and Mother went through the

same rituals. I wasn't excited about Christmas anymore. Mother had the prettiest decorations so our house was always lit up with Christmas ornaments and lights, but there was very little joy for us. It had been over two years since Mother put me in the basement so I had learned to adjust. I used the pail more often so I wasn't wetting the bed as much.

My eleventh birthday came and went. I didn't feel any different except that my body continued changing. Mother kept telling me it was a curse, and I was ashamed of my body. I hated myself probably as much as Mother did. I didn't have any friends, but some of the girls at school were trying to be my friend. I didn't trust them. I didn't trust anyone anymore. During recess I sat alone, ignoring the laughter of the other kids.

Spring came and I was glad that the cold winter was over. The longer days were a welcomed relief. Dad still made his daily visits, but I no longer felt anything because my mind was not connected to my body. I could feel myself floating above it all and I never looked down. I hated the smell of cigars because it reminded me of Dad. I hated the coughing spells he had and the heavy breathing too. It was nearing the end of school and I was dreading another summer living there.

The minute I heard Mother's feet hit the floor I knew trouble was coming. Brother Randolph hadn't been over in a few days and Mother seemed agitated. She yelled upstairs for the boys to come down into the kitchen. I knew that high-pitched voice; it was the one that suggested anger. I waited to hear my name. I felt I couldn't take much more of the abuse. I was hurting both inside and out, death was starting to seem like a welcomed blessing.

I heard Joe and Ralph's feet running down the stairs. When they were in the kitchen Mother began.

"You pissed in the bed again!"

I didn't know which one she was yelling at or if it was both. In the next instance I heard the sound of the whip. Ralph's screams filled the house. Sitting in the corner with my legs up to my chest I folded my hands under my chin and waited. It didn't take long before she called me.

"Joyce, get up here!"

I ran upstairs to the kitchen where Joe was on the verge of crying. Ralph was on the floor crying. She gave me an odd look before she started hitting Ralph again. She knew that I hated seeing her whip them. She made me stand there watching her beat Ralph while he begged for mercy. My heart thumped in my chest and my eyes watered. Joe hung his head. I guessed that he was crying.

It seemed to take forever before she let Ralph go. She was breathing hard. I was sure that Joe or I was next. Surprisingly she walked back into her bedroom. We stood in the kitchen afraid to move while Ralph was whimpering and moving around painfully. I hated this woman! I hated what she was doing to us! Ralph was barely able to stand up. His face was bright red and his eyes were pouring tears. I looked away afraid that I would start crying again. I don't know how long we stood there before she yelled for us to get out of the kitchen.

The phone rang just before it was time to leave for school. I thought it was Brother Randolph because Mother allowed me to walk to school that morning with Joe and Ralph who was in pain. Mother rushed us out of the house so quickly she didn't take time to examine Ralph like she usually did after a beating.

"We've got to get him out of this house!" I whispered to Joe after Ralph wouldn't stand up and walk. I was afraid to leave him home with her. If Mother knew how badly he was hurt she would keep him home. Mother was distracted by the phone call so we were able to get Ralph out of the house without her noticing him. Once outside he almost collapsed from the pain.

"We are going to run away and never come back!" Joe said the anger evident in his voice. His eyes were wide and filled with tears. "We'll go somewhere." Joe and I walked on each side of Ralph holding onto his arms to help him walk faster. Joe promised to tell us the details of his plan to run away after school that day.

165

In Years To Come

I was summoned to the office that morning about an hour after I arrived. When I walked into the office, the secretary motioned for me to sit on the bench. I didn't understand what was going on because I hadn't been late for school that day. I was really surprised when Joe came into the office.

""What are you doing here?"

I shrugged my shoulders.

""What are *you* doing here?"

Joe shook his head. I was sure Mother was behind whatever was going on. Was she coming to pick us up from school?

""You need to report to the nurse's office," the secretary said, interrupting my thoughts.

We followed the hall monitor to the nurse's office. A middle-aged woman with salt and pepper hair was sitting at a desk. She turned when she saw us.

"Are you Joyce?" she asked me.

I nodded.

"You must be Joe then."

He nodded.

I looked around the nurse's office because I had never been in there before. There were charts all over the wall showing food groups and body parts. I saw a picture of a kid brushing his teeth. Then the same eye chart that we had to say letters off of was on another wall. A small cot was shoved into one corner and someone was laying on it.

It was Ralph.

I felt myself breathing harder. What was going on?

"He's resting for the moment," she said.

"He told his teacher he was in a lot of pain so she sent him down here about thirty minutes ago."

"Do either of you know what happened to him?"

She looked from Joe to me. I couldn't find words to speak so I just stared at her.

"Your brother has some severe bruises on his body,"', she

continued. Joe shot me a look that showed he was scared. We weren't going to tell anyone anything. Mother would beat us when we got home.

"I've called a doctor to come here," the nurse continued. The Principal had walked into the room while she was talking, and he was leaning against the wall. I looked at him out of the corner of my eye.

I didn't know what was going on, but I didn't like it.

"Is Ralph going to be all right?" Joe finally asked.

"The doctor will examine him. You need to tell the doctor what happened to him if you know anything."

The principal stepped forward. "If either of you know anything, you need to tell the doctor or the nurse," he said.

We both shook our heads.

A tall man in a gray coat walked through the door. He had a black bag in his hand just like Dr. Dunlap.

The nurse stood up and introduced the man as a doctor and the two of them went into the hall to talk to the principal.

"What's going on?" I whispered to Joe.

"I don't know, but I'm not telling anything."

"Me either."

I tiptoed over to the cot where Ralph was lying. He was sound asleep.

"Hey Ralph," I whispered. But he didn't move. I reached out to touch him and he yelled.

I jumped back just as the doctor and nurse came back into the room.

The nurse looked at me.

"The doctor and I need to examine both of you," she said.

I was taken to another room while the doctor was left to examine Joe and Ralph.

"You will have to remove your clothes", she said. I didn't want to remove my clothes. What if she saw that I was growing hair?

I took off my dress but kept my panties and slip on. I heard the nurse gasp when I turned around. I could feel her hands moving over my back. They were soft and warm.

"Am I hurting you?" she asked.

I shook my head.

"How did you get these bruises and scars on your back?"

"I fell down," I whispered.

"What happened to your brother Ralph? Did he fall too?"

She left the room and brought the doctor back in with her. He looked at my back and made me lift my slip to look at my legs and thighs. He didn't say anything, but he kept shaking his head.

He was writing something on paper while he was looking at me. Finally the nurse told me to put my clothes back on. I joined Joe back in the nurse's office. Ralph was now sitting on the bed.

"I need you to tell me what happened" the nurse said, looking at me.

"I don't know," I said flatly.

The nurse was very patience and began talking to us. The doctor was out in the hall talking to the principal.

"Your brother has been hurt badly. We want to help him, but we don't know how he got those bruises." She looked concerned.

"You have bruises on you too and I know you didn't get them by falling down."

I started crying. The words started coming out and I couldn't stop them. I was telling everything. Joe and Ralph started talking too and when we finished the nurse hugged all of us.

"I believe you," she said.

There was a lot of talking going on between the nurse, the doctor, and the principal. Another man came in who identified himself as our temporary social worker. His name was Mr. Webber. He was a stocky white man with brown hair. We asked about Mr. Bergner but he didn't tell us anything.

The doctor took Mr. Webber into the exam room so he

could look at Ralph and Joe. When Mr. Webber walked into the principal's office where I was sitting, the look on his face told the story.

"I need you to keep these children here at the school", he told the principal. "They are not to go back to the Watson house and she cannot come here to get them."

I felt like a VIP the rest of the day because all the teachers watched us. They brought a police officer into the school to protect us. I kept expecting Mother to walk in, especially after we didn't go home for lunch. The teachers had us sit at the table where they ate so we were surrounded by teachers, but I kept looking over my shoulder. They kept assuring us that she was not coming to the school.

"Mother is going to be mad if we don't go home for lunch," I had told the Principal.

"Don't worry about it; we've already taken care of it."

I was glad we didn't have to go home to face Mother. I was sick of eating tomato sandwiches anyway. The food in the lunchroom was good and I ate everything on my plate. When we finished lunch we were escorted back to the office where we stayed until Mr. Webber returned to pick us up.

"You're not going back to live with Mr. and Mrs. Watson," Mr. Webber told us as we climbed into the county car.

I felt as if I was in a movie because it didn't seem real. I sat in the front seat staring out the windshield. Inside I felt strange like when Hon and Papa died. No one had died, but I felt like it.

"What about our clothes?" I blurted out.

"We'll make sure you get your clothes," he said softly. "You're not going back there for anything."

"We can't even say good-bye to Mother and Dad?"

I don't know what made me ask that question. I guess I wanted to be assured that I really wasn't going back.

He seemed to understand what I was hinting at. He looked at me with a sly smile on his face and shook his head.

In Years To Come

I leaned back in the seat, satisfied that I would never see them again.

I imagined the scene that was going on at Mother's house. I could see her playing the role once she was told we wouldn't be coming back. I imagined her crying and trying to defend herself. I saw the tears rolling down her cheeks and the fake sadness that usually overwhelmed people. Then I remembered what the nurse said. How would she explain the scars and bruises all over our bodies? How would she defend herself after what she did to Ralph who had suffered a fresh batch of welts that were open and oozing blood?

"Where are we going?"

"To another foster home."

The mention of another foster home made me feel uncomfortable. I squirmed in my seat.

"We are going to another foster home?"

Mr. Webber cleared his throat.

"Mrs. Williams is a very nice lady and Mr. Williams is a minister. They were willing to take all three of you in on an emergency basis."

I sat rigid in the front seat.

On an emergency basis? What did that mean? The ride felt too long. I looked out the window as we drove past houses, businesses, churches, and schools. I didn't recognize where we were going. I had not been to many places. When we first went to live with Mother and Dad we had ventured out more and went to movies, church, the park, and even the state fair that first year. Mother stopped taking us places after the first year.

Joe and Ralph were in the back. The doctor gave Mr. Webber medicine for Ralph to take and some cream for him to put on his open wounds.

I was nervous and jumped at the slightest noise. Mr. Webber watched me out the corner of his eye. I had mixed emotions about where we had been and where we were going. The tears wanted to come, but I continued fighting them. I didn't want anyone to see the weakness I was feeling. Wasn't I supposed to be happy? I didn't understand why I wanted to cry. I was finally free of Mother and Dad. All the things that were done to us over the years rushed through my mind like a bad movie. I saw myself swinging from the pipe in the basement; I saw the welts rising on my flesh with blood trickling from the wounds. I saw myself inside the cellar struggling for air.

"Please God, don't let met cry," I said to myself as the car pulled to the curb. I felt so much emotion and the tears only compensated for a small portion. The sky was a perfect blue with white clouds floating like balls of cotton. Trees swayed softly in the blowing wind. It was springtime and the flowers were starting to bud. The warmth of the sun on my bare arms felt good. The car stopped.

"This is it, children," Mr. Webber smiled at us. He got out of the car and opened the door. My legs felt weak when I stepped out. I looked up at the dark brown house that was so much different from Mother's beautiful white one. This was good. I hoped everything was different from that house.

We followed Mr. Webber up steep wooden stairs onto a small porch. I felt my heart pounding inside of my chest.

Mr. Webber rang the doorbell.

A woman opened the door. She was a tall, slim attractive woman with dark brown skin, long hair, and a nice smile. I was unprepared for what I saw next. She had a bulge in her stomach. *She is having a baby*, I thought to myself. I wondered for a moment about Vicky's baby.

We stepped into the small living room and sat on the sofa next to each other. It finally hit me that we were really leaving Mother's house. We made it out of there alive. Mr. Webber introduced us to our new foster mother. We listened to Mr. Webber tell her about what happened to us. I could see a look of shock on Mrs. Williams face. I took the opportunity to peek around at the house. The furniture wasn't new, but it was comfortable. The house was clean and everything looked okay. *I am going to help her with the baby,* I thought.

Mr. Webber chose his words carefully while explaining our emergency situation. I felt warmth in the house.

After Mr. Webber left Mrs. Williams tried to make us feel comfortable by talking with us. It was an awkward situation because I was a little apprehensive. I hadn't communicated with many people in the last few years, at least people I felt I could trust. Her eyes were friendly and she smiled a lot. I nodded or shook my head in response to questions. A part of me wanted to hug her and thank her for taking me into her house. She didn't look like a person who beat children. I stared at the walls filled with pictures of Jesus. I saw Bibles scattered in different places. Mother had also had Bibles and pictures of Jesus on the walls.

After about an hour we heard a noise coming from the back of the house. I turned around to see what it was. Two boys rushed into the house. They were breathing hard as if they had been running. We stared at them and they stared back at us. Who were these boys?

"Hi Mama," they said. Mama? I was really surprised now. Mr. Webber didn't tell us there were already foster children in the home.

Mrs. Williams smiled and introduced them. "This is Michael," the older boy nodded, "and this is Ricky." The younger one seemed shy. He looked at the floor instead of us. We responded with a shallow hello.

Mrs. Williams explained to the boys that we were going to be living with them. I thought to myself, *she already had two foster children in addition to the baby on the way; this lady must really love children*!

Michael and Ricky took Ralph and Joe upstairs while Mrs. Williams showed me my new bedroom. It was the most beautiful bedroom I had ever seen. It was small with a twin size bed pushed against the wall and a small chest. The walls were painted a pale green. The small closet was just the right size for my clothes. I finally had a bedroom just for me. There was a small window on the north side of the room where the sun beamed down making it brighter. This bedroom was a welcomed relief from the basement where I had spent most of the last three years.

Mr. Williams came home from work later that evening. He didn't look like the preacher I had imagined. He was a short man with a round face. The one thing I noticed right away was his funny eyes and the thick black glasses he wore. The first evening was awkward for everyone. The table was set with three plates on one side and three on the other side. At the end of the table near me was another plate. I expected Mr. Williams to sit in the seat on the end, but instead Mrs. Williams sat there. The food looked tempting, but everything that happened that day diminished my appetite. I closed my eyes while Mr. Williams blessed the food. His low voice was comforting. Dad always blessed the food. I couldn't help wondering what the reaction was when he came home to find us gone. When I opened my eyes after the prayer I still couldn't believe I was with a new family.

Michael sat directly across the table from me. He grinned at me shyly as he passed the plates of food around the table. I hadn't talked much to him. When Ricky spoke he had a cute stutter just like my baby brother, Louie. It was funny, but at the same time it was amusing because Michael also stuttered.

It caught me off guard like a slap in the face when I found out that Michael and Ricky were the Williams' biological children. I don't know why I assumed that they were foster children like us. I didn't think people with children of their own wanted to take in someone else's children. I couldn't help thinking now that they must not want us because they had their own children. It felt strange. I can't say it was jealousy that I felt, but I know it would have been easier to accept if they had been foster children too.

Mrs. Williams was a good cook. After dinner, Mrs.

173

Williams told us that we would all take turns washing dishes. We were paired together it was Ralph with Michael, Joe with Ricky, and Mrs. Williams with me. It was so good to know that the boys would be helping with the chores.

Mr. and Mrs. Williams slept in a large bedroom across from mine on the main floor. There were two more bedrooms and Mr. Williams' study upstairs. Michael and Ricky shared one bedroom while Joe and Ralph shared the other one.

I had to pinch myself to make sure I wasn't dreaming when I climbed into bed. I woke up in the middle of the night from a bad dream. The moonlight was streaming in through the window so I got up to look out. I believed we were safe. I went to the bathroom because I didn't want to pee in my new bed.

Chapter Five

The Williams

I was thrilled to have a bedroom that was perfect for me. I was like a little kid opening the closet and empty dresser drawers the first few days. The bed was comfortable and felt like lying on a pile of cotton compared to the hard cot that Mother had me sleeping on in the basement. Ralph and Joe liked their room too, but more importantly they got along well with Michael and Ricky. I couldn't fight off the nightmares about Mother and Dad coming to the house and kidnapping us. I once thought I had seen her car drive by and ran as fast as I could to school. For the first few months the nightmares were bad, but as time passed I stopped having them. Sometimes just knowing I wasn't in the basement anymore was enough relief to get me back to sleep. The bedwetting happened occasionally but not like when I lived with Mother. I learned how to pray to God, so every night I got on my knees and prayed before crawling into bed.

Even though we were out of that foster home our reactions were still there. Every time Mr. or Mrs. Williams made a gesture by lifting an arm, pointing a finger, or anything physical, we reacted by jumping or putting our arms over our face in defense. I tried to be more conscious of what I was doing, but my body automatically reacted. It was embarrassing, but they seemed to understand.

I was helping Mrs. Williams in the kitchen a few days later when she said: "Your other foster mother refuses to give the social worker your clothes."

"What are we going to wear?"

I had worn the same dress for three days even though Mrs. Williams washed our clothes every night in her automatic washer.

"I was given clothing vouchers so we will go shopping at Sears so all of you can have clothes to wear."

I smiled at Mrs. Williams. I liked her and her voice was soft when she spoke.

Mother had told Mr. Webber that she bought all our clothes, so she was going to keep them. Mrs. Williams took us to Sears and we bought a new wardrobe. I was glad because I didn't want anything reminding me of Mother or Dad.

Mrs. Williams enrolled us in Brown Elementary school, a couple of blocks from the house. All five of us walked to school and home together. Michael and I were only a few months apart in age so we ended up in the same fifth grade class. I was surprised to see Michael helping students in the classroom with their schoolwork. Michael was not only the teacher's favorite, but also the smartest kid in the class. Some said he was the smartest in the whole school. At school it was definitely about Michael and at home I had to listen to praise being given to Michael constantly. I had a sudden urge to compete with him. I refused to allow him to help me with class work or homework. When I received a good grade on my schoolwork I made sure the Williams's and Michael were aware of it.

The house wasn't big, but it was comfortable. The three of us settled into their routine and it didn't take long to find out all the rules of the house. The rules in the house were simple. We walked to school and home together. Household chores were shared among all of us. Mrs. Williams did the cooking and helped me with laundry although I did most of the ironing. Washing was much easier with the automatic machine. We didn't have time to play outside so I didn't have any friends in the neighborhood. Because I wasn't allowed to play outside when we lived with Mother I didn't miss it. I didn't bother watching TV because I didn't understand football and I grew tired of watching Bonanza. Mr. Williams said most programs weren't appropriate for us to watch so those were the only two programs we were allowed to watch. I did miss listening to the radio because I liked music and Mother had kept the radio on most of the time.

Sundays started with a breakfast of grits, bacon or sausage, and homemade biscuits. I looked forward to breakfast on Sundays when Mrs. Williams would make homemade biscuits. I watched her roll the dough and wanted to help, but she made it clear that only she would do the cooking.

Next, we would pile into the blue Volkswagen bus and go to Sunday school. I enjoyed riding in the mini bus because we each had our own window. After Sunday school we had regular church and after that we went home until the evening services. I had never gone to church so much in my life! I learned quickly that being a minister's daughter meant being in church most of the time. It seemed like we were in church every night because during the week we attended Bible classes, prayer meetings, or some sort of Bible study. Mrs. Williams knew the Bible really good too, so she taught Bible classes when Mr. Williams would be working. I never knew where Mr. Williams worked, but he did have a job somewhere. We were asleep when he left the house in the mornings, but he came home every evening in a pair of jeans and a work shirt.

We didn't just sit down and eat dinner. It was a time for talking, praying, and reading Bible verses out-loud. We took turns blessing the food. After we ate dinner each of us were expected to say a Bible verse we had memorized. Stacks of cards were placed in the middle of the table with Bible verses on them. We would select a card and read the verse on it out loud.

I was absorbed in reading the Bible so I spent most of my

free time in my bedroom. Michael and Ricky had a large collection of books upstairs in their bedroom. My love for reading expanded from the Bible to reading all the books that were on the shelves in their bedroom. Even though Ricky was barely seven years old he could read almost as well as me. The books were helping me be a better reader and I wanted to learn everything about the Bible, not only to please my new parents, but also to answer questions the way Michael and Ricky did.

Monday through Saturday Mrs. Williams cooked a pot of oatmeal in the winter and during the summer we ate cold cereal for breakfast. We walked home from school at lunchtime to eat. She fixed us a half of a peanut butter and jelly sandwich, a cookie and if it was during the winter, a small cup of soup. Our meals were usually balanced, but the portions were small so most of the time I was still hungry.

The small church where Mr. Williams was the Pastor was located on 20th and Center St. It was a house that had been converted into a church. The church was one floor with several rooms. An old upright piano stood in one area of the church. There were crosses and pictures of Jesus hanging on the walls. I recognized some of the Bible verses that were on various posters. Single metal chairs were lined evenly in the largest room facing a podium in the middle of the room. The windows were big so sunlight filtered in making it very bright.

We went to church early in the morning because we attended Sunday school. We always sat in the front row seats while Mr. Williams preached. There weren't very many members in the church. An older white man with no teeth was a co-preacher at the church. We called him Bother Bob. He looked more like a priest in his back suits. He always smelled like candy because he ate lifesavers one after the other. Brother Bob was nice to us, but sometimes he spit when he talked because he had no teeth. He had the coolest blue eyes and funniest laugh. Despite being toothless he always smiled. I had a great admiration and respect for Brother Bob.

Joyce A. Ford

Most churches I attended in the past had preachers who were loud and preached with so much emotion I seldom understood what they were preaching about. Mr. Williams was a different type of preacher. He looked the part of an intelligent man when he dressed in his Sunday suit and white shirt. He had a firm voice that was clear and easy to listen to. When he spoke you couldn't help being drawn into his story. He didn't do all the dramatics that I usually saw Baptist preachers do either. He was more like a teacher who explained the Bible. *What kind of church is this?* I wondered the first time I attended.

Outside of my bedroom door in the dining room was a piano. It wasn't a big upright like the one at Mother's house, and it seemed just right for a kid. I still yearned to play the piano, so when Ricky and Michael started taking piano lessons I begged Mrs. Williams to include me. I was disappointed when she kept making excuses why I couldn't take lessons. I would lie in my bed listening while Ricky and Michael did private piano lessons from a stout woman with a grandmotherly face. When they practiced their lessons the music flowed inside my bedroom. It soon became obvious that there were several things we were denied that Michael and Ricky were privileged to have. At church they sung solos. If we dared to ask if we could sing a solo we were told outright "no."

The last day of school came quicker than expected and this time I looked forward to summer vacation. I didn't know what to expect over the summer because we were so busy going to church and Bible study classes. When I was given my report card I could hardly contain my excitement. I couldn't believe my grades and kept staring at it. I had worked hard trying to keep up with Michael, but I didn't realize I was doing so well. I had not seen a good report card since living with Hon and Papa. I smiled to myself and imagined the look on their faces when I handed it to Mr. and Mrs. Williams. I didn't care about Michael's report card because I knew he would get a good one, but at least they would know I was just as

179

smart as he was.

The walk home seemed longer than usual that day. It took all I had to keep from running home. All of us had manila envelopes tucked in our hands, but no one talked about their grades so neither did I.

When we walked through the door, Mrs. Williams was in the kitchen cooking dinner. I wanted to be first so I ran to her and handed her my report card. She set it aside on the table so I saw the others pile up on top mine. I had hoped she would open it right then.

"I did really well in school," I said to her.

Mrs. Williams smiled and picked up the envelopes. Mine was now on the bottom. I was anxious for her to see my report card so I waited while she looked at them one at a time. The boys had scattered to their rooms. She finally opened mine. She read the grades and the comment on the back.

"This is good," she said looking at me.

"That's the best report card I ever got," I answered.

"I am going to have to show this to John when he gets home."

We were at the dinner table when Mr. Williams mentioned the report cards. He looked directly at me when he talked.

"That was a very good report card," he said. I wanted him to mention to everyone that I had gotten all A's and B's.

I looked away from him, smiling. I wanted to stand up and be given an ovation, but of course that didn't happen.

"You did well too Ricky, but you could have done better in a couple of subjects."

Ricky had gotten a couple of C's and it was obvious they were disappointed about it.

"Ralph and Joe, I expect a better report card from both of you next year."

"Yes sir," they both answered.

Then he turned to Michael. I was looking at him too because I wanted to hear about him. He may have gotten a few extra A's, but what could he possibly do that would top what I had done?

"I'm very proud of you Michael," he said. "You've done so well in school that they are skipping you a grade. You'll be going to junior high next year."

My mouth fell open.

Promoted to junior high school? How did that happen? I didn't hear the rest of the conversation as I tried to figure out how he managed to get skipped a grade. At that moment I wanted to grab my report card and tear it up in small pieces.

As the days passed we gradually stopped calling our foster parents Mr. and Mrs. Williams and began calling them Mom and Dad the same as Michael and Ricky.

Summer Vacation Bible School was beginning at the church. I listened intently as Brother Bob explained how we could win a week to Bible camp.

"Whoever brings the most kids to Vacation Bible School will win one week at Bible camp." He said looking at each of us.

I scanned the room looking at my brothers. This was going to be easy for me to win. I mentally checked each of them off beginning with Joe. He was shy around strangers and going to camp probably didn't interest him. Michael probably liked the idea of winning because he usually did, but he couldn't compete with me because his ability to communicate wasn't that great. I almost laughed out loud at the thought of him trying to talk to people with his stutter. Ralph probably wouldn't want to go either because he still had a bed-wetting problem that would embarrass him, so I knew he wouldn't try to win. Ricky acted like a baby so I felt he wouldn't get many children to come to church either. It came down to a contest between Michael and me.

I wet the bed a couple of times a month, but either Joe or Ralph was wetting the bed almost every night. The bedroom they shared was starting to smell. Mrs. Williams was upset about it and began complaining. I prayed to God to cure us of this curse, promising to be good if we could stop wetting the bed. Mr.

Williams assured us every week in church that God does answer prayers.

Ralph, Joe, and I were getting spankings for wetting the bed. Mrs. Williams spanked all of us, but Mr. Williams only spanked the boys. He never touched me. I didn't like getting spankings, but it was a lot easier than the beatings I got from the Mr. and Mrs. Watson. Mrs. Williams would make us bend over a couch while she slapped us on the butt with a belt. I almost laughed the first time because it was no comparison with what we had gone through. Sometimes Mrs. Williams made the boys drop their pants and would hit them a lot harder than she did me. I could hear their fake screams in my bedroom and just grinned to myself. We didn't do anything wrong except wet the bed. Sometimes we got in trouble if we got distracted at church.

Brother Bob sent us out every day to begin our recruitment for Vocational Bible School. The boys paired up together while I went my own way. I had already decided on how to win the contest. I would recruit large families. I walked the streets talking with children about coming to our Vacation Bible School. I spent time talking with mothers about how much fun the children would have learning about Jesus. I was surprised how easy it was to get the mothers and children excited about coming to our church.

I sat in church among the many children I had brought in. The smile on Brother Bob's face let me know he was happy as his blue eyes scanned the room. I was far ahead of everyone and the church was full of children. I was looking forward to defeating Michael. I made sure the kids got to church on time by helping mothers comb the girls' hair and dress the younger children.

Once Bible school started I enjoyed it. Brother Bob and Mrs. Williams made learning about the Bible fun as they illustrated stories using felt boards with cut out characters. We sang songs with Brother Bob who taught us one song using colors to sing to. When he flipped to the red he explained it as being the blood of Jesus and when he flipped the color to gold he sang about walking the streets of gold in heaven.

The day finally arrived. Vacation Bible School was almost over so Mr. Williams called me to the front of the church. I was feeling very emotional. It was the first time I was getting recognized for anything. Mr. Williams praised me for my efforts in getting the children to come to church. The kids clapped and yelled for me. He announced that I had won a free week at Bible camp. While still feeling victorious I heard him call Michael's name. I watched Michael walk up and stand on the opposite side of him. My mind began spinning as I listened while he told the kids that Michael was also going to camp. I wanted to scream. I said nothing as I stared at Michael who was grinning. I felt like the stupidest kid in the whole world. They had planned to send him to camp the entire time. Suddenly I didn't want to go to camp. I was planning on faking an illness or something just so I wouldn't have to go.

Susan was one of the girls I had recruited to come to church.

"I am glad you will be at camp because my mother is paying for me so I can go too," she said.

I looked up into her face and saw excitement in her eyes. I knew then I had to go. The day arrived for camp and I was ready. I had reasoned with myself all week that it was the right thing to do. We met the bus in the small town of Oak Creek. Susan was anxious to get there. We were the only two kids of color attending camp that week.

The mornings at camp began with a prayer, breakfast, and then games. After the first day I was glad I went. Susan and I shared a bunk bed, ate together, and were always on the same team whenever we played games. I couldn't swim so I watched as the other kids dived into the clear water at the creek. At night we had church service in a tent while warm summer breezes drifted in. The sound of religious music filled the air with an overwhelming excitement.

It was mid-week at Bible camp when something amazing happened to me. I was sitting on the bench in the tent during one of the services listening to a hymn I knew fairly well when the artist began drawing a picture of someone drowning in water. Tears began streaming down my face. I heard the music playing softly in the background. I was aware of myself singing along, "Let the lower lights be burning..." The artist drew a lighthouse in the middle of the water with lights reflecting on the water and in the middle of the water was the person, desperately trying to keep from drowning. For whatever reason I felt I was that person. It all seemed so real; I was drowning, not in water, but in something else. I said a prayer asking God to help me and pull me ashore like the preacher was saying. That image has never left my mind.

Camp was over too soon. The next week Michael went to camp. I was glad that he didn't go the same week as me. I think Mr. Williams knew how unhappy I was about him going to camp.

I remember the day the baby was born, I was secretly hoping that it was a girl, but a beautiful baby boy, Timothy, came home from the hospital with Mrs. Williams. I was amazed at how tiny he was. I wanted to help her with the baby. Everyone in the house was excited about the new baby and Mrs. Williams was protective of him.

I was told not to touch the baby while Michael and Ricky were allowed to hold him, pick him up, and feed him. The rejection was overwhelming and I began to feel as if I had a disease they weren't telling me about. I pretended it didn't hurt or bother me, but deep inside it did. I wanted to hold the baby and feed him, but she wouldn't let me. Mrs. Williams sometimes put him on the table in his little seat and I would make him laugh. He was a cute baby who didn't cry a lot.

Change is sometimes sudden and everything began to change around the house after Timothy was born. It felt like the family was being divided after Mr. and Mrs. Williams moved upstairs into the bedroom where Ralph and Joe had slept. They moved Ralph and Joe downstairs into their bedroom. They didn't offer any explanation for the change and we didn't ask. The move definitely separated us from them.

"We don't want you going upstairs," they warned us. It was clear what was going on. Mr. and Mrs. Williams, Ricky, Michael, and Timothy, were the only ones allowed to be upstairs. Of course nothing changed with Ricky and Michael so they were allowed all over the house. I resented Michael and Ricky because they let us know their position in the house. I pretended to ignore them but inside I was hurting. I knew we would never be equal with them and it made me more aware of our status as foster children. The words "Roy's crazy kids" rang in my head. Was that all we were ever going to be?

I could hear them when they were up and moving around. It always seemed to take a long time for them to come downstairs, especially on the weekends. I wondered what they were doing up there. I knew that Michael and Ricky had toys upstairs, but of course everything up there was off-limits, so no one else was allowed to play with them. The Williams family spent more time upstairs than they did down. I could hear Timothy crying, I could hear laughter from Ricky or Michael. I could even hear voices when they talked even though I couldn't understand the words. Sometimes I would go to Ralph and Joe's room or they would come to mine, but we didn't have a lot to talk about. We couldn't watch TV or listen to the radio. We couldn't touch the piano or fix anything to eat, so we waited for them to come downstairs. I continued reading books and spending most of my time in my bedroom. I began feeling isolated from the family.

It was a bright summer day and we were invited to a church in Burlington, Wisconsin. The drive didn't seem long before we pulled in front of a large, striking church. I marveled at the beautiful paintings and stained glass windows inside. It reminded me of Antioch Baptist Church. Mr. Williams was invited into the pulpit and we sat near the front pews. I looked around as people filled the seats. Most of them were staring at us. Mrs. Williams was greeting everyone with a smile or a nod of the head. When the service started

In Years To Come

I took another look around and noticed that everyone in the church was white except for us.

Mr. Williams was the guest speaker. He looked like Dr. Martin Luther King jr., as he stood erect behind the pulpit. His voice was sound and his message was powerful. Mrs. Williams was smiling at him so I knew she was feeling proud. When he finished speaking he pointed in our direction.

"I would like to introduce my family," he said. I sat stiffly in my seat because I knew all eyes were on us.

"I would like to introduce my wife, Williemae," Mrs. Williams stood up. "My sons, Ricky and Michael." I was sitting when Michael stood up at my right side and so did Ricky who sat further down. "And our three foster children, Joyce, Joe, and Ralph."

I felt glued to the seat. He told them we were foster children. I felt a lump in my throat and could see Joe and Ralph already standing. Why did he have to introduce us like that? I finally stood up and I could hear the people clapping around us. When I turned to face them I saw the pitiful looks on their faces. Why did he have to tell them we were foster children? I fought the tears that were about to fall. When I sat back down I didn't look up anymore. I felt ashamed that they knew I was a foster child.

The Pastor of the church thanked Mr. Williams for a great message and talked about how wonderful it was that they had taken us into their home. It reminded me of the days when Mother took us to church and made sure that everyone knew we were foster children.

We ate dinner at the Pastor's house that afternoon. I was impressed with the large brick house with the finished basement. I marveled at the pool table and the ping-pong table in a basement that looked as nice as the main floor of the house. I had never seen a basement with finished walls and ceilings like that. These people had to be rich to have such a beautiful home. How did they get a pool table inside of the house? I wanted to ask but I didn't want to be impolite. We were warned to be on our best behavior.

Mr. Williams drove to Mississippi that summer to visit his family and took Ralph and Ricky with him. They felt lucky to be going out of town even though I was reminded that I went to summer camp. All of us went somewhere that summer except for Joe. I wanted to go to Mississippi because I knew that was where my real parents were born. Uncle Ben had talked about Mississippi. Mr. and Mrs. Williams were from a small town where their parents still lived. After a couple of weeks they returned home loaded down with all kinds of vegetables and nuts. Ralph told us about meeting the grandparents and how nice they were to him. We spent the next few days shucking corn, snapping beans, and picking greens to put into the freezer for the winter. We ate roasted peanuts warm from the oven and they were good. The freezer was full when we finished stuffing it with all the vegetables that Mr. Williams had brought back.

It was near the end of the summer when we got a surprise visitor. It was on a Sunday afternoon after church. I was in my room reading when the doorbell rang. I could hear the football game that was playing on TV in the living room but I couldn't make out the voices.

"Roy jr. is here!" Ralph shouted to me when he came to my bedroom. At first I thought I must have heard the wrong name. I got up and went into the living room. Roy jr. was sitting on the couch wearing his trademark dark glasses. Everyone said he looked like Ray Charles with the glasses on. I hadn't seen him in almost four years, but I still knew who he was. Roy jr. dressed nice, always drove a late model car and seemed to have money.

"Hi."

"How are you doing young lady?" he asked in that voice that everyone referred to as proper. I thought he just sounded funny. I was grinning so hard I couldn't find my tongue.

We sat near Roy jr. on the sofa while he told Mr. and Mrs. Williams that he had been trying to visit us for a while, but our other

187

foster parents wouldn't let him in the house. Mr. and Mrs. Williams and the social worker gave him permission to pick us up on Sunday afternoons. It felt good to show Ricky and Michael that we had someone who cared about us too.

About a month later Roy jr. took us to see Sara at her school in Delevan. I was happy to see her and all of us clung to each other. The school was impressive. The entrance hallway had a large picture of several children playing. A small black girl about five years old stuck out in the crowd of white children. Sara told me that she was the little girl in the picture that was taken during her first year in Delevan. She took me to the bedroom she shared with another girl. It was small with twin beds. Everything was clean and shiny throughout the school. I met a lot of Sara's friends that day. She cried when we had to leave and so did I. Sara did not go back to Ruby's house and was placed in another foster home over the summer. She described her foster parents as a nice couple.

Roy jr. took us to his house most Sundays where we played with his two stepsons or watched TV. I was upset that we didn't get a chance to visit other relatives.

Ralph was telling Roy jr. about his visit to Mississippi when Roy jr. told us that our Grandmother Irene was still alive and living in Mississippi. I was shocked because I had forgotten about her.

"She's still alive?" I asked Roy jr. several times. He confirmed that my mother's mother was alive. I wanted to ask him why she hadn't come to visit. I held my tongue because I didn't want Roy jr. to get mad and stop coming to pick us up. Roy jr. finally got tired of me questioning him about Grandma Irene.

"Why don't you write her and ask her these questions yourself?" he said one day.

"Could I?" I asked, my mind racing ahead.

"Sure, you can write her, she can read and write."

He gave me her address. I must have written my first letter over about fifty times before I thought it was just right to send to her. What do you say to a grandmother you didn't even know was alive?

I danced around the room several times when I finally received a reply from her. The first communication between grandmother and granddaughter had started. I asked her lots of questions about my mother. I wanted to know what she was like as a little girl. Was she pretty? Was she smart? Were there any brothers or sisters of my mother's? There were never too many questions for me to ask. Grandma Irene continued to write back every time. I would read the letters out loud to Ralph and Joe. They didn't write her, but wanted me to ask questions for them. She didn't tell me much about my mother, which was disappointing. She did send a letter containing a few pictures a couple of them were of us as little kids. I laughed at Joe's big head. My real mother! I cherished the pictures as I showed them to everyone. My real mother had a slight resemblance to one of my teachers at school. She was thin but short; they had the same skin color and almost identical hair. My real mother had been the most beautiful woman in the whole wide world. I asked Grandma Irene to send me a picture of her but she never did. I was left wondering what she looked like. I slept with the pictures underneath my pillow so I could feel close to my real mother. When I told Roy jr. that Grandmother Irene had sent pictures he wanted to see them. Somehow he talked me into letting him keep them so I wouldn't lose them.

After a few months of correspondence I got up the courage to ask if we could come visit her. I told her that I would love to move to Mississippi and live on the farm with her and her husband.

When her reply letter arrived I felt my heart pounding in my chest. It was the letter that would be the answer to our dreams. Ralph, Joe, and I had all agreed to ask her if we could move to Mississippi. The letter began with the usual sentences, How are you? I love you. It was an unusually long letter. I finally read the part where she answered our question. She said she was too old to raise us.

I had a hard time dealing with the disappointment. I believe that disappointment was obvious in the other letters I wrote. The letters gradually diminished until one day she didn't answer any more of my letters. I quit writing to her too.

Summer was over almost as quickly as it started and we were back in school. There was a lot of talk about the school Michael was going to attend. I found out that he wasn't going to the junior high school in our district and was being bussed to a predominately white school in the suburbs. It seemed odd that Michael was going to the seventh grade; he was younger than Joe and even a few months younger than me.

The grade school we attended the year before was shut down so we were transferred to Twentieth Street School a few blocks in another direction. I began sixth grade anxiously hoping to be promoted. I had gained a lot of knowledge while reading books over the summer and hoped it would help me in school. Joe and I ended up in the same grade because Joe had failed a couple of times. Ralph was in the fourth and Ricky in third grade. Joe, Ralph and I were eligible for free lunch at school, but we never ate at school because Ricky had to come home everyday. They paid for Michael to eat lunch at school or sometimes he took a lunch with him. I didn't mind because at least peanut butter and jelly sandwiches with cookies were a lot better than the tomato with mayonnaise sandwiches that Mother fed us. I finally gave up trying to compete with Michael because he was doing just as good in junior high. He was so smart that he really didn't have to study and I spent all my time studying just trying to keep up with him.

The sixth grade wasn't too bad though. I made a few friends and managed to get decent grades. Going to school was different from when I lived with Mother because I was able to get a full night's sleep and eat a warm breakfast. I was more alert in the classroom. No one at this school knew me so my foster home identity wasn't known.

Joe was the tallest one in the school and he became a school safety cadet helping the children cross the street. He was so caring with the kids and knew how to direct traffic as well as a police officer. He became very popular and the teachers liked him as well. Joe was gentle. He didn't like arguing or fighting even when bullies challenged him. But at home, Joe didn't get along with Mr. Williams. I have no idea what fueled the animosity between them.

Mrs. Williams was cool towards me so I got the feeling that she would prefer me not being there.

Before Timothy was born she said to me, "After having you here I'm not sure I want this baby to be a girl." I hadn't done anything for her to dislike me. She never repeated it or said anything more. I was thankful she helped me take care of my hair because it had grown back long enough for me to put into a ponytail. Sometimes Mrs. Williams allowed me to roll it up and wear curls to church. Mrs. Williams wasn't mean to us, but there was something about her that reminded me of Aunt Lea. I panicked at the thought that she didn't want us there anymore. I didn't want to leave this foster home because I at least felt safe there. Mrs. Williams had a sister who lived close to us. She was an attractive woman who was a couple of years younger than Mrs. Williams. She had a cute two-year-old toddler named Rex. She didn't say hardly anything to me but she and Mrs. Williams talked for hours. I caught bits and pieces of their conversation. The soap operas were at the top of the list for gossip. I was usually left out of conversation so I retreated to my room.

That awful feeling of being the devil's child was slowly creeping back up. I was disappointed that all the praying and going to church did not stop the hair from growing on my body. One day I was taking a bath when Mrs. Williams walked in. I quickly covered myself with my hands because I didn't want her to see it. My heart was beating fast because I was scared. She looked at me and shook her head as I curled myself up in the tub with my hands still covering my private parts. After getting what she came for in the bathroom she left. I prayed that she hadn't seen anything. I believed if she knew about the hair growing on me she would have the social worker come and get me right away. I was relived when there was no indication that she saw anything.

A few months later she gave me a book to read about how my body was going to change. Nothing I read made sense to me because I didn't understand the big words in the book. I couldn't even pronounce menstruate. I got scared. The book didn't mention anything about hair growing. Did she know about me and was pretending she didn't? Over the next few weeks I avoided looking at her, believing she must know my secret. I prayed every night for God to get rid of the hair but it kept growing.

I finally got some matches and decided to burn the hair off of me. One day she walked into the bathroom after I left. I was in there burning my hair.

"What's that smell? She asked sniffing. I didn't say anything. She gave me a strange look, but I didn't say a word and quickly ran to my bedroom. After that I wouldn't do the burning until late at night. A few times I burnt my skin and had to endure painful blisters that finally healed.

I hated ironing. It was the worst chore on my list. I had to iron clothes for everyone in the house. Mr. Williams' shirts were always white and crisp. I made sure the pants were creased just right. I spent half of Saturday ironing clothes. I was glad that Mrs. Williams didn't make me iron sheets or underclothes.

Mrs. Williams cooked her best meals on Sunday. My mouth watered thinking of the deep-dish pies she baked. Pork chops were tender, chicken was fried crispy, and vegetables were tasty. I wanted to learn how to cook like her but she never taught me.

I would stand near the piano watching Ricky and Michael practicing. But it was Michael who showed me how to properly place my fingers on the keyboard. He showed how the notes worked and it didn't take long before I learned how to play a couple of Christmas songs. Ricky acted as if he didn't like to practice his lessons so I offered to do it for him, but I never did. I had to sneak to play the couple of songs I knew because I didn't want to get Mrs. Williams angry.

In the middle of the school year everything seemed to fall apart. The kids at school found out we were foster children and the harassment began.

"Foster kid! Foster kid! Foster kid! You're a creepy foster kid!" they chanted behind our backs as we walked home. I felt the shame all over again and hated the world. The kids didn't bother Ricky who strolled home with us. There were times when I wanted the ground to open and swallow me. I knew how mean and relentless kids could be. I had gone through that already at the other school. Their words hurt as bad as a sharp object being poked into me. We tried to ignore them by walking straight ahead and not saying anything, but that didn't stop them. We were pushed from behind. The more we ignored them the worse they became. Soon they were throwing rocks at us. Once they chased us all the way to our back door while rocks were flying past us. We got hit many times.

One day I decided that I wouldn't take the rock throwing, the name-calling, or the shoving and pushing anymore. I stopped and turned to face my enemies. They were all boys. Dennis was the ringleader and he sneered at me and pushed me down. I got up angry. Out of desperation I fought back, pulling, scratching, and punching. When we were finally pulled apart he was bleeding. It was the first time in my life I had ever fought back. It was also the day that I learned I could fight back. I got into a few more fights that semester because of the teasing, but the rock throwing stopped.

As nice as Joe was, it was hard to imagine the school kids turning against him. Joe didn't like fighting and avoided violence if he could. If he were cornered he would kick at the kids rather than fight. I got angry with him because I thought he was a big sissy. I started fighting his battles too because I was an angry girl. It never occurred to me that my brother just didn't want to hurt another kid.

Once again I was alone at school. I yearned for just one girl to be my friend. They avoided me because it was unpopular to be with the foster kid.

In Years To Come

Things weren't getting much better at home as days, weeks and months passed. Michael and Ricky were doing better than we were. They had their piano lessons, a new baby brother, hugs, kisses, and praises while all we did was exist in the house. Michael was getting straight A's on his report cards while I stayed an average student. Joe was a concern now because he had become withdrawn and very quiet. When we were alone he talked to us about leaving there. He believed that Mr. Williams didn't like him. While I agreed with Joe to leave deep down I wanted to stay. I didn't care that they treated me differently, I didn't care that Mrs. Williams acted as if she didn't want me around, and I didn't care that Michael and Ricky always reminded us of how much better they were. The only thing that mattered to me was that I wasn't being stripped naked and beaten like I was at Mr. and Mrs. Watson's house. I didn't have to worry about being molested either. I felt safe in this home. We ate three times a day and I had a bedroom of my own. The sores in my head had healed and the hair had grown back. Nothing else mattered.

Thanksgiving came and went with us celebrating with a big feast cooked solely by Mrs. Williams. It was close to Christmas-time so we were allowed to listen to Christmas songs on the radio. I sang along with the Christmas songs. A few times I sat down at the piano and played the two Christmas songs I knew, *Silent Night* and *Joy to the World*. Christmas was my favorite holiday. I remembered how Mother decorated her house with gold and silver. All the candy bowls had been filled with candy, peanuts, and chocolate. Mother had even hung mistletoe from the ceiling. It was the one time of the year that she would stay in a good mood. The scent of cinnamon, spice, and peppermint were overwhelming and bowls of fresh fruit spilled over. The outside of the house would be decorated with lights and shinning tinsel. The smell of pine from the fresh Christmas tree was welcoming and neatly wrapped presents were underneath it. Mother sure knew how to celebrate Christmas. We would tear our gifts open on Christmas morning, unwrapping clothes, toys, and other things. We didn't play with the toys long because Mother threw them away. Eventually those beautiful clothes we got were ripped off of us. Mother said she loved celebrating Christmas because it was Jesus' birthday.

I was sure that Christmas at the Williams's was going to be a greater event because Mr. Williams was a minister. I imagined nice gifts and how surprised all of us would be on Christmas morning. I wanted a doll to play with. It had been years since I played with a doll. I didn't care that my brothers thought I was too old for dolls. I was only eleven years old.

When Mr. Williams put the artificial tree up I was disappointed. It was small and looked like it had branches missing from it. The ugly tree sat on the end table in the living room. It was the smallest Christmas tree I'd ever seen. How were they going to fit gifts under it? It was decorated with small bulbs and a few lights. There were no flashing lights in the window either. The only indication in our house that Christmas was near was the tree and Christmas songs blasting from the radio. I still was being optimistic and looked forward to Christmas day.

We were usually out of the bed, washed up, and dressed by the time the family came downstairs. Dad went to work early in the morning. Michael was always rushing because he had to catch the bus and the rest of us waited until she cooked the oatmeal. On the weekends they came down whenever they wanted to. We could hear them moving around and the sound of the baby crying.

Christmas finally arrived. I had been looking forward to this day for weeks. On Christmas Eve I noticed a small wrapped gift tucked beneath the tree.

"They are going to put everything out tomorrow," I thought to myself. I had long gotten over that there was no real Santa Claus. I didn't blame them for putting gifts out on Christmas day; they probably assumed we were going to peek or unwrap the presents early. How would they know if we did? They were all upstairs. I got up early Christmas morning and met Joe and Ralph in the dining room. We looked at the small tree again and saw the same single gift.

"Where do you think the presents are?"

"They probably haven't brought them down yet."

We moved from the dining room to the kitchen, waiting for them to come down. We heard laughter floating downstairs. What were they doing up there? The laughing and noise kept going on for a long time.

It seemed we waited forever before they finally came downstairs. Michael was carrying Timothy, who was about three months old. I was amazed at how much they trusted him with the baby. I didn't want to appear eager so I waited for them to give us our gifts. That morning Mrs. Williams fixed a great breakfast. With each passing hour my disappointment grew, until someone finally gave Joe and Ralph the gift from under the tree. When they tore off the paper we saw a model car kit. Tears stung my eyes when I realized there was nothing under the tree for me. Ralph and Joe were disappointed about the cheap model car too. The only ones who didn't seem disappointed were Michael and Ricky. Did that mean they always celebrated Christmas like this? How could they be so content when they didn't get anything for Christmas? That's when I suspected that they had exchanged Christmas gifts upstairs without us. They had taken a long time to come downstairs, and I heard the laughter and playing.

I went to my bedroom and cried most of the day. Even though Mother was mean and abusive she always gave us gifts on Christmas.

The New Year came and we felt more divided than ever from the family. Timothy was getting bigger, but we were still not allowed to hold him. I watched Ricky, who was younger than me walk around the house carrying the baby. I watched the brothers play with him. Timothy smiled and made noises back to them. My birthday came and I turned twelve years old.

Joe was a thief. At least, that's what he was called by Mr.

Williams. It started when he stole a bag of cookies and ate them. Mr. Williams bought food in bulk including cookies. Joe was caught and confessed. Mr. Williams was angry so he took Joe upstairs to his study. We heard Joe's screams all over the house. That was the beginning of a deteriorating relationship between Joe and Mr. Williams, who didn't hide his feelings of anger and disgust towards Joe. I don't remember the first time I stole a cookie. I was getting up during the night to use the bathroom and passed through the kitchen to get there. Mrs. Williams kept the cookies inside of Tupperware containers. My stomach growled from hunger because we weren't getting enough to eat. I was able to reach the cookies that were on top of the refrigerator. I helped myself to the cookies and returned to my room to go back to sleep.

In the beginning it was just one or two, then three or four. When Mrs. Williams found out about the missing cookies she told Mr. Williams, and he confronted us at the dinner table. Mr. Williams had a lazy eye and sometimes when he looked at you it seemed like he was looking somewhere else. That evening at the dinner table Mr. Williams looked around at us. We could see anger in his eyes and when he spoke it reinforced our thoughts. He said each of our names asked us one by one if we stole the cookies. Ricky was sitting next to him on the left.

"Did you steal the cookies?" he asked him.

Ricky was quick to answer.

"No, I didn't do it."

"Michael, did you steal the cookies?"

"N-No. I-I didn't do it." Michael always stuttered when he was afraid or upset.

I felt my heart pounding long before he came to me.

"Joyce, did you steal cookies."

I was able to look him in the face and remain calm. In a controlled voice I said, "No sir, I didn't steal any cookies."

I was relieved when he moved to Ralph who was sitting next to me.

"Ralph, did you steal the cookies?" Ralph's eyes were large and unblinking.

"No, I didn't steal any cookies."

Joe was the last one in the circle. He sat directly across from Mr. Williams. I didn't look at him because I didn't want to see his face. I knew he was scared.

"Joe, did you steal the cookies?"

Joe looked around the table at us. I turned away from him because his eyes seemed to be silently pleading for someone to tell the truth. I couldn't look at him because of the guilt I felt.

"No," he whispered.

Mr. Williams' voice changed each time he asked Joe the same question.

"Joe did you steal the cookies?"

Again Joe denied it.

Mr. Williams became angrier each time Joe denied stealing the cookies. It sounded more like an accusation than a question. Joe was already crying when he answered, "No, sir," for the third or fourth time. Joe was asked over and over again about the cookies until he was finally ordered upstairs to the study.

Though I knew Joe wasn't responsible for the theft of the cookies, I never said a word as he was led upstairs to the study. I wanted to confess that I too had taken the cookies but I kept my silence and prayed that God would forgive me. The rest of us sat there looking at each other. Within minutes we could hear a scuffle and the sound of the belt hitting Joe's bare flesh. I cringed each time he cried out. I was the one who stole the cookies and Joe was getting punished or it.

When Joe came downstairs later his eyes were red and puffy from crying. His head was down and he wouldn't look at any of us. That night before I crawled into bed I got on my knees and prayed to God for forgiveness.

For a while I stopped stealing cookies, but the urge to eat something kept nagging me so I started stealing cookies again. Mr.

Williams didn't bother questioning us and Joe was the only one who was blamed for the missing cookies. After awhile I didn't worry about being caught for stealing cookies so I kept on doing it. Joe started confessing to stealing the cookies because it didn't matter whether he did it or not, he was going to get punished anyway.

Once they set a trap to catch Joe. I had stolen a package of cookies from the box in the basement. I ate a few and hid the package in the basement so I could go down there and snack on them.

When we came home for lunch my mind was on the cookies. Mrs. Williams fixed sandwiches and gave us a cookie. I was still hungry and thought about the cookies in the basement. Mrs. Williams sent Joe downstairs to look for something. I didn't have a reason to be in the basement so I grabbed a skirt and made up something about having to wash it. I wondered why she didn't want me to go in the basement, but she told me to hurry back upstairs. Anyway, I saw Joe down there and when his back was turned to me I quickly grabbed a few cookies out of the hidden package, threw the skirt in the washer and hurried back upstairs to where Mrs. Williams and the others were waiting. When Joe came back upstairs it was time to go back to school.

That evening after dinner Dad looked directly across at Joe. "I don't even have to ask you, do I?" his words cut through the air like a knife.

A surprised look covered Joe's face.

"You stole more cookies?"

"I didn't do it," Joe said weakly.

"I know you did it!" He yelled at him. "We set a trap to find out if you did it." I winced as he told about the missing package of cookies and how they found it hidden in the basement. "We wanted to see if you would sneak back into the cookies because we already counted them. And as sure as I'm sitting here four more cookies are missing. You were the only one in the basement this afternoon."

Joe shook his head in denial while tears filled his eyes.

My throat tightened. That was why Mrs. Williams didn't want me to go in the basement. I was nervous because I was sure that she was going to mention that I was also in the basement, but she never did.

"You were the only one down there!" he screamed at Joe. "We purposely sent you down to the basement just to see if you would eat more cookies."

Joe kept shaking his head in denial while Mr. Williams continued to talk. I wanted to speak up. I wanted to confess, but the anger I saw in Mr. Williams frightened me. He had never hit me before, but I was certain he would make an exception this time. I reasoned with myself that the whipping Joe was getting now was nothing compared to what I went through when we lived with Mother.

But the whippings Joe got from Mr. Williams were getting longer and harder. Mr. Williams stopped in between hitting Joe to talk to him. Then the beating would start up again. Hours passed before Joe would come downstairs.

I felt bad about what was happening to Joe so I stopped stealing cookies. When cookies began disappearing again I was surprised because I wasn't doing it and neither was Joe. Who was stealing cookies this time? All of us were eyeing each other as if to ask the same question. It never occurred to me that all of us were stealing cookies; we knew that Joe would get blamed. I never found out for sure who else was stealing but I suspected Michael and Ricky.

"I want to leave" Joe kept telling me. I agreed to leave with him although I really didn't want to go. Everyone in the house felt the tension between Joe and Mr. Williams who acted as if he hated Joe. They couldn't even look at each other without the obvious distaste.

Joe became depressed. He didn't talk to anyone except Ralph and me. He barely ate his food. At church he went through the motions but it was clear that he wasn't happy. He wanted to leave.

"I'm running away," Joe told me.

"Where are you going?"

Joe didn't know where he was going. He just wanted to leave. When he came up missing Mr. Williams questioned us about it. I didn't know where Joe was. I suggested that perhaps he went back to Mother's house. I don't know what made me say that. I didn't really believe he would go back there. I just thought maybe that would throw them off-track.

Ralph saw Joe around the school a couple of days later. He told Ralph that he was staying nearby with a friend. A few days later Joe returned home. When our social worker visited us we had a long talk with him without Mr. and Mrs. Williams in the room. Joe told him he wanted to leave and the social worker agreed to work on moving him.

Joe was talking about running away again.

"I'm going to find Uncle Ben. I hate foster homes and foster parents. I want to live with my own family," he said.

Going back to live with Uncle Ben didn't seem like a good idea to me. The torture we suffered from Nate was still in the back of my mind.

"They don't want us," I reminded Joe. I couldn't believe that after all we went through he actually wanted to go back there.

"They don't want us here either." His face was serious when he spoke.

Despite everything they had done to Joe and the way they made me feel rejected I still liked living with them. I enjoyed going to church and reading books. I even liked Ricky and Michael. I knew things were not equal and I didn't feel like a member of the family. I kept these feelings to myself.

Joe decided enough was enough. The stealing continued and so did the whippings.

"Let's run away after school," he told me one day.

In Years To Come

That afternoon we avoided Ricky and met on the playground to plan our get-away. Joe masterminded a plan to run away.

"We can go live with Uncle Ben," he told us. "I've already talked to him he said we can come back."

I looked up to Joe not only as my big brother but also as someone who really cared about me. He always thought about us even though things were rough for him.

We left after school and followed him to Uncle Ben's house. Uncle Ben wasn't home, so Joe took us in another direction and we ended up on Vilet Street at Ike's tavern. I was reluctant to go into the tavern at first, but Joe told us relatives were inside.

The musty smell of liquor filled my nostrils as I waited for my eyes to adjust to the darkness. I heard our names being called. Sitting on a stool at the end of the bar was Lucille and Cousin Liza. I hadn't seen Lucille since Papa's funeral. She seemed happy to see us and listened while we told her about our foster home. It was Joe who had all the bad things to say about it. She was shaking her head as we updated her about our foster home.

I didn't talk much to Cousin Liza; I remembered the rumors I heard about Bro Tot being Louie's father. Liza avoided me anyway and I always believed that she didn't like me. We were excited to be among family anyway. She was shaking her head as we described some of the things we had gone through.

"Can't we just stay here?" Joe was begging.

I had mixed feelings about living there. Lucille took us upstairs to the apartment over the tavern. Ike was living there. Cousin Liza and Bro Tot had their own tavern on Fond du Lac Street. The noise from the tavern filtered upstairs.

"I don't know what to do," Cousin Liza told us. Lucille offered us something to eat, and we were eating when men wearing long white trench coats walked through the door. I knew immediately that they were detectives. It was the same thing all over again.

202

"I'm sorry, but you can't stay here." Lucille said. It didn't surprise me as much as it did Joe.

"Can you believe she called the police on us?" Joe asked me later.

I could only smile because it wasn't the first time. I hadn't forgotten about the time we left Mother's house barefoot.

"They don't want us," I reminded him.

Joe was defensive, even then. "I will go to live with Uncle Ben. He wants us, and he always wanted us. I would rather stay with my own people than in foster homes. They are not our family."

I knew there was some truth in Joe's words. "Mr. and Mrs. Williams don't even treat us like we are part of the family. Look what they are doing to us. We have to stay downstairs while they're doing other things upstairs with their own children. And we can't even touch the baby. They act like we are going to hurt the baby. You are a girl and she should want you to help with the baby." His eyes narrowed. "All you do is stay in that little room. Everything that Joe said was true, but I didn't care. I still wanted to stay.

Mr. and Mrs. Williams were upset about us running away. Mr. Williams showed his anger with a lot of words directed mainly towards Joe, who was still determined to leave.

I wanted to make up for running away, but there wasn't anything I could do. It was then that Mrs. Williams confessed to me that she never wanted to be a foster parent for older children anyway. She had asked the people at child welfare for younger children.

"The only reason you're here is because they didn't have any other place to take you." She made it sound as if the child welfare didn't give her a choice. It was clear even though her words were painful.

Joe asked the social worker to remove him from the Williams' house. I didn't want to leave, but I couldn't bear the thought of being apart from Joe. Ralph had already agreed to go with Joe; I was the only one who was reluctant. I suggested that we attempt to get in touch with our Grandma Irene in Mississippi with hopes that she would change her mind about us. She never responded to any letters I wrote, and in the end I agreed to move back in with Uncle Ben and Aunt Lea. It was one of the most tormented decisions I had ever made.

Joe left a month before school was out because he couldn't stay there any longer. It was hard watching him pack his clothes. It didn't seem right that he would be leaving without us. I agreed with the social worker that Ralph and I should stay until school was out then join Joe at Uncle Ben and Aunt Lea's house.

When Joe said good-bye he reminded us, "We need to live with our real family."

Ralph and I stayed until the end of the school year. I wasn't as brave as Joe, and my feelings of sorrow were evident in my face, voice and tears. It was hard to believe so much had happened in a short year. The following school year I would be going into the seventh grade. I had already asked Mr. and Mrs. Williams to send me to the same school where Michael was going, but they told me that I couldn't go there. Joe and I would be going to the junior high school in our district.

"Michael doesn't have to go to that school," I reminded them.

"Don't question me anymore," Mrs. Williams said in an irritated voice.

I went into my room and cried into my pillow. Why didn't she want me to go to a good school like Michael? Did she think I was dumb? Pain mixed with anger gripped me. How could she think that Michael was so much better than I was? How dare she reject me? I felt defeated. I had tried for a year to win her approval but all I received was rejection after rejection.

It was heartbreaking to leave my bedroom and I had become attached to my foster brothers, especially Michael. The jealousy I felt in the beginning was now gone and I had started admiring his knowledge. It was a tearful departure as I clung to each of them. I was going to miss them.

"I don't ever want foster children again." The words came from Mrs. Williams and I felt a chilling feeling.

Mr. Williams favored Ralph so I knew that if he could keep any of us it would be him. At least Ralph had someone who cared about him.

I took one last look at the brown house. It was hard to believe we were on our way back to where we really belonged, with our real family. I imagined Uncle Ben's smiling face. I sat back in my seat while Ralph talked with the social worker about his future plans. I decided I wouldn't share my true feelings with anyone.

The last face I saw before we pulled away from the curb was Michael's. He was standing in the doorway watching us. I would be back to visit them.

Mr. Webber was looking straight ahead when I began talking.

"I want you to know that every bad thing that we ever said about Uncle Ben and Aunt Lea wasn't true."

He turned to look at me for a moment and smiled.

Chapter Six

Back to Uncle Ben's House

The house on Hadley Street hadn't changed during the years we were gone. When we pulled up in front of the house it felt strange and I was still apprehensive about being back. I couldn't forget about when Uncle Ben had left us alone, cold, dirty, and hungry. The memories rushed back as soon as I walked through the front door.

"Don't think about those times," Joe told me when I mentioned it to him. "Things are different now." He was right. Things were different. At least we were back with family. Ralph didn't seem to care that Uncle Ben and Aunt Lea had sent him away so I decided that I would try to forget what happened too.

"I've missed you," Aunt Lea said, hugging me.

That evening Ralph, Joe, and I took turns telling Uncle Ben about our life over the past four years.

"I'll never let you live with strangers again," Uncle Ben promised.

When I saw Nate the old, familiar feeling came back. He looked much different now. He was taller than Uncle Ben, but he wasn't skinny. He looked even more intimidating than before. He had already graduated from high school and was working and

206

getting paid a lot of money. To my surprise he smiled at me.

"Hi Joyce," he said.

I smiled back. "Hi".

"Wait until you see Nate's new car," Joe said. Nate took us to the back of the house to see his car. It was a shiny black sports car that looked new.

"It goes fast," Joe remarked.

Joe told us later that Nate took him riding on his days off from work.

"We're friends now," he said in Nate's defense.

Uncle Ben worked downtown at the Plankinton Hotel. I admired the dark blue suit with yellow trim that he wore to work. Nobody could say, "Yes suh," the way Uncle Ben could. His smile charmed many people, so Uncle Ben brought home lots of tips. Aunt Lea worked in a downtown Department Store.

Uncle Ben told us that we were old enough to take care of ourselves while they were at work and we did. I knew how to do everything from fixing sandwiches to ironing clothes. I could clean a house better than most women. The one thing I didn't know how to do was take care of my hair. I watched Aunt Lea press her hair using a small mirror so I decided to do it too. I put the hot comb over the gas flame and waited until it was hot. I rubbed it on the tissue the way I had seen it done over the years. When I brought the comb through my hair I could hear it sizzle as my hair turned brown.

"You burnt your hair," Aunt Lea told me when she noticed it. By the third week I had burnt a lot of my hair so my ponytail was shorter. Nate was nice to us so I gradually began to trust him. It was good that Nate's focus was not on us. He was dating now, so when he wasn't working he was driving girls around in his new car. We went along with him when he took the girl next door to the Lake Front. I was afraid of the lake so I sat on the beach watching the others play in the water. Sometimes Nate took us to Burger King because he loved eating the whopper hamburgers they served.

Going to Burger King was a treat because we had never eaten hamburgers from a stand before. My eyes were wide with surprise when I saw how big those whoppers were.

"Nate must have a lot of money," I whispered to Joe after he had bought us food from Burger King.

When I first returned to Uncle Ben's house I was reading the Bible and praying everyday. Joe and Ralph didn't care about reading the Bible so they were outside playing most of the time.

One day I laid the Bible down and walked outside onto the porch. I could smell the scent of fresh cut grass. The sun was hot but felt good on my skin. I walked off the porch onto the sidewalk and continued walking to the end of the block. It had been years since I could do this. Then it dawned on me that I could play outside anytime I wanted to. I could walk to the corner store and buy candy if I wanted to. And I could eat it. The whole thing hit me like I was waking up from a dream. I never picked the Bible up again that summer.

Aunt Lea had to make me come inside every night because I wanted to stay out as long as I could. I became friends with the girls on the block and enjoyed jumping rope, playing jacks or just sitting on someone's porch talking. The sound of music was refreshing too. Nate had a lot of new records and when he put them on the record player I wanted the volume all the way up. I danced while Ike and Tina Tuner, James brown, Aretha Franklin, and Stevie Wonder blasted from the record player.

We could watch anything we wanted on TV so we never missed an episode of *Batman and Robin*. It was one of the television shows that were forbidden in the Williams house.

Things were going well until Little Ben moved in with us. I heard that he had been discharged from the Army after claiming a hardship.

Little Ben had surgery and came to our house to recuperate. I watched him lying on the couch in the den day after day. It didn't seem right that he was in our house when he had his own family across town. Little Ben was shorter than his siblings and was on the heavy side. He looked more like Aunt Lea than Uncle Ben. He wasn't mean to us, but I didn't like running to the store to get him cigarettes, soda or whatever snacks he wanted. He seemed lazy to me because he only moved off the couch to go to the bathroom. I wasn't even sure how often he took a bath or shower because there was a musty odor in the den. I didn't like him being there because he interrupted everything. We had to watch whatever he wanted to watch on TV.

He had been there a couple of weeks when his wife Emma came to the house. She was pregnant again. They already had four or five children and were living in the projects. Emma was dark with silky smooth skin and a round face. I stared at her large belly that was sticking out.

"Is Ben here?" she asked me.

I nodded my head and let her inside of the house.

Aunt Lea was in the kitchen and stopped what she was doing when she saw Emma.

"What do you want?" Aunt Lea's voice was loud and rude.

"I want to talk to my husband," Emma answered bluntly.

I didn't know what to make of this situation. I was aware Little Ben was married, but this was the first time I had seen his wife.

Aunt Lea rambled on about Little Ben being sick and needing to rest. But Emma was determined to see her husband, so she walked past Aunt Lea into the den where Little Ben was propped up on the couch smoking a cigarette. In the next few minutes an argument broke out.

"You need to come home."

"He's not going home!" Aunt Lea screamed at her.

"You're spoiling him. That's why he doesn't work," Emma spat at her. "He needs to be home with his family."

In Years To Come

I listened while the two of them went back and forth arguing about Little Ben. I felt sorry for Emma, who ended up leaving without him. He told her he couldn't rest at home because of the children. She was crying when she left through the back door. How could he do that to her? It was hard for me to like him after what I had just witnessed. He didn't seem to care about his wife or children. He turned over on the couch and went to sleep as if nothing had happened. It was a couple of weeks before Little Ben went back home.

Aunt Lea and Uncle Ben had a fight and she called the police on him. I watched as the police took him away. Uncle Ben came home later that evening. I prayed that they wouldn't fight again. It scared me when they fought and I was sure that Uncle Ben was going to hurt her. I had to agree with Joe that living with them now was much better than before.

I can't remember when the riots started but everyone was talking about it. We saw the uproar on TV. They showed people in different states marching in the streets and holding up signs. They showed militant groups like The Black Panthers and The Black Stone Rangers speaking out against injustice. They also showed protesters being beaten and arrested.

"What are the people doing?" I asked.

"They are marching for freedom," Nate told me.

"Why?"

"Because white people still treat us like we are slaves."

I remember reading about slavery in a book I got from the library.

Black people in Milwaukee wanted freedom too. Father Groppi was the priest of Saint Boniface Catholic Church located in the black neighborhood. Father Groppi was white but he helped gather people at the church to do freedom marches. I was curious about the freedom marches and decided to go to St. Boniface one afternoon. I didn't bother telling Uncle Ben or Aunt Lea. I walked to the church, and sure enough there seemed to be

210

millions of people lined up and eager to march. Uncle Ben had warned us to stay away from the marches.

I was amazed at the large crowd of people and impressed by the freedom signs they carried.

When the crowd started moving I fell into place and began marching with them. I wanted to march for freedom too.

"Where are we going?" I asked one of the ladies.

"We are going to march to the south side of town," she answered me.

"Why are we going to the south side of town?"

The woman smiled at me. "This is a freedom march and we want to have the freedom to live anywhere in this city we want to."

I smiled back at her.

It didn't take me long to learn the freedom song they were singing either.

"Oh, Freedom, Oh, Freedom over me and before I be a slave I'll lay down in my grave and go home to my Lord and be free."

The police were riding on motorcycles beside us as we marched towards the other side of town.

I walked bravely, swinging my arms and singing with the crowd. It was fun being in the freedom march until I saw the faces of the angry mob that had gathered along the sidewalks.

"Go back to the ghetto, niggers," someone shouted.

"Get your black asses out of my neighborhood," another person shouted.

There were many nasty comments made by the white people.

I stopped singing and started watching them. The women, men and even young children had smirks on their faces as we passed by. The racial remarks got worse.

I saw people spitting on the marchers. Some threw rocks at us so we had to duck to keep from getting hit. Now I was ready to go back home. I was scared of what the white people would do to us. Suddenly a loud noise could be heard. It sounded like something was blowing up.

"A sniper!" someone shouted, and some marchers started running. I ran as fast as my legs could carry me. I couldn't hear the singing anymore. I didn't slow down until I was back safely on our side of town.

When we arrived back at the church the crowd was angry.

"This was supposed to be a peaceful march," one man said.

Father Groppi talked to them. It was suppose to be peaceful, but apparently someone wanted to make trouble.

I slipped away from the church and hurried home.

"Where have you been?" Uncle Ben's face was solemn and his anger was frightening.

"I went on a freedom march," I whispered.

"A what?"

"I went on a freedom march with…."

Before I could get all the words out, Uncle Ben grabbed me and started whipping me with a belt he already had in his hand.

"I don't want you going on no damn freedom marches," he yelled between hitting me with the belt.

"I told you not to get involved in that mess."

I never went back again, but the unrest in our city escalated. Riots broke out and a lot of businesses in the black neighborhoods were burnt down. We were put under curfew and the national guards walked the streets in an effort to keep order in the city.

Rev. Martin Luther King was on TV talking about racial tension and riots were breaking out in cities all over the United States. Someone mentioned that the Black Panthers were coming to Milwaukee to help organize something in black community. I was curious to find out about it but Uncle Ben had warned me not to get involved.

I had been outside playing all day when I walked into the house for a glass of water. The phone rang. We were allowed to answer the phone so I did it every chance I got.

"Hello," I said into the phone.

"Hi," a woman's voice replied. "I would like to speak to Stephen Ford."

"Stephen?"

"Yes."

"That's my brother, but he's not here."

"Do you know where he is?"

I thought about it for a minute. I didn't know where Stephen was. "No"

"Are your parents there?"

That was a crazy question. I thought about it for a minute too.

"My parents are dead", I told the woman. There was silence on the other end of the phone.

"I'm calling because Stephen has been drafted into the US Army and he needs to report."

My hands were shaking when I put the phone down. All the memories about Michael came flooding back. He was drafted too and went to Vietnam where he got killed. I didn't want Stephen to go to Vietnam.

I told Uncle Ben about the phone call from the lady.

"Stephen is in Colorado," he said.

It was mid-summer when another call came to Uncle Ben's house about a different brother. I answered it, and a woman's voice on the other end began speaking.

"May I please speak with Henry Ford?"

"He's not here," I told her.

"Do you know when he will be in?"

"Henry doesn't live here. He's my brother, but he lives in Indianapolis."

"This is the social security office calling. We have a check in the amount of three thousand dollars for Henry."

I almost dropped the phone. That was a lot of money. Henry was going to be rich.

"He's not here," I told the lady.

"If you see Henry tells him he needs to get in touch with the social security office."

"Okay."

When Uncle Ben came home I told him about the phone call from the lady at the social security office.

"I'll take care of it," he said. "I'll give Sister a call."

The end of the summer came quickly that year and it was time to go back to school. It was my first year in junior high. I was in the seventh grade and enrolled in the school that Mr. and Mrs. Williams refused to allow Michael to attend. I preferred walking to school with my new girlfriends rather than taking the city bus because it was always crowded with undisciplined boys and girls. They would scream from the windows when the bus passed those of us who were walking to school. The school was several blocks away, but it didn't take us long to get there.

Robert Fulton junior High was a fairly new school, but had a reputation for being rough. It was a predominantly black inner-city school. Junior high school was a big adjustment for me. I had to keep up with so many things. I was loaded down with books from several classes that were on a class schedule. It was different from sitting in one classroom with one teacher day after day.

Joe was in my homeroom class and we were seated in alphabetical order by last names so he sat directly in front of me.

Joe was a joker, which is why everyone liked him. I remember he took a big bite out of my beautiful shiny red apple I had set on my desk. I was devastated when I saw the chunk missing out of my apple. The kids thought it was funny. At the time none of them knew Joe was my brother so when I reacted by hollering at him they laughed even more. After a few weeks I got used to the different classes and teachers.

My girlfriends and I stopped at the corner store one morning to buy candy to take to school when we decided to buy a pack of cigarettes.

"Let's put our money together and get a pack," Karen suggested. Cigarettes were twenty-five cents out of the machine. I was always curious to try smoking so I went along with them. We bought a pack of Winstons because they were the most popular. I put the cigarette in my mouth and puffed on it like I had seen Uncle Ben. I didn't finish the cigarette because it made me sick. The next day my friends smoked more cigarettes. I tried to smoke again, but the smell was bad so I quit and didn't try anymore.

I met Melody one day while I was walking to school and was lagging behind the others. I noticed her because she was walking alone. Melody was a tall, dark-skinned girl with oval eyes and long brown hair. I was fascinated with her hair because I had never seen that hair color hair on someone with her skin tone. Melody told me she hated her hair because people were always noticing it. Gradually I stopped walking with the other girls who were now smoking cigarettes everyday. I liked Melody because she was humorous and kept me laughing all the way to school. She became my best friend.

Uncle Ben and Aunt Lea were fighting again. They had fought a few times that I had witnessed over the summer. I felt something bad was going on between them when I walked into the den. Uncle Ben was sitting in a chair mumbling to him. I could always tell when he was angry because his mouth twisted in a weird way. Aunt Lea was in the kitchen cooking dinner. I was sitting on the floor of the living room when Aunt Lea walked in. She started shouting at Uncle Ben from the doorway.

"I'm not afraid of you!" she screamed at him.

Uncle Ben got up from the chair and walked into the

215

living room where she was standing. I held my breath as I watched them scream at each other. Uncle Ben's fist was balled up. It looked like he was ready to strike but Aunt Lea didn't move.

"Hit me if you want to! I'm not afraid of you anymore. Go on hit me if that's what you want to do!" Aunt Lea's fist was balled up too.

Oh, my God! They were going to fight.

Uncle Ben hit her in the nose. Blood started pouring out of her nose and dripping down on the white blouse she wore. Aunt Lea screamed and ran towards the back door, which Joe was holding open. Uncle Ben started chasing her, but Joe slammed the door when Uncle Ben approached it. I heard Aunt Lea screaming all the way down the alley. When Uncle Ben got outside she had disappeared. He went back into the den and waited for her to come home.

Neither Aunt Lea nor Nate came home that night. When we came home from school the next day the social worker was waiting for us.

"I couldn't leave you here," Uncle Ben said. I refused to believe we were leaving. Why was this happening to us again? It was like living in the twilight zone.

We went upstairs and packed our clothes. I was angry with Uncle Ben and didn't bother saying good-bye. As much as I wanted to I didn't cry either. I didn't bother looking back as we drove away.

"Where are we going?" I asked Mr. Nugent, our new social worker. He was a short man with a brown hair.

"To another foster home," he said.

I saw Joe tense up. I felt sorry for him because he believed so much in family and thought we were going to be with Uncle Ben and Aunt Lea forever. The car parked in front of a big green house. The yard was nice and the flowers were pretty.

The woman who answered the door was short, with sagging jaws and she wore a light brown wig.

"This is Mrs. Guy," Mr. Nugent said introducing us to her. I stared at the woman. She was old. An old man with gray hair and baggy eyes was sitting in a chair in the living room.

"Hello Mr. Guy," Mr. Nugent said to him. Joe, Ralph and I sat down on the couch together. I kept staring at the old couple. These were our new foster parents. One thing I knew for sure was that they were not going to beat us. Joe must have been thinking the same thing because he burst out laughing. Mrs. Guy just smiled at us.

Chapter Seven

Mr. and Mrs. Guy

Mr. and Mrs. Guy looked like foster *grandparents.* Maybe Mr. Guy had been taller at one time, but when I first laid eyes on him I saw him as a shrunken old man. His hair was completely gray with a few thinning areas. His hands were dry and shriveled up. When he smiled I thought his teeth looked too big for his mouth. One day he didn't have any teeth at all, so they must have been dentures. When he walked his pace was so slow that I would watch to see if he was going to make it to his destination.

Jeanette Guy didn't look as old as her husband and moved around faster than he did. The brown wig covered up her gray hair but she still had signs of aging. She talked constantly so I learned how to tune her out. Their house was a large two-story duplex with an upstairs and downstairs, but they used the entire house for themselves. He outside of the house was painted a light green with darker green trim around the windows and doors. The large porch wrapped around the entire front of the house. The yard in the front had a steep slope and the back yard was big.

Mrs. Guy was a neat person. Her house was well organized inside and tastefully decorated. While Mr. Nugent talked with Mr. and Mrs. Guy I looked around the living room and immediately

218

spotted a light colored cabinet with a TV inside. It was a beautiful piece of furniture. When I found out later that the TV was color I couldn't believe my luck. This was the first time I lived anywhere with a real color TV in the house. It didn't take long to realize that the TV set was for Mr. Guy, who watched it all day. He was retired from his job so he was at home all the time.

Watching TV in color was like being at the movies. I was amazed at how different everything looked. I especially loved The NBC peacock that showed beautiful colors when it spread its wing. There were some shows that Mr. Guy watched that I also liked. *I Dream of Jeannie*'s bottle was a pretty blue and her outfits were very colorful. It was the same with all my other favorite TV shows *Petticoat junction, Gilligan's Island,* and *The Beverly Hillbillies.* I got up early on Saturday mornings to watch cartoons in color. I never knew that Wilma Flintstone's hair was red or Barney Rubble's was blonde. Watching color TV was the best thing about living with them. I became a TV addict like Mr. Guy.

Joe and I didn't have to change schools because we were in the same school district even though we were further away. Ralph attended the elementary school down the street.

When I first walked into the bedroom that was next to the kitchen I didn't expect it to be so large. The walls had flowered wallpaper with a dark red background with window curtains to match. A light wood full size bed with a matching dresser gave the room an expensive look. Mrs. Guy told me it was my bedroom all to myself. I had never slept in a bed so big before nor had I ever been in such a large bedroom. I liked it.

Joe and Ralph had their own bedrooms upstairs. While looking through my new bedroom, I came across the picture of a girl who was smiling. She looked a lot like Sara. I picked it up for a closer look. It *was* Sara. When I showed the picture to Mrs. Guy she admitted that Sara had been living with them since we left the Watson foster home. Mrs. Guy smiled after seeing the surprised look on my face. The social worker never mentioned that Sara also lived there.

"She will be here on her next school break," Mrs. Guy said. I found other things that belonged to my sister, but I was careful not to bother them. Sara was protective about her things and I didn't want to upset her. I looked forward to the day when I would see her. It had been awhile.

I got involved with a gang of girls at school who had reputations of being tough. I wanted to fit in even though I knew they were not the right group. They also wanted me to be part of their group after seeing me beat up a girl after school one day. I got into a few more fights that my new friends pushed me into. They cheered me on and I fought with all my might. They called me Sonny Liston and I liked it.

One day while walking back to my seat in class one of my new friends whispered to me. "She was talking about your mama."

"Who was talking about my mama?" I acted the way I was supposed to. I pretended to be angry and balled my fist to let her know I was ready to fight the person. I knew it was all a set-up to get me to fight. "Who called my mama a name?" I asked her.

She pointed to a girl in the corner of the room. I knew immediately who she was because of the long brown hair. I looked at Melody and when her dark eyes met mine I looked away. I knew she would never say anything about my mama because she was one of the few people who knew I didn't have one. We went our separate ways because Melody didn't want anything to do with my new friends, but I still liked her.

"She better watch her mouth," I told Wanda. "Or next time I'll kick her ass."

"You are going to let her get away with it?"

I knew she was urging me to fight. I didn't want to fight Melody.

"If she says it again I'm going to get her."

"Oooh! She said it again!"

Wanda eyed at me with a crooked smile on her face. Her

hands were folded across her chest. She was the one I had to impress and if she wanted me to fight someone I was suppose to do it. She popped her gum loud enough to cause me to jump.

I knew what I had to do.

I walked over to Melody.

"Did you call my mama a name?"

Our eyes locked. We both knew what was happening. Melody looked away without saying anything.

"Meet me after school," I said to the cheers of my new friends.

The day seemed to drag as I waited for the time to come. I didn't want to fight Melody and was trying to think of what I could do to get out of it.

My friends were waiting for me after school and Melody was walking home by herself. My friends were walking behind me when I approached her.

"I don't want to fight," Melody said turning around to look directly at me.

I didn't know how to respond.

"Hit that bitch!" the crowd was yelling.

My arms felt heavy. I didn't want to fight her. A part of me wanted to run in the other direction. Suddenly I was shoved from behind and pushed into Melody so I began hitting her. I didn't think about what I was doing as I punched her over and over again. When it was over Melody lay on the sidewalk, her face puffy and lips bleeding. The blouse she wore was torn exposing her bra and she was crying. I couldn't believe I did this to her. I felt terrible as I stood over the girl who was once my best friend.

"You know I never did anything to you," Melody whispered through trembling lips. I ran away from the crowd, my own eyes filled with tears. I could hear them yelling. "Sonny Liston, Sonny Liston!"

When I returned to school the next day I was called into the principal's office where I denied everything. They couldn't do anything to me because I wasn't on school grounds when the fight occurred and no one pointed the finger at me except Melody. At lunchtime my friends hovered around me and I told them I was finished fighting. They continued to provoke fights between me and other girls, but when I refused to fight they no longer wanted me with their crowd.

Being an outcast was like going through a death sentence. No one talked to me. No one wanted to be my friend. Melody didn't even look at me, much less talk to me. I wanted so badly to apologize to her.

At the same time I was getting pressure from my gym teacher because I refused to participate in gym class. The hair growing on my body was now visible and I couldn't do anything to stop it. I was determined not to embarrass or humiliate myself by taking my clothes off. What would the girls think of me when they saw what was happening to me? Mother had said it was a curse and she was right.

"Are you going to join us today?" Ms. Calder asked me when I walked in.

"No," I said and took my usual place on the floor near the wall.

"Why don't you get dressed and join us?"

"I don't have a gym suit," I answered.

Ms. Calder was a tall black woman in her twenties with muscles like a man. She had long black hair that she wore pulled back in a ponytail.

"You can't continue to come in here and just sit," she said.

I leaned back against the wall. I couldn't participate in gym because it meant I would have to change clothes and take a shower. I couldn't let them find out about my secret. Just the thought that they would find out about it scared me. I couldn't let them know that I was cursed.

Ms. Calder didn't say anything else to me as I watched the other girls run through the gym doing exercises or playing basketball. They looked like they were having fun and I wished I could join them. Sometimes they would glance over at me sitting on the floor and I would look away.

One day I walked into the gym and Ms. Calder was waiting for me.

"I have something for you," she said. I stared at the blue gym suit in her hand.

"Take it and get dressed", she demanded holding it out to me.

My hands were shaking as I took the gym suit from her. All the girls had dressed and were gone when I went into the locker room so I slipped into the gym suit.

When I walked back into the gym the girls cheered and I felt myself smile. The exercises were fun and then we played basketball. I was having so much fun that I was sorry when the bell rang. The other girls rushed to the showers while I poked around. I wasn't going to take a shower.

Ms. Calder noticed me standing around when I should have been showering.

"That didn't hurt did it?"

I shook my head.

"Okay. Now get in the shower", she said.

"I'm not taking a shower," I said to her.

"You have to take a shower."

I shook my head. "I am not taking a shower."

"Here we go again," she said staring at me. "What the hell is wrong with you?"

Frustrated and fed up with my attitude she grabbed me. I fought, kicked and cried as she pulled me into the shower room.

Panic set in as I saw the girls watching me. I imagined myself being taunted and talked about once my secret was uncovered. I fought as hard as I could.

Ms. Calder was bigger and stronger than me and determined to get me into the shower.

"Help me with her", she told another student.
With the help of the other girl she pulled me into the shower room.
I pleaded to Ms. Calder not to make me take a shower.

"Take off that gym suit or I'll do it for you!" she yelled at me.
Being sore from the rough treatment I slowly peeled off the gym
suit, stopping at my underwear.

"I want to keep them on," I said. To my surprise she allowed
me to wear them into the showers. I stepped into the steaming hot
showers where four other girls were showering. When I turned to
look at them my mouth fell open and I was unable to speak. My
head felt as if it were spinning. I looked from one girl to the other
trying to understand what was going on.

"What are you staring at?" One of the girls asked me as I
backed away from them.

"Maybe she likes girls," the other girl said.

"Dyke," she spat at me.

I shook my head and felt the warm water on my face as I
sank to the floor.

"Why did she do this to me?" I repeated over and over until
Ms. Calder came into the shower area.

"She told me I was the devil's child, and I was cursed," I
cried.

By that time the other girls had gotten out of the shower and
were wondering what was wrong with me.

Ms. Calder sent them away and turned to me.

"Why did she tell me all those lies?" I asked her.

She helped me out of the shower and sat me on a bench.

"Why?" I kept repeating over and over.

"I'm sorry," she began, "I shouldn't have...."

"It's not you," I whispered.

"Then who is it?"

I told Ms. Calder what Mrs. Watson had told me when I first
started growing hair on my body. I told her how scared I was and
how I tried to get it off by scrubbing, burning, and cutting myself.

Ms. Calder held me close to her.

"What is happening to your body is normal. You saw the other girls in the shower so you know that it's not a curse on you. I don't know why your foster mother told you those lies." Mrs. Calder held me until I stopped crying.

"I don't understand why anyone would poison a child's mind unless they were evil themselves."

I was relieved to know that I wasn't cursed or the devil's child.

Something inside of me had changed after that episode in the gym. I never told any of the girls why I acted the way I did. Some of the girls told other kids in school so it felt like everyone was looking at me differently. I felt alone again. I started ditching classes, not wanting to go to school anymore. I became increasingly rebellious towards Mrs. Guy who received several notices about my attitude in school and missing classes. I hung out in the bathroom with the other girls who didn't want to go to classes. They were putting on makeup and brushing or combing their hair. Some changed clothes, others just gossiped. I sat on the toilet, jumping every time someone walked through the door.

After being busted a few times in the bathroom for ditching class, I decided it wasn't a good idea to stay around the school so I walked to a park or a nearby store. There were truant officers patrolling the streets looking for kids ditching school. I was constantly looking over my shoulders.

It wasn't long before I wasn't attending any of my classes. Those who ditched classes said that I should hang around a nearby high school where I could blend in with the other students. In high school some of the students had unscheduled class periods and they used that time to sit outside on the grass. I felt it was safe for me to be there so I would find a nice spot on the grass and reminisce in the fresh fall air.

I didn't miss going to school because I had grown to hate it. I didn't have any friends anymore and what happened in gym class left me feeling stupid.

"You're going to flunk!" a teacher yelled at me one day.

I didn't care if I flunked because being away from the school made me feel better.

I was sitting on the lawn at North Division High School when I noticed three girls sitting nearby. They kept looking in my direction, making me feel uncomfortable. One of them was a tall, skinny, light-skinned girl who wore glasses. Another one was shorter than me with a short afro and the last girl was dark-skinned with her hair pulled back in a small ponytail. The short girl had large eyes that stared at me. I looked away and hoped that they wouldn't bother me. Their laughter floated in my direction.

"They're laughing at me," I thought. I stood up, ready to move away when the tall, skinny one called me over. I was hesitant and didn't move until the short one came over to me.

"Why don't you come over and join us?" She was smiling and she looked friendly.

I followed her to where the other two girls sat.

"Hi, my name is Doris," the skinny one said.

The short one turned to me. "I'm Lois and this is Alice. What's your name?"

It was obvious Doris was the leader.

"Joyce."

"I know you don't go to this school because you look too young."

"I go to Fulton Junior High."

"You're skipping school?"

I don't know why I was cooperating with them. I didn't even know these girls.

I nodded my head.

They burst out laughing. "Sit down."

I sat on the grass with them.

"I got kicked out of school," Doris laughed as she said it.

"She's suspended for a week," Alice finished up.

"Did you get kicked out too?" I asked Alice

"I don't go to school."

"You already finished?"

"No, I just don't go anymore. I got pregnant."

"You did?" My eyes must have given away my thoughts.

"I lost the baby," Alice said.

I looked at Lois.

"I don't go to school either," she said before I could ask. "I hate school."

"Then why do you hang out on the school grounds?"

The girls laughed again. "We like the boys who go here," Alice answered.

I was disappointed because I didn't like boys. I would rather fight them than be nice to them. I didn't understand why girls liked them anyway.

"You want to hang out with us?"

I looked from Alice to Lois. Both smiled at me. I nodded.

"Okay, let's go." Doris got up from the grass with the other two following her lead.

"Where are we going?" I didn't really want to leave the high school. "Over to my house to get some food." Doris didn't wait for me to protest. She grabbed my arm and pulled me up.

We walked down the street towards Doris's house. I didn't understand why I was following these girls or why they wanted me to hang out with them.

Doris and I walked ahead of Lois and Alice. By the time we got to her house I felt better about my new friends.

Alice hurried over to the record player to put on some records while Doris ironed a pair of pants. Lois made sandwiches. I sat on the sofa, watching them.

Alice started dancing around the room moving her hips the way I had seen Cousin Liza do when I was a little girl. I laughed at her and she got mad.

After we finished eating and Doris had changed clothes we

left the house. I tried to hide my discomfort as we walked in the direction of Mr. and Mrs. Guy's house. Every step brought us closer to the house but I didn't tell the girls because I wasn't sure if I wanted them to know where I lived. What if Mrs. Guy saw me? I was supposed to be in school. We came within a block of my house before turning in the opposite direction. I was relieved because I didn't want to tell them I was scared to go down that street. I was glad we were close enough to my house that I could easily walk the short distance home. We walked to a small house on the next block. A man about twenty years old opened the front door after Doris knocked.

"Come on in," he said smiling at us. A younger guy came into the kitchen where we stood.

"Hi," he said. I looked up at him. He looked to be about eighteen years old.

Alice and Lois introduced Doris and me to the brothers. They were nineteen and twenty years old. Both were tall and handsome. The younger one had pretty wavy hair and light eyes. Alice introduced him as her boyfriend. We followed them down into the basement where there was a couch, a couple of chairs and the record player. The younger brother grabbed Alice and started kissing her right in front of us. I was embarrassed to look up. In the next minute he had her pushed up against the wall.

What were they doing? I tried not to look but my eyes kept drifting back to them. Doris put on some records and Lois began kissing the other brother. Wine surfaced from somewhere and Doris began drinking it. The couples left the basement with promises of returning, leaving Doris and I alone. A few minutes later another boy came down into the basement.

I watched Doris and him pass the wine bottle between them. I kept shaking my head when my turn came to drink it. Michael Norwood was a tall, nice looking boy with honey-brown skin. He told us he was seventeen years old. I could see that Doris liked him because she kept talking to him and trying to sit close to him.

If I looked up and noticed him looking back at me I would look away. I never had a boyfriend and didn't care about having one. I was only twelve years old.

Michael eventually came over to talk with me.

"What is your name?"

"Joyce," I said.

"I really like you," he whispered in my ear.

Could this really be happening? I had never even thought about having a boyfriend and this older guy was telling me he liked me.

"I'm only twelve years old," I confessed. He didn't seem fazed by my age.

He told me he was in high school and good friends with one of the brothers.

Finally Alice and Lois returned downstairs with the brothers following close behind.

The music was blasting by then and Doris continued drinking. I wasn't paying much attention to what Michael was saying. The music sounded good and I was lost in The Temptations.

We were all in the room together when Doris became angry.

"I don't like you anymore," she yelled at me.

I didn't know why she was mad at me. I hadn't done anything to her.

Doris came towards me with her fist balled. I felt my heart pounding. One of the brothers grabbed her.

"Get out of here," he told all of us.

"Take her home", the younger brother said, pushing Doris towards Alice and Lois.

"Where do you live?" Michael asked when I began walking towards the back door.

"A big green house around the corner," I said quickly.

By the time we got to the back alley Doris was out of control. She turned to me and began calling me bad names. What surprised me the most was that Alice and Lois sided with her. Doris was holding what was left of the wine and she wanted me to drink it.

"I said drink some," she insisted.

"I don't want it," I told her. The memory of how it felt when I drank that capful of whiskey that Papa gave me was still on my mind.

Alice and Lois held me down while Doris poured wine down my throat. The wine was bitter and it made me gag. I felt it burning and wanted to throw up. I was crying when they let me get up. Doris was laughing and I was mad.

Doris threw the first punch and all I could see was red. I got on top of her hitting her in the face. I grabbed her head and started beating it on the cement. I felt hands pulling at me. Alice and Lois managed to pull me off of her. I started walking in the direction of my house but Alice stopped me.

"You're coming with us," Alice said.

"I live around the corner and I want to go home."

The three of them eyed me with such contempt that I was afraid. I believed the three of them were going to jump on me. Doris was still mad but Alice and Lois promised that I wouldn't have to worry about her. She was drunk and staggered all the way to her house.

After walking Doris home we proceeded to a large department store on Third Street.

"Go steal us some clothes," Alice demanded.

I was intimidated by them so I went into the department store. I didn't know how to steal. I had never stolen anything. Once I walked out of the store with a candy bar unintentionally.

I went through the store searching for clothes for them. They had told me where to go and what they wanted. They told me they would be outside waiting. A security guard watched me so I panicked and ran out the back of the store right into Alice.

I confessed to her that I was too afraid to steal anything. We joined Lois who was standing near the front door just in case I came out that door. I pleaded with them to let me go home because it was getting late. They laughed in my face. Instead they made me go with them to the house of a woman with a lot of children. "This is my cousin's house" Alice told me.

"I need to go home," I told them.

I didn't like being in Alice's cousin's house. It was nasty and had dirty dishes piled in the sink, trash was everywhere and even the kids were dirty. They wouldn't let me go home so that night I slept between Alice and Lois on a hard dirty floor. It was a long restless night during which I don't think any of us got much sleep. The next morning they decided I could go home.

When Mrs. Guy opened the door she seemed happy to see me. I wanted to explain to her why I didn't come home the night before but before I could say anything Alice was telling her how they took care of me. They told Mrs. Guy I had run away and they talked me into coming back home. Mrs. Guy believed them and told me I was lucky to have nice friends. They promised Mrs. Guy they would visit again. After they left Mrs. Guy lashed out at me while Mr. Guy sat in front of the TV as if nothing was going on. I tried to explain what had really happened but she chose to believe them.

A couple of weeks later Michael Norwood showed up at my house.

"You have a visitor," Mrs. Guy said allowing him to come inside. I was shocked when I saw him standing there with a mischievous grin on his face.

"What are you doing here?"

Michael smiled. "I came to see you," he said.

"Sit and talk with the boy," Mrs. Guy said. "And don't be rude, offer him something to drink."

I rolled my eyes. What was wrong with her? I was only twelve years old and it was clear that Michael was older. I didn't like boys and I didn't know how to act around boys other than my brothers.

I spent the evening doing everything that Mrs. Guy told me. She thought Michael was nice so it didn't even bother her that he

In Years To Come

was seventeen years old.

"Can I take Joyce to a party Saturday night?" he asked Mrs. Guy.

My mouth almost dropped open when Mrs. Guy agreed to let me go with him on a date that Saturday.

"I can't go," I said.

"What time are you picking her up?" Mrs. Guy asked him as if I weren't even in the room.

I couldn't believe it. She was going to force me to go with him. I wasn't ready for these older friends I had met. I wanted to eat ice cream, not drink wine; and most of all I didn't want a boyfriend.

"He's a good-looking young man," Mrs. Guy said after Michael left. I didn't care what he looked like I didn't want to go anywhere with him. I didn't like boys and I tried the rest of the week to tell Mrs. Guy, but she was busy planning my date with Michael.

She bought me a pretty silk blue dress that was too sophisticated for me. I didn't even have breasts yet and the dress was low cut. She insisted that I wear it, saying I filled out other parts of the dress. I felt stupid when I walked into the living room to meet Michael in that dress with high heel shoes on. My hair was pinned up and Mrs. Guy had smeared bright red lipstick on me. I was planning to wipe it off as soon as I could.

"I like the way you look," Michael commented. "You look older."

We walked around the corner to his friend's house. Alice and Lois were already there and acted as if they were happy to see me. The dress brought more compliments from them. There was a lot of drinking and smoking going on. I passed up everything because I didn't want any of it. I watched while Michael rolled something in paper and started smoking it. It smelled funny and I turned my nose up. Michael only laughed and offered it to me. I shook my head.

"Just take a few puffs and you'll feel better."

I clenched my teeth and stared at him. I didn't want

anything and he wasn't going to make me smoke it.

I was not having fun at the party. The music was too loud and the room was smoky. The people at the party were acting stupid because of the liquor so I stayed close to Michael.

"Will you sit on my lap?" he asked.

"Why?"

"I just want you to sit on my lap."

I sat down in his lap.

"Kiss me," he whispered in my ear.

I had never kissed a boy before so I gave him a quick smack on his jaw.

"That is not a kiss," he said.

I refused to kiss him like I had seen Alice and Lois do with those brothers. Michael became impatient with me because I turned down offers to kiss, drink and smoke. He turned his attention to another girl. It hurt my feelings but I was ready to leave anyway. Alice and Lois were pushed aside by the brothers when more girls came into the party.

"Let's get out of here and go home," Alice suggested. I was tired and ready to go home. I hated the dress and my feet hurt in the shoes. Once we got outside they changed their minds.

"Let's take a walk."

"I want to go home," I whined. The two of them grabbed me and forced me to go with them. I took the shoes off because I couldn't walk in them.

"Who put that lipstick on you?" Alice was laughing.

"Mrs. Guy," I said, wiping it off.

"That is a weird lady."

We were walking down North Avenue when three guys approached us. I didn't say much to them allowing Alice and Lois to do all the talking. The rain came unexpectedly and one of the guys offered me his coat to cover my dress.

"I know a place to get out of the rain," he said. We followed him to an old abandoned house a block away. I immediately felt uncomfortable. It was dark except for the moonlight shining in through a broken window.

Lois and Alice went with two of the guys leaving me with the other one. He suggested that we sit on a mattress that was in the corner of the room. I refused, but he kept blocking me every time I moved.

"Where did my friends go?" I asked him.

"They went into another room. They're probably doing what we should be doing."

When he reached for me I jumped back. He tried to throw me on the mattress, but I fought him with all the strength I had.

"Lois! Alice!" I screamed, hoping they would come help me. "Help!" I screamed just before he punched me across the mouth.

"Get down," he demanded pointing to the mattress. I pretended I was going to obey, and instead I took off running. I couldn't see anything because of the darkness. I opened the door to the room where I heard laughter. The guy was close enough to grab me just as I swung open the front door. I felt his hands on my dress and I pulled away from him hearing the dress ripping in the process. I managed to get outside where the rain was pouring down. I had no coat and my dress was ripped.

I ran until I was sure he wasn't chasing me anymore. I recognized the street; it was only a few blocks from Uncle Ben's house. I walked to the familiar house on Hadley Street and saw a light on in kitchen. I hadn't seen Uncle Ben or Aunt Lea since we moved away. I banged on the back door while looking over my shoulder. Then I noticed the car was gone.

What was I going to do now? I was going to have to walk home with my dress torn up and no shoes on my feet. I had a pencil in the purse Mrs. Guy gave me that matched the shoes. I don't know how I had managed to hang onto the purse. I had left the shoes behind. I found a piece of paper and began writing a note to Uncle Ben. I wasn't sure what I was writing, but I did have a lot to say. I tucked the note inside the door so it wouldn't get wet. The first phone booth I saw I called Mrs. Guy who gave me directions on how to get home. When I walked through the door barefoot with my dress torn and tears running down my face she wanted to know what had happened. I wasn't aware of the cuts and bruises on my body. I refused to tell her what happened to me. I was angry about her sending me on a date I didn't want to go on.

"He seemed like a nice young man," she said. "I can't believe he did this to you."

"He didn't do anything to me," I told her. "It was someone else."

When the police showed up I had calmed down. I glared at Mrs. Guy because I knew she had called them. They talked with Mrs. Guy in private. When they came back into the room I was sitting in front of the TV.

"We have to take you with us," one of them said.

"Why?" I looked again at Mrs. Guy.

I was taken to the juvenile Detention Center. It was a large facility located on the outskirts of the city. I was blamed for everything that had happened to me. She was the one who insisted that I go on a date with Michael; she was the one who had liked Alice and Lois and said they were good friends for me.

I told the policemen about the guys who tricked us into going into the vacant house on North Avenue. I pointed it out to them when we drove past it.

Chapter Eight

The Detention Center

When I arrived at the Detention Center a woman gave me a bar of soap and shampoo that smelled horrible they said it would kill any lice I had. They took all my clothes and replaced them with two skirts, two blouses, a pair of pajamas and a few pair of white cotton underwear. Everything had the words *Detention Center* stamped on them. I was also given sheets, a blanket, towels, toothpaste, a toothbrush and a pillow.

After I showered and dressed in the pajamas a woman led me into another area of the building where I would be staying. It was at night so all I saw was a long hall with closed doors on the left and right. She opened a door on the right with a key and I stepped inside a small room with a bunk bed shoved against the wall. It was stripped of all sheets and covers. A toilet with a sink was in the other corner of the room. There weren't any windows except for the small one on the door. I made the bed on the bottom with the sheets they gave me while the woman watched. After I was done she closed the door, and when I heard the lock click I began hyperventilating. My heart was pounding and I couldn't breathe. The light in the hallway was turned off. I was alone and locked in the room. I began to pray to God to help me. I cried myself to sleep that night.

The next morning I woke up to a voice coming over the loudspeaker.

"Breakfast in fifteen minutes," the woman's voice said.

I washed my face, brushed my teeth, and waited. The sound of keys clinging together could be heard throughout the hallway. Then I heard a key turning in my door. I stepped out into the hallway welcoming the fresh air. I followed the other girls lining up against the wall. A middle-aged white lady with gray hair led us through several doors and down a stairway. I could smell food as we neared the cafeteria. We walked in on one side and another group of girls walked in from the other side.

I let out a squeal when I saw Alice and Lois among the group. How did they get in here? They waved at me and I waved back.

Later that day Lois was transferred to the same unit I was in.

"The older girls stay on that side," she told me. That was how I found out that Lois was only fourteen.

"We were in that house with those guys when the police picked us up for curfew. I've been in here a few times before," Lois told me. I felt better now that Lois was with me.

We had to go to the school that they had inside the facility. It was just a classroom with a teacher named Mrs. Lamb. I entered the classroom and sat down. It looked like a classroom for little kids with the small desks and simple words pasted throughout the room. The older girls from the other side also came. Mrs. Lamb was a middle-aged woman with short brown hair and a scowl on her face. She had no control over the girls, who deliberately taunted her. We never got much done because Mrs. Lamb spent most of the class time trying to maintain order in the classroom. I didn't care what was going on so I sat there until the counselor came back for us. This so-called schooling was nothing but a big joke and a waste of time. I ignored Mrs. Lamb just like the others did.

When Alice came to class the three of us talked about what happened that night. According to Lois and Alice, they had sex with the two guys in another room, but claimed that it was forced. The two guys were there when the police went to check the house out, but the policemen allowed the guys to leave after they said that the sex was consensual. It was Alice and Lois who were taken into custody because of curfew.

"Why are you here?"

"Mrs. Guy didn't want me living there anymore. She called the police and told them that I was out of control. I walked home and didn't get there until almost midnight.

It took me a few days to adjust to being in the Detention Center. We went through the same routine every day, beginning with breakfast. Afterwards we completed chores assigned to us; cleaning the bathrooms, the recreation room and the room we slept in. We swept and mopped floors, made our beds, and washed the sinks and toilets that were in our rooms. We took daily showers and were provided with clean clothes everyday. We were locked in our rooms for a short time in the afternoon, so I searched through the books available to us and began reading again. I started liking it in there after a few days. I began talking to Mrs. Brown, an older black woman who was always cheerful and encouraging. She taught me how to crochet, so I made scarves and hats.

Stacked on the shelves near the TV were lots of comic books so I began reading them. I took them to my room and read during lockdown. I enjoyed reading Archie, Casper, Ritchie Rich, and others that kept my imagination going. I read all of them. I had forgotten how much I enjoyed reading. Most of the girls watched TV, but I read. I decided that it wasn't so bad being there, so instead of being afraid I started feeling safe.

Mrs. Green was another counselor that I befriended. She was an older tall woman with flaming red hair. In some ways she reminded me of Lucille Ball. She advised me to not come back there once I was released. All the other girls were happy when they got released to go home, but I was hoping to stay forever.

I got a surprise visit from the social worker one day. "I am putting you into the Children's Home," he said.

The Children's Home was an orphanage a short distance from The Detention Center. When we drove into the parking lot of the Children's Home I saw that it was a cluster of brick buildings that looked like a college campus. We walked through the main doors into an office. The place was old and had a musty smell to it. The walls on the inside hallways were pale and the tile on the floor was worn. I was assigned to a large dormitory where rows of beds were lined up against the wall. The counselor directed me to a bed near the corner. Were they serious? I had to sleep in this big room with several other girls?

"This will be your drawer."

I looked at a two-drawer tin cabinet built into the end of the bed. "Where do I put my clothes?"

"You won't need many clothes around here, we wear uniforms."

"I'm not wearing any uniforms," I thought to myself.

They gave me a white blouse with a plaid skirt. I stared at the clothes in disgust. I decided that I didn't like this place. My attitude reflected my feelings as I mechanically moved about. I didn't socialize with the girls who shared the room with me. This was bad because we were together all the time except when we attended school. I became increasingly rebellious; refusing to do anything they asked me to.

Was there any hope of getting out of here? A family member could come get us on the weekends. My heart was crushed. Who would come get me? Who knew where I was? When the weekend came most of the girls in my area had visitors. I looked out the windows envious of them laughing and talking with relatives. We were allowed to walk outside on the premises during visiting hours. I was walking outside when I saw a boy who seemed to be about my age on the playground. I assumed he had no visitors either.

We began talking. I was sorry to find out he had been in

there for a while.

"I have a visitor sometimes," he told me. "Our sister comes to visit us. He didn't talk much about his parents. His sister was older than him and his brother who was also in there.

"Why can't you go live with your sister?"

He shrugged his shoulders.

"What's your name?" I asked him.

He looked at me and smiled for the first time. I smiled back at him.

"Kenneth"

"My name is Joyce. I've only been here for a couple of weeks."

Kenneth nodded.

"What is your sister's name?"

"Her name is Linda."

I looked at Kenneth again. He had that same look. No, it couldn't be the Linda that lived in Mrs. Watson's house.

"What is your brother's name?"

"Kevin."

I remembered all the things Linda told me about Kenneth and Kevin, and now we were together in the Children's Home.

"I know your sister," I told him excitedly. "We were in a foster home together."

"She's trying to get us out of here," he said.

I remembered when she told me how badly she wanted her brothers to live with her.

"I wish I had a sister like Linda."

"You don't have a sister?"

"My sister is handicapped. She can't hear or talk."

He looked puzzled, like most people do when I talked about Sara.

"She can't hear anything?"

"Nope."

"She can't say anything?"

240

"Nope."

"Why is she like that?"

"I don't know"

"Where is she?"

"In a school for the deaf"

"Where is that?"

"In Delevan."

I hadn't seen Linda since she left Mrs. Watson. I was eager to see her again. I didn't know what happened to her marriage, but she remained faithful with her visits to her brothers.

"She'll be here next Saturday," Kenneth told me. We decided to surprise her.

While I looked forward to Saturday, things were getting difficult for me in the Children's Home. I decided I didn't want to wear the uniform so I refused to get dressed one day. The counselor was a tiny white lady with mean looking eyes. She grabbed my arm and began twisting it. It hurt, but I was stubborn. Then she took a wire hanger and started hitting me with it. I wrestled the hanger from her and started swinging it at her. Her screams could be heard down the hall and it didn't take long before other counselors held me down on the floor until the police arrived.

"What happened?"

I could hear her voice as she described her version of what had happened.

"She refused to get dressed and when I insisted she put on her uniform she attacked me with the hanger."

"She hit me first!" I screamed.

"You cannot attack counselors. We cannot condone your behavior."

I passed her on my way to the waiting police car. I didn't care about leaving; I didn't mind going back to the detention center. In fact, I welcomed it.

The drive to the Detention Center was silent.

The only good part about being in the Children's home had been meeting Kenneth.

I wished I had a chance to say good-bye to him, and I really did want to see Linda again. Maybe Kenneth would tell her where I went and she could visit me in the Detention Center.

I had been through it before so I knew what to expect. After taking a shower and washing my hair in that awful smelling soap I was laden with blankets, sheets, and clothing. I expected everyone to greet me when I walked through the door. Instead, Mrs. Green shook her head and Mrs. Brown didn't have much to say to me. I hadn't been away long, but everything had changed. Most of the girls who had been in there had left including Alice and Lois. I hadn't expected everything to be so different.

I knew this time things were going to be rougher for me because no one was as sympathetic as they had been the first time I was there. I wondered now if I would ever get out. The social worker had warned me that the Children's Home was the only place left for me to go and now I had blown it. I wanted to go back and tell them I was sorry. I wanted to see Kenneth and Linda. Maybe I could go live with Linda too.

It was obvious that Mrs. Green and Mrs. Brown were upset with me. It bothered me that Mrs. Brown barely spoke to me. I waited everyday during visitor's hour hoping that Linda would come. I stood close to the door in case my name was called. I kept checking with the counselors to find out if I had any visitors. No one came to see me, not even the social worker. Time started running together, and I stopped even thinking about what day it was. I buried myself in books and crocheting everything that I could.

The day my name was announced over the loudspeaker for a visitor, I was shocked. I had almost given up on Linda. Then I remembered that the social worker hadn't been to see me either.

"Is it a man?" I asked the counselor who was taking me to the visiting room.

"A man and a woman," she said.

"Oh." I hoped she didn't notice the disappointment in my

voice.

I wasn't ready to face the social worker who told me that he had a hard time getting me into the Children's Home and that there were no foster homes available.

As we walked down the hallway, the counselor took long fast steps. We stopped in front of a small room. I looked inside and saw a man, a woman and a small child.

"Who are these people?"

I looked up at the counselor certain that she had made a mistake.

"Joyce?"

The man knew my name. I walked closer to get a better look at him. My mouth dropped open when I recognized him. It was my brother, Robert. He looked the same except for the facial hair that he was growing. I let out a big yell and ran towards him. I felt his arms to make sure he was real. It was true my brother Robert was here in Milwaukee. I had heard that he was living in Denver, Colorado. The last time I saw him was when he had the fight with Sonny while we were living with Uncle Ben.

"Why are you in here?" He asked after we settled down. I told him about what happened at the Children's Home and watched as his expressions changed. I was suddenly embarrassed that he had to come to the Detention Home to visit me.

"I'm getting you out of here." He said.

"You are?"

"Yes, as soon as possible."

Although my brother was young, there was something very mature about him. Maybe it was the beard he had grown.

"This is my wife Judy."

The woman was short and plump. She was holding a little boy about two years old. She smiled at me and I smiled back.

"Hi," she said

"Hi."

"That's my son, Tony." The little boy took a look at me and

held tighter to his mother. He was cute. He had chubby cheeks with dimples in them. I fell instantly in love with him.

I couldn't believe that Robert was married and had a son.

"You want to live in Denver?"

I couldn't believe I heard him correctly. "Denver?"

"Denver, Colorado."

"Where is it?"

"It's a beautiful place in the west with mountains, pine trees, and beautiful homes."

"Really?" My mind was already visualizing the place.

"You don't belong in here," he said.

I went back to the recreation room that day feeling confident that I was going to Colorado. I told all the counselors about my brother from Denver who was taking me to live with him.

A few days later, Robert returned with papers saying I could be released to him. I said good-bye to everyone and promised I would never come back.

After retrieving the few belongings I had, we were on our way to Denver. Robert was driving a late model blue Chevrolet that had plenty of room for all of us. The ride was longer that I had anticipated. I had never been that far away from Milwaukee. Robert talked constantly about Denver during the drive there. We stopped a lot and he bought whatever I wanted to eat.

"Stephen lives in Denver too," he told me.

I was excited. I couldn't wait to see him.

I was in the back seat asleep when Robert's voice woke me up. I was groggy and it was dark outside.

"Joyce! Wake up! Look at the lights! I want you to see how beautiful Denver is at night," he said.

I saw lights blinking in the distance.

"That's Denver," he said. Judy started clapping.

I stared at the beautiful lights. It reminded me of the Walt Disney movies when they showed a lot of lights blinking in the background.

"Yes," I whispered.
I was in Denver, Colorado.

Chapter Nine

Denver Colorado

It was mid October when I arrived in Denver. In less than four months I had moved five times. My attitude didn't help much because now I was an angry and confused twelve-year-old. Robert was renting a two-bedroom; one-story duplex in an attractive area of Denver called Park Hill. I woke up the first morning after I got there and walked around the neighborhood. I was astonished to see so many nice brick homes with green lawns and large beautiful pine trees. People of all races lived in the same neighborhood. This was something new for me to get used to because I had never lived in an integrated neighborhood. Milwaukee was still very much segregated with white people living on the south one side of town, and black people living on the northwest side of the city.

The sun was shining brightly that day and it was warm outside. Fall was my favorite time of year, but in Milwaukee the sun didn't come out much during the fall and winter months. We always braced ourselves for the blast of winter that usually came shortly after Thanksgiving in Milwaukee.

Robert took me riding around Denver and I couldn't help admiring the beautiful scenery. I had only seen neighborhoods like the ones he was showing me while riding on the bus to the county hospital. The mountains in the background were real and my eyes kept going back to them. We drove down a street called Monaco that was lined with beautiful homes sitting on large lots.

"This is where the expensive houses are," Robert told me.

We drove past the house where the famous boxer, Sonny Liston once lived.

"It's beautiful here isn't it?"

I looked at Robert and nodded my head. "This is the most beautiful city I have ever seen," I told him.

We stopped at Uncle Guy lee's shoe shop that was located on Sixth Ave close to downtown. When we walked through the door I saw a man bent over a machine doing something. The smell of hot leather filled the air along with chemicals that made me want to go back outside for air. The noise the machine made was loud so I knew he didn't hear us come in. Robert casually walked around the counter.

"Uncle Guy lee!" Robert shouted as loud as he could.

The man finally looked at us and I stopped breathing for a moment. He looked so much like Papa that I couldn't help staring at him.

When he turned off the machine Robert pointed to me.

Uncle Guy lee looked closer and said, "Is that Joyce?" He smiled at me and again I was taken back because it was Papa's smile plastered on his face.

"Hi Uncle Guy lee," I said.

I embraced the uncle I didn't know that well because it felt like I was hugging my grandfather. Uncle Guy lee acted like he was really happy to see me, and that made me feel good.

When Stephen came over to visit in his orange and white car I laughed at the gold letters on the side that spelled, *The Lover*. I was delighted to see him because I hadn't seen him since Papa passed away. He was no longer the shy boy that I once knew. Stephen's round face didn't have much hair, giving him a boyish look along with a broad smile displaying a nice set of teeth. He was a handsome young man. There was no doubt that he liked girls and they liked him. Stephen told me he dropped out of high school so he could work and was living across town with his girlfriend whose name was also Joyce. When I met Joyce I liked her even though she was a quiet person. I found it easy to communicate with her and she was very much in love with Stephen and pregnant with his first child. Stephen had a natural talent for humor so he kept everyone around him laughing. Sometime during that first visit I mentioned to him the phone call from the Army that came to Uncle Ben's house.

"I'm going to sign up for the Marine Corps," he said.

The first thing Robert did was buy two twin beds for my bedroom. Next we went shopping for clothes at a store in the Dahlia shopping center a few blocks away. I didn't have many clothes left between all the moving and needed something to wear to school. Robert enrolled me in Smiley Junior High, where I continued in the seventh grade. The school was several blocks from our house, but I was used to walking so it didn't seem that far. A school bus picked up a few kids at the corner, but I enjoyed walking. Everything about Denver was different than Milwaukee. The school was overcrowded so it split up the classes and we went to school in shifts. Some kids went early in the morning and others went later. I was put in the mid-morning group.

Uncle Guy lee lived with his family in a blonde colored brick house in Park Hill on Glencoe Street surrounded by two large Pine trees that grew straight up in the front yard. I remembered when they came for Hon's funeral. Uncle Guy lee and Pudding were doing well with the two businesses they operated. Pudding operated the shoe shop in Park hill not far from their home. Sometimes when I walked to school I passed by the shop.

There was so much to absorb living in a different environment. I settled in with Robert and his family although I wasn't sure if I liked his wife who was just a few years older than me. I didn't want her telling me what to do. Robert didn't put many

248

restrictions on me either so I didn't feel pressured. Robert and his wife both worked in a restaurant on Colorado Boulevard. He was a cook on the night shift and she was a waitress during the day.

I was living in Denver, going to a new school, and most importantly, living with my own family. I loved my nephew Tony and had fun taking him trick or treating that year. Halloween night was a little breezy, but not too cold. It was the most fun I'd had since moving there.

I wasn't readily accepted at school, the kids thought I talked funny. I said soda and they said pop. I laughed at them too.

"Don't you know that's soda?" I asked one girl who insisted it was pop.

There were other small differences in the way I talked compared to them. Also, the music and dances they were doing were different from what we did in Milwaukee. Most of the dances I was familiar with they didn't know about in Denver.

I woke up every morning to watch "All My Children" and I spent most evenings watching more television. I couldn't understand why Mr. Williams didn't allow us to watch *Batman and Robin*. He said it was a sin. It was as funny as it was stupid, but not sinful.

Then a girl named Beverly Tolliver came to Smiley. She was big for her age, not in the sense of being fat, but she had a very mature body for a seventh grader. Her dress stuck out in the front showing large breasts that weren't typical of most seventh graders. Being the new girl in school she endured some teasing. I thought it was strange that she wore the same orange shirtdress and brown desert boots to school almost everyday. I'm sure she felt humiliated because kids teased her about the dress and boots. Beverly was a cute girl with long hair that was always pulled back into a ponytail. I liked Beverly because in some ways she reminded me of Melody. We were ecstatic when we found out that we lived around the corner from each other and she became my new best friend.

"We moved here from Spain," Beverly told me one day

while we were walking to school

"You mean the country Spain?"

She nodded her head. I couldn't believe she had actually lived in another country.

"How did you get there?"

"We flew on a plane. My father is in the air force and he had to move to Spain so he took us with him."

I was impressed that I knew someone who had lived in another country.

I remembered when I was in fourth grade staring at the happy faces of people who had lived in Costa Rica and other parts of South America. I was hoping one day to visit there.

"What was it like?"

"It was a nice place to live. The people are nice and I learned how to count the money."

Beverly even spoke a few words in Spanish.

Mr. and Mrs. Tolliver seemed like a nice couple. Mrs. Tolliver was a thin dark-skinned woman with large eyes and a raspy voice. She smiled a lot and I enjoyed talking with her. Mr. Tolliver appeared to be a big man at first sight, but later I noticed that he was a short man with a large body. He was good-looking, with skin the color of light oak, dark wavy hair, and light colored eyes. His shoulders were broad, making him look bigger than he was. From the day I met him I was intimidated by the way he acted towards me. He never smiled, and those eyes looked at me in an accusing way.

"Your father makes me nervous," I confessed to Beverly one day.

"He makes me nervous too," she said.

Of course, what I usually noticed was the anger he displayed, especially the way he looked at me. I was afraid of him especially after Beverly told me that he beat her. I went to Beverly's house to visit her most of the time because she wasn't allowed to go anywhere. I felt sorry for my friend because she was so unhappy. When Mr. Tolliver was home he spent most of his time in the upstairs bedroom. I thought that was odd but I was relieved in some ways because I didn't have to see him. When I did see him I managed to mumble a hello and get out of his way as quick as possible. I was more relaxed around Mrs. Tolliver because she was easy to talk to; she usually joked and laughed with us when he wasn't around.

Mr. and Mrs. Tolliver had eight kids. The oldest two children, Dawna and Gene, were Mrs. Tolliver's children from a previous marriage. Mr. Tolliver had adopted them, but Beverly was actually the oldest of Mr. Tolliver's biological children with Mrs. Tolliver.

Mr. and Mrs. Tolliver slept in the big bedroom and the youngest two children occupied the second bedroom on the main floor. The finished basement had three more bedrooms and a recreation room. The two older boys slept in one bedroom. Beverly and her two younger sisters slept in the same bed in another bedroom while Dawna enjoyed having her own bedroom.

Beverly was convinced that her parents didn't like her because of the differences they made in the way they treated her and her older sister.

Dawna seemed to be the main focus in the family. For some reason everyone was mesmerized by her. Mr. and Mrs. Tolliver were always bragging and praising her. The younger children were always pulling on her or following her around like she was some kind of goddess. Dawna was a small-framed girl with large almond-shaped eyes. She was about five foot one and wore her hair in a cute short cut that fit her face. I thought she looked all right, but she wasn't a beauty queen.

I decided that I didn't like Dawna because she acted like she was better than the other children, especially Beverly. Even Beverly believed that Dawna was better than her and she adored her. Dawna was in high school and dating. When guys came to pick her up for a date, Beverly had to entertain them until Dawna was ready.

I was afraid of her brother, Gene, because he was always

acting strange and was always getting into trouble. Mr. Tolliver beat him, but it didn't do any good. I believed something terrible was wrong with him and I told Beverly that. Beverly told me that he was the reason they had to leave Spain. He was always getting into some kind of trouble with the police.

Beverly and I became like two peas in a pod and did almost everything together. We had a couple of the same classes in school so we sat next to each other. There were other girls I was friendly with, Judy and Helen Gunn, Pam, Pat Fox and a few more. By this time in my life I had become very angry and bitter. I didn't care about much of anything and that included school. I was always talking back to the teacher or refusing to do work assignments. I constantly disrupted the class and usually ended up in the detention room. I became a bully and welcomed a fight. My bad attitude spilled over into my home life and I started getting into fights with my sister- in- law.

Robert took me to visit Uncle Guy lee and Pudding right before Christmas. Pudding had decorated the house beautifully and had all sorts of candies, cookies, and other goodies around the house. I didn't have a taste for the German treats, but it reminded me of when I lived with Mrs. Watson.

"I want you to spend the night with us," Uncle Guy lee offered. "The girls will have a ball with you around." I felt good because I liked my cousins even though they were younger than I was. A short time after the holidays I went to spend the night at Uncle Guy lee's house. He had a big house with two bedrooms upstairs and a big basement that looked like another house. He had a kitchen in the basement just like at Mrs. Watson's except his entire basement was completely finished with two more bedrooms and a large recreation room.

The girls were playing with their dolls in the upstairs bedroom where they slept and I was talking with them when I heard him call my name.

"Come out here," Uncle Guy lee called.

I went into the neatly furnished living room where he was sitting. I knew that he was serious when his usual smile wasn't on his face.

"I've wanted to talk with you since you got here," he said.

The talk turned into a roar of accusations. I was shocked and hurt by his words. His final words caused me to react.

"All of you tore up my mama and daddy's house," he said. "They took all of you into their house and all you did was tear it up." The mention of Hon and Papa was enough to upset me.

"We didn't tear up nobody's house," I yelled back at him.

"Don't raise your voice at me!"

I stared at the face that looked so much like Papa.

"I don't care what you say. We didn't tear up Hon and Papa's house."

"I'll give you something you need," he shouted while groping for the belt in his pants.

"You are not going to hit me with that belt," I shouted back at him.

I looked up and saw Gil staring at us. His angry father was pulling the belt out of his pants about the time I ran out of the front door. I could hear his threats as the cool, breezy air brushed against my face. I ran several blocks towards my house and was glad to see Robert when I got there. Still trying to catch my breath I sat down.

"Uncle Guy lee tried to whip me," I announced to him.

Robert shook his head in disbelief. "What happened?"

"He said he wanted to talk to me and then he started saying things that weren't true. He said that we tore up Hon and Papa's house. He said we worried them to death."

"Don't pay any attention to him," Robert told me. "I've heard a lot of stuff from him too."

My relationship with Uncle Guy Lee was never the same after that. I loved Uncle Guy lee and felt terrible about the things I said to him.

When Robert wasn't there I ignored Judy because I didn't

like her telling me to do anything. Robert worked the late night shift so I was with Judy most of the time. I was glad when Robert bought a new color TV because they put the old black and white one in my bedroom. I spent most of the time in my bedroom and came out only to eat or go to the bathroom. Judy tried to talk with me, but I hardly ever responded.

Judy was watching TV. And tried to make conversation with me, but I exploded and threatened to beat her up. I was still mad that she told Robert about the trouble I was getting into at school. I was self-destructive and when Robert confronted me about the trouble in school I went into the bathroom that night and cut off all my hair with a pair of scissors. The next morning I looked like a plucked chicken with stands of hair in different lengths. The kids really laughed and taunted me at school so I got into more fights.

I was still acting up in class and after my third trip to the principal's office I was sent to see Mrs. Bell. She was a Dean for the girls. And a very strict well spoken black woman who was successful in handling children like me. I was sent to her office on more than a few occasions because of my behavior. I liked Mrs. Bell because she seemed to understand my problems. When she saw what I had done to my hair she offered to take me to a beauty shop to see if they could do something with it. I confessed to her that I cut it off because I was mad at my brother and sister-in-law.

I returned to school with a new look and new attitude that didn't last long, because my slick new perm turned into a nightmare. The perm not only burnt my tender scalp, but also caused the little hair I had left on my head to fall out. They were teasing and laughing at me because I looked like a boy with a dress on. There was nothing I could do to cover up my baldhead so I fought some more.

One morning I woke up feeling sick but decided to go to school anyway. I was in my second class when I had an awful feeling that I wanted to throw up. I rushed to the girl's bathroom with the worst pains I'd ever felt in my life. I was hurting so bad that

I couldn't stand upright. Someone in the bathroom noticed me and alerted a teacher who came to my aid. I was sent home with a note from the nurse saying that she didn't know what was wrong with me and suggested that I be taken to the doctor.

"It is just gas," Robert said later while I lay across the bed moaning in pain. "You will probably feel better once you use the bathroom."

I struggled to walk to the bathroom. I didn't feel the need to use it, but I was willing to try anything to make the pains go away. I strained to get rid of the gas my brother said was in me, but the pains only got worse. I returned to the bed and prayed for God to help me. I finally fell asleep and woke up later feeling better. I returned to the bathroom and it was then I noticed the blood. I started screaming because I was scared. I was sure I had blown a hole in my bottom with all the straining I did.

"What's wrong?" Robert asked from the other side of the door.

I was crying loudly by then, but refused to answer him.

I stuffed toilet paper in my panties trying to soak up the blood, but I kept using more and more. I was too embarrassed to tell Robert what I had done.

The next day I felt a little better except the blood continued to seep through the toilet paper. I didn't go to school and refused to leave my room.

"If you're not better in a few days I'm taking you to the doctor."

I nodded my head. I couldn't eat and only got up to go to the bathroom. I was disappointed to discover that the blood had not stopped. I felt better after a couple of days and told Robert everything was okay even though I still had not stopped bleeding.

The bleeding finally stopped a few days later. I was relieved and thanked God. I decided not to say anything about it. The next month the same thing happened to me again. I was at school when my stomach began hurting. I rushed to the bathroom where I started throwing up and again noticed the bleeding.

The nurse let me lay on the small cot in the nurse's office because I couldn't move without feeling pain. She took my temperature and announced that I didn't have a fever. I whimpered until I fell asleep.

When I woke up, it was an hour later the nurse was in the room with me.

"How are you feeling?"

"Better," I answered. I felt something warm running down my legs. I knew it was blood and I was afraid to move. I started crying. The nurse rushed over to me.

"Are you hurting again?"

"I think I blew a hole in my bottom," I told her.

The nurse looked at me oddly.

"My brother told me I had gas when my stomach was hurting like this last month so while trying to get rid of the gas I must have strained because I started bleeding. Now I'm bleeding again. I have blood all over me now because I can feel it running down my leg. I'm sorry I messed up your bed."

I was sitting up so she sat down next to me and put her arm around me.

"Has anyone ever talked to you about how your body will change when you become a certain age?"

"I found out that the hair growing on my body wasn't a curse," I told her.

"Who told you it was?"

"Mrs. Watson, my foster mother."

"Have you ever heard the word menstruate?"

I remembered the booklet that Mrs. Williams gave me. It had the word menstruate in it.

"My foster mother, Mrs. Williams, gave me a booklet to read that had that word in it, but I don't know what it means."

"Did Mrs. Williams ever explain the book to you?"

I shook my head. "She only gave it to me to read."

256

I listened while the nurse explained everything. I felt my heart skip a beat when she said that now I was capable of having a baby. She told to me about wearing sanitary napkins and how to put one on. I was both scared and thankful when Robert picked me up from school.

I wanted to tell him that what I had was called cramps, but he was a man. Since men didn't have babies they didn't menstruate.

The nurse talked to him and I was sure she told him what happened, but to my relief we didn't discuss it. Judy came to my bedroom that evening with a large box of sanitary napkins. I changed them just like the nurse had instructed me to. The belt was uncomfortable around my waist and the napkins were bulky, but I had to wear it.

I told Beverly about my change into womanhood and she laughed at me. She knew everything and I envied the fact that she had someone to explain it to her.

One day Beverly and I came home late from school after getting into a fight with two girls. We laughed all the way home about how we beat the girls up. I didn't fight with my fists. I fought the girls like they fought me with a lot of swinging and scratching. I did punch one girl in the face after pinning her on the ground. I walked Beverly home first because it was late and she was afraid to go home alone. We got out of school at five so getting home at 6:15 didn't seem so late. Mr. Tolliver met us at the door. He started shouting.

"What the hell are you doing coming home this time of day?"

Beverly didn't respond as she stood in front of him. I felt a shiver down my spine. I avoided looking at Mr. Tolliver's face because I knew if I had seen that angry look I would have ran out of the house right then leaving Beverly to face him alone. His massive body stood over Beverly and he was glaring at her. I moved to the sofa and sat down while he dragged Beverly into the bathroom. The first sound I heard was a slapping noise followed by a scream. My heart started beating wildly when I realized he was hitting her. The urge to run into the bathroom and help her was great, but I couldn't move. It felt as if something was holding me down. I felt awful listening to my best friend getting beaten. When she emerged from the bathroom shaking and crying, I looked at her with my own tears stinging my eyes. Mr. Tolliver followed her, breathing hard.

"This is what you need too," he yelled at me swinging the belt back and forth. Somehow my body took over and I jumped up from the sofa and ran home. I was shaken up by what had just happened. I couldn't believe what I had just witnessed. He beat her while Mrs. Tolliver did nothing to stop him. I went into my bedroom and lay across the bed crying for my friend. I should have done something to help her. I told Robert about what Mr. Tolliver said about me needing to be hit with his belt.

The next day Beverly refused to walk to school with me. Her father had ordered her to take the bus for the rest of the school year. She was quiet and cool towards me. I tried to talk with her, but she deliberately ignored me all day. I didn't have a pass to ride the bus, so I walked home alone thinking about everything that happened the day before. I suspected that her parents told her not to hang around me. I also noticed that Beverly moved around school like a robot. I wondered if her stiff movements were due to the beating. She retreated to the girl she was when she first came to school. I waited, hoping she would snap out of it.

Eventually she did. Within two weeks we were laughing and talking again. She told me about her brother, Gene getting in so much trouble that her father had his hands full dealing with him. She was as much afraid of Gene as she was of her father.

I was watching TV in my bedroom when I heard a scratching noise at the window. I looked out to see Beverly bent down on her knees. I opened the window to talk to her.

"What are you doing here?"

"Let me in," she said.

"Why didn't you come to the front door?"

Joyce A. Ford

"I don't want anyone to know I'm here," she whispered.

I helped her get in through the window. Her face was wet with tears and the blouse she had on looked as if it had been ripped off of her showing parts of her bra.

"He...beat...me...again." She said the words slowly as if forcing them out of her mouth.

"Who beat you? Your father?"

I knew who it was, but I wanted her to verify it.

"Yes," her tears came again with a loud sob. I did the only thing I could and hugged my friend. She winced and jumped back when I wrapped my arms around her.

"What's wrong?"

She slowly took what was left of her blouse off. When she turned around I felt myself gasp because her back was rippled with bloody welts. She cried out when I touched it.

"He did this to you?"

She nodded her head.

"I want to get out of that house," Beverly whimpered.

"How can you get out?"

She shook her head, "I don't know."

My best friend cried and vowed never to return home. I can't remember whose idea it was, but I do remember that I agreed to hide her in my house. The duplex we lived in had an attic with enough room to stand up in. I wasn't concerned about Robert or Judy coming into my bedroom because they seldom did. That night, Beverly slept in the other twin bed while my bedroom door was locked. Because Robert was home during the day I told her she would have to hide in the attic while he was there.

Early the next morning she went into the attic and I went to school as if nothing was different. Mrs. Tolliver showed up at our door that evening.

"Is Beverly here?" she asked. I peered past Robert, who had the door open wide enough to see Mr. Tolliver standing behind on the sidewalk.

259

"Why would she be at our house?" Robert asked.

"She ran away last night and I thought she would come here."

Robert shook his head. "Joyce?" He turned around to face me. "Have you seen Beverly?"

I denied seeing her.

Later that night after my brother went to work and Judy retreated to their bedroom, Beverly and I laughed about how well we were fooling them. Our plan seemed to be working fine. Beverly could easily get in and out of the attic without being seen. She was also able to eat dinner, take a bath, and sleep in my bedroom at night. Sometimes Beverly hid in the closet. Robert and Judy didn't seem to notice me carrying two plates of food to my bedroom where I started eating my dinner after getting into an argument with Judy. I had everything I needed in my bedroom: a TV and a record player. Beverly thought I was lucky to have my own bedroom with a TV.

A few days later Mrs. Tolliver returned to our house.

This time she had a worried, pitiful-looking face as if she were ready to cry.

"Please tell Beverly to come home if you know where she is."

It was harder for me to look at her this time, but I knew I couldn't give in to her pleas. Remembering the welts on Beverly's back made it easier to tell another lie.

"I saw her at school," I lied. "She was with some other kids." I went on to describe a car that never existed, hoping to throw her off-track. Robert was starting to worry about Beverly too.

"If you know where she is you better tell her mother," he said, looking directly at me.

"I don't know where she is!"

He nodded his head as if he believed me.

I walked back to my room and slammed the door as if I was angry. Beverly was hiding in the closet in my bedroom so she heard everything and giggled when I walked back in. I described to

Beverly how bad her mother looked.

"Was *he* with her?" I knew she was talking about Mr. Tolliver.

I nodded. He always came with her, but wouldn't come to the door.

"She doesn't care," Beverly snapped at me.

Mrs. Tolliver came to the house everyday to ask about Beverly and I continued to lie and deny any knowledge about her.

"No one else saw her at school," she told me. I shrugged my shoulders.

Robert was getting tired of the daily visits. "I'm glad she's not here," he told me after one of Mrs. Tolliver's visits.

We went to visit Uncle Guy lee one evening and came home to discover that someone had broken into our house and taken the new color TV Robert had bought a couple of months earlier from Sears.

"I haven't finished paying for that TV," he said.

He was so angry that he walked around the house cursing. I was concerned about Beverly, who was supposed to be in the attic.

"I'm going to ride around and see if I see anyone," Robert said. "Come on and go with me."

We rode up and down a few streets before turning on Monaco. In front of us was a red car. What got our attention were two antennas sticking up from the back seat.

"There is my TV!" Robert shouted. He pulled up close to the car and looked in. We saw the TV and it looked like the stolen one. The man in the red car saw us looking at him so he sped up. Robert followed close behind him. I didn't panic until Robert grabbed his gun from under the seat.

"What are you doing?"

"I am going to shoot that son of a bitch!" he shouted.

"Here, hold the steering wheel."

I tried to steer the car, but I didn't know how to drive and almost ran into a tree. Robert had to take over the wheel and the red car got away.

Robert called the police and gave a description of the car.

They found the man and the car, but no TV. To make matters worse, I didn't pick the right guy out of the lineup, even though Robert insisted it was the man in the middle. He was right.

We came back home without anything. The TV was gone and Robert still had to pay for it.

Beverly was in the attic unaware that we had been robbed. I told her about it when she came down.

"I want to get some fresh air," she said. "I need to get out of this house."

"Where do you want to go?"

"I just want to get out."

It had been over three weeks since she came to my bedroom window and she was getting anxious.

"Let's climb out the window," Beverly said.

It was springtime and the night air was warm. Everything was so quiet. We walked down a few blocks including the one where she lived. Everyone was asleep because all the lights were out. Beverly hurried past the house and didn't look back.

We climbed back in through my bedroom window about an hour later. At least Beverly was satisfied for now.

A few days later while Robert was watching TV in my bedroom we heard a noise.

"Shhhh," he whispered. I pretended I hadn't heard anything.

"I heard a noise," he said.

I shook my head, denying hearing anything. Then the noise happened again. There was no use denying it now. Robert rushed to his bedroom and grabbed the shotgun.

"What are you going to do?" I asked him. I started to panic when he stood under the opening leading into the attic.

"It may be only a mouse, but if someone is up there I am going to blow a hole in him!"

I wanted to stop him--to tell him that Beverly was up there.

Somehow the words couldn't find their way out. Instead I watched him climb up into the attic.

"Do you see anything?" I asked him.

"No I can't see anything."

He fired three or four shots into the attic.

"What is it?" I shouted up to him while my heart was pumping faster and faster.

He climbed back down.

"I didn't see anything, but I decided to shoot off a few rounds just in case. If anyone was up there they are dead now."

I watched as he covered the opening to the attic. What should I do now? My knees were so weak I couldn't stand up. My mind was cluttered and I tried to sort everything out. What should I do if Beverly was shot? I was nervous the entire time Robert watched TV in my bedroom. After their TV was stolen they started coming into my bedroom to watch TV. I was happy when Robert left for work.

I stared at the attic door wanting to go up there. I was lying across the bed trying to figure things out when I felt something pulling my arm. A shaken Beverly stood by my bed. We held onto each other, crying when we realized that she had come close to getting shot or even killed.

"Let's get out of here," she said. "I need some air. I'm afraid to go back up there." We climbed out the window again. While we were walking Beverly told me the only reason she didn't get shot was because she stood directly behind Robert and when he moved she moved with him.

Beverly still wasn't ready to return home. She believed that her father was waiting to beat her again. We walked in the direction of Monaco Street, crossed the railroad tracks, and ended up on the backside of the Monaco Theater. We met two guys who were also walking in the back of the theater.

They walked along with us for a while before we turned into another direction.

In Years To Come

When we crossed the vacant field behind the Drive-In, bright lights flashed in my eyes blinding me momentarily. I could hear the scrambling of feet while I stood in the light trying to shield my eyes. I heard a man's voice.

"I almost shot you!" he said. When my eyes adjusted I saw two policemen.

"Two guys just robbed a nearby hotel," he said to me. I don't suppose you came across them while you were out here walking."

My thoughts were already racing inside of my head as I thought about the two guys we had met.

Two more police cars drove up. "We've got the suspects," he told the policeman who was talking to me.

"Why are you out here this time of night? Is there anyone with you?"

I felt Beverly must be safe because they had the two guys in the back of the police car.

I shook my head and stood while they took their flashlights and searched the area.

"I didn't find anything," one of them said.

I was charged with curfew violation and taken home. Robert had just gotten home from work and climbed into bed when they knocked on the door. He was surprised that the police were bringing me home. I didn't sleep well that night because I kept waiting for Beverly to knock on my bedroom window.

The next morning there still wasn't any sign of Beverly. She finally showed up hours later at my window.

"Where were you?" I whispered to keep Robert and Judy from hearing us.

"I spent the night at the Drive-In."

"They were looking all over the area."

"I know. I saw them, but they didn't see me. A bullet went right pass my head," she said.

I was shocked because I didn't know they had fired their

264

gun. This was the second time she was almost shot.

"We can't go out anymore at night."

She agreed with me.

I could hear footsteps coming toward my bedroom, and Beverly jumped into the closet. I was lying across the bed when Robert rushed into my bedroom and turned on the TV. I hated that his TV got stolen because now he was always watching mine.

The closet door was still open. I tried to get past Robert so I could shut it, but then Judy ran into the bedroom to watch what was happening on the TV.

"Dr. Martin Luther King jr. has been shot!" Robert said aloud.

"Who?"

"Dr. Martin Luther King jr."

I knew about Dr. Martin Luther King Jr. because he was always involved in Freedom marches. He gave speeches and people followed him. Sadness swept over me as I stared at the TV and the picture of Dr. Martin Luther King jr. fixed in the background. They showed a mob of angry, mainly black people, starting to riot.

"Oh my God," Robert kept saying.

The distraction allowed me to get to the closet and shut the door before they could see Beverly who was in clear view sitting on the floor.

We heard later that evening that Dr. Martin Luther King jr. was dead. A part of me wanted to go out into the streets and riot too.

"There is going to be a riot," I told Robert.

He laughed at me. "This is Denver," he said. "People don't riot here."

Suddenly I missed Milwaukee because it was different in Denver. The people in Milwaukee were angry and ready to riot, while in Denver they didn't seem to be doing much of anything. I began feeling that I didn't belong in Denver. I missed Joe, Ralph, and Sara. I wanted to go back home because I understood the people back there.

In Years To Come

Beverly and I talked about Dr. Martin Luther King jr. I told her about the riots in Milwaukee and how they burned everything down on Third Street. We both wanted to do something so we decided to take another walk. We didn't get far this time because the policemen drove up and immediately jumped out of the car. We had violated curfew and they discovered that Beverly was a runaway. I was taken back home again and Beverly went to juvenile Hall.

When Robert found out that Beverly had been staying with us all along he was upset with me. Things were starting to get tense between us. He was especially shaken after learning that she was in the attic when he fired off those rounds.

"I could have killed her!" he repeated over and over again.

Mrs. Tolliver was shocked that I had blatantly lied to her.

"You are a bad influence on Beverly," she told me.

Robert and Mr. and Mrs. Tolliver agreed that it was best if Beverly and I stayed away from each other. When Beverly got out of juvenile hall she went home to her family. When I saw her in school she told me she couldn't talk to me anymore.

"Things have changed at home," she told me.

I didn't understand why her parents preferred the friend she met in juvenile hall to me. Everyone, including Robert, blamed me for Beverly's decision to run away. They wouldn't listen to me and I was constantly reminded of how close Robert had come to shooting her.

"How could you stand there looking up at me so calm knowing she was in the attic?" he asked me.

I had no answer.

I became withdrawn and alienated myself from everyone. I cursed at the teachers, refused to do any work at home or school. I didn't listen to what anyone said including Robert.

"It's a girl," Stephen informed us when Stephanie was born on the last day of April. I fell in love with her the moment I saw her. She looked so much like her father with the wide smile, tiny eyes, and beautiful round face.

266

"Can I hold her?"

It felt so good when they placed the tiny bundle in my arms. I wanted to cry as I stared down at my niece. I had never held a tiny baby before. Stephen was proud of the daughter that looked so much like him. When I held her close the baby smell was sweet. I could almost feel her heart beating.

"She likes you," her mother said, making me feel really good.

Joyce joked about how we would have the same name once she and Stephen got married. She clung to Stephen and treated him as if he were a king. I felt sorry for her because I knew Stephen was seeing another woman who lived in Englewood. He brought her to our house a few times and introduced her to us. I was hoping that with Stephanie's birth things would change between Stephen and Joyce, but they only got worse. He continued to see other women while she stayed home with the baby. Although Joyce was older than me we had a great friendship. Sometimes I spent the night at their house to keep her company while Stephen was gone. I would sit and hold Stephanie for hours, glad to be away from Robert and Judy.

Judy was telling me I wasn't the bad one and I didn't need Beverly as a friend. As time went on, I came to rely on Judy to make me feel better about myself, which was a big mistake. We ended up in a big fight and I had such a dislike for her that even Robert couldn't change it. Judy admitted that seeing me lose my best friend gave her the opportunity to take advantage of me. Her admission made things worse. I was miserable and wanted to go back home to Milwaukee.

Hurt by Beverly's coolness towards me, angered by Judy's betrayal, and confused by my brother's attitude, all contributed to my desire to leave Denver. I was sure that Robert really wanted to help me, but maybe he was just a few years too late. So much had happened to me that he didn't even know about. The anger, the hate, and the shame I was feeling were buried inside of me. My last fight with Judy sent me to juvenile hall

I stood before the judge with a face of stone and a smoldering anger inside of me.

"I don't want her to live with me anymore," Robert told the judge. "Send her back to Milwaukee."

Although those were the words I wanted to hear, I was still filled with an internal pain.

"So much has happened to me in thirteen short years," I thought as I looked out the window of the plane. It was my first plane ride and I was too mixed up to be scared. An older man sat in the seat next to me reading a newspaper. I was going back to Milwaukee where I belonged. Robert's life was different from mine. He had his wife and a son to take care of and there was no room for me. It had been several months and I still didn't get to know him or Stephen. He never knew what I had gone through or that the past was still haunting me. At least he tried to help me and for that I was grateful.

Stephen had visited when he could, but he also had his own life. He had finally gone down to the recruiting office and signed up to join the Marine Corps. I prayed that he would not be sent to Vietnam.

Uncle Guy lee may have had good intentions when he tried to discipline me, but I didn't know him that well either. I was certain that he had judged me without getting to know the real me.

I decided that I hated Denver. Its beauty was deceitful. I thought about Beverly and I knew it would be just a matter of time before her father started beating her again. I wouldn't be there next time so they couldn't blame it on me.

The plane landed at General Mitchell Field in the early afternoon. It was springtime and I couldn't wait to see the flowers blooming. Milwaukee had beautiful flowers and large trees that were scattered throughout the city. I especially loved the tulips that came in a variety of colors and the smell of lavender from the bushes. I walked off the plane with the other passengers onto the concourse. A man in a tight suit with an old trench coat spotted me right away.

"Are you Joyce?"

I nodded at him. He looked funny with his large head and freckled face.

"I'm your new case worker, Joe McCormick."

I smiled at him. I was home again.

Chapter Ten

Adams Hall

Mr. Mc McCormick drove an old, beat-up 1955 Buick that was a light green. The noise from the car was loud as we drove through the city. The car stopped in front of an old house that was as tall as an apartment building. I heard later that it had once been a mansion. The outside was a dark brick, almost black in color, with ivy growing up the walls. The house had lots of windows in different sizes. Many tall trees and bushes surrounded the large lot hiding most of it from view. The house was situated on a busy street amid tall apartment buildings. At first glance there was spookiness about the place that made me shiver.

"This is Adams Hall," Mr. Mc McCormick said as we were getting out of the car. "This house was donated to the city and converted into a place for kids to live while in transition to a foster home. It is named after the person who donated the house."

I nodded and followed him as we climbed the concrete steps up to the house. The place looked gloomy from the outside, but once we stepped through the double doors, sunshine glinted from every window and the brightness lit up the place. The foyer was big with a high ceiling. I marveled at the winding staircase that was on my left. I almost expected to see a life-size picture of someone on one of the walls with eyes that followed you around the room like I had seen in the movies.

Mr. McCormick walked down the hall to a room that had been turned into an office. An older black woman with a short afro mixed with gray was sitting behind a desk. She looked up at us through thick glasses.

"May I help you?" Her voice was low like a man's.

"I'm Joe McCormick and this is Joyce Ford. I am her social worker."

"Hello, I'm Joann Hopkins." the woman said giving us a pleasant smile and extending a hand towards Mr. McCormick.

The woman pointed to the chairs in front of the desk. We sat down while she thumbed through some files. She pulled one out and glanced over it.

"Okay, we have everything we need for Joyce to become a resident of Adams Hall," the woman said looking up at us with the same smile. McCormick answered all the questions while I looked around the room noticing stacks of papers throughout the room. Two more desks took up space in the office, and there were file cabinets in one corner and a typewriter on one of the desks.

Mrs. Hopkins turned to me. "We have rules here at Adams Hall, and if you break them, depending on how serious the offense is, you could end up in the Detention Center."

I listened carefully while she went over the rules. Most of them seemed okay, but a few were stupid. I nodded anyway. The next thing she did was an inventory of everything I had brought with me. I was embarrassed that I had to empty my suitcase of clothes in front of Mr. McCormick. Mrs. Hopkins wrote everything down including color and size on an inventory list. "We inventory everything you bring into Adams Hall and everything you take when you leave," she told me. Mr. McCormick looked relieved when he was finally able to leave.

I followed Mrs. Hopkins down the hall to another area of

the house.

"This is the only bedroom on this floor," she told me. "I am putting you in here because we don't have any more beds upstairs."

The room was small and didn't have a window. I felt closed in, but I wasn't going to let her know it. I took my things I had out of the suitcase.

I was especially impressed with all the activities she told me about. It had been awhile since I had been to the movies and Friday was movie night.

Another counselor came into the hallway just as Mrs. Hopkins was taking me on a tour of Adams Hall.

"Do you want me to show her around?"

Mrs. Hopkins smiled. "That would be nice if you could, Mr. Holt."

Mr. Holt was a tall, younger man with short brown hair and matching eyes.

"Where did you live before coming here, Joyce?"

"Denver, Colorado," I answered quickly.

Mr. Holt looked puzzled.

"I was in living in Denver with my brother. I went there almost a year ago, but things didn't work out so I'm back here."

Mr. Holt nodded as if he understood.

"I heard it is beautiful in Colorado," he said.

"Yes, it is."

"All the residents are in school right now," he told me. "So we can take a quick tour."

My shoes were slippery as we walked across the polished ceramic tile floors. I followed him up the wide, winding staircase and could hear the wood squeaking in some places. The first landing was the second floor.

"This is where the boys sleep," he told me. "Girls are not allowed on this floor. There are severe consequences if we find any girls on this floor."

We continued up another flight of stairs.

"This is where the girls sleep and no boys are allowed up here either."

I saw three large open rooms with several beds lined against the wall like a dormitory. Each resident had his or her own bed with a small nightstand. The closets and dressers were shared. There were bathrooms on each floor.

All of the beds were neatly made and some were decorated with pillows or stuffed animals. I took a deep breath of the spring-like scent that was in the air. The place was clean.

"Everyone is assigned chores," Mr. Holt said when I commented about the cleanliness.

I stared at the large crystal chandelier hanging off the ceiling as we walked back downstairs. It was a beautiful chandelier that sparkled like glass.

The main floor had a big recreation room with a black and white TV, record player, and a table with chairs. A large stack of records was near the record player. I took a moment to look through them. I recognized a few, *The Temptations*, Smokey Robinson, and Stevie Wonder.

The kitchen was close to my bedroom and I could smell the food even before we walked through the door. I was surprised to see the biggest kitchen I had ever laid eyes on. An older woman with a white apron tied around her waist and a net covering her silver-streaked hair greeted us.

"This is Mrs. Campbell."

"Hi," I said.

"This is our new resident, Joyce," Mr. Holt told her. I was staring at the small bowls filled with chocolate pudding that she was putting in the large refrigerator.

"This is where we eat," he said pointing to a large table with several chairs around it.

"Everyone eats at the same time?"

"Yes," he said. I remembered how important it was for all

of us to eat together when I was in the children's home.

"What time do we eat dinner?" My stomach was empty because I hadn't eaten anything. I should have eaten something on the plane, but I wasn't thinking about food at that time.

Mr. Holt checked his watch, "We eat dinner at five o' clock. The residents should be coming in from school soon. You can watch TV or listen to some music in the recreation room if you want."

When we were back in the hallway he pointed to a door that was across from my bedroom. "That is the cooler; we put kids in there to cool off." I walked to the door of the cooler and peeked in through the opening at the top. It was dark in the room. My mind went blank as I flashed back to the cellar room where Mrs. Watson put us. I knew that I didn't want to ever be put in the cooler.

I decided to lie down on the bed. I fell asleep and woke up when I heard loud voices and someone screamed. I sat straight up on the bed.

"Hi."

I turned around to see a girl standing in the doorway. She walked into the bedroom. "My name is Tammie."

She was a Puerto Rican girl with a warm brown complexion and jet-black wavy hair that hung down her back.

"My name is Joyce."

"They put you down in this room huh?"

I nodded.

"You want to sleep or do you want to go watch TV?"

I got up and followed Tammie to the recreation room where some of the other kids had gathered.

Tammie introduced me to several of them and told me about each one of them. I knew which kids came from broken homes and which kids were rebellious.

"I couldn't get along with my mother," Tammie told me of her situation. "The last time I was home we fought like two

274

high school kids." She laughed at the thought. "Anyway, I ran away from home and when they caught me my mother told them to take me away."

"What's going to happen now?" I asked.

"My mother and I are talking again so maybe we will work things out. I might have to go to a foster home though."

Tammie and I hung out together that evening. I met more counselors when the shift changed. Mrs. Campbell proved to be a good cook and I wolfed my food down like I hadn't eaten in days. My eyes lit up when I saw the small bowls of pudding placed by each plate. Tammie pointed out a tall white boy with blonde hair and greenish eyes who was sitting across from us with another boy.

"He's seventeen," she whispered to me. Tammie was only fourteen.

I didn't see anything special about him.

"I think he's cute." She giggled like a silly girl.

"I kissed him a couple of times."

I looked at her and this time I laughed. His name was Alan and he seemed to be into himself. I suspected he didn't really like Tammie because he ignored her the whole time we were in the recreation room.

"He didn't say anything to you," I reminded her later.

"He said that we shouldn't be seen talking together."

"Why? Everyone else talks to each other."

"He's shy," she said.

"There is nothing shy about him," I told her. "Could it be that he doesn't want anyone knowing he's kissing a Puerto Rican?"

Tammie eyes narrowed. "He likes Puerto Ricans."

Alan's main friend was another white boy named David. He was shorter than Alan and wore a black leather jacket all the time. He used something in his brownish hair that made it shine. I suspected it was some type of grease because it made his hair slick. He kept it combed back off of his pimpled face. David was definitely not an attractive boy. From what I heard he didn't like anyone who wasn't white.

The controversy started when we were in the recreation room listening to music. I was tired of hearing all white music. Sometimes I enjoyed The Beatles, Rolling Stones, and other white bands, but I also enjoyed listening to black music.

"I'm playing James Brown," I announced after the last record in the stack that David had put on the record player finished. I was ready to replace the other records with a James Brown one when he walked to where I was standing. I looked up at him.

"What are you looking at?" he asked.

I rolled my eyes at him and turned away.

"We don't want to hear James Brown."

"Well I do".

The silence in the room hung over us like a curse. I stared into his eyes. I would not allow him to intimidate me.

"We outnumber your ass and we don't want to hear no dam monkey looking James Brown song."

I ignored him and proceeded to put on my record anyway. Everyone was watching us. I was the only black face in the room and there were only two Puerto Ricans.

"Say it loud, I'm black and I'm proud," screamed from the record player. I started singing along with the record and pointing at him. I was dancing across the floor all by myself. I saw his face turn red and I smiled to myself. Then I heard the dreadful sound of the needle scratching the record when he took it off.

"I'm black and I'm proud, you're white and you're foul," I spat at him.

"I would rather be white and foul than to be black and proud any day," he said with a smirk on his face.

The heated argument that followed landed us both in our

276

bedrooms for the rest of the evening. The counselors decided that equal time would be divided among all residents so that all of us got a chance to listen to the music we liked. I replaced the James Brown record that David had scratched and played it over and over just to irritate him. He left two weeks after I arrived. He went back home to his parents. I had heard that he was from a middle class family on the south side of town, but had gotten into trouble with two other teenagers so instead of going to the detention center, they sent him to Adams Hall for a couple of months.

Things were better at Adams Hall after David left because he was the main person who initiated the segregation among the kids. After he left we were like one big family who watched TV, danced to music and went on trips to the movies or other places. Most of us had one thing in common: we were displaced either because of abuse, neglect, or other problems. I was in the system because I was an orphan, and it seemed I was always the only orphan. Over the next few weeks kids left and others replaced them. We weren't separated by color; the whites, Puerto Rican, and blacks ate together, slept together, and shared all the facilities together. When I had come back to Milwaukee there were still a few weeks of school left before summer break, so I was enrolled in Lincoln, a junior and high school combination that was only a three-block walk from Adams Hall. The school was integrated although it was mostly populated with Puerto Ricans. I liked the school because of the older kids who went there.

I woke up early every morning to the sound of music playing on the radio near my bed. After the alarm went off the music started and that is what usually woke me up.

"I beg your pardon; I never promised you a rose garden, along with the sunshine, there's got to be a little rain sometime." I thought it was strange that this song would play every morning at about the same time.

One morning I was singing along with the radio. "The day my mama socked it to the Harper Valley PTA," I sang at the top of my voice.

Tammie clapped and fell on the bed laughing.

Tammie met Alan in back of the house that evening. She didn't bother to tell me where she was going and I was looking all over for her. She showed up a couple of hours later and I could smell the liquor even before she got close.

"What the hell happened to you?"

"I was in the back drinking with Alan." Her words were slurred and she was weaving.

I caught her before she could fall down. It was hard getting her into my room because Tammie was a big girl.

She was crying and talking at the same time.

"Alan knows I love him," she said.

"He doesn't love you, Tammie."

"I know it," she said. "He only wants one thing from me." She started crying again. "Tonight he was giving me something to drink to relax me, but what he wanted was to have sex with me."

"Did you do it?" I stared at Tammie in disbelief.

She shook her head. "I couldn't."

I knew it was one of the counselors when I heard the knock on the door. I wasn't supposed to have the door closed except when I was changing clothes.

I opened the door and Mrs. Johnson saw Tammie lying on the bed. I was sure she smelled the liquor.

"What's going on?"

Tammie started crying again. This time I knew she was busted. Mrs. Johnson grabbed her off the bed. She took her screaming and crying and put her in the cooler. Tammie kept screaming and looking through the hole in the door.

Alan left the next day. I heard he was sent to the Detention Center for having liquor on the premises.

I stayed in Adams Hall for about six weeks and in that time I made many friends. Tammie eventually returned home to her family.

All the other kids had come and gone but I was still there. I was getting comfortable being there so it didn't matter anymore if I went to a foster home or not.

I was called to the office one day and saw Mr. McCormick sitting there. I knew he had come to take me away. A sense of sorrow overwhelmed me.

"We've made the arrangements for you to return to your Uncle Ben's house," Mr. McCormick told me. "They called when they heard you had returned to Milwaukee."

I couldn't believe it. I was going back to Uncle Ben's house! A part of me was happy, but another part was apprehensive. Joe had already moved back and was waiting for me to join him. The thought of being reunited with Joe was so great that I didn't care about anything else.

I stayed in Adams Hall until the end of the school semester. It gave me time to say goodbye to all my friends. My last day at Adams Hall was good because we had a small celebration. I thought about Robert a lot and wished I could apologize to him and Judy for some of the things I had done. I also thought about my friend Beverly, who I missed. I wondered if I would ever see her again. I wanted to believe this was going to be my last stay with Uncle Ben and Aunt Lea. I was tired of moving around and wanted desperately to stay in one place forever.

I had missed Joe, Ralph, and Sara and wanted to see them. When we pulled up in front of the familiar pink and turquoise house my excitement was genuine. I prayed this would be the last time I would have to move. Uncle Ben and Aunt Lea met me at the door with open arms and I ran into them. We hugged each other tightly. Nate was watching from across the room, and when I looked up, he smiled at me.

Chapter Eleven

Uncle Ben's house the third time

Nate was still working at the factory and making even more money than before. He had replaced the black car with a newer one. Joe and I talked for hours, catching up on what happened during the year we were apart. I told him about Denver and how pretty it was there.

"I wish I could go there," Joe said. We agreed to return to Denver together when we were grown.

"I couldn't stay with Mr. and Mrs. Guy either because I didn't get along with him."

We laughed about how strange the couple was. He told me that Ralph and Sara were still living with them.

"They are doing okay," Joe said.

Uncle Ben kept talking to us about opening a restaurant on Third Street.

"You and Joe will be working in the restaurant and I'm going to pay you".

Aunt Lea and I had our first disagreement.

"You better not get pregnant," she said to me. I wasn't sexually active but she didn't believe me and kept checking to make sure I had a period every month.

Three weeks had passed when I ran into Alice and Lois on the street corner. I hadn't seen them since we were in the Detention Center together.

"You're coming with us," Alice said grabbing my arm.

"I'm living with my aunt and uncle," I told them. "I can't go with you." They still intimidated me so I allowed myself to be led away. First, we went to Alice's cousin's house on Brown Street. The house was dirty and her cousin had at least six or seven kids who were running around, so it was very noisy. I begged Alice to let me return to my uncle's house but she wouldn't. I ended up staying all night in her cousin's house sleeping on the end of the couch while Alice slept at the other end. Lois didn't stay with us that night.

The next day Alice kept me close to her. We walked to her house a few blocks away where we showered and changed clothes. We returned to the cousin's house where Lois was waiting for us. We spent most of the day talking. I listened mostly to the two of them talk. Alice promised that I could return home the next day.

That evening after Lois left I went with Alice to a street corner where two guys were waiting for us. Victor was a cute guy about nineteen years old. He immediately grabbed my arm when we approached them.

The four of us walked down the street to another house. Victor tried to make small talk, but I was shy and didn't say much. Victor was pulling my arm and I followed him up the stairs into the house. He immediately led me to a bedroom with two beds in it. My heart was beating so fast I could hardly catch my breath. I wanted to run, but I couldn't move. My legs felt heavy and my head was light.

Victor slammed the door shut and pulled me down onto the bed. I sat there stiff and afraid. Alice and the other boy were already on the other bed kissing.

"What's wrong with you?" Victor asked kissing on my

neck. I pulled away from him. I saw what was going on in the other bed.

"I don't want to do it," I whispered.

He looked at me as if he was seeing me for the first time. "How old are you?"

"Thirteen."

"Have you ever done this before?"

I shook my head and started crying.

Victor jumped up from the bed. "Damn," he said. "You're still a virgin," he spat at me. He shook his head, "I don't have time for this."

He opened the door and practically threw me out of the bedroom. I was alone in the hallway waiting for Alice who was in there with both of them. I sat on the floor and waited for her.

When Alice finally came out the four of us walked back down the street to her cousin's house. Alice was mad at me when we got back to her cousin's house.

"Why didn't you tell me you've never done it before?"

I shrugged my shoulders.

The next day I was sitting on the porch of Alice's cousin's house when a group of girls approached me. The girl who was leading the pack had a stomach that was sticking out far enough that I could see she was pregnant.

"I heard you were with Victor last night," she said to me.

I shook my head.

"Yes, you were. Someone told me that they saw you with him and I'm going to kick your ass."

I couldn't believe I was in the middle of this big mess. The door opened and Alice came out on the porch.

"Leave her alone," she told the group of girls. When the pregnant one started arguing with Alice I found out that she was Victor's girlfriend and was pregnant with his baby.

The girl and Alice knew each other and somehow they resolved it without me getting beat up. I was ready to go back to

Uncle Ben's house.

"You're right," the girl said loudly. "Victor wouldn't want anything to do with her ugly ass." She and the group of girls laughed as they walked away.

I didn't want anything more to do with Alice or Lois. I didn't like boys and couldn't do the things that they were doing.

"I'll let you go back home after today," Alice promised me when Lois showed up.

Alice's other cousin had three kids, two were toddlers and the other one was a baby.

"I need a babysitter," the cousin told Alice when we went over to her house. I felt their eyes on me and knew they would volunteer me to baby-sit.

"Joyce will watch your kids," Alice said.

"Thomas should be home from work in a few hours and he can watch them until I get home," the cousin told me. Thomas was her boyfriend and the father of the last two.

Babysitting was fun. I enjoyed playing with the kids. They were so cute after I gave them a bath and combed the girl's hair. I played with them until they got tired. The baby was the one who needed the most attention. I held her and walked around the house singing to her. It was the first time that I was alone without Alice or Lois, so it was nice. If it weren't for the kids I would have left and found my way back to Uncle Ben's house, but I couldn't leave the kids alone.

I was watching TV when I heard the door open. I was enjoying the time alone with the kids, but now the boyfriend was home. I looked up and saw a big man walking through the door. He eyed me with suspicion.

"I'm the babysitter," I told him.

He grunted something and went into the kitchen. The kids were taking naps so it was very quiet in the apartment. I heard noises in the kitchen and assumed he was looking for something to eat. I had fixed something for the kids, but I didn't really know how to cook food.

The man returned to the room where I was watching TV. He had a beer in his hand that he was sipping on.

"What's your name?"

I looked up at him. "Joyce," I murmured.

"How old are you?"

"I am thirteen," I said.

He smiled and drank more beer.

I got up off the couch because I was beginning to feel uncomfortable.

"The kids are taking a nap, so I better go now."

"You are the babysitter so you better stay here with the kids," he said.

"She told me to stay here until you came home," I told him.

He laughed. "I'm not babysitting."

I wished she had had come home before he did. I didn't know what to say to this man. He finished off the beer and walked over to where I was standing. I could smell the liquor on him and suspected that he had more than just the one beer.

"I just got paid today," he said, smiling. "How much would you charge me to have some fun with you?"

I backed away from him. Again, I could feel my heart beating fast. I knew what he was talking about.

"I just want to leave." I told him.

He took a wad of money out of his pants pocket and showed it to me. "Look at this."

I kept backing up trying to get closer to the door.

He reached out for me and I began fighting him. He tried to throw me on the floor, but I was fighting hard. I screamed out, hoping someone would hear me, but he put his hand over my mouth. I bit his hand and he let me go. I ran for the door with him on my heels. I opened the door and started down the stairs. He was close to me. He caught me again halfway down the stairs and

284

turned me around, trying to kiss me on the mouth. He was laughing and trying to raise my dress up. The money was sticking out of his shirt pocket so I grabbed it. He stopped what he was doing and tried to get the money back, which gave me an opportunity to run again. This time I made it out the door and kept running until I reached the house where Alice was. I was out of breath and crying by the time I walked through the door.

"What the hell happened to you?" Alice asked me.

I tried to catch my breath to tell her, but she saw the money in my hands. I had forgotten about the money until then.

"Where did you get that money?"

I told her what happened.

"We are going shopping."

I refused to let go of the money so Alice and Lois decided I could keep it and pay for their purchases. We walked to a nearby Sears store a few blocks away. I sat in the chair while the two of them tried on different clothes.

A security guard passed by and I ran to him while they were in the dressing room.

"I'm in trouble," I told him. "Please help me. There are two girls who brought me here and they are trying to make me pay for clothes with money I grabbed from a man who was trying to do something bad to me."

The security guard took me to a room to wait while he called the police. When Alice and Lois came out of the fitting room and saw I was gone they left the store. The police arrived and listened while I repeated my story of how Alice and Lois made me go with them for two days. I told them what happened with the man and showed them the money I took from him.

One police officer took the money from me and counted it. "We'll take you back home," they promised.

I sat in the back of the police car, rubbing my hands together. I felt as if I had been in a fairy tale the last couple of days. We pulled up in front of the house and I breathed a sigh of relief. I was happy to be back. The policemen escorted me to the door. Uncle Ben and Aunt Lea were obviously upset with me and thought I had run away because of the disagreement with Aunt Lea. I repeated my story to Uncle Ben and Aunt Lea in front of the policemen. They told me I was welcomed back home and everything was all right.

"Thank you," I whispered, grateful that they believed me.

The policemen left and immediately Uncle Ben started yelling at me.

"What do you think they are doing with that money you gave them?" he asked.

I shrugged my shoulders. I had taken the police to the house where the man lived, but no one had answered the door.

"They are going to split the damn money and keep it. You should have at least kept the money. You didn't have to tell them about the money."

I didn't want to keep the money. I wanted them to arrest the man because he was trying to do something bad to me.

Uncle Ben shook his head. "We could have used that money. How much was it anyway?"

"They said it was over eighty dollars."

Uncle Ben was shaking his head. "We sure could have used that money," he repeated.

I felt that all he was concerned about was the money. I had been through a terrible ordeal, but no one cared about that.

The next morning Aunt Lea and I had another disagreement. "You were probably out there messing around with boys," she said to me. "I hope you don't come up pregnant."

Nate was sitting at the table eating and I was embarrassed by what she was saying.

"I'm a virgin," I blurted out to her.

Aunt Lea looked at me as if she didn't believe it.

"I am a virgin," I yelled at her.

Aunt Lea took me to a doctor who confirmed that I was

286

still a virgin, which surprised her because she really believed that I was sexually active. I was glad to prove to her that I was telling the truth. I didn't hear any more of Aunt Lea's remarks about me getting pregnant.

Uncle Ben and Aunt Lea opened Ford's Barbeque Pit on Third Street a couple of weeks into the summer.

"You will work with me in the evenings and Joe will work with Lea during the day," Uncle Ben said.

Joe and I were both excited about working in the restaurant because it seemed like it was going to be fun. I didn't care that my summer would be spent working. I didn't want to risk meeting Alice or Lois on the streets again.

The restaurant was a big success when it opened. Aunt Lea cooked greens, beans, cornbread and other soul food and Uncle Ben barbequed the meat that we were famous for. The restaurant stayed opened until two O'clock in the morning and if it was a busy night it didn't close at all. Weekends it was open twenty-four hours.

The location of the restaurant was perfect. It was on a busy street and next-door to a teenage club. The music coming from the club could be heard through the walls. I was too young to go into the club because you had to be at least eighteen to get in.

After the club let out, teenagers crowded into our restaurant to listen to the jukebox, talk and eat burgers and French fries. Uncle Ben taught me how to cook hamburgers on the grill and cut up potatoes for French fries. We were busy from the time the club let out to early in the morning. There wasn't a lot of business in the early morning hours from one until four a.m. except on weekends. Sometimes people wondered in off the streets for something to drink.

The end of the first week Uncle Ben handed me a crisp ten-dollar bill and I almost fainted. I was glad to get the money and spent all of it in the stores further down Third Street. Joe was also getting ten dollars a week to work there.

Uncle Ben and I went straight to bed when we got home in the mornings. I didn't sleep long and was up within a few hours. Uncle Ben slept a lot longer. Nate also worked the night shift so he was sleeping at the same time we were.

Sometimes Nate got up and left the house or he would just hang around and talk to me. Our conversations were strange because Nate told me about having girl friends. He told me he had a lot of girlfriends, but he never brought them home. I didn't know how to respond to him so I listened while he talked. He also claimed to be friends with many of the teenagers who hung out at the restaurant.

There were two popular guys who were brothers and about twenty-one and twenty two years old who went to the club every week. They were nice-looking and the girls liked them. The older one, Stephen, was cute and he always smiled at me. Nate knew the brothers and told me they were his friends from high school. Stephen always played the flip side of the Dells popular ballad *Stay in My Corner* and would sing along with the record.

The restaurant seemed to be the best thing that could have happened to all of us. Nate was friendlier towards me and any trace of the meanness he once had was gone. He was still working at the factory and making lots of money.

I was in the bedroom when Nate walked in. Uncle Ben had left to go somewhere that day so it was just the two of us. He started talking to me about the things he did with his girlfriends. I was listening to him just like I always did.

"Maybe I should show you what we do," he remarked. The next thing I knew, I was being held down on the bed by his massive body. I couldn't breathe or move because he was a strong man. He was on top of me and I knew what was going to happen. I couldn't do anything to stop it so I just lay there. Then it happened, the thing I had fought off so many times. I felt a burning sensation mixed with pain and cried out. My cry went unheard and what followed was a nightmare. I felt a lot of brutal pushing and my body moving involuntarily. When it was over I stood up and blood ran down my leg.

I locked myself in the downstairs bathroom and that is where Aunt Lea found me hours later when she came home. Nate had already left for work. She told me to clean myself up and never asked me what happened. I took a long, hot shower, carefully washing my bruised body. I wanted to die right there in the shower because I felt so ashamed of myself and cried until I couldn't shed another tear.

Uncle Ben didn't notice anything different when I went to work that evening. I tried to act as if nothing had happened but everything kept flashing through my head like a bad movie. I kept running to the bathroom so he wouldn't see me burst out in tears. I tried my best to control myself. I had to do it because I couldn't let anyone know what happened. I believed it was my fault so I had to try to forget about it. I didn't know that it wouldn't be the only time.

It was impossible for me to stop Nate from attacking me so he did it whenever and wherever he wanted to. I knew it was wrong and I wanted to tell someone but I was too afraid. I didn't like coming home anymore because I never knew when it was going to happen again. I fought sleep, even though I was tired from being up all night because he usually woke me up to sexually assault me. I couldn't look at anyone anymore and kept my eyes downcast. I felt different and hated myself even more. Nate didn't care; sometimes he raped me two or three times in one day. I panicked at the thought of missing a period because I knew what that meant, but thankfully I never missed.

I stayed close to Joe and followed him around whenever he was home because I felt safe being with him. I didn't tell Joe what was going on because of the shame and guilt I felt. One night Joe and I were lying on the floor in the living room. When it was hot we would put a stack of records on the record player, turn off the lights, lie on the floor and listen to the music. I never heard Nate come into the room and was surprised when I felt another body lying next to me on my right side. I knew it was Nate. I prayed that he would leave because I was not going to go upstairs with him. I felt him pull me, but I wouldn't move. I pretended to be asleep, hoping he would leave me alone. Then I felt his hands tugging at my panties. I tried to stop him and when he pried my legs open I kept closing them, but he was stronger than me. He rolled over on top of me and I felt myself stiffen. He knew Joe was lying on the floor next to me, but it didn't seem to matter to him. I couldn't believe he was doing this to me while Joe was there. I prayed that Joe was asleep during the assault. When it was over he got up, leaving me lying there with my panties off and my dress up. I didn't want to move. I cried, but no one could see my tears. I wanted Nate to stop, but I knew he wouldn't. I never thought my own cousin would be doing this to me.

Joe and I never mentioned that night on the floor so I assumed that he was asleep. I became withdrawn from everything and everyone. It was hard talking to anyone, including Aunt Lea and Uncle Ben. I couldn't look anyone in the face and jumped whenever a man came close to me. I had crying spells and couldn't function at times. Uncle Ben yelled at me a lot because I forgot things. Memories of the times in the bathroom with Michael and the feel of Mr. Watson's hands all over me came back.

I had to tell someone. I needed to talk to someone who would believe me. The only person I could think of was Little Ben's wife, Emma. She had come with him and their children to visit a couple of times. She was nice to me, and although she and Aunt Lea didn't get along, I liked her. I was sure she would listen to me.

I walked to their apartment one afternoon when I didn't have to work. She was feeding the kids when I walked through the door. I had already rehearsed what I was going to tell her, but when I got inside I just started crying. My body was shaking with sobs and I couldn't stop.

Emma held me and told me everything was okay. I kept shaking my head and telling her it wasn't.

"What is going on?"

"Something bad," I murmured to her.

Emma stared at me. "What is it?"

I looked up at her and realized I couldn't tell her. The words wouldn't come out.

"Is someone doing something bad to you?"

I nodded my head.

"You can tell me," she said.

I started crying all over again.

"It's okay," Emma said.

"Is someone forcing you have sex with him?"

Her words took me by surprise. How did she know?

"Please don't say anything," I told her. "I don't want to get in trouble."

Emma had tears in her eyes too. "Is it someone in the family?"

I nodded.

"That son of a bitch," she said out loud. I didn't tell Emma the details of the abuse or who it was because I couldn't talk about it. I told her when it started and how afraid I was to tell anyone.

About a week after my visit with Emma, Uncle Ben and I came home from working all night at the restaurant and found the house empty. Joe, Aunt Lea, and Nate were all gone and so were their clothes. Uncle Ben was furious because he didn't understand why she left this time. They hadn't had any arguments or problems that he could think of. I was upset because they had taken Joe with them.

Uncle Ben had to close the restaurant at night because he

didn't have anyone to work in it and we started working during the day. It was the first time in a long time that I had actually slept soundly.

Later that day, Ike called Uncle Ben and told him to bring me and meet him at his tavern. I sat in the front seat listening to Uncle Ben curse all the way down to the tavern. "I don't know what the hell Ike wants," he said to me. "He wants both of us to come down there. I got enough problems with Lea gone and losing business at the restaurant."

I shrugged my shoulders. It had been awhile since I last saw Ike.

When we walked into the dimly lit tavern, Ike was waiting for us. Cousin Liza and Lucille were also in the tavern.

Ike took us to a small area to talk. He lit into Uncle Ben quickly.

"What is this I hear about you messing around with Joyce?" he stared straight at Uncle Ben. I saw the anger in Ike's eyes. "She is your niece, how could you do it?" He kept staring at Uncle Ben.

"What are you talking about?" Uncle Ben was puzzled.

"You know what I'm talking about!" Ike shouted at him. "I could kill your ass for doing something like this to Joyce."

"Messing with Joyce?" he asked.

"You know what I'm talking about." This time he said it bluntly.

My heart almost leaped out of my body.

"Hell No I'm not!" Uncle Ben shouted back at him. "And who the hell told you that damn lie?"

Uncle Ben was now angry and I shrunk back.

Ike looked at me. "I want you to tell me the truth," he said.

I was shaking and ready to cry.

"Has Uncle Ben ever messed around with you?"

"Uncle Ben would never do anything like that to me," I said with tears running down my face.

"Are you sure?"

"Uncle Ben never did anything to me."

Uncle Ben was crying too. His tears were mixed with anger. "Where did you hear something crazy like that? He asked Ike. "As God is my witness I would never do such a thing." Uncle Ben raised his hands up in a swearing manner.

Ike pointed to Cousin Liza who walked over to where we stood. She was between Ike and Uncle Ben.

"That daughter-in-law of yours is the one who said Joyce told her you were messing around her and Lea must be messing with Joe and that is why she probably took him with her when she left town this time."

"That's a lie!" Uncle Ben shouted. Then he looked down at me. I kept on crying.

"I didn't tell her it was you," I said weakly.

I felt all the eyes on me. I looked up at them with tears streaming down my face. Uncle Ben was shaking his head.

"Go sit down while we talk," Ike said to me. I sat at the other end of the bar while the three of them talked.

Lucille was sitting next to me.

"What's going on?" she asked.

I hunched my shoulders. I didn't want to tell her anything.

"I heard Lea left town again."

I nodded my head. Lucille laughed. "It seems every time you go back to live with them she leaves."

Uncle Ben didn't say anything while he drove back to the house. Before we got out of the car he turned to me. I could see his eyes were red from crying. His face looked old and worn. I suddenly felt sorry for him. I didn't mean for anyone to attack him for what Nate had done to me.

"I will make sure that Lea sends Joe back," he said. "I know you want to be with your brother."

I nodded and tears came flowing again. I missed Joe.

"Lea and Nate are not coming back this time," he finally

said. Joe was back two days later. He told me that Aunt Lea had the whole thing planned when they got home from working in the restaurant. They packed their clothes and drove all the way to Ohio. Joe never heard why they were leaving and he didn't ask them. They asked him if he wanted to go and he said yes, so they took him.

"Nate quit his job," Joe said.

Uncle Ben assured us that we would stay together and run the restaurant. Roy jr. finally married his longtime girlfriend, Mary and she helped cook food at the restaurant. Several other family members pitched in to help to keep the restaurant going. Uncle Ben placed a *help wanted* sign in the window.

The sisters who answered the sign were from Flint, Michigan and had been in town just a short time. They were renting a room in a house. When the two girls came in to inquire about the job Uncle Ben's eyes lit up and his smile widened. There was only one job available, but both of them ended up working there and within two weeks Uncle Ben had moved them into our house on Hadley Street. It was a strange arrangement, but Uncle Ben seemed happy with them so I didn't complain either.

The sisters, Karen and Katie, were twenty-three and twenty-one years old. The first time I saw Uncle Ben lying in bed between the girls, I was shocked. The sisters were supposed to be working in the restaurant, but after awhile I was doing more work than both of them. They only worked when they wanted to and spent most of the time having fun with their new friends.

One day I came home from working at the restaurant and the house was full of people. I could hear the music from the street. Joe was playing records and watching the people who had filled our den.

"They are having a party," Joe said. I didn't care that they were having a party and I joined Joe at the record player. We watched while they danced and drank liquor. Uncle Ben was tired when he came home later from the restaurant so he went to bed despite the noise from all the people.

Most of the crowd went home later, but a few were too drunk to leave and passed out on the floor of the den. When Uncle Ben got up during the night he saw people scattered all over the house and got mad. He made them leave and woke up the sisters and made them leave too. I was glad they moved out because things went back to normal. Uncle Ben hired another lady who worked hard in the restaurant and business started picking up again.

A young African student, Mezinga, who was twenty years old, started coming to the restaurant every day to eat. He talked to me about Africa and I was intrigued with all he had to say. He was a short man with chocolate brown skin and a small afro. He had a funny accent when he talked and sometimes I had to strain to understand his words. He told me he spoke several different languages.

"Mezinga wants to take you out on a date," Uncle Ben told me one day while I was wiping off the counter. Mezinga had just been there and I had seen the two of them talking.

"I don't want to go on a date with him." I remembered the terrible night I went on that date with Michael.

"He's a nice young man and a good customer. He asked me if he could take you to the movies."

"He's twenty years old," I whined. "I am only thirteen. I don't want to go anywhere with him."

"He is a good fellow. He's going to school, working a decent job."

"He's too old," I blurted out.

Uncle Ben laughed, "You're thirteen years old, a teenager, and I don't see anything wrong with you going to the movies with him. Go with him. He's one of our best customers."

I couldn't believe Uncle Ben was serious.

Uncle Ben's eyes stared into mine. I looked away, afraid to say no. I didn't want to go out alone with Mezinga, but Uncle

In Years To Come

Ben wanted me to.

"I'll give you a few extra dollars to buy a dress."

I managed a weak smile and Uncle Ben seemed happy.

I bought a white dress with puffed sleeves and a scarf to wear around my head. It was hot the evening Mezinga picked me up at the restaurant. We went to the movie, but I couldn't concentrate because Mezinga kept putting his hand on me. I felt uncomfortable around him and wished the movie would hurry up and end.

I had always enjoyed talking with Mezinga when he was at the restaurant, but this was different. The way he talked about Africa I imagined it to be a beautiful place. I could almost see the elephants, tigers and lions that roamed in the wild. We walked out of the movie hand in hand because he insisted on holding my hand. We were walking down Third Street towards the restaurant when we passed by an alley.

Mezinga was talking but I was paying little attention to him because I wanted to hurry back to the restaurant. I felt myself being pulled and before I could really say or do anything I was in the alley pushed up against a wall. Mezinga was trying to put his tongue in my mouth. I pushed him as hard as I could, but he was stronger than me. Then I felt my dress being pulled up. I knew what that meant, and all the strength I had seemed to come out. He told me I was acting like a big baby. I was able to push him away and run from the alley back to Third Street. I kept running until I reached the restaurant. I didn't even know I had been crying until I walked inside.

Uncle Ben was in the kitchen of the restaurant, and Darlene had just taken a customer a plate of food. She saw me walking in.

"What is wrong with you?" she asked.

I shook my head.

"Why are you crying?"

"I don't know," I answered, and hurried to the bathroom

before Uncle Ben could see me. I cried a few minutes longer, then washed my face and straightened out my hair. I had lost the scarf during the struggle.

Uncle Ben was surprised to see me.

"Where is Mezinga?" he asked.

"I think he went home," I told him.

"Did you enjoy the movie?"

"Yes," I lied.

Uncle Ben's words to me were, "That boy looked like he might have some money being from Africa."

Mezinga never came back to the restaurant and Uncle Ben never mentioned him again.

Aunt Lea and Nate had been gone for over two months but every time I heard Nate's name my body would automatically stiffen.

Uncle Ben started dating a light-skinned woman who sometimes came to the house. She was about his age and was nice to us. "Maybe this time Uncle Ben is really going to move on with his life," I thought.

One day when we had just gone through a rush hour crowd, I was putting napkins in the holder and taking a moment to relax. Uncle Ben was putting a couple of slabs of ribs on the barbecue pit. A guy came in. He wasn't as tall as Uncle Ben, but he had some height. He had a pigeon-toed walk and large brown eyes and a smile that made me look at him again. Judging from the nice suit he wore I was sure he had to have some money. He had never been in the restaurant before, I was sure of that. He sat down at the counter and I couldn't help noticing his goatee and full sideburns, just like Elvis Presley. His skin was peanut butter brown, his face was round, and his lips were thick.

"I would like a cheeseburger and fries," he said to me in a voice that was so deep I was taken back. I hurried to the kitchen with his order.

"Go ahead and cook it," Uncle Ben told me. I threw the

297

meat patty on the grill and placed a new batch of cut up potatoes in the fryer.

When I came back with his cheeseburger, the song *Stay in My Corner* by the Dells was playing on the jukebox.

"I love that song," he told me, smiling.

I was cautious not to say much to him. The incident with Mezinga was still fresh in my mind. I watched from the corner of my eye as he took a bite of the cheeseburger.

"Mmmm, this is good," he said with ketchup dripping down his mouth. He quickly wiped his chin.

"I made it myself," I said to him.

He nodded because his mouth was full of food.

"There are two more selections left on the jukebox. Go play another song."

I hurried to the jukebox and selected my favorite songs.

"*You make me feel like a natural woman!*" Aretha Franklin's voice filled the room as she belted out the words. He smiled at me and I looked away.

Uncle Ben came from the kitchen.

"How are you doing today?" Uncle Ben's voice surprised me and I jumped back. He was talking to the guy who ordered the cheeseburger and fries. I laughed at how funny Uncle Ben looked. His skin looked darker than usual because he wore all white. The shirt, pants, apron, and even the hat he wore were all white. He reminded me of the man on the Cream of Wheat box. "This is very good," he answered.

Another customer sat down at the counter, so I hurried over to take his order. After the guy finished the cheeseburger and fries I watched him get up and leave. I picked up his plate to take it back to the kitchen and was surprised to see a whole dollar tip. Uncle Ben told me to give it to him because he got all the tips.

"I hope he comes back," Uncle Ben said, stuffing the dollar into his pocket.

The next day he showed up again and ordered the same

thing. This time I didn't cook it for him. He gave me two quarters to play the jukebox. There were other people in the restaurant so I didn't get a chance to talk much to him.

"My name is Matthew," he said.

"I'm Joyce," I replied, not looking directly at him.

"Why do you hold your head down all the time?" he asked.

"I don't like looking at people," I said.

"You need to keep your head up and show everyone that cute smile."

I felt myself blush.

"I like your name. How old are you?"

"I'm thirteen," I whispered to him.

"I'm seventeen," he whispered back.

I jumped away from the counter to look at him. He couldn't be seventeen years old. He looked older than Nate. He put his finger to his lips.

"Don't tell anyone."

"You look older than seventeen," I told him.

He laughed. "Everyone thinks I'm older because I tell people I'm twenty-three. You're the only person other than my family who knows my real age.

When Matthew left I found another dollar tucked under his plate. Uncle Ben smiled when I handed it to him.

"I hope he comes back again. Whatever you are talking to him about, just keep it up. We need good customers like him."

I was happy that Uncle Ben was pleased. I felt responsible for losing a good customer like Mezinga so I hoped Matthew would make up for it.

Matthew came in everyday and ordered the same thing and always left a dollar tip.

One day he asked me what I was doing with the tip money he left.

"I give it to my uncle," I told him.

"What?"

"Uncle Ben told me to give all tips to him."

"No, when people leave tip money it's for you, not your uncle. How much is he paying you?"

"Ten dollars a week."

"Ten dollars?"

I nodded my head.

"Your uncle is getting more in tip money than he's paying you. I am not leaving any more tips if you are going to keep giving it to your uncle."

"He'll get mad if you don't leave a tip."

"Okay, I will leave a dollar and a quarter. You give him the quarter and keep the dollar."

"But you always give a dollar."

"Tell him I lost my job."

I laughed at Matthew because he was funny. I gave Uncle Ben the quarter and told him what Matthew said.

"I hope he keeps coming in here. I don't care about the tip as long as he buys a cheeseburger and fries. Quarter tips are good enough.

Matthew became one of our best customers and Uncle Ben was always happy to see him. I don't know why I felt comfortable with Matthew, but I did. I hardly talked to most of the guys, and after the incident with Mezinga, I was really afraid.

Matthew and I talked about everything and I actually started looking forward to him coming in. I added extra fries to his order and sometimes I even gave him an extra cheeseburger when Uncle Ben wasn't looking. I was saving the dollars he gave me and started keeping a portion of all the tips that other people left.

I worked afternoons until late in the evenings. Joe worked from early morning to late afternoon. Uncle Ben worked all day into the wee hours of the morning. We were usually asleep when he came in from the restaurant. He had hired another lady to help with the overnight shift now that the restaurant was being kept open twenty-four hours. At the end of my shift I was tired from being on my feet all day. Uncle Ben usually took me home and went back to the restaurant.

Matthew walked through the door later than his usual time. He saw me sitting near the door.

"You're not working?"

"I'm waiting for Uncle Ben to come get me so I can go home."

"Where is home?"

"I live on tenth and Hadley Street."

He grabbed my hand. "We can catch the bus."

I shook my head. "I better wait for Uncle Ben."

Matthew called to Darlene, "Tell Mr. Ford that Joyce is catching the bus and I will make sure she gets home safe."

I followed Matthew to the bus stop. After a few minutes passed Matthew became restless.

"Let's start walking and we'll catch the bus further down the street."

We started walking down Center Street in the direction of my house. My feet didn't seem as tired as they had been in the restaurant and I started perking up.

Matthew and I were talking and laughing the entire walk and before I knew it we were standing in front my house.

"This is it," I said sadly. I didn't want him to leave. The house was dark so I knew Uncle Ben wasn't in there.

"Do you want me to stay until your brother gets home?"

I nodded.

We walked into the quiet darkness and he helped me turn on all the lights. I turned on the TV and we watched it until I fell asleep. When I woke up, he was gone and Uncle Ben's Cadillac was parked outside.

Matthew came by the restaurant every evening to see if I needed him to escort me home. Uncle Ben liked him and encouraged our friendship. I wasn't sure if it was because he had become our new best customer. He was different from Mezinga. Matthew started coming to the house to visit and every time he came he brought my favorite candies. He even brought candy for Joe. He was so easy to talk to and I enjoyed the stories he told me about how he passed for someone older. I told him what happened between Nate and me. After I finished he looked as if the color had drained from his face.

"I'll look after you," he promised. "I will never let him or anyone else hurt you again. If he ever lays another hand on you it will be his last."

I believed that Matthew really cared about me and I felt safe with him around. I was sure that if Nate ever did come back and try to do anything to me Matthew would keep his promise. I would sit on Matthew's lap like a little girl and he would wrap his arms around me and hold me until I fell asleep. I was still having nightmares that had started after the sexual abuse. Matthew would hold me tight if I cried out from a bad dream.

"I'm here with you," he would say. I didn't like going to bed and preferred to sleep on the couch or in a chair. The bed only reminded me of what had happened so I believed that if I slept in that bed I would wake up with Nate standing over me. Most of the time when I woke up Matthew was gone. I would be trembling and wishing he was there.

Matthew never touched me uncomfortably nor did he make suggestions about having sex. For the first time in my life I met someone who really cared about me. I believed that Matthew truly loved me and I loved him back. It wasn't the kind of romantic love like on TV or in the movies. It was like he was my guardian angel. We held hands while taking long walks together.

"I'm living with a woman," he confessed to me one day. "She's older than I am and we have a little girl together."

Matthew was a father? He told me that his girlfriend thought he was older too.

"I love my daughter," he said, showing me a picture of a little girl who looked very much like him.

I felt a stab of jealousy, but I understood. I didn't have anything to offer a sophisticated man like Matthew. He owned his own business and was making enough money to dress like a businessman.

The restaurant closed down before the end of summer so Joe and I were out of a job. Uncle Ben seemed depressed and was away from home a lot. He mainly stayed in Ike's tavern. Joe and I were glad that we had Matthew to depend on. He brought us food and made sure that we weren't alone in the house all the time.

One day I found a check from the social services department. It was a large sum of money and I was shocked. I didn't know Uncle Ben was getting that much money for us to live with him. I tucked the check underneath my Mattress. Uncle Ben looked all over the house for the check. When he couldn't find it anywhere he threatened us because he was sure one of us had it. I put the check in his bedroom the next day.

When Uncle Ben sat in his chair one evening I knew that something was terribly wrong. A few days later a dark-skinned man dressed in black slacks and a white shirt showed up at our door.

"I'm Mr. Carter, your new social worker." Joe and I didn't like Mr. Carter from the beginning because he looked mean.

"Your uncle asked me to come by and get you."

Joe and I looked at each other. It was happening again.

Mr. Carter told us that Uncle Ben had called and told him that he was moving to Ohio and never coming back. We packed the few things that we had and left with Mr. Carter.

He waited until we got into the car before delivering the bad news. "They don't have room for you at Adams Hall where I'm taking Joe, so you will have to go to the Detention Center."

Chapter Twelve

Adams Hall the Second Time

I spent two weeks in the Detention center before Mr. Carter returned to get me. He took me to Adams Hall, where Joe was.

The atmosphere in Adams Hall was different than when I had stayed there before. Adams Hall seemed to be more balanced with an equal share of boys and girls from all ethnic backgrounds: white, Puerto Rican, and black. I shared the upstairs dorm room with several other girls. My bed was closest to the door.

Cheryl was the first person I met when I arrived; she was the same age as me and was five foot two, with dark skin and bowlegs. Wilma was also in the room that we shared. She was a light-skinned black girl with a small build, medium brown eyes, and a cute face. Cheryl, whose sense of humor kept me laughing, was pleasant to be around. Her personality sparked a great friendship between us. Neither of us liked Wilma who thought of herself as a raging beauty queen. Wilma was a couple of years older than us and in high school.

The way Wilma acted was sometimes unbearable. It didn't surprise me that she had a boyfriend. I had met girls like her in school, and they craved attention, especially from boys.

Wilma's boyfriend never came inside of the building so I never met him face to face. Wilma would sneak out to meet him almost every day, even though we weren't supposed to have visitors' everyday.

"Where is she going?"

Cheryl looked at me "She's going to meet David."

"Where are they meeting?"

"In his car, it's probably parked in a dark alley," she would laugh.

"Why would they want to be in a dark alley?"

"You can't be that stupid. What do you think they are doing?"

I didn't have to answer that question because Wilma didn't mind telling us how far she went with David. When she returned after spending an hour or more with him her hair was always messed up and her face was flushed. She had a purposeful walk that caused her to butt to wiggle. She would walk past us with a smile on her face and wiggle her butt.

"Nasty thing," Cheryl would say when she was out of earshot.

My clothes had dwindled down to almost nothing. I had bought a few things while living with Uncle Ben, but I didn't have the essential things I needed like underclothes. I was glad when one of the counselors took Joe, Cheryl, John, Amy, and I shopping in a large department store downtown. I found out that all the stores accepted the welfare clothing vouchers and wondered if Mrs. Watson had used clothing vouchers the time she took Joe and me shopping. I was amazed at how easily Cheryl could steal clothes. She walked right out of the store with the bag of clothes that the counselor bought and another bag of stolen clothes including a beautiful white rabbit jacket she had admired all evening. We laughed later about how smooth she was at stealing those clothes. Amy was a small white girl with an innocent look who came to Adams Hall a few days before me. She had stolen clothes too, but I didn't even attempt to steal anything because I was too afraid. Cheryl offered me a blouse because she had stolen two of the same kind.

Raymond was Italian, seventeen years old, and didn't look like he belonged in Adams Hall. He fell head over heels for Cheryl. He was average height and sort of stocky, with thick wavy black hair and olive skin. Cheryl took advantage of his feelings and strung him along for a while. He gave her money and presents and she took everything. He told her he was in Adams Hall because of an unstable home environment, but never talked about his family.

The relationship between Cheryl and Raymond ended when he returned home to his family. Although they promised to keep in touch, I knew from experience that it would be short lived. Joe made friends with Eddie and Keith. Eddie was tall and thin like Joe and about the same age. Keith was shorter with a huge afro that made up for the difference in height. He was brown skinned with a handsome face and beautiful smile.

Eddie got into a lot of trouble and was in and out of the Detention Center. This time they decided to put him in Adams Hall. I liked Eddie because despite his obvious problems he was a nice guy and got along with everyone. Eddie talked Joe into running away with him. I was worried and mad at the same time when I heard about it. They stayed out all night and returned the next day. Joe was put in the cooler underneath the stairs. Eddie was sent to the Detention center. Joe told me later that he came back because he didn't like eating cold beans out of the can.

Shortly after that Mr. Carter placed Joe into a foster home. His new foster mother was a single woman named Mrs. Perkins. I had hoped that they would find a place where we could live together, but Mr. Carter said it was hard because we were older. Joe was happy to be leaving Adams Hall because he didn't like it there, but he was sad about leaving me behind.

"I'll be all right," I promised him. I wasn't even sure if Mr. Cater was looking for a foster home for me. He didn't seem to like me.

"My foster mother is nice to me," Joe told me during one of his visits. I was glad that Joe had finally stopped talking about Uncle Ben and accepted the way things were. His disappointment about being betrayed a third time was worse than anything Uncle Ben had done as far as he was concerned. He also complained about his little foster brother, Cary. "He makes me mad, Sis."

Living in Adams Hall was good for me. I liked the counselors, the residents, and the school. We were given special privileges and they made sure we were busy with activities. I didn't feel the pressure like I did the short time I had lived in the Children's Home.

Residents came and left Adams Hall all the time. I never knew when I was going to wake up and see a new face or come home from school to be greeted by a new roommate. I got use to seeing new faces all the time, but one morning when I went downstairs to eat breakfast I saw a face that caused me to pause. He was sitting in the recreation room. I stopped on the stairs and stared at him, feeling paralyzed. His honey brown skin seemed to lighten the room. I took in all his brawny facial features and found it hard to pull my eyes away.

"You're going to eat breakfast, right?" I turned to see who was speaking to me.

"Yeah," I said to Keith. "Who is the new boy?"
Keith laughed. "You got your eyes on the new boy already? He came in this morning."

I couldn't help staring at him. He had a serious look on his face as if he was thinking about something.

I wanted to get a closer look at him. I walked towards the recreation room while trying not to stare at him. He didn't seem to notice me when I walked in. I pretended I was looking through some records and just happened to look up and see him.

"Hi." I said.

He looked at me as if I had interrupted his thoughts. His

eyes were a light color and looked like two marbles.

"Hi," he said and looked away.

I was smiling when he looked back in my direction, but apparently he didn't want to talk.

I put the records down and walked out. My legs felt like jelly with each step I took. I managed to walk back upstairs to find Cheryl sitting on her bed.

"Where have you been?" she asked.

I ignored the question. "Have you seen the new boy?"

Cheryl frowned and shook her head. "What new boy?"

"There is a boy downstairs in the recreation room with light brown skin, light eyes and an afro."

"You really checked him out," Cheryl teased me.

"Yeah," I said, more to myself than her. I fell backwards onto my bed and stared at the ceiling smiling.

Cheryl rolled her eyes upward. "Girl what is wrong with you?"

"You have got to see him."

We walked back down the stairs together and he was still sitting in the chair.

My heart started fluttering when I saw him again.

"There he is," I whispered.

Cheryl laughed at the way I was acting. She pulled me down the rest of the stairs and together we walked into the room.

The TV was on now and other residents had gathered in the room. Cheryl walked over to him.

"Hi," she said boldly. "My name is Cheryl and that is my friend Joyce. What is your name?"

He looked up at her. "My name is Norris." I immediately decided I liked his name.

The rest of the morning I stole glances at Norris who spent most of his time in the recreation room. He moved only to go to the bathroom or to eat. Later that evening at the dinner table, I kept looking up at him, but I never saw him look my way. That night I told Wilma and Cheryl I was in love with Norris.

I had never been interested in boys, but Norris was different. I was attracted to him and didn't understand why. I was curious to know why he was there. I tried to make small talk with him, but he seemed more irritated with me than anything else. Cheryl would laugh and shake her head because I talked about him non-stop.

"The boy doesn't even know you exist," she told me one day.

I continued to try to build a friendship with Norris, despite what Cheryl had observed. He was strange because he didn't want to be friends with anyone. I probably should have given up, but I really liked Norris and talked to him every time I had an opportunity.

After a few weeks he loosened up and began talking back to me. I hung on every word he said. He was fifteen years old and had come there from a foster home he didn't like. He enjoyed the same music I did but didn't care much about dancing. He didn't smoke cigarettes, but liked to drink a little wine. The first time I saw him smile I thought I was going to faint. It was the most beautiful smile I had ever seen.

"That boy is going to have you dropping your drawers," Cheryl said one night before we crawled into bed.

"I don't care."

"What? Oh, now I know you've lost your damn mind."

"I'm in love."

Cheryl shook her head. "I don't know what you see in him. Yes, he is cute, but I wouldn't lose my mind over him."

Wilma walked into the room with a towel wrapped around her. She had just stepped out of the showers and caught the last part of our conversation.

"Norris is cute," she said staring at Cheryl. "He looks a lot better than that white boy you were all hung up on."

I saw Cheryl's nostrils flare and knew she was mad.

In Years To Come

"For your information he was Italian. And I wasn't hung up on him; he was hung up on me."

Wilma bobbed her head, freeing the towel that was wrapped around her hair.

"Uh huh, and I know he wasn't giving you those gifts for nothing."

"I'm not like you," Cheryl spat out. "I don't do it just because they ask."

Wilma laughed out loud. "I don't do it just because they ask either. I do it because I like it."

I didn't say anything as the two went back and forth with their smart remarks. I couldn't understand how Wilma could enjoy having sex. The only feelings I had about it were disgust and shame. I wondered how it could feel the way that Wilma described.

"Keep your virginity for as long as you can," Cheryl said to me.

I didn't reply. She assumed I was still a virgin and I didn't try to convince her otherwise. I wondered how she would react if she knew the truth about me. I could still hear Wilma's laughter when I fell asleep.

It was a beautiful summer day, the sun was shinning and I looked forward to going on a fieldtrip the staff had planned for us. Norris was in the recreation room when I came down. He looked handsome in his white pants with a black and white striped shirt and bright white tennis shoes.

"Are you going with the group today?" Norris was smiling when he asked me. I felt my heart fluttering again.

"Yeah, I'll probably go. Are you going?" I was hoping he would.

"No, I am going across town to visit my sister. She had a baby a few weeks ago."

I didn't know he had a sister because he never talked about her.

"You have a sister?"

He nodded.

"Would you like to come with me?"

He was asking me to go with him to his sister's house!

"Yes," I mumbled.

I couldn't believe he wanted me to go with him. I ran back upstairs to get my things. Cheryl was putting on some lipstick.

"I am going with Norris to visit his sister!"

Cheryl turned to face me. "He asked you to go with him to visit his sister?"

I nodded my head. I was so excited that I could hardly gather my things.

"Well, have fun, but not too much fun."

I laughed. "And you have fun at the lake."

I rushed downstairs to where he was waiting.

Mr. Denson was standing near the door. He had on a pair of shorts, a T-shirt, and sandals. "You're not going with us?"

"We are going to my sister's house," Norris answered. "She just had a baby."

Mr. Denson smiled. "Congratulations, Uncle Norris," he said.

We walked past him through the door. Norris talked about his life growing up when he lived in Harlem. I was fascinated with the stories. I could even imagine him sitting on the rooftop on hot summer nights looking at the stars.

"I'm going back to Harlem when I turn eighteen," he said.

"I would like to go to Harlem with you," I blurted out.

He kept on talking. The walk didn't seem as long because we talked about a lot of things and it was the first time Norris had really opened up to me. I liked everything about Norris, the way he held his head to one side, the smile that showed his beautiful teeth, and his hearty laugh.

We made it to his sister's apartment way too soon for me.

"This is where she lives," he said. "I've never been over here, but it is the address she gave me."

I sucked in my breath and stood with him in front of the door. He knocked loudly.

"I'm coming," a woman's voice replied.

Norris smiled at me and I smiled back. I was glad that she was home even though I was nervous about meeting her.

The door swung open and she stood there looking from him to me. My mouth dropped open and I couldn't speak.

"Joyce?"

Norris looked at me realizing his sister had just said my name.

"Nita?"

We hugged for a long time. Then she grabbed Norris and hugged him.

I was surprised to learn that Nita was Norris's big sister. I hadn't seen her since she left Mrs. Watson's house. She still looked the same with beautiful skin and a shapely body even though she had just given birth.

We both talked about our experience in Mrs. Watson's foster home. "I'm sorry I didn't help you," Nita said to me. "I didn't know she was doing those things to you." I was glad that Nita knew the truth now about Mrs. Watson. Norris kept shaking his head in disbelief.

Her baby, a cute little boy, was asleep in the crib. I watched Norris playing with the baby's tiny fingers. Norris was more handsome than ever that day and I stole glances at him when I thought he wasn't looking.

We spent the entire day with Nita and the baby. She fed us a hearty lunch and allowed us to take turns holding the baby.

"It's time for us to get back to Adams Hall," he said. I was sorry that we had to leave. I promised Nita that I would visit again with or without Norris. The walk back to Adams Hall was as pleasant as the one going to Nita's house. This time I did most of the talking. I told Norris about Mrs. Watson. I could see genuine sorrow in his eyes and that made me like him even more. I left out the part about his sister sneaking into Freddy's bedroom.

We made it back to Adams Hall before dark. I was lying across my bed when Cheryl walked in.

"How was your day?"

"It was the best day of my life."

"What about his sister?"

I jumped up. "His sister use to be my foster sister when I lived with Mrs. Watson."

Cheryl gave me a puzzled look. "No shit?"

I crossed my heart.

"I was shocked when the door opened and Nita was standing there."

"You get in good with the sister you just might get your man," Cheryl laughed. I bounced back on the bed, laughing.

When Joe came to visit I told him about going over to Nita's house. He had a smile on his face as if he too had some news to share.

"Okay, what is it?"

"Would you believe that my foster brother, Cary is also Norris's brother?"

"What?"

Joe nodded. "My foster brother is Norris's brother." I couldn't believe it. The brat that was getting on Joe's nerve was Norris's little brother.

Norris confirmed that Cary was his baby brother. He seemed relieved to know where he was. Now I was convinced that it was meant for Norris and me to be together. I kept suggesting that we take another walk to Nita's house, but he didn't seem interested.

The counselors planned another trip to the lake. Norris came to me a couple of days before the event.

"Are you going to the Lake?"

I smiled at him. "Yes, I am"

He smiled back.

"I want to ask you a favor."

I felt myself tighten. Norris wanted a favor from me?
"Sure."

He was acting shy which wasn't really part of his character.

"Well, I want to ask Wilma to be with me on the beach, but I don't know how to approach her. Will you give her the message for me?"

Was he serious? Did he really expect me to ask Wilma to be with him on the beach? I felt as if someone had punched the air out of me.

"Yes, I'll tell her," I heard myself say.

Wilma smiled when I gave her the message. "You're not going to go with him are you?" Cheryl asked.

"I don't know," Wilma answered.

"You know Joyce likes him."

I sat on my bed. I was on the verge of tears. How could he like Wilma and not me?

"Joyce is the one who told me the boy wanted to go with me." Wilma said defending herself.

"If Norris wants to be with Wilma I'm okay about it," I heard myself say.

Cheryl shook her head and didn't say anything else.

Saturday morning came and I decided I didn't want to go to the lake. For two days I watched Wilma sucker Norris into her web and it made me sick. She put on a short set and wrapped a beach towel around herself. The rollers she put in her hair the night before produced curls that hung down into her face.

I hated Wilma. She knew how I felt about Norris because I had poured my heart out to her and Cheryl.

"She's a no good hoe," Cheryl told me.

After Wilma and Norris started seeing each other, nothing was ever the same between Norris and I. Wilma used him for attention. He cared about her so I didn't tell him that she was seeing David.

It seemed like everyone started leaving Adams Hall at the

same time. I was glad when they found a foster home for Wilma. Norris started getting into trouble and eventually ended up in the Detention Center. I wrote him letters every day until I finally got one back from him asking me not to write him anymore.

I became the resident with the longest time in Adams Hall. It seemed strange to be the only one without a place to go. I felt alone except for the times when Joe came to visit. He had gotten lucky with Mrs. Perkins. She lived on the North side of town in a single-family home. Joe liked Mrs. Perkins, but didn't get along with Cary. According to Joe, he was a little terror.

"He calls me names and does stupid things to irritate me," Joe said.

"He's just a little boy," I said in Cary's defense.

"He talks about you too. He calls you names and says that his brother never liked you." I shrugged my shoulders. The words hurt, but I knew that already from the letter that Norris wrote to me. I had only seen Cary once. He looked like Norris with those same pretty eyes.

A young soft-spoken guy named James Patton came to Adams hall. He liked Cheryl and I thought they made a cute couple.

I was devastated when Cheryl had to leave. James and I were the only two left of the original gang so we became closer. James was a good dancer and we spent a lot of time in the recreation room playing records and dancing.

Fall was still my favorite time of year because I loved the crisp cool air and the colorful leaves that crushed easily beneath my feet. It was on a fall day that James asked me to go on a date with him. I was apprehensive because I still remembered the previous times with Mezinga and Michael.

"Where would we go?"

"I want to take you somewhere special." he smiled at me and it warmed my heart.

James was a good friend and I did like him. I trusted him too so I agreed to go out with him Friday evening.

In Years To Come

Everyone in Adams Hall knew we were going out on a date. They thought that James and I were a couple and since I wasn't sure what we were, I never corrected them.

Friday evening came and I put on my two-piece skirt outfit with matching shoes and pulled my socks up high to my knees. I combed my Afro into puffs and tied ribbons around them. I didn't wear makeup so I oiled my skin and was ready to meet James. He stood at the bottom of the stairs waiting for me. He was neatly dressed as usual in a pair of dark slacks, a dress shirt, and a pullover sweater. His hair was neatly trimmed and combed and he displayed bright white teeth when he smiled. I knew the others were looking when we stepped out into the cool evening air. A counselor reminded us that our curfew was at eleven.

James took my hand and his grip was so tight that I almost cried out. I stepped as quickly as he did down the street. The first place we stopped at was a small café. When we walked into the place music was blasting from the jukebox. Hippies were sitting all over the place in small groups. They looked up at us, but no one said anything. I was nervous because we were the only black ones in the place.

"Don't worry about them," James said. "The hippies don't care about us being in here."

I followed him to a booth where we slid in across from each other.

White Room by Cream was playing by the time James ordered a large strawberry shake with whipped cream and fresh strawberries on top.

"And two straws," he said, winking at me.

I glanced around the room, trying not to stare at the hippies who were slouched on the seats. Most of the guys had long hair with bands or scarves tied around their foreheads and the girls wore beads, flowers, or other colorful things in their long straight hair.

Hey, Jude came on the jukebox just as the shake arrived.

316

I loved that song and every time I heard it I wanted to cry. We shared the shake and looked into each other's eyes. I had to look away because I was thinking about Norris.

When we left the café about an hour later, James grabbed my hand again.

"Where are we going now?"

"To my math teacher's apartment."

I thought I had heard him wrong.

"Where?"

"We are going to my math teacher's apartment. He lives in a high-rise a couple of blocks from here."

The apartment building was as tall as the buildings downtown. I had never been inside a tall apartment building before.

He rang the buzzer and a deep voice came over the box. He let us in. We took the elevator to the fifteenth floor.

A tall, dark-skinned man with a big afro and wearing a colorful dashiki let us in.

"This is Joyce," James introduced me.

The teacher shook my hand. He filled the table with cookies, soda, and other snacks for us to eat. We listened while he told us stories about his travels around Europe.

"Have you ever gone to South America?"

"I will someday," he said.

The time passed quickly and we had to leave.

Once we were outside I told James that I had a great time with him. He gripped my hand and we walked back to Adams Hall holding hands. We were standing outside of the building squeezing out a few more minutes before going inside.

"I really like you," James told me.

"I like you too."

Then I felt his lips brushing against mine. He had just kissed me. Before I could react he was pulling me up the stairs. Over the next few weeks we became closer which made it harder when it came time for him to leave. I went to my room because I couldn't say goodbye to him.

James left with promises of coming back to see me. I knew he wouldn't be back because no one ever came back except for Joe. Cheryl had promised to stay in touch, but I hadn't seen or heard from her either. That familiar lonely feeling came back. I missed the old Adams Hall crowd that I had had so much fun with. Things had changed since they left and most of the residents coming in stayed only a short time.

It was a Saturday afternoon when Matthew showed up at Adams Hall. I was both surprised and happy to see him.

"How did you find me?" I asked him.

Matthew winked at me and smiled. "I have my ways," he said. He handed me a large sack of all my favorite candies.

We took up the relationship where we'd left off. He came faithfully every week to visit with me and I looked forward to seeing him. When Matthew couldn't visit he called me and we talked on the phone until someone made me hang up.

Linda Garcia was a sixteen-year-old Puerto Rican girl with long jet-black hair that was ratted on top and held in place with lots of hairspray. She wore heavy makeup including bright blue eye shadow. Linda and I became good friends and I introduced her to Matthew. He brought his friend Robert with him on the next visit and introduced him to Linda. I didn't think Linda would like Robert, but they hit it off and began dating. The four of us would take walks around Adams Hall holding hands and talking.

Matthew broke up with the woman he had lived with and moved into his own apartment. He had just turned eighteen. He took me to his apartment. It was sparsely furnished, but was very clean. He put on some music and sat close to me on the couch. We spent the evening in awkward conversations. I enjoyed his company and really did like him, but I felt he was treating me like a child. He was telling me what I should and shouldn't do. Eventually Linda and Robert broke up. She said he was pressuring her to have sex and she wasn't ready for it. Linda left Adams Hall shortly after that to go into a foster home. I introduced Matthew to another girl, Barbara, and gave them my blessings.

The new girl, Sue Hackbarth, was sitting in the recreation room by herself. She had been in Adams Hall a week, but this was my first time talking to her. Everything about her was strange. She was taller than me, and thin with long brown hair and hazel eyes. She had thin lips, a pointed nose and pale white skin. It always took awhile before new residents warmed up, but she was still quiet. I introduced myself to her.

"I'm Joyce Ford."

She smiled at me.

"My name is Susan Hackbarth," she said. "You can call me Sue.

There was something about her that made me want to be her friend. I found out that she was seventeen years old and had been kicked out of the house after her parents found out she was pregnant. She had spent time in a home for pregnant girls and gave birth to boy she named Jeffrey.

"Your parents kicked you out of the house?" I asked.

This seemed odd to me because I didn't think that white people treated their kids like that. I was quickly learning that white people weren't too much different from other races. "Jeffrey's father was popular in school," she told me. "He had his choice of almost any girl, but he chose me." Sue still looked like she was love struck when she talked about him. He abandoned her once he found out she was pregnant. He left her to deal with the emotions and shame all alone. I felt sorry for Sue and wondered what type of parents would turn their backs on their own daughter.

Sue was turning eighteen soon and was getting her own apartment so she could take care of Jeffery. Sue and I became good friends. When she turned eighteen the social workers helped her find an apartment for her and the baby.

Sue rented a furnished one-bedroom apartment on the second floor of a three-story apartment building. I was glad that it was only a few blocks from Adams Hall and around the corner from the school I was attending. I spent most of my free time at Sue's apartment. I watched the baby while she ran errands or just to give her a break. She was a good mother and very attentive. I adored Jeffery with his baby fat cheeks and large thighs.

"I don't know how he can crawl with those big ham hocks," I would tell her.

I was just starting to feel like life was good again when my new social worker showed up at Adams Hall one day.

"We found you a foster home," she said.

I wasn't ready to leave but I had no choice.

"You're finally leaving!" one of the counselors commented.

I smiled weakly and wondered how I would get back and forth to visit Sue and Jeffery. The girls gathered around my bed while I packed my things to leave. I had really enjoyed living in Adams Hall and was going to miss everyone.

I knew I had to leave someday because Adams Hall was only a temporary place. I was still thinking about Sue and Jeffery when I climbed into the car with the social worker.

Chapter Thirteen

Mrs. Oglesby

We pulled up in front of the small wooden framed house on a side of town I wasn't familiar with. The curtains on the front window were off track and I could see the unevenness from the street.

"This is your new foster home," the perky young social worker said. I couldn't remember having a female social worker except for Mrs. Gray when we lived with Hon. She seemed happier than I was about the foster home.

An older woman opened the door and invited us in. I stepped into the semi-dark living room. It was small and furnished with an old green couch, a coffee table, and two end tables with lamps that didn't match. A curtain that was pulled across the opening blocked the entrance into the other room.

"Another old woman," I thought to myself. Mrs. Oglesby looked like she was at least sixty years old. She was short and wore a wig with curly hair that was too big for her face. She dressed like an old woman in baggy pants and a sweatshirt. I could tell that the teeth she displayed when she smiled weren't hers either.

The social worker didn't stay long.

In Years To Come

"I'll show you to your room," Mrs. Oglesby said. I followed her through the curtain that she pulled back. I was shocked when I saw piles of junk throughout what was supposed to be a dining room. There were stacks of newspaper and piles of mail. I saw paper sacks and boxes with more stuff in them. We passed by the kitchen on the way upstairs. I was again shocked to see the large kitchen with junk all over the place. I noticed stacks of clean plates and pots all over the kitchen counter. Canned goods and other things were scattered throughout the kitchen. Then I noticed a pile of unwashed dishes in the sink. I had never been in such a junky foster home before.

I followed Mrs. Oglesby upstairs to an attic area. The room where I was to be sleeping was a big open space with two beds in opposite corners. The unfinished attic reminded me of the one at Hon and Papa's house. There was no way I was going to live in this house. I had only been there a couple of hours and I hated it already.

I was relieved to find out that I had a foster sister. Anna told me she was born and raised in Chicago. She had moved to Milwaukee with her family and ended up in the foster home system. She had been living with Mrs. Oglesby for a few months. Anna was only a couple of years older than I was, but looked older. She was tall and thin with light brown skin. She was so experienced in life that I sometimes forgot her age. I was stunned when she told me that she was already a mother and that her daughter was born when she was twelve years old.

"She's in a foster home right now. I visit her on the weekends." I couldn't imagine a mother and her baby being in different foster homes.

Later she told me, "Mrs. Oglesby doesn't care what you do. As long as you go to school you can do whatever you want. Her main concern is about getting that check every month." We both laughed about that.

"She's old and sometimes she gets on my nerves, but

overall she's a good lady."

I complained to Anna about the house and the junk, but the more Anna talked about Mrs. Oglesby the more I thought about staying put for a while.

Everything that Anna said about Mrs. Oglesby was true. She allowed us to do whatever we wanted to as long as we went to school. I seldom ate at the house and spent as much time and I could over Sue's apartment where I ate and often slept there. On the weekends I stayed away the entire time.

When the checks came every month Mrs. Oglesby gave us a few dollars to buy things for ourselves. Mrs. Oglesby's twenty-three year old daughter, Audrey and her daughter lived with us. Binky was a cute little toddler that kept us entertained. Audrey was a single mother and told me that her mother was furious when she found out she was pregnant. I didn't understand why Mrs. Oglesby would be so angry because Audrey was over twenty-one. Audrey catered to her mother by buying things for her. She never talked about Binky's father either.

Audrey worked, and for fun she spent time at the corner tavern shooting pool. She was good at it and had her own pool stick that she kept carefully stored in a case.

After awhile I regarded Mrs. Oglesby as a strange woman who believed in using home remedies I had never heard of before. Audrey had long pretty hair and Mrs. Oglesby told me it was because they rinsed it with beer and conditioned it using mayonnaise. I couldn't believe it.

"Don't wash your hair when you are on your period," she warned me. You can become seriously ill or die. It scared me so bad that I was afraid to get my hair wet when I was on my period. I also allowed them to use the beer and mayonnaise treatment on my hair to see if it worked. I didn't see a significant difference in my hair except it did feel softer.

Mrs. Oglesby had a son that came by the house. I was still leery of grown men so I never felt comfortable around him. He always wanted to dance so he would put a record on the record player. It was during the time when Marvin Gaye's, *I Heard It Through the Grapevine,* came out. I smelled liquor on him even from a distance, but I never said anything. I usually ignored him and stayed out of his way when he was there.

I was enrolled into Wells Junior High School, a few blocks from the house. I was in the eighth grade and Anna was in the ninth. We walked together in the mornings and the cold winter winds seemed to go right through us.

One morning after a big snow and a deep freeze we were walking across the playground that was now covered with ice. It looked like a skating rink because the ice was so thick. Anna took baby steps to keep from falling and I walked with caution. We had almost made it across when she fell hard on the ice. I turned around to see her sitting on the ice with her legs in a distorted position.

"Help me," she cried out. I managed to help get her off of the ground and we held on to each other until we made it to the other side of the playground.

Later that evening Anna complained of not feeling well. I saw her going in and out of the bathroom. It was early in the morning around one or two o'clock when I was fast asleep that a loud scream woke me. Anna's bed was in the far corner of the room, but I could see it because the light was on. I sat up and saw that Mrs. Oglesby and Audrey were by her bedside.

"It hurts!" Anna screamed out. "Oh God, help me!"

I jumped out of my bed and hurried over to where Anna was. The covers were pulled back and Anna's knees were pulled up. Sweat was pouring from her forehead and tears were streaming down her face.

"It hurts!" she screamed again.

I saw Mrs. Oglesby changing a sanitary napkin that was stuck between Anna's legs. I almost screamed when I saw how much blood it was soaking up.

324

"Go back over there," Mrs. Oglesby said to me. I wasn't going to move because I wanted to know what was going on.

"I am going to call the ambulance," Audrey said. It was obvious that she was worried.

A short time later I heard the sirens and in the next few minutes there were people in the room. I moved out of the way while they attended to Anna, who was still screaming.

"She's probably having a miscarriage."

I couldn't believe that Anna was pregnant. She told the paramedics about the fall on the ice that morning at school. They took Anna to the hospital in the ambulance and I couldn't go back to sleep. I was wondering who got her pregnant because she never talked about having a boyfriend. Anna came home after a few days in the hospital. I stayed away from the house as much as I could.

Sue had a better relationship with her parents and they were coming to visit her and Jeffrey. I wasn't there when they came because Sue thought it would be best if I weren't around. I took the hint that her parents would have a hard time accepting her being friends with me because I was black.

Sue got involved with a guy named Ricky who lived on the first floor of her apartment building. Ricky was a tall, handsome Puerto Rican with slick coal black hair and dark features. He had a killer smile that even I couldn't help staring at. Sue fell head over heels in love with Ricky and he seemed to like her too. Sue kept her involvement with Ricky a secret from her parents. I babysat Jeffery when Sue went down stairs to Ricky's apartment.

She talked about him all the time as if he was a type of God. "I love him so much", she told me one day. Sue waited for him to return when he left and was in his face when he got back home. When Ricky came upstairs to her apartment they would disappear into the bedroom.

Sue was crying one day I when I went to visit her. Ricky

had told her that he wanted them to slow down and Sue felt she was going to die without him. I felt sorry for her, but she wasn't being reasonable. I told her she had to look after Jeffery and let Ricky do whatever he wanted to.

"I love him," she whispered between sniffling and tears.

I didn't like living with Mrs. Oglesby especially after Anna had the miscarriage. I was sure they were keeping things from me with all the whispering the three of them did. I began to suspect that Mrs. Oglesby's son was the one who got Anna pregnant. It made me sick to my stomach to think about his grown ass messing with her especially since he was already married. I had heard enough of the talking to understand it. I never said anything about it to Anna nor did I ask her. She did confirm that she was pregnant and had a miscarriage.

"It hurt like hell," she told me.

I was ready to move on and just before spring I was taken to another foster home.

Chapter Fourteen

Mrs. Walker

There were several older houses on the north side of Milwaukee that were family duplexes. These houses were split into two levels, a downstairs complete with a living room, dining room, bath, and kitchen, and an upstairs complete with bedrooms, bath, dining area, kitchen, and a living room. Each side had its own address and front entrance.

The back entrance led into a hallway that allowed a person to go either upstairs, downstairs, or to the basement. The separate entrances into the actual living areas had private locks. Both families could enter through the backdoor and share the basement, because the washer and dryer were down there. Sometimes people turned these split-level houses into single families' home just like Mr. And Mrs. Guy had done. Mr. and Mrs. Walker did the same thing with their house.

Mr. and Mrs. Walker owned the biggest house on the block. It was a white house with a large porch on the bottom and a full porch that extended the length of the house across the top of the house. There was no garage, but the driveway went all the way to the rear of the house to accommodate more than a few cars. In the back of the large house was a small two-bedroom, single-family cottage. Mrs. Walker owned the entire property and rented the cottage house to her younger sister, Bea.

Mr. Burgner was now the supervisor of all of the new social workers who were in and out of our lives. He didn't do home visits anymore, but if we wanted to talk to him we could. I didn't bother contacting him after leaving Mrs. Watson's house because I didn't trust him.

The social worker talked non-stop all the way over to the foster home.

"You will be living in a group home with several other girls. I hope that you settle down and fit in with them. I've known your new foster mother for some time and she's a wonderful woman. Her name is Mrs. Walker and I'm sure you will like it there. The other girls are a little older than you, which may be a good thing because you seem to need a little guidance."

I didn't say anything. I preferred to stare out of the car window.

When we pulled up in front of the massive-looking house all I could do was stare at it. It was located off of Seventh and North Avenue across from the freeway that went through town. I followed Mrs. Graham up the stairs to the front porch. I took a deep breath while she rang the bell.

The door swung open and Mrs. Walker, a large woman with huge jowls that hung down, greeted us. Her eyes were large and looked as if they would pop out at any moment. I couldn't help noticing the yellowish tint in her eyes that glared back at me. Her large fat lips were puckered as if she was ready to kiss someone and she licked them constantly, probably out of habit. When she spoke her voice was a mixture of hoarseness and deepness. A part of me wanted to laugh because she really did look funny. She wore a thin housecoat with deep pockets that showed the outline of a pack of cigarettes.

"Mrs. Walker, this is Joyce," Mrs. Graham introduced me. I could hear Mrs. Walker's heavy breathing from where I stood.

Joyce A. Ford

Then she lit a cigarette that was already in her hand and I watched her suck on it with her big lips. I finally looked away when she glanced at me though those big eyes.

This was my first experience living in a group home and it was exciting when I found out that we had the entire upstairs to ourselves. We didn't have to come to the main floor except to eat. We had our own entrance through the back door so we didn't even have to bother Mrs. Walker when we came home from school.

"I demand respect from all the girls," she said. I nodded my head in agreement. I peeped around the house as I usually did when I went to a new foster home. It was nicely furnished and clean. That was a welcomed relief after living with Mrs. Oglesby.

Mrs. Walker showed me around the house after Mrs. Graham left. The main floor is where Mr. and Mrs. Walker lived. There were two bedrooms and they slept in the biggest one. The kitchen had been remodeled to accommodate the group of girls. A big square table with at least ten chairs around it was in one part of the kitchen. The other part of the kitchen was nice too, with new looking appliances where Mrs. Walker cooked our meals. She did all the cooking in the house and we were not allowed in the kitchen other than to eat or clean up. I was impressed with the house even though Mrs. Walker didn't seem like a typical foster mother.

When we went upstairs Mrs. Walker walked so hard that it sounded like she was stomping instead of walking. The stairs creaked loudly under her weight.

The upstairs was as large as the main floor of the house. The dining room and kitchen had been replaced with other rooms. There were five bedrooms, a bathroom, and a den. When she opened the door we walked into the den. It was furnished with a couch, a couple of chairs, a TV, and a record player. A large window overlooked the side of the house where we could look out to see who was coming to the back door. We walked past all the other bedrooms and ended up in the front of the house. This is your bedroom. You will be sharing it with Elsie," Mrs. Walker told me after the tour. I nodded and walked into the large room with my small suitcase. I was relieved when Mrs. Walker walked back downstairs. I winced with each pounding of the stairs and thankful when she made it to the bottom. I could still hear her stomping around downstairs. Four beds could have easily fit in the bedroom I was standing in. The small bed on the other side of the room left a lot of space between us. I was nervous about meeting my new foster sisters that first time and hoping they would like me. I could smell the food that Mrs. Walker was cooking and my stomach growled, reminding me that I was hungry. I unpacked my things and put them away. The furniture was old but in good condition. It was a bright bedroom with large windows and the door leading to the outside porch.

Elsie was the first girl to show up. She was a thick, big-boned girl, with dark skin, bushy eyebrows, thick hair, and long eyelashes. She was friendly and soon put me at ease. As I relaxed she told me about living with Mrs. Walker. Elsie was in the eighth grade and attended St. Boniface, a catholic school in Father Groppi's church. That first evening I was in for a surprise when my new foster sisters came in from high school. I came face to face with Wilma who smiled when she saw me. Deep down I wanted to scratch her eyes out. Wilma was the one person I hoped never to see again. Memories of Norris rushed through my head when I saw her. I pretended to be happy to see her although I had not forgiven her for what she did to me. We hugged I think more for show than any true affection for each other. I could see that nothing about her had changed. She was the same girl who talked frankly and openly about guys, sex, and of course, herself. I still didn't understand why Norris was so taken by her.

The bedroom closest to the back door was where Sheila slept. Sheila was seventeen. Her bedroom was small, but she didn't have to share with anyone. In some ways she reminded me of Olive Oyle because she was tall, thin and plain looking. She wore glasses, very little makeup, and clothes that were plain. Her teeth were slightly bucked because she still sucked her thumb. Sheila's mother had passed away and her father couldn't take care of her and her siblings, so they had all ended up in foster homes. She visited her father and siblings all the time, though. Sheila had a good-looking boyfriend named Dave who came over more than Mrs. Walker knew about. They were always on the couch cuddled up together kissing and hugging. I don't think they went any further than that because she always said she wanted him to marry her first. Sheila was in her last year of high school and planning to get married as soon as she graduated.

Wilma had moved to Mrs. Walker's house after leaving Adams Hall. She attended North Division High School along with the other foster sisters. Her bedroom was next to Sheila's and she shared it with sixteen-year-old Candy, who was the comical one in the group and kept us laughing.

Wilma always had to have a boyfriend and the latest one Carlos, was a senior at her school. He was handsome and came regularly to visit her. They usually ended up in the bedroom with the door closed. Wilma wasn't ashamed or embarrassed to admit that she was sexually active.

Candy was a mystery because she hid her true feelings and joked about everything. She was a pretty girl, but didn't seem as interested in guys as Wilma was. She claimed to be in love with a guy named Russell. He came over for a few visits, but I didn't see the two of them cuddled up the way the other girls and their boyfriends did.

The next bedroom also had twin beds and seventeen-year-old Barbara English and sixteen-year-old Connie slept in there. Barbara was a shapely brown-skinned girl with short hair that she wore either in an afro or in a short pressed style. It didn't matter which way she wore her hair because it always looked good on her. She was more serious about everything than the rest of the girls. She was in high school too, but wasn't as involved with boys. She had a boyfriend, but they didn't seem serious because he only came to the house a couple of times. She was secretive about everything, including her family. I liked Barbara because she was nice to me. Sometimes I asked her opinion about things that confused me. She seemed to be the smartest of all of them even though she didn't always get along with everyone. Barbara and Connie smoked cigarettes, which is why they shared a bedroom. Mrs. Walker didn't care about us smoking as long as we were sixteen years old or more.

Connie was tall with a large structure and looked older than her age. She had a mature body that could easily pass for a grown woman. Connie told me she preferred older men and didn't date guys in high school. Connie attended High School with the others even though she didn't like school. She loved music and dancing and was an easygoing person. My foster sisters would argue among themselves about anything but I always tried to stay out of it.

Barbara Cole was the oldest and her bedroom was on the opposite side of the hall from the other bedrooms. Everyone liked and respected her. Barbara had a one-year-old son who was living with his father. She was a cute brown-skinned girl who was already eighteen years old. Barbara reminded me of a singer or someone who should be famous because she had that look about her. I admired her more than any of the other girls because she didn't participate in the gossip or petty things that went on in the group home. She didn't have any guys coming to visit except the baby's father who usually picked her up in front of the house and seldom came inside. Once in a while Barbara would bring her son upstairs and all of us would crowd around him. Because Barbara was going to vocational school and working she was gone most of the time. She didn't share her bedroom with anyone either so it was locked when she was away.

The bedroom I shared with Elsie was in the front of the house at the end of the hallway. It was the biggest bedroom upstairs. Our bedroom had the large front porch that we could walk onto in the summertime. Mrs. Walker warned us not to go out there, but we did it anyway especially on hot summer nights.

Elsie had lived with Mrs. Walker for a long time, so they had a good relationship between them. I think she was the first foster child to come there.

Elsie and I were the youngest in the group home, and vowed to stick together after Elsie told me that a couple of the girls were mean to her. Mrs. Walker had prepared a great feast and I enjoyed every bite as I wolfed down my food. It had been awhile since I had enjoyed a good home-cooked meal. I very seldom ate at Mrs. Oglesby's house, and neither Sue nor I knew how to cook, so we mainly ate sandwiches. Mrs. Walker did have heavy feet so we could hear her downstairs stomping around the house. When we did come face to face with her she usually had a cigarette dangling from her mouth. Mrs. Walker had a voice that was loud and she talked continually, especially while we were eating.

I was enrolled in Roosevelt Junior High, a few blocks from the house. I wanted to go with Elsie to St. Boniface, but there was a tuition charge, so I had to go to public school. I tried my best to get along with my foster sisters, but I was teased and called names by them. Wilma and Candy were the worse ones.

I turned fourteen in February. There wasn't much for me to do on the weekends after I stopped visiting Sue and Jeffery because the bus ride was too long. Mrs. Walker was very strict about curfew and I didn't have time to go to Sue's place and get back home before my curfew. Being closer to Joe's foster home was good because we began hanging out together again. Most Saturdays he walked over to Mrs. Walker's house. My foster sisters all knew Joe and liked him.

My most memorable time was the day Joe and I decided to walk near the river. I was amazed at how easily Joe moved around town and his sense of direction was incredible. We walked along the rocks near the water, looking at the fish that were swimming close to the edge.

"I want a fish to take home," I told Joe.

Joe caught a big black fish with eyes that popped out. He put it in a plastic bag and we went to Woolworth's and bought a fish bowl. My foster sisters hated the ugly fish and insisted that it was not the kind that you kept as a pet. I didn't care about what they thought and fed it fish food and changed the water every day until the fish died.

St. Boniface began having teenage dances so I went with Elsie to the dances. I met all the teenagers she went to school with and talked to me about. They were mostly boys, James Golden and a couple of other guys. Elsie had a crush on James. He was a good-looking boy, tall and thin with a big Afro. When he smiled he was even cuter. I danced with him once and felt like I was going to melt on the dance floor. He was popular and most of the girls were trying to get his attention.

I found out about another place on Third Street that hosted a teenage dance so Elsie and I started going there. It wasn't long before all of the teenagers started going there too. The dance was in the basement of a large church. Elsie and I had the same curfew so we walked to the dance and back home together.

Two weeks later I was standing outside in the long line waiting to get into the dance when I saw him. He was standing near the entrance dressed in a pair of shorts, a sleeveless T-shirt, an open vest, and sandals. I looked away for a minute, and then back again. He saw me and when I looked at him again he was motioning for me to come forward. My knees felt weak as I made my way to the front of the line. When I got closer we stood face to face staring into each other's eyes. Then he smiled at me. I had just bought a pair of white bell-bottom pants with a navy and white matching blouse. I wore a white cap that was turned to one side.

"How have you been?" He had the same warm smile.

"I've been doing okay."

"Where are you living?"

334

"I live in a group foster home on North Avenue."

Matthew nodded.

"I'm not going to let you leave here without giving me a phone number or an address."

"Go on in," he whispered in my ear. "I'll talk to you later."

The girl collecting the money moved aside to let me pass. I felt special as I strutted past everyone. That evening Elsie and I had left the house together, giving Mrs. Walker the impression that we were going to the dance together, but she had gone somewhere else. I suspected at that time she had a boyfriend that she wasn't telling anyone about.

The music blasted from the speakers on the wall. One of my favorite Temptations songs was playing. Being one of the first ones in the place had its advantages; I found a seat near the wall. The next song was a slow song and I saw a few couples on the floor *grinding*, as we called it. Some teenagers were drinking sodas while others stood in dark corners, talking. I was ready to dance with someone. The dance was getting crowded as teenagers made their way into the basement. I had turned around to talk to a group of girls standing behind me when I saw one of them staring at something with a strange look on her face. When I turned around to see what she was staring at Matthew was standing there. *I Can Sing A Rainbow* by The Dells was the next song that played.

"May I have this dance?" I took Matthew's outstretched hand and followed him onto the dance floor. I could feel all eyes on us as he held me close. I glanced over to the girls I had been talking with and saw the shocked looks on their faces. Matthew didn't seem to notice anyone but me.

His strong arms felt nice wrapped around me. It had been so long since anyone hugged me. I wanted to cling to him just for the sake of being held.

"When can I visit you?"

I thought about the rules Mrs. Walker had given me. No boy company for Elsie or me. She said we had to be at least sixteen before we could have boys over. The only males allowed to visit me were Joe and Roy jr.

"I can't have any company," I told him.

"What's the address?" He began nibbling on my ear.

I laughed because it tickled. I rattled off the address sure he wouldn't remember it.

It didn't surprise me that Matthew was the one who had organized the dance because he was a hustler. He was making money by having the dances, which was popular among the teens. I watched him as he made his rounds, keeping everyone in line. He carried something that looked like a bat and he did look intimidating because he was a big guy. Girls pulled on him and made gestures at him as he passed by them. He was so popular that I wondered why he kept wasting his time on me.

He asked me to stay after the dance so he could walk me home.

"I don't want you walking home alone," he said.

I let him walk me within two blocks of my house, where I met up with Elsie on the corner.

I could see him waving at me as I continued walking with Elsie in the opposite direction.

"He's too old," she said.

"I know," was all I could say. She wouldn't believe me if I told her he was only eighteen. The full beard he had grown made him look even older. I didn't ask Elsie where she went that evening.

Matthew always let me in the dance for free. It felt good to have him back in my life because I could still talk to him about anything. He had his choice of girls, but it was me that he seemed interested in. He sought me out to dance with him.

"You still my girl?" Matthew asked while holding me close.

I believed that he truly cared about me.

"Yes," I heard myself saying.

One Saturday morning, and we had just finished cleaning our rooms. I was lying across the bed reading when I heard all the commotion.

"Look who's coming up the walkway!" Candy was almost screaming.

"Who? Who?"

I turned over in bed to get a better position. I was used to guys coming over so it didn't excite me. They could visit but also had a time to leave. Most of the times the girls would sneak them back in and ask me to sit on the stairs so I could warn them in case Mrs. Walker decided to pay one of her surprise visit. I didn't mind being the lookout because the job usually came with a sack of candy. I peeked out the window to get a glimpse of the person Candy seemed to be excited about. There were two of them; one guy was wearing a blue suit that matched the hat that was pulled down on his head. He had a cane in one hand and a bag in the other. The other guy was tall and thin and dressed casually. I recognized the one in the blue suit. It was Matthew. When I heard the knock on the back door my heart damn near skipped a beat.

How would I be able to explain Matthew?

Wilma opened the door and began flirting immediately.

I heard her ask him a series of questions before he walked through the door.

I walked into the hallway so I could hear what was going on.

"Where's Joyce?" I heard Matthew ask in his deep baritone voice.

"Who?" Wilma asked, with a hint of surprise.

He repeated my name, unaware of her sarcasm.

I heard laughter. "You came to see her?"

"Yes, doesn't she live here?"

More laughter followed. "What do you want with her?"

"Does she live here?" Matthew repeated. I could imagine that he was getting frustrated with them. I decided it was time to walk into the den. Most of my foster sisters were in there with their freshly made up faces and cute little outfits.

337

Matthew smiled when he saw me and stood up from the chair he was sitting in. I was aware of all eyes on me when he hugged me.

The smile on his face was genuine.

"I don't believe this," I heard one of them whisper.

I ignored the remark. Matthew handed me the bag filled with the candy that I liked.

"This is my brother, Bernard," he said, introducing me to the guy who came in with him. I could see that his brother was getting mushy over Wilma.

Matthew sat back down and I was about to sit in another chair when he pulled me onto his lap. I knew what was going on between us was shocking to the other girls.

I knew they were looking, so I deliberately kissed Matthew passionately on the lips. Matthew was even taken back by it. I did it more for my foster sisters' benefit.

Sitting on Matthew's lap felt natural just like it had during those times at Uncle Ben's house. I didn't pay much attention to my foster sisters and began taking to Matthew as if we were the only two in the room. He was whispering jokes about them in my ears. I laughed so hard I almost fell off his lap a few times. From the corner of my eye I saw them shaking their heads in disbelief and whispering among themselves. I was sure he understood how insecure they made me feel.

We were talking when Mrs. Walker came through the door with the fury of a dragon. I didn't hear her coming up the stairs. When I looked up she was standing in the doorway. It was obvious from the way she was reeling that she'd had a few drinks. It was mid-afternoon on a Saturday and she was drunk. My reaction didn't help either. Aware that things may have looked bad to her I jumped off of Matthew's lap.

"What's going on up here?" She glared at me.

"Nothing," I said.

My foster sisters had smirks on their faces, ready to burst

into laughter at any moment.

Her eyes focused on Matthew.

"Who are you?"

He looked up at her, "My name is Matthew."

"Do you know how old she is?" She was pointing at me.

"Yes, I do," he said.

"Then you know she's too damn young for you. How old are you?"

"I've known Joyce since-"

"I don't give a damn how long you've known her, she's still too young for you."

From the look on Matthew's face I was sure he was in disbelief.

"I want you and your friend to leave right now and don't come back here anymore!" she shouted at him refusing to let him get a word in. "I don't allow boys coming to see her. She is only fourteen years old and still a baby. You look at least twenty five years old so you have no business coming to see a fourteen-year-old girl."

Tears filled my eyes. I hated Mrs. Walker at that moment. How could she do this to me?

Matthew stood up and motioned for Bernard to do the same.

"This is your house so we will leave." He turned to me.

"If you need anything, you know where to find me."

I nodded.

He kissed my forehead, heightening the fury of Mrs. Walker.

"Good-bye," I whispered.

Mrs. Walker stood in the doorway staring at him walking down the stairs with anger in her eyes.

"What did you say, young man?" she yelled down the stairs.

The only answer she got was the slamming of the door. She turned to me.

"I am surprised at you having grown men coming to see you.

I thought you were different, but I was wrong about you. The only virgin in this house is Elsie because I know the rest of you aren't."

Sheila took her thumb out of her mouth as if she was going to say something. She had sworn to us that she and Dave were waiting for marriage before they had sex.

I didn't know what to say.

Mrs. Walker always had her moments after she had been drinking. She would come upstairs and talk until she was out of breath.

"That old ass man is out for one thing," she shouted at me.

I wanted to tell her Matthew wasn't like that but I couldn't speak. Mrs. Walker continued her verbal assault on me while my foster sisters smiled as if they believed I deserved it.

I hated all of them. I wanted to run away. I knew Mrs. Walker had every right to tell Matthew to leave. I knew the rules so I deserved the lashing that Mrs. Walker gave me. It was the way my foster sisters laughed at me that humiliated me. I was put on punishment for two weeks.

I saw Matthew when I went to the dances but I wouldn't let him walk me home. He kept assuring me that Mrs. Walker didn't bother him. It bothered me a lot.

One night Elsie and I were at the dance when she saw a friend who went to school with her. Jack was about sixteen and cute. He asked me to dance and before I realized it we were dancing almost every song. Jack walked us home that night and I enjoyed talking with him. He said things that a young girl like me enjoyed hearing. I didn't fall head over heels in love with him, but I did like him.

Only Elsie knew about Jack and even though our relationship was limited to talking on the phone, sometimes I would meet him at Roosevelt Junior High School where we would kiss and he would rub up against me. I used Jack to help me avoid Matthew. I still liked Matthew, but I didn't want to get him in trouble.

That summer I discovered a café around the corner that

served the best ice cream I had ever tasted. I would lean on the glass trying to decide which flavor to buy each time. There were two sisters, Cheryl and Brenda who lived next door to Mrs. Walker and I would take them with me to the café. The younger one, Cheryl was my store buddy. We walked to the corner store all the time to buy candy.

One evening I had a craving for strawberry ice cream so I decided to walk around the corner to the café. It was a hot summer night and a lot of people were sitting outside on their porches. I turned the corner and noticed two guys sitting on the porch of a big house that was across the street from the café. They were well dressed in the popular suits that young people were wearing. I guessed them to be between sixteen and eighteen years old. At first glance I didn't notice anything special, except that there seemed to be something familiar about one of them.

While waiting for my ice cream cone, I stared through the large glass window at them. When he looked up I felt my heart flutter. There was no mistake about it: the one in the dark suit was definitely Norris.

My legs could hardly move during the walk back home. I deliberately crossed the street so I could walk in front of the house where they were sitting. Neither of them looked up as they laughed and talked. When I glanced back after passing by the house I knew for sure that it was Norris. Mrs. Walker was friendly with the woman who lived there so I asked her questions and found out that the house was a group home for boys.

I immediately started to devise a plan to gain access into the group home. I couldn't believe I had found Norris. All those familiar feelings came rushing back and I felt obsessed about seeing him. I remembered he told me to stop writing him when he was in the Detention Center. He also said he didn't like me the way I liked him, but maybe now he felt different. I wanted him to know that I lived around the corner just in case he wanted to see me. Over the next few days I ate a lot of ice cream just hoping to get another glimpse of him sitting outside. When I did see him he was always well dressed, that added to his good looks. He looked more mature than I remembered him being. He was definitely taller. I quit calling Jack and focused all my energy on finding a way to see Norris. I stopped going to the dances too.

I tried to get Norris's attention once when I passed by and he was on the porch. If he did notice me, he ignored me. Mrs. Walker agreed to talk to the foster mother who was her friend. I pretended that I wanted to talk to her about my brother Joe moving in there. The foster mother invited me over one Sunday. I put on a pretty print summer dress that fit nicely and everyone complimented me about it. I had my hair pressed and rolled it up, getting rid of the afro that I usually wore.

I paced in front of the house trying to ease my nerves for at least five minutes. Each step that brought me closer to the front door weighed me down. I finally made it onto the porch and knocked on the door. A woman with a friendly face greeted me.

"Come on in," she said. "You must be Joyce. Oh, don't you look pretty?" I smiled at her. Her house was very similar to Mrs. Walker's. She began telling me about the boys in her group home and how long she'd been a foster mother.

"Can I have a tour?" I asked in my sweetest manner.

She couldn't resist an innocent-looking girl who appeared to be interested in her foster home.

My legs were weak as we walked up the stairs. I could hear music floating down.

Baby, I'm For Real by The Originals was ending when we made it to the top.

I stood behind her, trying to resist the urge to open the door. *What Does it Take to Win Your Love?* By Jr. Walker and The All Stars was now playing on the record player when she opened the door. Then I saw him. Norris was sitting on the couch clad only in underwear. Our eyes locked momentarily before he jumped up and rushed off. I sensed he was embarrassed. I had to catch my own breath because Norris had a body that was rippling with muscles and I actually felt something just looking at him.

The foster mother turned to me, "I told the boys a young lady was coming to visit and asked them to be up and dressed."

I could hear laughter coming from the other room. The other boys were teasing Norris. Apparently, he had gotten out of bed late after being out most of the night.

I was introduced to the boys who were fully dressed. I politely shook each of their hands. *What Does it Take to Win Your Love* played again on the record player. I tried to stall for time, hoping Norris would come back out. He never did.

The foster mother served me tea and cookies once we were back downstairs.

"What about the boy who was sitting on the couch?" I asked her.

"That's Norris. He's the shy quiet one. He's only been here a couple of months."

I smiled at her.

"He's a handsome young man."

I nodded my head in agreement. I tried to focus on our conversation but my mind was on Norris and seeing him sitting on the couch with his bare chest exposed. Norris knew who I was; he also knew where I was living. I didn't care that Mrs. Walker would disapprove about him coming to visit; I was more concerned about Wilma being there.

I made more ice cream trips hoping to see Norris. A few times he was on the porch. He waved at me twice, but for the most part he ignored me. *My Cherie Amour* by Stevie Wonder was a smash hit and I adopted that song as Norris's and mine.

Jack was upset because I wouldn't meet him on the playground anymore. How could I meet Jack with Norris living around the corner? I told Joe about Norris moving into the group home around the corner and suggested that he could move in there since he was having trouble with Cary. Joe assured me that he was fine living with Mrs. Perkins.

I stayed close to home hoping that one day or night Norris would come over. Mrs. Walker probably wouldn't fuss about him because he was close to my age. I didn't even care if he saw Wilma. I just wanted him to come by and talk to me like he used to. There was something about Norris that I hadn't felt for any other boy. All I wanted was for him to like me.

Mrs. Walker's favorite saying was "I'll tell you what," followed by whatever she was going to say. My foster sisters mocked her when she wasn't around. They would stomp through the house saying, "I'll tell you what" and making their face look like hers. I would laugh because it was funny.

Mrs. Walker made noises that we heard all the way upstairs. It was a moaning sound usually followed by her saying her husband's name, Dewitt.

"You know what they're doing," the girls would say as they chanted, "Ooh Dee, ooh Dee." Candy was the best one who could imitate her. We laughed until we couldn't anymore.

I'm not sure where Mr. Walker worked because he never talked to us. He left early in the mornings and came home in the evenings but never socialized with us. He didn't even eat at the dinner table with us. I couldn't believe that they were a couple when I first saw him. He was a tall thin attractive man who looked a lot younger than her. It was easy to imagine how handsome he had been as a young man. While we heard Mrs. Walker's voice all over the house we seldom heard anything from him. He was a quiet reserved man who hardly ever smiled. I heard them argue a few times.

"He married her for her money," Candy said.

I listened as she told me the story of how Mrs. Walker was once married to another man.

"They had a baby boy".

It was hard for me to imagine Mrs. Walker with a baby. They were in a train accident and Mrs. Walker's son and husband were killed. She got a big settlement out of it and that is how she bought this house."

I cringed at the thought of Mrs. Walker loosing her family in a tragic accident. It had happened several years before she became a foster mother and she never had any more children.

"Mr. Walker is a flirt and is probably fooling around on her", one of the girls said. None of them trusted Mr. Walker and neither did I.

Tension began mounting between my foster sisters and me. I took a lot of my frustrations about Norris out on Wilma and we argued a lot. I was jealous of her and believed that if I looked like her, he might like me.

One day I jumped up ready to fight Candy because I was tired of her teasing me. It had been awhile since I fought anyone, but I was sure I could beat her up. We didn't fight but I complained to Mrs. Walker about her.

Elsie came home after going to the dance alone that night. I was certain she had met with a boy. We were in the den listening to music when Elsie came out of the bedroom dressed in her gown. "You smell funny," Candy said to her.

Elsie didn't reply.

"You smell like you've been screwing somebody," Candy said laughing.

Elsie denied it and left the room in tears.

"She needs to take a bath or shower next time her ass go out screwing," Candy said, making everyone laugh.

A few days later Mrs. Walker came upstairs in one of her moods. This time Mrs. Walker came directly to our room with the other girls on her heels. She was fussing at Elsie who had been sneaking out of the house at night.

"Look at that bed," she said. The bed was lumpy.

Mrs. Walker pulled the covers off the bed and pulled the top Mattress to the floor. Something big and red and made out of rubber fell to the floor. The other girls gasped when they saw it.

"That is the biggest douche bag I've ever seen in my life!" Candy remarked. The other girls were laughing. I stared at the thing.

"She sure can't be a virgin using that thing," one of the girls remarked.

Elsie was embarrassed and ran out of the room. Mrs. Walker made a few more stops at the other girl's bedrooms before going back downstairs. Elsie admitted to me that night she had been having sex. I promised her I wouldn't say anything.

I wanted to watch TV and the other girls wanted to listen to music. I was defiant and didn't back down. Mrs. Walker came upstairs to settle the dispute, and of course she sided with them. I was angry about it and wanted to move out. I don't know what happened between Mrs. Walker and Barbara Cole. I just remember that one day she was gone. Mrs. Walker was now making threats about shutting down the group home. There was a lot going on that I didn't understand. She had fallen out with her sister, Bea, who moved out of the cottage in the back. There was also a rumor that she and Mr. Walker were separating because he was cheating on her.

Everything happened quickly. I didn't know anything until my new social worker came to the house that day.

"What is going on?" I asked.

"You are moving to Adams Hall," she told me.

Mrs. Walker was sitting in the living room with the social worker.

"Mrs. Walker is closing down the group home and wanted to make sure that you had a place to go."

I looked at Mrs. Walker in disbelief. She looked worn and her eyes were red. I could smell stale liquor on her.

"I had to make sure you had a place to go," Mrs. Walker said.

The other girls were gone when I packed my things. I gathered everything, trying hard to control my emotions. The bedroom walls seemed to close in on me as the actuality of what was happening began sinking in. Despite everything with my foster sisters I was going to miss them. I wished I could tell them good-bye. How long had it been since I had come to live with Mrs. Walker? Months? A year? I couldn't calculate the time. It felt as if a lifetime was spent there. I realized then that I was emotionally attached to Mrs. Walker. Although my foster sisters laughed at her, talked about her and even taunted her, I believed they had a genuine fondness for Mrs. Walker too. Images of my foster sisters rolled through my mind as I passed by their bedrooms, Wilma, Candy, Barbara English, Connie, Sheila and of course Elsie. Barbara Cole's room was now empty and the door was open. I assumed she had moved somewhere with her baby. As I hobbled down the stairs I started crying. It felt different being in a foster home where saying good-bye was breaking my heart. My foster sisters weren't always nice to me and sometimes they hurt my feelings, but we did bond. When I returned to the living room my eyes were dry. I couldn't let them see me cry. I hugged Mrs. Walker and prayed for control.

"It's time to go." The social worker had already picked up one of my bags. She seemed annoyed by my slowness. I knew this was her job, yet it seemed so cold. I was sad when I walked away from Mrs. Walker's foster home. I waved goodbye to her before getting into the car. Mrs. Walker was having problems that I wasn't supposed to know about. She probably didn't know how thin the walls were in the house. My mind wondered back to my foster sisters. I wondered what would happen to them.

The social worker tried to start a friendly conversation as we rode to Adams Hall.

"It's really a nice place."

I glanced out the window. I felt as if I was going to cry again. I didn't want her to see me cry.

"I think you'll enjoy being with this group of kids. There are several kids in there that are on my case load."

I nodded still looking out the window. I didn't want to talk to her. For some reason my mind went back to when I left the Williams foster home. I felt again I was leaving a place I wanted to be. We rode in silence, giving me an opportunity to prematurely think about the next foster home. What would it be like? Will I like them? Would they like me? Adams Hall was just a stepping-stone until a foster home was available.

Joe constantly talked about us being together as a family again, but I couldn't see it happening. I was sure they had deliberately separated us. Joe had been living with Mrs. Perkins for a long time now. He didn't complain much, so I assumed he was happy there. I met Mrs. Perkins once and she wasn't friendly to me. Suddenly I wondered if Joe would know where to find me. I had to tell the social worker to let him know.

"Will you tell Joe where I'll be?" I blurted out.

"Sure," she said without hesitation.

At least Ralph and Sara were together. Last I heard they still lived with Mr. And Mrs. Guy. I was a little jealous that the Guys' foster home worked out okay for Ralph and Sara. It probably would have worked out okay for me too if I had been more willing to accept them. Anyway, I was on my third residency at Adams Hall.

"I've been to Adams Hall twice," I told her. I was tired of her going on about how nice it was there.

We pulled up in front of a large brick building that I had never seen before.

"Where are we?"

She smiled. "You will like the new Adams Hall."

Chapter Fifteen

The New Adams Hall

When I was told I was going to the New Adams Hall I wasn't expecting the building to be too. The new Adams Hall was a modern, three-story brick building amid a cluster of single-family homes on the Northwest side of town. It looked like an apartment building. Wall to wall carpet greeted us when we walked in through the front glass door and tiled shiny floors in the hallways. The first floor was garden level and was the full length of the building with a huge recreation room filled with game tables. In the back of the building were a parking area and an outdoor basketball court.

The office was on the main level. It was a large room with new office furniture. A secretary was hired to take care of the administrative work. She greeted us when we walked in; I listened while she repeated the rules of Adams Hall. I had heard the speech two times before and could recite it as well as she could. After the social worker left the secretary did a quick inventory of my clothes. I was taken upstairs to the third floor by one of the counselors. There were several bedrooms with twin beds in them. We had our own recreation area on the floor complete with a television, record player, and a card table with chairs. There were several bathrooms with baths and showers to accommodate all of us. I was glad that we no longer had to sleep in one large room. Two residents were assigned to each bedroom. I was given a bedroom in the back of the building overlooking the parking lot and basketball court. I loved my bedroom and was thankful for the privacy. Everything about this Adams Hall was nice and I could still smell the newness of the place.

I had put away all my personal things and was walking through the recreation area when I saw her. We stared at each other for what seemed like forever before the shock wore off. It was Anna. I hadn't seen her since leaving Mrs. Oglesby's house. Anna and I ran into each other arms hugging and squeezing each other. Anna said that she left Mrs. Oglesby's house soon after I did. The next surprise was seeing Barbara Cole in there. They were the two people I least expected to see in Adams Hall. I assumed that Barbara was on her own after leaving Mrs. Walker's. It felt good having two of my foster sisters in Adams Hall with me. I proudly told everyone that I was Barbara and Anna's little foster sister. Barbara was the oldest girl in there and all of us looked up to her.

Barbara was still working at the hamburger place where she got the job while living with Mrs. Walker. She told me that she was saving up money so that she could move into her own apartment. She continued the weekend visits with her son. Barbara told us stories about things that happened on her job that sometimes had us rolling with laughter. One day she took me aside and told me she knew about the problems going on in Mrs. Walker's house.

Anna was waiting to go into another foster home, but was hoping she could return home to her mother. I never knew what the problem was with her mother, but it must not have been so terrible since she wanted to go back to her.

"I'll take my daughter out of foster care," she said. "We will move back to Chicago." I wanted to ask Anna about the miscarriage because I still wondered if Mrs. Oglesby's son was the father, but I didn't have the nerve to ask her. She seemed happy and wanting to move on with her life.

I settled into the new Adams Hall nicely. The counselors had changed along with the new building. They were younger, more energetic, and to my surprise, many of them were black. There were also more male counselors. I would watch from my bedroom window while Mr. Love, Mr. Johnson, and Mr. Williams played basketball with the boys. We also had more activities going on. There was a movie night, which was one of my favorites. We had our own in-house dances and sometimes even live bands came to play. We would dress up and go downstairs to the garden level. We could invite our friends from all over the city so it was always lively. At the movies we no longer had designated seats to sit in, which made it fun. I liked to sit in the balcony while some kids preferred to sit lower level or up close. There were fewer restrictions at Adams Hall and they no longer had the cooler room.

You still had to be sixteen years old to smoke cigarettes and the boys and girls still slept on separate floors. Alcohol and drugs were forbidden but they still had ways of sneaking them in. Curfews depended on our ages. Every month we were given allowances to do whatever we wanted with.

The new cook was a short black woman. She was really good and cooked whatever we wanted to eat. The cafeteria was also on the garden level and connected to the recreation room. The cook told us what was on the menu in advance so we could pick what we wanted to eat. There was always plenty of food so we snacked between meals.

Joe found me after the first week and came to visit every chance he got after that. Some counselors and residents thought he lived in Adams Hall because he was there so much. Joe was able to move around Adams Hall as if he were a resident. Eddie was back in Adams Hall and so was Keith. Both of them had grown a lot since the last time I saw them. Keith now sported a voice that was really low.

I found Jack's phone number in one of my books so I called

him. We had pay phones in the hallway downstairs that we could use. It cost a dime to make a phone call so I called only two times a week. He called me too and whoever answered the phone would usually go find the person the phone was for.

I gained a lot of respect from the other kids just because Barbara and Anna were my foster sisters. I was upset when both of them left about the same time. I felt alone even though by then I had made many new friends. One day I tried to contact Sue and Jeffrey but it had been over a year and she had moved away from the apartment.

The longer I stayed in Adams Hall the more I liked it. That summer we went on all kinds of field trips including a barbeque in the park. Being popular was a benefit when the Johnson sisters came. Brenda was a year older than me and Debra was my age. I knew them from Robert Fulton Junior High. Brenda looked mean and had a reputation of being rough. She got into a lot of fights at school. There was a story about how Brenda jumped out of her shoes so she could run a girl down. Brenda was more laid back than her sister. She wore her hair pulled back in a single ponytail. I never saw her wear any dresses. Her wardrobe was limited to jeans with big shirts and tennis shoes. The scar on her face didn't help soften her look. Being in Adams Hall didn't stop Brenda from fighting either. She was always on restriction for fighting.

Debra was very feminine and prettier. She wore her hair pressed and curled. She was opposite of her sister and wore makeup and dresses. Debra and Keith liked each other so they both claimed to be going together.

Linda Garcia also returned to the New Adams Hall. She looked the same as when I last saw her with long straight black hair that was ratted at the top and held in place with lots of hair spray. She was now wearing the Marla Thomas, That Girl; look with bangs in the front. Her makeup was still heavy with shades of blue or purple eye shadow and black eyeliner. She was almost eighteen but looked older with the makeup on. They assigned Linda as my roommate.

We would stay up late at night talking, laughing and joking with each other. We talked about Matthew, Robert, and the old Adams Hall. Linda was a smoker so we sat under the window with it open while she smoked because we weren't supposed to be smoking in our bedroom. Linda would spray cologne to camouflage the smell.

The biggest problem at Adams Hall was the clothes stealing. Most of the kids living in Adams Hall had families they could spend the weekend with. So they would take the stolen clothes home and leave them there. If clothes came up missing no one ever saw them again. If a resident ran away or didn't return after a home visit his or her clothes were stolen out of the closet and divided between those who wanted them. Those who were leaving to go to a foster home also stole clothes to take with them. I kept my bedroom door locked even though it was against the rules. I had managed to stockpile a lot of nice clothes and I didn't want anyone taking them. I didn't loan out my clothes and I wasn't concerned about Linda wearing my clothes because she was a lot bigger than I was. My wardrobe was probably the largest in Adams Hall. Some clothes still had store tags on them.

One mid-summer night it was too hot to sleep, so Linda and I took the screen off of the window to let more air in. It didn't help cool off our room but at least the cigarette smoke was going out faster. Linda sat under the window smoking and watching it go out. That was when I decided that I wanted to try smoking again. Linda laughed, but gave me a cigarette. I lit the Salem and began puffing.

"You have to inhale the smoke," she whispered.

I almost choked when I inhaled. She laughed a little.

"You have to get use to it."

I took another puff. Within minutes my head was spinning. Soon a sick feeling filled my stomach. Linda laughed when I sprawled across the bed complaining of the dizziness. I wasn't old enough to smoke so I couldn't tell the consolers what was wrong.

Finally as my stomach began turning I made a rush for the bathroom and began vomiting. I vowed to never touch another cigarette.

I didn't even think about being in Adams Hall anymore. I became close with a lot of the residents because all of us were in the same situation, unsure of our future while we waited for someplace to go. Some went to foster homes, others returned to their real parents or some went to live with relatives. I was the only true orphan in Adams Hall. Going back to live with my parents wasn't an option for me. Even going to live with relatives didn't seem to be a possibility. I hadn't seen any of my siblings other than Joe in a long time. My uncles, aunts, and cousins were just a blur of a memory. Linda and I got emotional as we began comparing our feelings and sharing stories. It was as if all of us were being recycled through the system. We knew that most of us would meet again, either in a foster home or an institution.

"We are recycled children," Linda said.

Jack and I began talking more on the phone and each night I pledged my dedication to him. I started keeping a dairy in which I recorded our conversations as well as other secrets. A few times I met Jack behind Roosevelt Junior High, where we would kiss and rub against each other fully clothed. I didn't tell anyone about my secrets except the diary I wrote in every night. Many times my imagination ran further than my reality.

Linda left to go back home so I was given another roommate named Tara. She was about seventeen years old with pale skin and hair that was dried out from too much blonde dye. She admitted to me that she liked to get high on drugs. Her thing was popping pills. She loved LSD and wanted to take what she called a trip on it all the time. At night Tara talked to herself and paced the floors in the bedroom. She scared me the way she acted. I blended in more with the others and kept my distance from Tara.

When Anna, Barbara, and Linda left, they all promised to keep in touch. But I knew how far those promises went. They were out on their own with apartments, boyfriends, and jobs. Why would any of them think about me? I didn't expect them to.

Eddie was more like a brother than a friend. He was older and more mature than any boy in Adams Hall. I didn't want to get involved with any of the boys in Adams Hall, until Richard Reynolds arrived. When he came to Adams Hall he immediately got my attention. He reminded me of James Patton with his good looks and savvy ways. It wasn't long before he and I began passing notes to each other. Sometimes I wrote notes to Richard while talking on the phone to Jack. The only one who really knew about my confusion was the diary. I liked them both; Jack was older and mature, while Richard was cute and a lot of fun. Jack always met me at the school when I could get away so I asked him why we couldn't go to his house, but he only laughed. I was getting tired of Jack. When I did see him all he wanted to do was rub his body against me and lately he wanted to do more, but I wouldn't let him. Richard and I started spending more time together. We even held hands when we went to the movies with the group.

So now it was Debra and Keith, Eddie and Lisa, and Richard and I. We sat in the movies holding hands or sharing popcorn while the counselor sat nearby. Everything seemed to be going okay the evening we went to the movies to see Sidney Potier in *To Sir with Love*. I can't recall what the dispute was about, but it spilled over into the movies. Debra was home for a weekend visit and I was mad at Richard so I sat with Keith during the movie. When we returned to Adams Hall someone told Richard that I was with Keith.

I was on the basketball court when Richard came outside to argue with me. We both said foul things to each other and Richard shoved me. I felt something fall at my feet and looked down to see a shiny object. Richard continued shouting threats at me. I looked at the crowd that was gathering around us. I felt like I needed to do something. I could feel my hands picking up the razor. Richard came closer to me. Somehow the razor found its mark across his cheek. I screamed as blood began trickling down my hands and

Richard let out a loud cry. I was sure he was dead when he fell to the ground.

The crowd began shouting something to me. Someone took the razor from my hand, as I stood, frozen, looking down at Richard. I could hear voices in the background shouting for me to leave but my feet wouldn't move. I was still there when Mr. Love came outside. All I saw was blood. I heard the screeching sound of an ambulance in the distance as I was being led inside to wait for the police to arrive.

"You've done it this time," Mrs. Lacy kept saying to me while I gathered my clothes from the closets and drawers in my room. She allowed me to pack my clothes myself. I called Roy jr. and asked him, to come get my clothes and keep them at his house so they wouldn't get stolen. I was going to take my diary with me, but decided to hide it inside the box of clothes. Roy jr. promised he would pick up my clothes.

I had my head down when the police led me to the waiting police car. I could feel the eyes of everyone on me and I knew something bad was going to happen to me. I was scared. I prayed that Richard would be okay.

Chapter Sixteen

Back to the Detention Home

Time passes either quickly or slowly when you're locked up, but for me the time didn't matter anymore. I couldn't keep up with the days or weeks as they came and went. I spent most of my time making things. I loved stuffed animals so I made stuffed teddy bears in all different colors and spread them around my bed. I also enjoyed reading the endless supply of comic books. I was there when girls came and was still there when they left. Sometimes girls were released and came back twice and I was still there. It was as if I didn't exist to the outside world anymore.

Mrs. Brown talked to me about God to keep my sprits up and even convinced me to crochet. I started making hats, potholders, and other little things with the yarn they provided. I'm sure she felt sorry for me because during the entire time I was in the Detention Center, the only visitor that came was the social worker. Her visit was a waste of time because I knew about the charges against me and understood they were serious.

"We will decide what to do with you when we go to court," she said, hinting that I would probably end up in Oregon, the State correctional facility for girls until I was eighteen years old. Some of the girls coming through the Detention Center had been to Oregon and told me that it wasn't a good place to be.

When I told Mrs. Brown about the conversation with the social worker she suggested that I find out the name of the judge who would be over my case and write a letter to him. I found out that it was Judge Foley. The girls who had been in his courtroom gave me little hope that Judge Foley would go easy on me.

"He is going to send your ass straight to Oregon," the majority of them said. When I had the pen in my hand I tried to think of what to say to Judge Foley. Mrs. Brown told me to write what I felt and explain what happened. I started off writing an apology letter, but as I began writing a feeling swept over me and the words flowed. By the time I finished the letter there were tears drops all over it. I didn't read it once I was finished because I didn't want to change anything. I knew everything I wrote came from within so I left it that way. Mrs. Brown told me that she would continue to pray for me.

Months passed and I was still in the Detention Center before I finally went to court. Mrs. Brown and Mrs. Green were both angry that I had been in there so long. The courtrooms were located inside of the juvenile facility. Most of the kids wore street clothes when they went to court so Mrs. Brown bought me a nice dress to wear. I was nervous in the courtroom because it seemed so strange. I had appeared before a Judge a few times before, but today was different. I didn't know anyone in the courtroom. The social worker and probation officer sat near me on one side while another lady and man were on the opposite side. I got a visit from the probation officer the week before. She told me she would be in court with me. She was about thirty years old with a harsh face from too much sun. Her hair was blonde and eyes were light brown. The time she spent with me was awkward and I was glad when she finally left.

"Your honor, this girl needs to be sent to the State Facility for Girls until she is eighteen," I heard the man say. I felt my pulse rushing and my head was light. I looked at the man who went on and on giving more reasons why I should be put away. Judge Foley was an average looking man with black-rimmed glasses that slid down over his nose. He didn't say anything while the man talked about how bad I was. He mentioned that I was dangerous and quoted how many times I had been in the Detention Center.

"We have no idea why she was in here at least three times," the probation officer interrupted him. I squirmed in my seat and looked at the woman sitting next to me. I didn't want to go to Oregon. I looked around the courtroom. There was no one else there. I was alone again in a time in my life when I needed someone to help me. Judge Foley looked at the papers he had in front of him. He too was baffled about three stays in the Detention Center. He also wanted to know why I was left in there so long. No one could answer his questions. The social worker could hardly talk when he asked her how many times she had visited me. I thought about my own family now. Most of the girls who went to court had at least a family member with them.

The probation officer also had a hard time explaining why she only visited me once but she did describe parts of my life to the Judge and mentioned that the cut to Keith's cheek was an accident.

"She isn't dangerous to anyone. Joyce did not have the weapon when she and the young man started fighting. Someone in the crowd threw the knife to Joyce and she picked it up because she was afraid. We are talking about a boy fighting a girl."

I breathed a sigh of relief because at least someone believed me. I couldn't tell what the Judge was thinking because he didn't show any type of emotion.

The two people on opposite side began whispering to each other. It seemed like an argument to me, but I didn't really know. The woman took over and began to repeat much of what the man had already said. She recommended that I be put into Oregon too. I was glad when it all ended and the judge began to speak.

In Years To Come

He looked at me and I smiled at him. I was sure he smiled back. He referred to the letter I wrote him.

"I have never in my life received a letter that was so touching. I must have read that letter a dozen times and I want you to know that it touched me. I receive letters all the time from juveniles, but never such an emotional one. The young man that you cut refused to testify against you and he refused to press charges against you. He said that it was his fault because he started the whole commotion."

I couldn't believe what I was hearing because it was the first time I had heard that he refused to press charges against me. It felt good to know that Richard didn't blame me.

"The cut on his face was superficial and has probably healed by now, and according to the records it will not leave a permanent scar. There was no permanent damage to his face." I was almost in tears by the time the Judge finished talking. He spoke about how mature I seemed and how he believed that I was truly sorry about what happened. Mrs. Brown, Mrs. Green, and Mrs. Patterson had sent Judge Foley a file on me that showed him how well behaved I was.

"Why can't she be put into a foster home?" he asked the social worker.

"Your Honor, we didn't know what was going to happen because the charges against her are very serious."

Judge Foley gave me probation and ordered the social worker to find me a foster home or somewhere else to go within a week.

It was hard saying goodbye to Mrs. Brown and Mrs. Green because they were my favorite counselors. I had many stuffed teddy bears and other things I had made while I was there. A couple of counselors had to help me carry them as they escorted me out to where the social worker was waiting. I was turned over to the state and was going to my first State foster home.

Chapter Seventeen

Miss Vera

Miss Vera was a single mother with two young daughters. She had a son but he was grown and out on his own. It was a strange arrangement living with Miss Vera. Her elderly parents and two daughters, Merry and Juanita lived in a single-family house on North Avenue. I was to live there with them. Miss Vera owned a small restaurant on Twelfth Street and above the restaurant were bedrooms that she rented out to people. That is also where Miss Vera slept every night. I saw Miss Vera every day because we went to the restaurant after school to eat dinner. Miss Vera's parents helped her in the restaurant. Her father worked behind the candy counter selling penny candy. I remembered his face from the few times I had gone into the restaurant before to buy candy. Her father was a rough looking man with an unsmiling face and eyes that seemed to stare right through you. My perception of him was that he was mean and old. I stayed out of his way most of the time and cringed when he yelled at Merry and Juanita.

Miss Vera's mother was sweet with a smiling face. She had watery eyes like Hon. I wondered how such a sweet woman could be married to a grouchy old man, but there was a lot of love between them that glowed like a bright light. I was sure that I saw the old man smile a few times when he was around her. Her mother helped Miss Vera with the cooking. The food was delicious and I looked forward to eating every day when I came home from school. I was enrolled back in Roosevelt Junior High to finish up the eighth grade.

Merry and Juanita attended the elementary school down the street. After awhile it didn't seem any different eating at the restaurant than at the house. There was a room in the back of the restaurant where Merry, Juanita, and I went for privacy. We did our homework back there. An old brown upright piano was in the middle of the room and I listened while Merry played and sang church songs. I especially liked when she sang *blowing in the wind*, a song made popular by Stevie Wonder. Merry was the oldest, she was twelve and Juanita was eleven.

I never told Miss Vera about my experience working in a restaurant because I didn't want her to make me work. I did chores around the house and if I was needed to do small chores at the restaurant, it was okay too. I didn't want to work the way I had at Uncle Ben's restaurant.

There was a basic respect between Miss Vera and me so we got along just fine. I had made a couple of friends at school and invited them to the restaurant where we would sit in a booth and talk about boys like most girls did. There was a jukebox in there and Miss Vera let me operate it without having to put money in so I played a lot of music.

Just like at Uncle Ben's restaurant, Miss Vera had customers who faithfully came to eat everyday. I never mingled or talked with the customers.

One day while my friends, Loretta and Diane, were visiting me in the restaurant, two guys walked through the door. A bell went off every time a customer walked in so the three of us looked up.

"The one in the trench coat is cute", Diane said. I looked

362

over to where the two men were standing and smiled.

"He is cute," I agreed.

When the other guy turned around I almost gasped. It was, Roy jr.

"The one in the front is my brother," I told them.

Diane laughed. "Find out about the guy with him," she whispered.

"Roy jr.!" I shouted rushing over to him.

"Hey girl," he said to me. Roy jr. never hugged anyone so we stood looking at each other.

"Do you know who this is?" He pointed the guy with him.

I turned around to look at him. He was short, cute, and had a nice smile.

I shook my head and smiled back.

"This is your brother, Henry." I could hear *These Eyes* by Junior Walker and The All Stars playing on the jukebox in the background. I had not seen Henry since in years so all I could do was stare at him.

"Hi Joyce," he finally said.

"Henry?"

He nodded. "I live in Indianapolis with Sister and her family."

I introduced Roy jr. and Henry to Miss Vera, who invited them to stay and eat. My friends left while the three of us sat at table talking. I forgot about being mad at Roy jr. for not picking up my clothes from Adams Hall. When I went to Miss Vera's house I was given a small sack with two dresses and a pair of pants. They didn't know what happened to my clothes or the diary I had carefully put in the box. I was mad at Roy jr. because he never showed up to pick up my clothes.

Roy jr. told me that my social worker gave him the information about where I was living. Miss Vera's mother was at the house when he stopped by so she directed him to the restaurant.

In Years To Come

"I'm coming back to see you again," Henry promised before they left.

There was quietness around the house that reminded me of when I lived with the Williams. It was good for reading, but I loved to listen to music. The Temptations had a new song out called *Psychedelic Shack* that I played on the jukebox in the restaurant.

It was strange to see two sisters who were so different. They even looked different. Merry was on the plump side with a round face, dark skin, and thick hair. Juanita was thin and taller. Her hair was short, but it looked nice with her oval face. She liked dressing up and seemed to be more feminine than Merry. Their attitudes were different too: Merry was quiet and obedient while Juanita was rebellious and talked back to her grandparents. It seemed like Juanita should have been the older sibling.

Miss Vera had rented out all the rooms above the restaurant, so when a young couple came for a room there weren't any left. It was a young black girl named Bernice and her boyfriend, a Puerto Rican named Hose. They had moved to Milwaukee from another state. Miss Vera felt sorry for them and decided they could rent a bedroom in the house. Juanita and Merry had to share a bedroom when the couple moved into Juanita's room.

I started talking with Hose and Bernice after school one day. She was a short, thin, homely looking girl with a small afro and bowlegs. Hose was average height with beautiful black wavy hair and red eyes. It looked like he was crying all the time. I liked Bernice and we became friends. I spent a lot of time talking with her when she was home. Bernice was the only one working so we didn't see each other that often. Hose spent most of the time in the bedroom and only came out when Bernice was home. Sometimes he would leave the house and go somewhere. I soon found out why he had red eyes. He drank a lot of liquor that Bernice usually supplied. I was surprised when she told me she was only seventeen years old; she told most people she was twenty-one. She got involved with Hose when she was sixteen, and they had to leave town because of their mixed race relationship. I couldn't tell anyone because they had told Miss Vera they were married. In Milwaukee it was against the law to live together if you weren't married.

It was clear from the beginning that Hose controlled Bernice. She told me she loved Hose even though her family didn't approve of the relationship. Her older brother, Ezell, and his family had moved to Milwaukee a couple of years earlier.

"We wanted a fresh start," she told me. "So we moved here. I was able to get a job, but Hose has had a hard time finding work."

I didn't understand why he was having a hard time finding a job because he was a healthy man. At twenty-eight he looked older to me, but nevertheless he was still young enough to get work. My own theory was that Hose didn't want to work, but I never suggested that to Bernice. There was something hidden behind those red eyes that made me feel uncomfortable around him. I didn't like him or the way he treated Bernice. I wasn't sure what went on behind the closed bedroom door, but Bernice was always upset.

I went to visit Mrs. Walker who lived a couple of blocks down the street. She acted like she was happy to see me. She told me she had closed down the group home, but Elsie was still living with her. When Elsie walked into the room a few minutes later I was shocked because she was pregnant.

"What happened to you?" I whispered to her when Mrs. Walker left the room.

"Remember that boy I talked about named Maine?"

I nodded my head. She had talked about him all the time.

"Well, I let him talk me into doing this and now I'm seven months pregnant. I'm staying here with Mrs. Walker until after I have the baby, then I'm going back to live with my mother."

"Are you and your baby both going to live with your mother?"

She nodded.

I didn't even know that her mother was still alive because Elsie had never said anything about having a mother. I was surprised that she even had a relationship with her mother.

"Wilma is having a baby too," Mrs. Walker told me.

That didn't surprise me, but I laughed at the thought of Wilma being fat and out of shape. Most of my foster sisters had gone to other foster homes or were returned to their families. Sheila turned eighteen, graduated from high school and married Dave. They were expecting their first child. I visited Mrs. Walker and Elsie a few more times.

Merry didn't talk much with either Bernice or Hose, but Juanita was always hanging out near their door. I thought it was strange the way that she was always acting around them, but I never said anything to her.

I came home from school early one day. I knew the grandparents and Mrs. Vera would be at the restaurant. I used my key to let myself into the house. It was quiet. All the shades had been pulled down so it was dark. I walked upstairs to my bedroom and heard a strange noise. It was coming from Bernice and Hose's bedroom. It was unlike Bernice not to go to work, but she must not have I thought. The door was closed so I didn't bother to investigate. I was in my room when I heard more noise and this time I decided to knock on the door. Hose opened the door and stood there looking at me. I looked past him and saw Juanita sitting on the floor.

"What's going on?" I asked him.

"Nothing," he said. I knew he was lying. Juanita got up off the floor and I noticed that her clothes were wrinkled and her hair was messed up. From all the evidence I saw I knew more was going on in that room.

Juanita brushed past me and ran into the bathroom. I

confronted her later.

"What were you doing in his room?"

"Leave me alone!" she shouted at me. Her eyes narrowed and her lips curled.

"I am going to tell your mother," I shouted back.

"You don't know anything!" she shouted.

"What are you doing with him?" You're an eleven year old girl!"

Juanita looked at me. "I may be a little girl, but Hose loves me and I love him. I am doing whatever he wants me to do," she answered.

I felt like I was going to throw up. Memories of what happened to me flooded my mind and I wanted to hurt Hose. How could he do this to an innocent girl like Juanita? I realized that my suspicions were true. He was molesting her. What puzzled me the most was why Juanita was a willing participant. I remembered how horrible I felt and how badly I wanted someone to find out about me so it would stop.

"Juanita, he has a wife and besides that he's an old man."

"He loves me," she repeated. Then the tears came. "I love him too," she whispered.

I was caught up with so many issues that I couldn't sort it out. I liked Bernice and didn't want to hurt her by telling her that Hose was molesting Juanita. I also didn't know how I could tell Miss Vera about it because she trusted them enough to allow them to rent a room in her house. The biggest problem of all was the way that Juanita was acting. I didn't understand it. I knew what was happening to her had to stop, but I wasn't sure what to do. I confronted Hose and told him I was going to tell Miss Vera and Bernice if he ever did anything to Juanita again.

Juanita confessed to me that she and Hose had been doing things for a while. She also begged me not to tell because she didn't know what her mother would do.

"You're only eleven years old," I kept saying to her. "It is wrong for a grown man to be messing around with a little girl." I knew that much.

A week later I told Miss Vera about Hose and Juanita.

The look of shock on Miss Vera's face told me how she felt. Things were really shaken up in the household after that. Miss Vera put Bernice and Hose out of the house. Bernice was upset when she found out too, but forgave him and they moved into an apartment a few blocks down the street. Juanita was a mess and cried for Hose. She really believed that Hose loved her. Tears were in Miss Vera's eyes when she held her daughter in her arms and tried to comfort her. The relationship between Miss Vera and me went downhill and I felt as if she was blaming me for what happened to her daughter.

Eventually, I was taken out of the foster home. When we said goodbye, Merry clung to me and cried out loud. I felt sorry for her because she cried a lot lately. Juanita didn't look or behave like the eleven-year-old girl I had met when I first came there. I already knew that she would never be the same.

Chapter Eighteen

Mr. and Mrs. Reed

The scent of vanilla filled the air when I stepped through the door of the large two-story green house. The woman who opened the door smiled at me and invited us in. She was an attractive older woman with a girlish look. Her face was almost perfectly round.

"Come in," she beckoned to the social worker and me.

I had made up my mind that I wasn't going to be nice to her or anyone else who lived there. The social worker told me that this was another group home so I decided I wasn't going to make friends with the other girls in there either. I deliberately turned my nose up and put a frown on my face.

"You can call me Mrs. Reed," the woman said to me.

"I'm Joyce," I mumbled.

The social worker looked at me nervously before she sat down on the sofa. I slid into an overstuffed chair. My eyes scanned the room while the two of them talked. I peeked into the adjoining dining room and was amazed at how tastefully furnished the house was. The beautiful dining room table was a light colored wood that sparkled. The house was full of beautiful oak wood. Mrs. Reed watched me out of the corner of her eye and when I found myself looking at her I quickly turned away. The house was extremely clean and I couldn't see a speck of dust anywhere.

I almost jumped when an older girl walked through the front door, interrupting the conversation between Mrs. Reed and the social worker.

"Hello," the girl said, waving at Mrs. Reed.

"Hi Pat."

I looked at the tall girl who could have easily passed for a grown woman.

"This is Joyce," she said pointing to me.

"Hi," Pat said, smiling.

"Hi."

"Pat, take Joyce upstairs and show her the bedrooms so she can decide which one she wants."

Mrs. Reed smiled at me again, but I looked away and jumped up to follow Pat.

The oak banister leading to the upstairs was shining like it had just been polished.

"Where are the other girls?"

"I'm the only one living here," Pat said when we made it to the top of the stairs.

I was surprised. "How long have you been here?"

Pat looked as if she were adding the days.

"About a month."

It dawned on me that Mrs. Reed must be a new foster mother.

The first bedroom on the left was a small room with a twin bed and matching dresser. A large window overlooked the front of the house and I could see below into the streets. The room was painted a pale pink.

The next bedroom was large with three beds in it.

"This is my bedroom," Pat said. "I like to have a lot of room so I chose this room."

Pat slept in the bed closest to the door. I thought it was odd that she would sleep in this huge room all by herself.

Another large bedroom was next to Pat's bedroom and it also had three beds in it. At the other end of the hall was another single bedroom that was the mirror image of the first one.

"I like the first bedroom," I told Pat.

I sat down on one of the beds in Pat's room. I hadn't intended on making friends with her, but since she was the only one in the group home I felt we might as well be friends.

Pat said she was seventeen years old and had just gotten out of the State Home for girls in Oregon. I told her she looked older and she agreed with me, saying that most of the men thought she was at least twenty-one. Pat was five foot seven with a well-developed body. She wasn't fat but had big breasts and hips. She was going to a vocational school downtown and making plans to move when she turned eighteen. Pat talked fast and I had a hard time keeping up with her conversation.

The social worker left so I brought my things upstairs to put in my new bedroom. I loved the bedspread and when I spread out all my stuffed animals it looked good.

"Come on down to dinner," a woman's voice yelled upstairs. I rolled my eyes.

"She's all right," Pat said.

"I'm not hungry."

"She's a good cook," Pat told me.

I followed her downstairs to the kitchen. The food smelled good and I felt myself weaken.

I ignored Mrs. Reed when I sat down at the table. I was talking to Pat, but I wasn't going to say anything to her or her husband.

Mr. Reed was a dark-skinned man who looked a lot older than Mrs. Reed. He sat down at the table with us but was quiet.

"This is Joyce," Mrs. Reed said breaking the silence.

I looked at him for a moment and turned away without

saying anything.

"Hi, Mr. Reed," Pat said.

"Hello Pat," he said. "How was your day?"

"It's the same thing every day," she answered.

Mr. Reed shook his head before bowing and blessing the food. Mrs. Reed was a great cook and I enjoyed the food.

Over the next couple of days I ignored Mrs. Reed and spent most of my time in my new bedroom. I would sit and look out the window watching the neighbors.

Pat spent most of her time downstairs in the basement, listening to music on the record player. A small room in the basement had been converted into a place for us to watch TV or listen to music. A TV, couch, chair, and record player were in the room. Mrs. Reed also allowed us to smoke down there. We were allowed to talk on the phone and receive phone calls. My curfew was ten and Pat's was midnight on the weekends. We weren't allowed to go out on school nights.

An album by Isaac Hayes had just been released and Pat bought it.

"You have to hear this song," Pat said when she came through the door with the new album under her arm.

"Who is it?"

"Isaac Hays."

I had never heard of him.

"Come on down and listen," she said.

I was sitting in the chair while Pat sat back on the couch smoking a cigarette.

The first part of the song he was talking. I liked his low, vibrating voice. Then he began singing: "I stand accused of loving you too much…."

I nodded my head in agreement. I liked the song.

A week had passed without me speaking to Mrs. Reed when she grabbed my arm after dinner.

"What is wrong with you?" she asked me.

I pulled away from her. "I don't have to talk to you if I don't want to," I growled at her. I could feel my pulse increase as I stood glaring at her.

Mrs. Reed seemed surprised for a moment.

"You want me to call the social worker and tell her to come get you?"

"Yes," I said, walking away.

When I walked downstairs Pat was listening to another album. I sat down.

"Who is that?"

"That is Wes Montgomery. The album is called *A Day in the Life*. Do you like jazz? Wes is a jazz musician."

I closed my eyes and listened to the music that floated through the room.

"Why are you acting like you don't want to be here?"

I opened my eyes and looked at her.

"Mrs. Reed is the nicest person I know. If you go to another foster home who knows what kind of people you will be with."

Deep down I wanted to apologize to Mrs. Reed because actually I really did like her and her house was beautiful, but something inside of me wouldn't allow me to confess it.

"I'll be eighteen in a few months and out on my own," Pat said blowing out smoke from a cigarette. "But you have a long way to go before you're eighteen, so you better think about what you're doing to yourself."

I was on my way upstairs to my bedroom when Mrs. Reed stopped me. I stood in front of her wanting so badly to say something smart, but the words wouldn't come out. She grabbed me again and this time I leaned on her shoulder while the tears flowed. I could smell a sweet scent like flowers as she held me and allowed me to cry. I wasn't sure what the tears were for, but the anger I was feeling began to seep away. When Mrs. Reed released me I apologized to her.

"I know you've been through a lot," she said. "I won't call the social worker."

"Thank you," I whispered. I went to bed that night feeling better.

Over the next few months several girls came and left the group home. Most girls who came to Mrs. Reed's house were on probation or coming from Oregon. I remember Pricilla well because she came straight from Oregon to the group home. Pricilla was an attractive girl with fair skin and long dark wavy hair. She shared the bedroom with Pat. Pricilla was a year younger than Pat. The two of them were inseparable and spent a lot of time in the basement. Sometimes I got mad because when I went down there they treated me as if I wasn't in the room. I began feeling left out so I stayed upstairs in my bedroom. A couple of other girls came, but none stayed long. Cathy came from another foster home. She moved into the bedroom next to Pat's. She had a great sense of humor and kept me laughing. Cathy stayed on the phone too long, leaving less time for the rest us. There were about six foster girls living in the house by the time Cathy joined us. Helen and Barbara shared the bedroom with Cathy because it had three beds in it.

"Let's go down and listen to some music," Cathy suggested after we had been upstairs all evening talking. I didn't mind going down with the other girls because at least I would have someone to talk to. The basement was dark except for a small light beaming from another part of the basement. We could hear the music, but nothing else. Cathy turned on the lights and we were shocked to see Pat and Pricilla embracing each other the way a man and woman did. They were kissing each other. My mouth dropped open because I had never seen two women entangled the way they were.

Cathy laughed at them.

Pat jumped up and Pricilla was clearly upset.

"We caught you," Cathy said. "I knew something was

going on between the two of you."

Pricilla ran past us and up the stairs. Pat stood up smiling. "Yes, I like her," she said.

"Are you a dyke?" Cathy asked her.

"If you really want to know what I am, I'm a hoe," Pat said sarcastically. "I turn tricks on Third Street for money, but I prefer to be with women."

"I'm telling Mrs. Reed about you two."

I stood there while Cathy and Pat stared at each other with looks of hatred until Pat walked out of the room.

"What were they doing?"

Cathy looked at me. "You know damn well what they were doing. Pat is a dyke, can't you tell?"

Cathy never told Mrs. Reed about the incident in the basement, but when other foster girls came she told them. I couldn't get the image out of my mind. I would never have thought that Pat was a dyke. She did have short hair, but when she put on her wig and makeup she was a gorgeous woman. I always thought that real bulldagers looked like men.

Pricilla was embarrassed because Cathy was telling the other girls about what happened. The teasing drove Pricilla to run away. I never saw her again. More girls came and left, but Pat and I were always there. The beds in Pat's bedroom filled up as well as the other beds in the next bedroom. Cathy left and was quickly replaced. Just like at Mrs. Walker's house, all the girls were older than me. Pam was almost nineteen years old. I wondered why she was still in a foster home at her age, but I never found out. This group of girls was different and I didn't get close to any of them.

I did get closer to Mr. And Mrs. Reed though. She seemed to have a spot in her heart just for me. The two of us had long talks and I felt I could share things with her the way a mother and daughter did. Mrs. Reed acted like she understood me. She kept reminding me that it wasn't my fault that I didn't have parents. I went shopping with Mrs. Reed and it wasn't long before my wardrobe grew to include a black and white snakeskin coat with a matching hat. Mrs. Reed had an extra closet downstairs where I kept my best clothes because my foster sisters borrowed everything from personal things to clothes. I didn't like anyone wearing my clothes, but they sometimes went into my closet and helped themselves without my permission. When they borrowed my clothes they were either damaged or not returned.

Sana came to Mrs. Reed's group home after I was there about five months. She was fifteen, a year older than I was. She was a short brown-skinned girl with long hair and features that reminded me of an Indian. I called her a black Indian.

Sana had lived with her grandmother for a while, but they had had problems and now she was in a foster home. Sana was already the mother of a two-year-old girl who lived with her grandmother. She told me she was twelve when she got pregnant by her boyfriend that she called Joe Pig. Her daughter and grandmother lived in a two-bedroom apartment in the projects.

I became good friends with Sana. We went to the same school so we walked there and home together. On the weekends Sana visited her grandmother and she would meet her boyfriend there. Sana told me she would sneak him into her bedroom so he could spend the night with her.

Sometimes I went with Sana to her grandmother's apartment. We called her Big Mama. She was a tall woman with a deep voice. She always had a cigarette in her hand and smoked them one after the other. Big Mama was a caring woman. I admired the way she took care of Sana's daughter, Torina. It was plain to see that Torina adored her grandmother too. I met the rest of Sana's family including her mother Delores, her uncle Howard, and her brother Marcus. Her father lived in Minnesota.

I remembered her sister, Valerie from Twelfth Street School but she was going by the name Annette now. She had changed and looked different. She was a beautiful girl with shiny thick hair. She had changed from the skinny little girl I knew in grade school. Annette was always a pretty girl but now she was beautiful.

"She could be a model," I told Sana.

When I met Sana's boyfriend, Joe Pig I liked him. He wasn't the best looking guy, but he was nice and the three of us had a lot of fun talking and joking on Big Mama's back porch. Joe Pig was older than Sana by just a couple of years, but he seemed much older. I questioned Sana about why he wasn't going to school or working. "He's a hustler," she told me.

Mrs. Reed was overprotective of me. She didn't want me going out on the weekends like the other girls, but she couldn't make me stay home either. In the beginning I would sit at home with Mrs. Reed and we would talk. I enjoyed talking with her, and because of the time we spent together, we became very close. I told her things that I hadn't discussed with anyone. After Sana came I started hanging more with her and going with her on weekends to visit Big Mama.

Sana and I met Billy at a dance one Saturday night. He was funny and danced with the two of us all night. Billy was going to walk us halfway to Big Mama's house and then he was going in the other direction to Galena Street where he lived. The three of us were crossing the street. Billy was walking between us when a police car drove up, cutting us off from the other side of the street.

"You're jay walking," the police officer in the passenger seat said to us. We didn't move. Tensions were high in the black neighborhoods because of police brutality. I had heard about it, so I stood there waiting for him to give us an order. The police car had attracted a lot of attention from the other teenagers who were leaving the dance.

The police officer got out of the car. He was a tall man with reddish hair and an unpleasant look on his face.

"Step back onto the sidewalk," he said to Sana and I. Billy turned to walk back with us, but the police officer grabbed his arm.

"Hey man, let me go," Billy said before he was thrown on the top of the police car.

"I'm arresting you for jay walking," the police officer said.

Billy protested while Sana and I looked on in disbelief. The policeman was slamming Billy's head against the hood of the car.

"Let him go!" I yelled out.

Then we saw a bottle fly through the air and land next to the police car. The other police officer got out of the car with his gun drawn.

"Leave him alone," I heard a person shout and before long more bottles flew through the air. The crowd was picking up anything they could find and throwing it at the police officers.

"Go to my house, 3049 Galena Street, and tell my sister what happened," Billy yelled before he was thrown in the back seat of the car. I heard the sirens in the distance and knew more police were coming. Most of the teenagers started running, including Sana and I, while others stayed and continued to throw things at the police.

I could hear the noise all the way up Center Street.

The next day I walked to Galena Street. The house with the address 3049 was a large wooden house painted a dull gray. There were two kids outside playing in the dirt. The boy looked up at me when I walked up the stairs to the porch. There was a lot of trash on the porch. I rang the doorbell. A girl about twelve years old opened the door.

"Is this the house where Billy lives?"

"He ain't here," she said, almost closing the door in my face.

"I know he's not here," I said to her. "I came to talk to his sister. Are you his sister?"

The girl nodded.

"Billy was arrested last night on Third Street."

The girl's mouth dropped open and she began shouting, "Cookie! Cookie!" The girl rushed from the door, leaving it open enough for me to peek inside. There was clutter everywhere in the house. Trash and food were on the floor, the coffee tables, and the furniture. I could see several children, and a baby that looked a few months old was propped up on the couch.

An older girl replaced the one who had opened the door.

"What happened to Billy?" She was looking serious and angry at the same time.

"My name is Joyce and I was at the dance last night. Billy, my friend, and I were trying to cross Third Street when the cops pulled up. They arrested Billy for jay walking."

"Damn," she muttered.

"They were beating on him with a stick. Everyone started throwing bottles at the police but they just called more cops to come help them. Billy gave me this address and said to come here to tell his sister about it."

"I'm his sister, Cookie. Come on in," she opened the door for me to walk in. I almost felt like holding my breath as the smell of urine filled my nose. I could see the kids clearly now. There were five of them including the baby. "I have to go call Mama," Cookie told the girl who had opened the door. "Joyce, this is my sister, Fanny. Have a seat."

I looked at the dirty couch where the baby was propped up. "No thanks."

"I am going to the phone booth so you have to watch the kids," she told Fanny. I was still standing when Cookie grabbed the baby from the couch and walked out of the house.

Fanny started fussing at two little boys.

"How many of you stay here?"

"There are ten of us all together," she said.

"These are your bothers and sisters?"

Fanny nodded. I glanced around the house and saw more

mess. Worn bed sheets covered the window in the living room. There was only a couch and chair with a few end tables. Trash was piled in one corner of the house and I couldn't tell what color the walls were because of the dirt.

"I hope Mama comes home," Fanny said.

I turned to look at her. "Why did you say that?" I asked.

"Because mama lives somewhere else with her boyfriend and we live in this house. Billy and Cookie watch us. Mama brings us food and other stuff, but she always leaves."

I knew Billy had just turned eighteen. "How old is Cookie?"

"She's sixteen and tries to act like our mama," she said.

"She has a baby?"

"No, that's my little sister, Dana. Mama brought her here after she was born for Cookie to take care of."

I couldn't believe what she was saying. "How old are you?"

Fanny smiled. "I'm thirteen. I go to Robert Fulton Junior High School." Fanny was a pretty girl with pretty skin for a teenager.

"What school does Cookie go to?"

"She can't go to school because she has to watch Timmy, Daniel, Amanda, and Dana."

Cookie and the baby walked back into the house.

"Mama said she is going to go check on him." She thanked me for coming over to tell her.

I couldn't get the scene out of my mind as I walked back home. A couple of days later I went back there to give them some food and clothes. Fanny was smaller than me, but I had a few things I was sure would fit her. The clothes she had on were worn.

You would have thought I had brought her clothes worth thousands of dollars the way she screamed and jumped up and down when I handed her the bag. Cookie thanked me for the cookies and moon pies I had brought for the little ones.

Cookie kept me updated about Billy and I promised that Sana and I would testify for him. The public defender told me Billy was charged with resisting arrest. I sat in the courtroom waiting for my turn to be called to the witness stand. When Billy came out with the other prisoners I almost choked at the sight of him. His face was swollen with a black eye, cuts and bruises were all over his face and neck, and he was limping. I knew the policemen had beaten him up.

Billy went before the judge when they called his name. We waited for our chance to testify for him. He pleaded innocent, but it didn't Matter because the Judge didn't allow us to testify. Billy went to trail and was found guilty. He was sentenced to sixty days in the house of corrections for resisting arrest.

I visited Cookie, Fanny and the rest of the kids at least once a week bringing them whatever I could. They were always grateful.

One day as I turned the corner on my way to visit them I saw a woman standing on the sidewalk. She was ready to get into a waiting car, but Fanny was holding on to her. I quickened my steps and made it to the house while the woman was still there.

"Mama, don't go," Fanny was saying. The lady looked much younger than I thought she would be and certainly didn't look as if she had given birth to ten children.

"Fanny, you have to quit this nonsense. You know that I have to leave." The woman looked at me when I walked up. The man who was sitting behind the wheel of the car beeped the horn. The lady pried Fanny's hands away. Cookie stood on the porch holding the baby and the other kids were standing near her crying.

The woman managed to get away and jumped in the car. The wheels screeched as he pulled away from the curb.

Fanny stormed back into the house crying.

"Hi Joyce," Cookie said when I walked upon the porch. Cookie didn't have a tear in her eyes and didn't look like she was upset.

"Was that your mother?"

She nodded. "Sometimes I wish she wouldn't come around because it always upsets the kids. The younger ones don't know her that well, but they still get upset."

I visited the family when I could because I knew it was hard for Cookie to manage those kids by herself. Fanny had to miss several days of school to help her with the kids while Billy was in jail.

The day that Billy came home everyone was happy. I went to see him. He had healed up from the beating, but he was still mad.

"My mama doesn't care about nothing but that boyfriend of hers," he told me. "She didn't come see me one time while I was in jail. She only comes here to pick up her welfare check or bring us food. She pays the bills, but I don't even know where she lives and all we have is a phone number if something happens. We don't have a phone in the house so we have to walk to the tavern on the corner to use the phone."

I couldn't understand why a mother would leave her children and live somewhere else. It didn't make sense to me.

I became good friends with Cookie and Billy and was just as upset as they were when Fanny got pregnant.

It was dangerous hanging around on Galena Street, but I guess I was too ignorant or too young to realize it. I met a lot of junkies and people who didn't have much of anything. I bought the junkies clothes and food too because I felt sorry for them. They looked forward to my visits because I always had something for them, a warm blanket, a pair of pants, or a soda. I felt they were people too, but watching them deteriorate made me realize how bad drugs were and I swore I would never use them.

Fanny had a baby girl and dropped out of school to help Cookie with the little ones. Billy had moved out after he met his girlfriend. They moved into a small apartment together. Their mother moved the family into another house further away so I stopped going on Galena Street and I never saw them again.

I ran into Bernice one day on North Avenue and rekindled our friendship. She gave me her address so I started going over there to visit.

I never recovered my lost diary or my clothes that Roy jr. never went to pick up. The people at Adams Hall claimed they put them in storage where everything disappeared. I was angry with Roy jr. for a long time. I started keeping another dairy and wrote everything in it, my thoughts, dreams, and passions. Sometimes I wrote things in my dairy that were fantasies, but they felt real to me.

Bernice's brother, Ezell, worked at the Coca Cola Company. He was short like his sister and laughed a lot. I liked him so I started hanging out with him. He was twenty-eight years old and I went with him to the neighborhood taverns where I sat on the barstools while he drank beers. He gave me quarters to play the jukebox. I didn't like the stale smell of liquor that most taverns had, but Ezell was fascinating to be around. Mrs. Reed was suspicious of what was going on with me, but I didn't tell her about my friends.

Friday evenings were busy in our house. We had to almost pull numbers to take showers or use the iron. Everyone was getting ready to go out. A couple of my foster sisters had steady boyfriends who came to pick them up.

A cheap wine called Ripple was popular at the time. It tasted like kool-aid to me. I don't know why each of us bought our own personal bottle of ripple. At least Ripple didn't taste like that bitter white pork wine that Alice poured down my throat. I didn't drink much of the wine, but I felt that I needed my own bottle so the other girls wouldn't think of me as a baby. We weren't old enough to purchase the wine, but there was always someone who was willing to buy it for us.

After leaving Mrs. Reed's house on foot, we split up in different directions to hitch rides to our various destinations. We never stuck our thumbs out like hitchhikers because guys would always stop and offer us a ride. At the time we didn't believe it was dangerous to catch rides with strangers. A couple of times we got into cars with a man who wanted more than just to take us to where we were going, but we always managed to get away from them. The rule among us was to never get in a car alone, but some of the girls did it anyway.

I was home alone when the probation officer showed up at the house. I was on probation because of the incident that happened in Adams Hall when I cut Richard. She ordered me to go with her. I wanted to leave a note for Mrs. Reed but I didn't get a chance to do that either. I was taken to the detention center for violation of probation. They didn't tell me what I had done. I was in the detention center for a couple of days before they transferred me to Oregon school for girls. I hadn't done anything wrong and didn't know why they were doing this to me.

During the first week I was put in isolation and not allowed out of my room except to eat. That's when I met Julie. Her room was next to mine. When the doors were unlocked we could sit on the floor in the doorway and talk to each other. She was kept in isolation because she was in there for murder.

I remembered the incident because it had been all over the news.

"I don't remember grabbing the knife or sticking it in him," she told me. "All I wanted was for him to leave me alone." Julie was thirteen years old, but when she killed the man she was only eleven.

It was on all the news channels and in the newspaper. Everyone was talking about the eleven-year-old girl who stabbed a man to death. I had never heard of a child killing a grownup before. The man's body was at Williamson's funeral home so a group of us had gone to see him. The funeral home was only a few blocks from the school. I was afraid of dead people or at least I thought I was, but I wasn't going to let my friends know it.

Williamson's funeral home was across the street from O'Bee's funeral home. All the people in my family who had died were taken care of by O'Bee. My legs felt wobbly when we finally made it to the doorsteps of the funeral home. I swallowed hard to get rid of the lump that was forming in my throat. None of us talked about the dead man or the girl who had killed him because I think we were afraid it would scare us more than we were.

I opened the door and sucked in the familiar odor that I hated so much. This funeral home was a lot bigger than O'Bee's, but it had the same feeling and smell. The others followed behind while I walked down the red carpet towards a casket that was visible from the door. I could feel my heart beating faster with each step, and a part of me wanted to turn and run. The four of us stood side-by-side looking down into the face of the man who was killed by eleven-year-old Julie. I stared at the face wondering what really happened that night.

Julie claimed that the man tried to force himself on her. . I was sure he was guilty. He was a large man with a thin black mustache and a neatly trimmed short afro. I guessed him to be thirty something. He was dressed in a dark suit with a white shirt.

It never occurred to me that a child was capable of killing a grownup until that moment. It occurred to me that I could have easily hid a knife underneath my pillow and plunged it into Mr. Watson when he came downstairs. I remembered how I felt after hearing about Michael being killed in the war. All the people who had hurt me over the years flashed before my eyes and I imagined all of them with knives in their bodies.

"Let's get out of here," Loretta said, backing away towards the door. I saw how frightened the other girls were and nodded. We were a few blocks away before anyone said a word.

"Mama said that she stabbed him through the heart."

All of us looked at Diane, who was talking.

"Mama said the man died instantly."

"He didn't look mean to me", Loretta said.

I turned towards her. I was thinking about what happened to Julie because I understood. I knew they didn't have to look mean to do bad things to you.

"You don't understand that he got himself killed because he was trying to rape Julie?"

"Mama said--"

"I don't care what your mama said. She wasn't there so she doesn't know anything."

"Well, I don't think I could ever kill anyone," Loretta said.

I stopped walking. The three of them turned to look back at me.

"I believe I could kill someone who was trying to hurt me," I said.

The rest of the walk home was silent with each of us thinking our own thoughts. I didn't know what was on their minds, but I was thinking that the man deserved what he got. The man who chased me down the stairs would have raped me if I hadn't gotten away from him. Although I won that battle I still wasn't safe. For the first time in years I wondered about Nate. He got away with what he did to me. He had a mother and father who protected him. Uncle Ben moved to Ohio with them and none of them ever returned to Milwaukee. Loretta and Diane didn't understand about a hurt inside of you that never goes away.

Two years had passed since the murder and here I was in the room next to Julie. When I arrived in Oregon they told me I had to spend two weeks in solitary before I was put in a unit with the other girls.

"Don't talk to her about the murder," I was warned.

When I first saw Julie I was surprised. At thirteen years old she was very developed.

"My name is Julie," she said the first time we were out of our rooms and in the common area. She had sad eyes that looked innocent.

"I'm Joyce." I smiled at her. I wanted to ask her about the stabbing even though I knew I wasn't supposed to. I noticed that she walked around like a robot, and I felt sorry for her. When Julie was allowed out of her room she spent her time watching TV.

"I'm sick of this place," she told me one day. "I miss my family and my sisters."

I did what I could to bring some comfort to her. After all she was just a little girl. I didn't believe it was fair that she was locked up. She did what she had to do because the man was going to rape her.

My anger mounted as the days passed by and Julie confided in me about the murder. I never told anyone what she said.

"He was a big man and I was scared so I ran and got the butcher knife. He saw the knife but all he did was laugh. He was stronger than I was and almost took it away from me, but I fought hard and the next thing I knew the knife was in him. He dropped to the floor and I saw all this blood seeping out of him."

I didn't tell her that I had gone to see his body at the funeral home. Julie had enough on her mind, so I didn't want her to think about it because it seemed to haunt her.

When I found out that Cheryl was Julie's big sister I was shocked. Julie talked a lot about her and finally said something that helped me put two and two together. When I told Julie I knew Cheryl her eyes seemed to light up.

"If you see her again tell her that I miss her."

"I will," I promised.

Julie became very special to me and I vowed to protect her as long as I could. The two weeks went by speedily and I was taken out of isolation leaving Julie alone again.

"The time will pass quickly," I told Julie, who cried when she found out I was being moved. The last time I saw her she was sitting near a window looking out. It reminded me of myself when I was a little girl looking out of the large picture window of Hon's living room.

I was assigned to a cottage where I quickly became friends with a couple of the girls. When I first arrived at Oregon I had to go through a lot of examinations including a pregnancy test. I felt humiliated going through it because the doctor was an old man who wasn't sympathetic at all.

Girls from all over the state of Wisconsin were placed in Oregon. It was a diverse population of blacks, whites, Puerto Ricans, and even a couple of Indians. Most of the girls did petty crimes such as running away from home, drugs, prostitution, and shoplifting. I was the only one who wasn't sure why I was in there.

The place looked like a college campus with several small buildings spread over a large lot of land. A certain amount of girls were assigned to each building along with counselors who worked three different shifts. It reminded me of the detention center except here we were able to walk around outside.

We lived and ate in the cottages that we were assigned to. The counselors were like housemothers because they were with us everyday. The counselor who worked the day shift did not like me, and I didn't like her either. I got along with the girls in the unit, but the one counselor who didn't like me sent me to my room almost every day, where I would spend time alone. The rooms were lined up next to each other like in the detention center, except there were no locks on them. We had our own space and wore our own clothes. Each building had its own kitchen where our meals were cooked.

There was a recreation room in each cottage with a television and a radio to listen to music. Some of the girls went off-campus to school. It was still August when I arrived so school had not started yet. We did daily chores that were shared. We were responsible for washing and ironing our own clothes.

Annette was watching television when I walked into the recreation room one day. She had a scarf wrapped around her head, but I knew who it was even though I hadn't seen her in awhile. Annette was still the prettiest girl I had ever seen. "Annette? What are you doing here?" I don't know which of us was more surprised.

"I've been in here for a couple of months."

"What are you here for?" I couldn't imagine her getting in any sort of trouble.

"I ran away. How's my sister?"

I missed Sana and wondered how she was doing too. "If I know Sana she's okay."

Annette smiled, showing her perfect teeth.

"I don't know what the hell I'm doing here." I said.

Joann was a tall, thin, black girl from Sheboygan, Wisconsin. My room was the last one on the right and Joann was my neighbor. She was a funny girl who kept everyone laughing. She talked about how strange it was being from a small town with just a few black people. She was a shoplifter and it finally landed her in Oregon.

"I'm never going to steal another damn thing," she promised. I liked Joann and we became friends. I was getting anxious to get out of Oregon because things were getting heated with the counselor who hated me. She not only sent me to my room, but also denied me a lot of other privileges. The two of us argued constantly and she kept threatening to send me to isolation. I never backed down even though I was afraid of her.

Three weeks passed and I was still asking about leaving there. Finally, the fourth week came and so did hope. I was told that I was needed in the main building.

I froze when I stepped inside the building and saw Mrs. Reed standing there. I didn't know whether to shout or cry. Mrs. Reed opened her arms and I went to her.

"I'm sorry I didn't get a chance to say good-by. They

made me leave with them."

Mrs. Reed didn't say anything, but held me.

"I didn't do anything so I don't know why they brought me here."

Finally I heard her soft voice talking. "I'm here to pick you up," she said.

I pulled away and looked at her.

"They're going to let me go back home?"

Mrs. Reed nodded. "When they told me that you were sent here I had a fit. I did everything in my power to get them to release you."

"Thank you," I whispered.

The other girls were surprised to see me leaving so quickly. I was thankful that Mrs. Reed had come just in time. It had been a long three and a half weeks, but I was finally on my way home.

It felt good to be home again and everything was just as I had left it. Mrs. Reed said she made sure all my personal things were locked up while I was away.

I told my foster sisters everything that had happened to me during the time I was gone. They were surprised about the lady picking me up at home without any notice. They especially liked the part about Mrs. Reed showing up to take me home.

Sana was upset when I told her Annette was there.

"What the hell did she do this time?"

"She said she ran away."

"I'll ask Big Mama."

Sana and I were enrolled in Lincoln High School that year. I was fifteen and in the tenth grade. Pat was still going to vocational school. When we walked to school we took short cuts through an alley. It was usually me, Sana and Tonya who lived across the street. Tonya was a year older and in the same grade with Sana. We saw a man in the alley putting out his trash one day. He stared at us when we passed by. Sana and Tonya said I was paranoid because he made me feel uncomfortable. The next day the man was in the same spot as if he was waiting for us. This time he spoke.

"You sure are pretty," he said. He was staring at Tonya. All of us laughed because the man was at least thirty years old.

Every day for the next week the man was in the alley waiting for us to pass by. He propositioned Tonya with money one day, holding out a bunch of bills. Tonya turned her nose up and walked on past him.

"That's not enough money," she shouted over her shoulders after we had reached the end of the alley. We laughed, but I was nervous because there was something about this man that didn't seem right.

"He just an ugly old man," Sana assured me. "That man isn't going to do nothing to us."

Sana had been sneaking to see Joe pig and missing a lot of school. One day she didn't come home. She had runaway to be with Joe Pig. Mrs. Reed didn't take her back into the foster home so she ended back with her grandmother.

A few weeks later I was sick and stayed home from school.

"Don't walk through the alley when you're alone," I had warned Tonya.

"Alright, I'll go the long way and walk down Richardson," she promised me.

When she hadn't arrived at home by four o'clock I knew something was wrong. Her mother was already pacing the floor.

"Where could Tonya be?" everyone asked when we sat down to eat that evening. I watched as the hours ticked away. My thoughts kept going back to the man in the alley. Tonya didn't just disappear; I knew she was in that house.

I couldn't sleep that night because I felt I had to help rescue her. I told Mrs. Reed about the man in the alley.

"Did he ever try to hurt any of you?" she asked.

I shook my head.

I didn't tell her about the money he offered to Tonya. What if Tonya took the money and went with him? I didn't want Mrs. Reed to know about that.

"Tonya ran away," she told me. We knew that Tonya had started dating a boy named Ray that her mother didn't approve of. She said Tonya was too young to date at sixteen years old. I told Mrs. Reed about the man in the alley, but she didn't seem interested in what I had to say either.

"She's probably somewhere with that boy," she said. Everyone thought Tonya was with Ray and I couldn't convince anyone about the man in the alley.

The next day I passed by the alley and didn't see him.

Stephen had moved back to Milwaukee from Denver with his wife, Gwen and his son Stephen jr. He married Gwen instead of Joyce even though she had waited for him while he was in the military. He served a couple of years in the military and told me he had been to Vietnam. I knew that Stephen was more interested in my foster sisters than visiting with me, but that day it gave me the chance to use him. I convinced Stephen to take me to the house where the man lived by telling him that we were going to pick Tonya up.

Stephen pulled up in front of the house and turned up the music on the radio. I knew he had a crush on Tonya after meeting her at the beginning of the summer.

I couldn't believe my eyes when I saw the man who was in the alley leave the house and walk towards the corner tavern. I jumped out of the car and ran to the back of the house. I peeped through the windows but I couldn't see anything. I pushed on every window until one of them opened. I was shaking when I climbed through the window and landed hard on the wooden floor. If anyone were in the house they would have definitely heard me.

The house was almost bare of furniture and had a musty

smell. I was scared when I walked from the kitchen into the other rooms. I heard a moan and called out Tonya's name.

The noise was coming from a closet so I opened the door. Tonya was sitting on the floor of the closet on a pile of clothes. She was naked. There was a wild look in her eyes that was frightening and her hair was all over her head. She screamed when I reached in to pull her out.

"It's me, Joyce," I said.

I grabbed a shirt that was hanging in the closet and helped her put it on. It hung on her tiny body like a dress.

"I knew you would find me," she said in a small voice. She could hardly walk and winced as if she was in pain. An awful smell filled my nose and it was making me sick. It was then that I noticed stuff all over her body and in her hair as if someone had deliberately smeared it on her. I knew what it was. I tried to wash it off with a washcloth I found, but we didn't have much time.

"We have to get out of here," I screamed at Tonya who looked as if she would fall down.

"I can't walk," she said.

"You have to walk. I can't carry you." We were both crying.

It seemed to take forever for us to make it to the front door, but we did. I turned the knob, and when the sunshine hit her face, she blinked and shielded her eyes. I found a renewed strength once we were outside and practically dragged her to the car.

Stephen looked surprised when he saw us. I put Tonya in the front seat between us. Then I saw the man was coming towards us. I froze. I wanted to jump in the car, but my body wouldn't move. Tonya saw him through the back window and began screaming. That is what snapped me out of it, and I quickly jumped inside the car. The man began running towards the car and I started screaming while pushing the inside locks on the doors.

"What the hell is going on?" Stephen asked.

"Just drive!" I screamed at him.

The man made it to the car and was pounding on the window.

Tonya was still screaming.

"Go Stephen!"

Stephen put the car in gear. The man was still holding onto the car while it was moving. He ran along with the car. Stephen pulled away from the curb and the man hit a lamppost and fell to the ground.

Stephen dropped us off at Tonya's house. We were lucky that her mother was gone. I helped Tonya take a bath and washed her hair.

"Don't tell anyone what happened."

I looked at Tonya. "They think you ran away with Ray."

"Let them think whatever they want to. Just don't ever tell anyone what happened."

I nodded my head. "Okay, I won't."

Tonya found one of her mother's cigarettes and lit it.

"What happened in that house?" I asked her.

Tonya didn't look at me. She inhaled the cigarette smoke and exhaled it slowly.

"He did whatever he wanted to do to me," she said. I noticed the red marks on her wrist and knew she had been tied up.

"I thought he was going to kill me." The tears came quickly and she cried until she couldn't squeeze any more water from her eyes. I cried with her because I felt her pain.

Tonya took a pair of scissors and went to the mirror where she started cutting off her hair.

I didn't leave until her mother came home. I could still hear her fussing at Tonya when I closed the door. I prayed that she would be okay.

Tonya never told anyone what happened to her and seemed to be okay. I walked past the man's house a couple of days later and saw that it was vacant. I was glad he had moved away. Tonya's mother put her on punishment for a long time. I didn't see much of Tonya who became withdrawn and was sick all the time.

Pat had a new boyfriend she wanted me to meet so I agreed to skip my last class and walked with her to his apartment. Moose was a big guy with a flat nose and lots of facial hair. He seemed nice, but it was hard to imagine them together. Moose's apartment was around the corner from Tot-Ta-Wa, my Uncle Ike's tavern. About six or seven other guys were also there.

"He's forming a singing group," Pat told me. "Those guys are here to practice."

It was entertaining watching them practice. The guys were doing dance moves and singing. I was surprised that they sounded good. They seemed to rely on Pat and I for approval so we clapped, yelled, and nodded our heads. It was fun and the time passed by quickly.

I stopped going to my last class altogether and met Pat over at Moose's house everyday. I would sit inside of the window ledge that overlooked the street. I was looking out the window daydreaming when I saw a guy walk into the apartment across the street. I had seen him the day before going in and out of the apartment, each time with a different girl. A short time later a girl showed up and knocked on the door. I watched her disappear inside of the apartment. I was still sitting there when she came out about an hour later followed by the guy. He walked with her down the street. When they passed by Moose's place I could see him clearly. He wasn't a tall guy, but the afro he wore was so big he appeared taller. He wore a pair of wide bell-bottom jeans with a tight-fitting white T-shirt, which showed off his large muscles.

I smiled to myself as my eyes followed him down the street until he disappeared around the corner. About fifteen minutes later he walked back to his apartment. Then I saw him get into a silver car and drive away.

The next day I was watching from the window and saw

the same guy come out of his apartment with a different girl. He kissed her on the lips and she left. It wasn't long before another girl appeared at his apartment. This seemed to be a daily routine because I watched him day after day.

"Who's that guy?" I asked Moose.

He looked over my shoulder. "That's Lonnie Johnson," he said laughing. "He's got more girls than all of us put together."

The group of guys laughed with him.

"He's bad news," Moose said more seriously this time.

I smiled in spite of myself. It was fascinating how well he coordinated them. I spent the next couple of weeks watching him. He drove a Buick, entertained lots of females, and left his apartment everyday in the late afternoon and never returned before Pat and I left Moose's apartment.

I was at home alone when I heard the doorbell ring. Mrs. Reed had an appointment and the other girls were gone. I was on punishment because I had missed curfew again and wasn't supposed to go anywhere. I walked to the door and was shocked to see Robert standing outside.

"Joyce!" he said with enthusiasm. I opened the door and the two of us hugged.

"I can't invite you into the house because Mrs. Reed isn't home."

Robert smiled. "It's good to see you," he said.

I looked past him at the beautiful red convertible parked in front of the house.

"Is that your car?"

Robert nodded. "I just bought it." I drove it here from Denver.

I walked outside onto the porch and pulled the door without shutting it all the way. The lock was on and I didn't have a key to get back in. Robert and I were laughing and talking when I heard the clicking sound I knew immediately I had locked myself out.

396

"Damn!" I cursed out-loud. Mrs. Reed is going to really be mad at me now. "I just locked myself out."

Robert laughed at me. "She'll understand."

I sat down on the steps of the porch to talk. I hadn't seen Robert since leaving Denver, but he still looked the same.

"I've been here a couple of days, but I just found out today where you live."

"It's good to see you, Robert."

He leaned back and had a faraway look in his eyes.

"I like your new car."

Robert smiled. "Yeah, I like it too. I always wanted a red convertible car with a white top."

"How long are you going to be in Milwaukee?"

He turned to me with a serious look on his face. "I'm thinking about moving back here," he said. "I can quit my job and get a meat-cutting job here."

"You cut meat?" The thought made me queasy.

"Yes, I'm a meat-cutter for Safeway."

Both of us heard the sound of the car at the same time. Mrs. Reed got out of the car and looked up at us. Mr. Reed followed her up the steps to the porch.

"This is my brother, Robert," I said.

Mrs. Reed looked from me to Robert.

"I just got here from Denver." Robert tried not to be nervous.

"You need to leave," Mrs. Reed said unflinching and staring at Robert.

"Ma'am, I came by to see my sister."

"I don't believe Joyce is your sister and you better get off my porch."

"But Mrs. Reed--"

She gave me a look that made me stop talking.

"Get in the house!" She shouted. Mr. Reed had unlocked the door so I walked into the house. It was clear that she didn't believe either of us.

Robert tried again to explain to Mrs. Reed who he was, but she stood her ground and made him leave. I watched Robert walk down to the car. I could tell by the way he slammed the door that he was mad.

I introduced Stephen to Mrs. Reed when he first moved back to Milwaukee. Mrs. Reed already knew Roy jr. because he came to visit and he always talked with Mrs. Reed just like he had done with Mr. and Mrs. Williams and Mrs. Walker. Roy was good at playing the big brother role but it was all talk. I knew both Stephen and Roy jr. were more interested in my foster sisters than visiting me.

Stephen was especially interested in my foster sister, Barbara. He was going to a party one night and asked Barbara to go with him. I threaten to tell his wife if he didn't take me to the party. It was obvious that Stephen didn't want his fifteen-year-old sister trailing behind him. He had a friend named Walter that I liked and insisted that I be included. Stephen picked us up that evening in Roy jr's T-Bird. I sat in the back with Walter who had very little to say to me.

When we arrived at the party the music was nice. Most of the people at the party were Stephen and Walter's age. Barbara was almost eighteen so she fit in a lot better than I did.

"Why did you have to bring your little sister?" I heard Walter ask him. "I am not going to spend the evening babysitting her."

"All you have to do is keep an eye on her," Stephen argued. "I promise I'll make it up to you."

I sat in a chair watching other couples on the floor dancing. Walter would hardly look at me, much less dance with me. Stephen and Barbara were in a dark corner, hugged up together.

Walter was standing by the food table so I went over there to get something to eat and drink. I watched him pour something

398

into a cup.

"Can I have some?"

He looked down at me. "You're too young to drink liquor," he said.

"No, I'm not."

"Your brother would kill me if I gave you any of this."

"I'm not a baby and I want a cup."

Walker handed me the cup. "Drink it down fast so your brother won't see you."

I grabbed the cup and gulped it down, even though it burned my throat.

"Want some more?" He was laughing at me.

"Yes," I said. I didn't really want more, but he was laughing and I was going to show him.

He poured more liquor and I gulped it down. I don't know how many times I did it before everything went black.

I was passed out in the back seat of the car when I felt the need to throw up.

Stephen was arguing with Walter, but I couldn't understand what they were saying.

I ended up throwing up in the car. Barbara helped me up the stairs and into the house. I was throwing up all night so Mrs. Reed stayed with me. I felt like I was going to die that night.

"I don't understand how your brother could let this happen to you!" she screamed at me the next day. Now she didn't believe Stephen was really my brother. He couldn't come over anymore. Barbara told me I embarrassed him at the party because I went to the bathroom and broke the zipper on my pants so they were falling off of me. She and Stephen had to hold my pants up.

I was walking to Ike's tavern one afternoon after leaving Moose's house. I was trying to stay away from Bernice and Hose's house. I had also stopped hanging around with Ezell. I turned the corner and saw his car parked on the street. I walked past the car and was startled when a voice called out to me. I turned around in time to see him get out of the driver's side of the car.

"Where are you going?"

"Are you talking to me?"

He was smiling at me and I felt like I was going to melt.

"Come over here," he said.

I hesitated before walking towards him. My legs felt as if they were going to collapse, but I maintained a sturdy walk. I didn't stand too close to him but I felt my body tremble. He smiled again and I couldn't help smiling back.

"I'm going to visit my uncle."

"Come talk to me for a minute." I felt myself moving towards the car as if I were in a trance. Then I heard a woman shouting and that brought me back to reality. I looked across the street and saw an older woman leaning over the porch of a broken down house. She was shouting to him.

"Bring me some beer," she yelled.

"Mama, stop it," he yelled back. "I told you I don't have any money."

He had already opened the car door for me. I climbed into the front seat of the Buick. It was a nice car, silver with bright red interior. I couldn't believe I was actually with him. I had been watching him from Moose's apartment for over a month now. He slid in an eight-track tape. I didn't know what to say to him. Less than an hour ago I had seen him with another girl.

"How old are you?" he asked, looking directly into my eyes.

I turned away from him. "I'm seventeen, I will be eighteen in a few months," I lied. That was what Pat usually said, so I decided to use her line, even though she really was going to be eighteen.

I didn't have to talk because he kept the conversation going. His voice was smooth and I hung on every word he said. My heart felt as if it were going to jump out of my chest any moment.

"I live around the corner."

I nodded my head. I knew where he lived, but I wasn't going to tell him that.

"I have to go to work in a few minutes. I work in a flour factory from four until midnight." So that was why he left every afternoon.

"I don't really l like my job, but it pays alright."

He smiled again and I couldn't help giggling like a schoolgirl.

"I'll drive you to your uncle's house."

"I'm going to his tavern around the corner."

I saw his eyebrow rise. "What tavern?"

"Tot-Ta-Wa."

His facial expression changed. "Tot is your uncle?"

I nodded. Most people called Ike Tot.

"I know him."

He drove me around the corner and dropped me off in front of the tavern.

"I hope to see you again around here."

I nodded. "He will definitively see me again," I thought to myself.

I saw Lonnie every day and after about a week he added me to the list of females coming and going from his place. The first time I stepped into the small, one-bedroom apartment I was nervous. I wanted to turn and run out, but he was charming. I was surprised at how respectful he was with me. He talked a lot and I listened.

We became very close and I believed I was falling in love. Lonnie would pick me up from school during my lunch hour and we would go to his apartment. He thought I was a senior in high school. I enjoyed the attention I got from the other students who watched me get into his nice car. I saw the envy of other girls when we drove away together.

In Years To Come

I felt comfortable with him, but for some reason my mind and body seemed to be disconnected. It was nice being with Lonnie and I felt good when we were alone together, but I still had problems with too much intimacy. I wanted to will myself back to reality but I couldn't. Lonnie didn't say anything about my inability to be more romantic and I was thankful.

Mrs. Reed immediately noticed the change in me. I tried to act the same way, but I couldn't. I was on the phone a lot and always eager to leave on Friday evening. I was making up lies to stay out all night while spending the weekend with Lonnie. He couldn't pick me up at Mrs. Reed's because she didn't allow me to date, so he picked me up around the corner. My foster sisters kept asking me if I had a boyfriend, but I denied it.

I wrote in my diary that I kept under my pillow. I was in love so I wrote about him every day. He was twenty-two years old so I couldn't tell anyone about him except my diary and Sana. I stopped going to Moose's apartment and started going over to Lonnie's instead. The other girls he was seeing were dwindling.

One of my foster sisters's found my diary and she passed it around. I didn't know everyone in the house was reading it until we sat down to dinner one evening and one of the girls made a smart remark.

"Someone in here is messing around with a grown man." I didn't look up from my plate because they always teased each other. "Someone thinks she's in love with a twenty-two-year-old man. Yeah, and she sees him during school, after school and on the weekends." I heard a giggle.

I thought I was going to choke on my food. I looked up to see several pair of eyes staring at me, including Mrs. Reed. "He's sweet and his lips are so soft," Janice said in a high-pitched voice. I felt my head swimming. This couldn't be true. They were quoting from my diary.

"His arms are well-built and he carried me to the bed and--"

I jumped up from my seat. "You've been reading my diary!" I shouted at all of them. "You went into my bedroom and took my diary from under my pillow and read it." I looked around the table at all the faces. "How could you do this to me?"

"Yes, I read it, and I told Mrs. Reed everything that was in it."

I heard laughter as I fled from the table. I slammed the door to my bedroom and reached under the pillow for my diary.

I was hurt and angry too. I wanted to do something to make them sorry for what they did to me. I searched the bottles on my dresser and found a small bottle of hair tonic and decided to drink it. It had a terrible smell and tasted even worse but I managed to drink some of it.

When my stomach started churning I opened the door and ran into the hallway. I was doubled over in pain. One of the girls saw me and ran to get Mrs. Reed. When she came up to my room she saw the opened bottle and the brown stuff around my lips.

"Did you drink this?" I nodded my head.

"Oh my God!" she shouted. "Get an ambulance!" Mrs. Reed helped me downstairs to wait for the ambulance. I remember being in the back of the ambulance and then on a cold hard table in the emergency room.

"Drink this!" someone was shouting to me. I couldn't because my stomach ached. I felt the liquid being forced down my throat and dripping off my lips. The next thing I felt was my stomach bubbling and it came out. A pan was put under my mouth. I felt as if my insides were coming out each time I bent over the pan. I thought I wasn't ever going to stop vomiting, but finally it was over and I was exhausted.

"Were you trying to kill yourself by drinking that hair tonic?"

The doctor was looking at me with stern eyes.

"They stole my diary and read it and were teasing me about it." I started crying.

"That is why you were trying to kill yourself?"

"I didn't want to really kill myself I just wanted to get back at them."

"We are going to keep you in the hospital for a few days."

I woke up the next morning feeling worse than I had the night before. There were four other women in the large room with me.

"It's time for breakfast," a nurse said to us. The thought of eating food made me nauseous.

I was still in the bed when the nurse came later and told me I had to go see a doctor.

I walked through a large room with a TV in it. Several patients were sitting in front of it.

The doctor was an older man with a thin mustache.

"You came in here last night because you drank some poison?"

I nodded my head. I was feeling ashamed of myself now.

"Were you trying to kill yourself?"

I shrugged my shoulders. "I was mad at my foster sisters because they stole my diary and read it."

"I'm sure that upset you."

"I wrote some very personal things in my diary and they had no right to read it."

"I agree with you." I looked up at the doctor and believed he meant what he said.

"Were you trying to get their attention or were you trying to kill yourself?"

"I was trying to get their attention. I was mad and wanted them to feel sorry for what they had done." I started crying. "I don't want to die, but sometimes things are hard."

The doctor nodded. "Life is hard Joyce, and you're only fifteen years old."

"That was a stupid thing that I did."

The doctor agreed. "Fortunately, you didn't drink enough

of it to harm yourself, but I bet you're feeling lousy."

"I am."

"We will keep you a couple of days to make sure you're okay and then you can return home. I don't believe you'll be drinking any more poison for a while."

"No sir," I whispered.

I was in the mental ward of the county hospital. I climbed back into the bed and slept. I felt better by dinnertime. I showered and put on fresh pajamas because that was all I was allowed to wear.

I was walking with other patients to the table to eat dinner when I saw someone who looked familiar. She was sitting in a chair near the window with her head down. She had on pajamas and a robe. Her feet were bare and curled under her. She looked like a little girl at first glance. I moved closer to get a better look. When she looked up I stared into a set of lifeless eyes.

"Sue?"

She jumped as if saying her name brought her back to reality. It took a few minutes before she recognized me.

"Joyce?"

I nodded.

"What are you doing in here?" She sat up in the chair.

"What is wrong with you?"

I took at good look at her and tried not to look as shocked at I felt. What had happened to her?

Her eyes were puffy, she wore no makeup, her skin was pale like death, her hair was greasy and hung down in her face, the pajamas were dirty as well as the bottom of her feet. She was thin. She looked at me through her swollen eyes. She didn't look twenty years old and reminded me of the female junkies who hung around on Galena street begging for their money.

"Ricky doesn't want me anymore," she said in a voice that was high pitched like a little girl. "I love him so much."

So, this was about Ricky Rodriguez.

"What about Jeffery?" I asked.

She shook her head. "He's with my parents. They've had him for awhile."

I couldn't believe that she was in this bad of shape.

I talked her into coming with me to the table so she could eat dinner. I watched her bony hand lift the fork full of food only to put it back down. She did manage to take a couple of bites of food and wash it down with juice.

I listened to her talk about Ricky for about an hour. He had really hurt her bad.

"He treated me like I was garbage," she said.

"Sue, you need to clean yourself up. You can't function when you look like this. Please take a shower and I will help you wash your hair. I washed her hair in the sink and she washed it again in the shower. I tried not to stare at the cuts on her wrist while I was washing her hair. They were deep cuts and several of them were in a pattern across both wrists. I inhaled to keep my hands steady. She was definitely serious about dying.

After Sue got out of the shower I combed and brushed her hair until it was shining.

"I love him so much," she repeated. "He doesn't want me. I don't think he ever really wanted me." She started crying again. I didn't say anything as the tears rolled down her face. She was probably right about Ricky. I warned Sue about getting involved with him in the first place.

"Sue, you have to think about Jeffrey." I repeated to her. I kept talking to her about Jeffery who was now two. I wanted her to know that she had to get better and get out of the hospital so she could take care of him. She kept nodding as if she understood.

I was spending all my time with Sue and saw life slowly creeping back into her. The nurses told me that they were having a hard time getting Sue to take care of herself before I came. Sue told me she attempted to kill herself three times by slashing her wrist and taking pills and almost succeeded the last time.

She talked more about Ricky than Jeffery. I wondered if people could really love another person that much.

"Where is Ricky?"

The tears came again, "I don't know. He moved away from the apartments." I was glad he was out of her life, but she had to pull herself out of this despair she was in. I wrote down my phone number. "Give me a call," I told Sue when they released me to go home. I never saw or heard from her again. That month flew by quickly and the next month I began feeling sluggish. I hadn't missed a period since I started having them, but I did in October. I was standing in the kitchen leaning against the wall after making a phone call to my brother, Roy jr., but the call didn't go through because the phone was busy. I could feel someone's presence even though my eyes were closed. I opened my eyes to see Mrs. Reed standing in front of me.

"You're pregnant," she said to me. "You know what that means."

I couldn't speak because her words surprised me.

"I cannot keep pregnant girls here so you will have to leave," she said.

I was going to protest, but she didn't allow me to speak.

"You'll be okay," she said. Then the tears flowed down her face and she kissed me on the forehead. I felt my own wet tears flowing as I watched her walk away.

A week later I was in the doctor's office getting examined.

"You're pregnant," the doctor told me.

I wasn't surprised, but I had a hard time digesting the information. I interpreted what the doctor was saying. I was going to have a baby, which meant that I was going to be a mother. The thought frightened me because I didn't know anything about being a mother or the responsibility of taking care of a baby.

When I told Lonnie about it he seemed happy. He had a couple of kids already, including a little girl who looked just like him. Then I had to admit to him that I had lied about my age and that I was really only fifteen.

"Do you realize what you've done?" He was angry because his eyes had narrowed.

I stared at him because I thought he was talking about the baby.

"You told me that I couldn't get pregnant because you knew how to stop it." I reminded him.

He shook his head.

"That's not what I'm talking about. You are only fifteen years old and that means I can go to prison if the authorities found out I got you pregnant."

"I won't tell anyone."

"You lied to me. You told me you were almost eighteen years old."

I did deliberately lie to him. I wanted so many times to tell him the truth but I was scared that he would dump me.

"If you knew I was only fifteen you wouldn't have had anything to do with me." I started crying.

"It's too late for that," he said, showing no sympathy.

Lonnie was upset with me, but promised that he would stay with me as long as I didn't tell anyone about him being the baby's father.

"I will deny it," he said.

I felt bad about disappointing Mrs. Reed who kept encouraging me to finish school and do something constructive with my life. She told me several times that having a boyfriend and a baby wasn't the smart thing to do; yet here I was with a boyfriend she had never met and a baby on the way.

I didn't want to leave Mrs. Reed or the private room at the top of the stairs that I loved. I sat on the bed looking around the room after packing my things. The social worker was waiting for me outside when I came out with my bags. Mrs. Reed had tears in her eyes too. I had never felt as close to any foster mother as I had to Mrs. Reed. She was the only foster mother who I felt emotionally connected with.

"You take good care of yourself," Mrs. Reed told me while I was walking away.

"You're going to a foster group home for pregnant girls," the social worker told me while we were driving to my new destination. I arrived at Mrs. Perry's house early in the afternoon while the other girls were gone.

Chapter Nineteen

Mrs. Perry

Mrs. Perry lived in one of the better neighborhoods near Capital Drive. Her house was a large three-story brick on a nice street with rich green lawns and two car garages. I arrived at Mrs. Perry's group home a few weeks after the test confirmed I was six weeks pregnant.

Mrs. Perry was a tall; light-skinned black woman married to a quiet man. She greeted us at the door with a smile.

"Hello Joyce," she said as if she already knew me. "I'm Mrs. Perry."

"Hi." I said.

I looked around the beautiful house and elegant furnishings. The big formal living and dining rooms were gorgeous and the kitchen was big enough to accommodate a large group of people.

The upstairs was nice too with several bedrooms that were shared two to a room. Mrs. Perry showed me to my bedroom located close to the stairs. It was a nice bedroom with a matching set of twin beds. I liked the bedspreads and the window overlooking the backyard.

I was putting my things away when the other girls came in

from school. I heard a familiar laugh, but I couldn't put a face with it. I was sitting on the bed when a girl walked into the room. Her belly was huge and looked as if she could deliver any second. I couldn't help staring at it.

"Hi," she said. "My name is Charlene."

"I'm Joyce."

I heard that strange laughter again. I was going to see who was laughing just before she walked into the bedroom.
She was short, dark, and bow legged. I stared at her until she finally looked up at me.

"Cheryl?"

"Joyce?"

Cheryl ran to the bed and I jumped up in time to grab her. We hugged each other as tight as we could.

"You two know each other?"

"Know each other? We lived together in Adams Hall a couple of years ago," Cheryl told Charlene.

Nothing had changed about Cheryl except the small bump in her stomach.

"I'm five months," Cheryl said rubbing her stomach.

"I'm only six weeks," I said looking down at my flat stomach.

"You have a long ways to go," Charlene commented, shaking her head. "Thank God I only have a few weeks left."

She had my full attention now.

"Where are you and your baby going to live?"

"I'm giving the baby up for adoption," she said nonchalantly.

I couldn't believe my ears. The social worker had been pressuring me about giving my baby up for adoption since finding out I was pregnant. I told her I couldn't do it.

I looked at Cheryl who shrugged and turned back to Charlene.

"Are you really giving your baby up for adoption?"

411

"Yes, I am," she said. "Then I'm going back home to live with my family. I will finish high school and go on with my life."

"What about the baby?"

"The baby will have parents who can take care of him or her."

She didn't seem upset about giving her baby away. Before she walked out of the room she turned to me and said, "This has been the longest eight and a half months of my life, and I will be glad when it's over."

I turned back to Cheryl after she left. "What about you?"

"I'm not giving my baby up if that's what you're asking, but it will go into a foster home until Charles and I get married."

"So, we can live here with Mrs. Perry until we have our babies?"

Cheryl nodded. "Most babies will end up in a foster home. Charlene and Vanessa are giving their babies up for adoption. The only girl in here who is going home with her baby is Jackie."

I spent a restless night tossing and turning because I couldn't get Charlene and her baby off of my mind. In the next couple of days I thought of nothing else but what would happen to my baby and me.

Cheryl was happy to be pregnant because she was in love.

"Charles is an older man," she told me. "He's sweet and wonderful and loves me very much."

I was happy for Cheryl. She reminded me of myself a few years earlier when I talked about Norris to her. I still thought about Norris but Lonnie was now the love of my life.

"I met your sister Julie when I went to Oregon a few months ago." I saw the sadness in Cheryl's eyes when I mentioned her sister.

"Is she doing alright?"

I nodded my head.

"I don't understand why she had to go to jail," I said, shaking my head. "She stabbed him because he was attacking her."

Cheryl was very quiet. I knew she was thinking about Julie.

"I wish I could have been there to protect her," Cheryl said."

I understood that this whole situation with Julie went deeper than anyone knew. We never discussed Julie again.

Charlene went into labor a week later during the late evening. Mrs. Perry rushed her to the hospital while we waited at the house. I was nervous and paced the floor of our bedroom. We didn't see Mrs. Perry until early the next morning and she looked exhausted.

"Charlene had a baby girl," she informed us.

I wanted a baby girl. I smiled at the thought of having a daughter. I was going to name her Stephanie, the same as my niece in Denver. Charlene returned to Mrs. Perry's house a few days later to pick up her things and no one mentioned the baby. Charlene had lost most of the baby weight and I barely recognized her because there was no evidence that she had just had a baby.

I was enrolled into a school for pregnant girls. It was nice because they provided us free lunch. We were all under eighteen years old and there were a couple of girls having their second or third baby. Denise was sixteen and having her third child. She told me she had her first baby at twelve with her boyfriend, Daniel, who was also sixteen and the father of all of her children.

After a couple of months of living with Mrs. Perry I was ready to leave. It was strange watching pregnant girls move in, have their babies and leave. Some girls came to Mrs. Perry only days before giving birth. Most of the babies went into foster care. A few were adopted. I wanted to believe that I could keep my baby with me. I was sure I would find a way even though I was getting pressure from the social worker to put my baby up for adoption.

"A sixteen year old cannot take proper care of a baby." She would tell me on the way to a Dr. Appointment.

I'm sure I can take better care of my baby than a stranger could," I answered.

I ignored the sounds she made to let me know she disagreed with me.

"You need to think about the baby instead of yourself. What kind of life can you possibly offer a little baby? You haven't even completed high school yet."

Her words bounced off me like a rubber ball. I was determined not to allow her to change my mind. I was going to keep my baby even if I had to run away with it.

"I want to move," I blurted out. "I don't like being in a foster home with nothing but pregnant girls."

Cheryl had already left. She ran away to be with Charles. I knew wherever she was she was okay.

I liked Mrs. Perry but it was time for me to leave there.

"Mrs. Perry can't have any kids because she went through the change of life when she was in her early thirties," Cheryl had told me. I felt sorry for Mrs. Perry because she would have made a wonderful mother. I was very happy the day I moved out of Mrs. Perry's home.

Chapter Twenty

Mrs. Whitehead

My new foster mother was an old woman with white hair who walked with a cane. She was even older than Mrs. Guy and Mrs. Oglesby. I was sure she was probably on disability. She lived in a two-bedroom apartment on the second floor of a duplex.

Mrs. Whitehead's apartment looked as if she had lived there forever. It was cluttered with all kinds of old stuff. She had a little poodle that ran around the house yelping at everyone.

My bedroom was probably once a closet because it was just big enough to hold a twin size bed and a small dresser. It reminded me of the room I slept in when I lived with the Williams. Dorothy was my new foster sister. She was seventeen years old, tall, and thin and wore a short afro that was neatly trimmed. We got along okay although she was very secretive. When I told her I was having a baby she was surprised.

"Mrs. Whitehead is old and doesn't care what we do as long as we are here when the social worker comes to visit."

I laughed with Dorothy. In some ways, Mrs. Whitehead reminded me of Mrs. Oglesby with all the clutter. Unlike at Mrs. Perry's house it was a more relaxed atmosphere. I knew that it was going to be easier living with Mrs. Whitehead. I was excited because now I would be able to see more of Lonnie. Mrs. Whitehead didn't have any rules in her house so we did whatever we wanted to. It was clear to me that Mrs. Whitehead was in it for the money. I suspected that she lived off of a pension check and needed money. When I spent the night over at Lonnie's apartment I told Mrs. Whitehead I was visiting a relative. She never checked on me so it really didn't matter.

Lonnie and I were amazed when my stomach finally started swelling. There really was a baby in there and I loved it already. I couldn't give my baby up for adoption nor did I accept the idea of it going into a foster home. What if my baby ended up with someone like Mrs. Watson?

"You can continue to live here with Mrs. Whitehead after you have the baby." The social worker told me one day.

"What about my baby?"

"We will find a good foster home for your baby."

I thought about how lucky Elsie was that her mother had allowed her to return home with her baby. There had to be someone who would be willing to take in my baby and me. Then it occurred to me that Mrs. Walker had allowed Elsie to stay with her until she had her baby. Maybe she would let the baby and I live there too. I decided that I would visit Mrs. Walker and ask her to let me move back in with her so I could keep my baby.

Mrs. Walker was home when I knocked on the door. Her eyes were bulging out of her head, and she had to stare for a while before she recognized me. I smelled the liquor the minute I stepped inside the door.

"Hello Joyce," she said in that loud boisterous voice of hers.

"Hi Mrs. Walker," I said.

She looked at me from top to bottom. I saw her eyes resting on the middle part that was starting to show.

"You've gone and got yourself pregnant I see."

I nodded my head.

The house was quiet and had an eerie feeling about it. Mrs. Walker began talking about other girls who once lived there.

"Wilma and Elsie both had baby girls. Shelia had a baby boy. Elsie is pregnant again." I saw the disappointment in her face when she mentioned Elsie.

"I don't understand why you young girls are having babies."

I let Mrs. Walker vent about everything from her former foster girls to her ex-husband, Dewitt.

"I did everything for that man," she said. "And he left me for another woman in the church. Those so called sisters in the church will snap your man up just like that!" I watched her snap her fingers and noticed her hands were shaky.

I nodded my head and listened.

Finally Mrs. Walker looked at me. "I know you want something," she said. I was going to protest, but I thought it was as good a time as any to ask her.

"I want to come back here to live with you," I blurted out.

Mrs. Walker looked as if I had just cursed her out. Her fat head began shaking from side to side.

"No, I am not going to take in any more foster children."

"But, Mrs. Walker if you don't let me come live with you they will take my baby away from me."

Her head was bent and her eyes were closed like she was praying.

I kept talking to her. I told her about the social worker wanting me to give my baby up for adoption.

"It's the only thing I have," I told her.

When she opened her eyes she stared right at me.

"You are barely sixteen years old. How do you expect to take care of a baby?"

I stood up.

"I am not going to let them take my baby. I will runaway

417

if I have to and never come back here again. All I'm asking for is a chance to keep my baby."

Mrs. Walker knew I was serious when she looked into my face. Tears were stinging my eyes and a part of me felt like dropping to my knees. Mrs. Walker was my last hope to keep my baby and I needed her to say yes.

"I've closed down my foster home and I don't have a license anymore."

I stared at her, pleading with my eyes.

Finally she said those magic words.

"Okay, you can come live with me."

I jumped for joy and kissed one of her fat cheeks.

"I don't know why I'm doing this," she fussed.

It took the social worker two weeks before I could move back in with Mrs. Walker.

Chapter Twenty-One

Back with Mrs. Walker

I moved in with Mrs. Walker and she allowed me to sleep in the bedroom downstairs next to her bedroom. I didn't stay at home much and Mrs. Walker didn't seem to care because she was drunk most of the time.

"What damage could you possibly do now?" she would remark.

Mrs. Walker had turned the upstairs into a boarding house. She rented the rooms out and everyone shared the single bathroom in the hall. There were several borders coming in and out of the upstairs rooms. A young boy who claimed to be a college student befriended Mrs. Walker, but I never trusted him. She liked him and said he was good company for her. Once I came home and found him downstairs. He claimed he was helping Mrs. Walker get into bed, but I was suspicious of him because she was passed out on the bed with her dress pulled up and she didn't have on any panties. Her legs were wide open. Mrs. Walker wore a lot of thin gowns, but I had never seen her butt naked. She reeked of alcohol so I knew she had been drinking. An empty bottle of Johnny Walker Red was on the nearby nightstand. I made him leave and pulled the covers over her.

I spent most of my time with Lonnie, but he was getting more paranoid about me being over his place. We were watching TV one night when we heard banging on the door.

"Stay here," he said.

I sat on the couch while he went through the kitchen to open the door.

"Get away from here!" I heard him say.

"I know she's in there," a woman's voice answered. I peeked in the kitchen and saw Lonnie pushing to keep someone from coming in through the door.

"Let me in," the woman said.

"Get the hell away from here,"

I saw him struggle with someone on the outside of the door.

"I know you have her in there," she screamed after he successfully shut the door in her face. "I'm going to kick her ass." He was leaning against the door when I walked into the kitchen. I didn't say anything.

"I am going to call the police and tell them you have an underage girl in there".

Sweat was pouring off of Lonnie's face and he was breathing hard. I stood there looking at him.

"It's okay," he said. "Go sit back down." My stomach was a round ball by now. I rubbed it and walked back into the living room. The next banging we heard on the door was louder.

"Open up, Police." Lonnie ran into the living room.

"Hide behind the couch and stay quiet," he said.

I heard the door open and Lonnie talking with the police.

"That woman is crazy," he told them. "I don't want her around my house. I won't let her in so she's making up stories."

"You need to go in there and search," the woman screamed. "I know she's in there and she's only about fifteen or sixteen years old. He's a twenty-two year-old man."

"Do you mind if we look around?"

"No, come on in."

I held my breath as footsteps walked through the house. They were in the living room now. I was relieved when I heard them walk back to the kitchen.

"Sorry to have disturbed you. We will talk to her outside and if she disturbs you again we will take her in."

"Thanks," Lonnie said.

The woman didn't return, but it was a long, restless night.

Mrs. Walker and I had some heated disagreements. I didn't want to stay home and she didn't want me going and coming as I pleased. I usually waited until she passed out from drinking and left the house anyway. I was getting up to go to the bathroom one night when I saw her. She was standing near her dresser with the bottle in her hand. I watched her turn up a full quart of Johnny walker and drink from it. She wiped her lips with the back of her hand. She was already drunk and could barely stand up. I hurried to the bathroom and crawled back into my bed.

I was always spending the night over Lonnie's apartment. He gave me money to buy food, but I didn't know how to cook. I made the mistake of telling Roy jr. where Lonnie lived and he showed up there early one Sunday morning to take me home after I had been gone for three days.

"Tell Joyce that I'm here to take her home," he told Lonnie when he opened the door.

I got dressed and left with Roy jr.

"You are not a grown woman," he said scolding me on the way back to Mrs. Walker's house. "I know you're going to have a baby, but you're still only a teenager. Mrs. Walker told me that you've been gone for a few days."

When I got home Mrs. Walker was there but she was drunk again. Roy jr. enjoyed the praise he got from her and left me there with her. I went to my room and closed the door.

By March I was five months pregnant and could feel some life because the baby was starting to move. Lonnie would put his hands on my belly and smile when he felt movement.

Lonnie started making excuses for me not to come to his apartment. I suspected that he was involved with someone else. He kept denying it. He had told me that he wasn't going to be home one evening, but I decided that I was going over to his place anyway. I wanted to see if he was with someone else. The memories of those days when girls were going in and out of his apartment flashed before me.

I was walking along Walnut Street when I saw Matthew. He was dressed in a nice suit and his sideburns were connected to a full beard now. I wanted to turn around but he saw me.

He stood in place as I walked towards him.

"Hi Matthew," I said, trying to sound normal.

"Hi Joyce." He smiled at me and I saw his eyes scan me from head to toe resting on the budge in the middle. I felt ashamed of being pregnant at that moment. I wished I could have hidden my stomach but it was too late.

"So, who is the father?"

I swallowed hard because suddenly my throat was dry.

"His name is Lonnie Johnson"

"Lonnie?"

I nodded.

I saw the look on his face.

"I know him and his brothers." Matthew shook his head. "How the hell did you get involved with him? Of all the guys in Milwaukee, you got involved with him?"

"He's not that bad!" I said.

"Joyce, he is older than me. He has to be at least twenty-one or twenty-two."

"He just turned twenty three."

"This is my pool hall," Matthew said, changing the subject. "I bought it about six months ago."

I looked up at the sign. I couldn't see inside the dark windows.

"Where are you living?"

"I'm living back with Mrs. Walker."

"Can I visit you there?"

"I'm sure she won't have a fit now if you do."

"Where are you going?"

"To my uncle's tavern on Vilet Street."

"Do you want me to walk with you there?"

I shook my head. "It's only two more blocks".

"Take my phone number," he handed me a piece of paper. "Call me if you need anything."

"Okay." I took the paper and put it in the small purse I had. I wrote down Mrs. Walker's phone number and address and gave it to him.

"I'll be in touch," he promised.

I walked down Walnut to twelfth and turned. It was good to see Matthew again, but I couldn't shake that feeling of embarrassment about being pregnant.

Lonnie's car was gone and when I knocked on his door I didn't get an answer. I walked to his mother's house around the corner. She was sitting in a chair near the door talking with an old man they called Cowboy.

"Hi, Miss Hattie," I said when I got closer. She smiled at me showing several missing teeth.

"That's my son's woman, and she is carrying my grandchild," she said to Cowboy.

The old man smiled at me.

Lonnie's oldest brother, Shirley, interrupted us. He lived with Miss Hattie. I didn't like him because all he did was get drunk and beat women. He didn't have a job so he never had money. I suspected that he didn't like me either.

"What you doing over here?" he asked me with a mean look on his face.

"She can come over here any time she wants," Miss Hattie

shouted.

"Lonnie ain't here so she doesn't need to be over here either."

"Leave her alone, Shirley."

He glared at me before disappearing into the back room.

"You got any money?" Miss Hattie asked me.

I did have a few dollars. I pulled out the money I had stuffed in my pocket.

A wide smile came across her face. "Go buy me a six-pack of beer," she said.

"Is that gal old enough to buy beer?" Cowboy was looking me up and down.

"Hell, yeah," she answered. "She's eighteen or nineteen years old."

"Go get some Pabst," she said.

I hurried down the stairs and walked towards my uncle's tavern. I knew that if I told him I was buying it for her he would sell it to me.

Ike's tavern was crowded that evening. The jukebox was already spinning records and people were drinking. I made my way through the crowd to the bar. I didn't see Ike but a cousin was behind the bar. I remembered when my cousin, Football use to be a bartender. He wasn't old enough to even be in a bar but he knew how to serve drinks.

Anyway, one day Football opened a bottle of beer that exploded in his face. He survived but an eye. The beer company paid out a good settlement to him.

"Lonnie Ford was the youngest of Uncle Guy Lee's children by his first wife Mag. He was behind the bar. "I need to buy Miss Hattie a six-pack of beer," I whispered to him. Miss Hattie was happy when I returned with the six-pack of beer. She gave Cowboy one, and after taking one for herself, hid the rest from Shirley. I sat on the porch listening to the old couple argue. Miss Hattie drank the other beers by herself and by the time the sun started going down she was drunk. Cowboy went to his apartment next door leaving the two of us.

"That Lonnie is a lowdown dirty dog," she said to me. "I don't know why you put up with him." I didn't respond. "He isn't gone nowhere. He's in that apartment with another woman." I felt like I couldn't breathe. "His car is parked two blocks down from the house. He is hiding it from you." Miss Hattie looked at me.

"Come on," she said. I followed her through the house. She stumbled a few times, but stayed on her feet.

She showed me a key. "We are going over to his apartment. I can get in with this key."

I followed Miss Hattie to Lonnie's apartment. It was dark and didn't look like anyone was home. If Lonnie were home he would have the lights on. Miss Hattie slipped the key into the lock. I sucked in my breath when the door opened.

"Lonnie! She shouted as she walked inside. I slipped inside the apartment. Miss Hattie turned on the light and the kitchen became so bright I had to close my eyes. I heard a noise and Lonnie came running into the kitchen. He was wearing only his underwear. The look on his face when he saw me standing there was clear that he was surprised to see me.

"Mama, why did you bring her here?" He was looking at his mother and I rushed past him to the bedroom. I wanted to see who she was. Lonnie ran after me but not before I flicked the light on. I didn't know what to make of what I saw. There were two women in the bed. They both stared at me and didn't bother covering themselves up.

"What is going on?" I asked Lonnie. The tears were falling because I couldn't help myself.

"Come on," he said to me, dragging me towards the door.

"You a low down dirty son of a bitch," Miss Hattie yelled in her drunken voice. "I brought her here so she could see for herself."

Lonnie managed to push both of us out the door. "I know

you don't understand, but I'm making money. These women pay me to do this. I'm going to get a couple of hundred dollars from these ladies. I tell you what; I'll give you at least half to buy stuff for the baby."

I couldn't stop crying. What was he talking about? I knew girls were prostitutes, but men?

My head was still swimming when Lonnie called me the next day.

"We have to talk," he said. He came to Mrs. Walker's house and I went to the car to meet him.

"I'm sorry you walked into what was going on last night."

I stared out the windshield.

"I'm going to have to do something that you're not going to like." He pulled me close to him. "I'm moving in with another woman. I have to establish a relationship with someone else. I know you probably won't understand, but that is the way it is going to have to be. I will still be with you and I will be there for the baby.

"Who is this woman?"

"Her name is Marion and she works for the telephone company and she has two kids."

I couldn't respond so I sat there listening.

"She was the one at the door that night and called the police on me." He held me tighter and I cried harder. "I'm not going anywhere and I still love you."

Lonnie moved in with her, but he came to see me almost every day. I was jealous of him living with her, but I accepted it.

Matthew showed up at Mrs. Walker's one day with candy, fruit. I didn't know if I was having a girl or boy, so Matthew bought a lot of yellow and light green clothes. Every time Matthew came to visit he brought something for the baby and me. I started feeling comfortable being around Matthew again Matthew didn't talk about Lonnie, but I knew he didn't like me being involved with him.

Mrs. Walker and I weren't getting along because I felt like our roles were reversed. I was the one making sure that she was taken care of.

When I was six months pregnant, Mrs. Walker made me move upstairs to one of the border rooms. I didn't feel safe around the strange men who rented the rooms, so Lonnie stayed with me until I fell asleep at night. I was in my seventh month when Matthew took me to see James Brown in concert. I had never been to a concert. I felt people staring at me but Matthew didn't pay any attention to them.

"I'm not ashamed to be with you, so don't worry what other people think," he told me.

Mrs. Walker talked all week about the church picnic. She was cooking the greens. If there was one thing that Mrs. Walker could cook, it was greens. My mouth watered in anticipation of eating Mrs. Walker's greens.

I didn't like her church or the people who went there. Her Pastor came over to the house for a visit. He was a short, middle-aged man with an ugly smile. I was sitting in a chair in the living room.

"When are you coming to church?" He asked me. I shrugged my shoulders. It had been a long time since I had attended church and I had no desire to do it now.

He licked his nasty lips and smiled at me.

"I like young girls like you. It doesn't bother me that you're pregnant either. In fact that turns me on even more." I looked at the man in disbelief. He was supposed to be a preacher. I couldn't believe he had said what I just heard.   "If you want I can come back when you're by yourself," he said, winking at me.

The thought of being around him made me sick. I hurried out of the room, rushing past Mrs. Walker who was coming back with something to give the preacher.

I knew if I told Mrs. Walker what he said she wouldn't

believe me.

Roy jr. came to visit me towards the end of April at Mrs. Walker's house.

"Your grandmother Irene has passed away."

I stared blankly at him. I didn't feel anything at all.

"Jerry, Joe, Stephen, Henry, Ralph, and I are going to the funeral. I know you're in no condition to travel so I won't ask you to come along." I was almost seven months pregnant. She had stopped writing me years before. I thought about her once in a while, but it didn't bother me anymore.

"That's too bad she's dead," I finally said when I could speak.

Sana's baby was born the middle of May so I went by Big Mama's house to see him. He was a big baby with a round face. Annette was also pregnant and expecting her baby by the end of summer.

Memorial Day was on a Sunday that year. I woke up at five o'clock in the morning with stabbing pains in my lower back. I didn't want to wake Mrs. Walker up so I waited until I heard some movement, about 7:00am. Mrs. Walker locked her door at night so I had to wait until the next morning to talk to her.

"I'm having some kind of pain," I told Mrs. Walker.

Her eyes rolled upward and she shook her head.

"You probably got gas," she said. "I know you aren't going to have that baby today. You're not due until July fourth and you are not going to ruin the Memorial Day picnic I've been working on."

"Okay," I said weakly, and walked back upstairs to my room.

The pain didn't go away and as another hour passed by I returned to the kitchen where Mrs. Walker was stirring the greens she had cooked. Another woman had come over and was helping with some other things.

"I'm still hurting," I told her.

"Call your brother and see if he will come get you," she said.

I stood in the kitchen a few minutes watching while she and the other lady continued to prepare the food.

A pain hit me hard when I sat in the chair to make the phone call. I didn't know what to do.

I called Roy jr.

"What is it?" he asked.

"I think I'm in labor, I'm having some pains."

"Here," he said, giving the phone to his wife.

"What's going on?" she asked.

"I think I'm in labor, I'm having pains and I've had them since about five this morning."

"How bad are they?" she asked.

"They seemed to be getting worse," I said.

"How far apart are they?"

I hadn't timed them. "I don't know."

"Time your pains and call me back," she said.

I hung up the phone just as another pain hit me. I looked at the clock and watched it until the pain subsided and I waited for the next one. About fifteen minutes later another pain hit.

I called Roy jr. again and told his wife the pains were fifteen minutes apart.

"You're in labor," she said.

I told Mrs. Walker my pains were fifteen minutes apart.

"Call your brother back and tell him to take you to the hospital. I don't have time to take you today."

I called Roy jr. again.

"I'll be there to pick you up," he promised.

I packed everything I needed for the hospital and sat in the chair watching the clock and wincing with every pain.

The pains started getting worse and I began crying. Mrs. Walker started cussing. It was clear that she was upset about me being in labor. I knew she was drinking when she disappeared behind her bedroom door.

"Why did this have to happen today?" she asked her friend.

"Did you call your brother?"

I nodded my head because a pain was just starting and I couldn't talk.

I called Roy jr. several more times, but got no answer. The time seemed to move quickly and it wasn't long before Mrs. Walker had to leave.

"I can't leave you here," she said to me. "Will you drop her off at the hospital?" She asked her friend.

I tried to remain calm during the ride to the hospital.

Mrs. Walker and her friend were talking about my untimely labor.

There were no other cars in front of Saint Mary's hospital when they dropped me off. I climbed out of the car with my small overnight bag in my hand. "I don't think she's in labor," Mrs. Walker said. We can drop her off so they can check her out and come back later."

"I will check on you later," Mrs. Walker said before they sped off to the church picnic leaving me standing near the curb.

Another pain hit just as I started walking towards the door. I walked to the information counter.

"I'm in labor," I told the woman sitting behind the counter. She looked up and stared at me.

"Have a seat," she said, looking at me as if her eyes were glued to me. I was grateful when someone showed up with a wheelchair.

"How old are you?"

"Sixteen."

"Where are your parents?"

I wanted to cry, but was determined not to. "I'm here alone."

I was sitting in the chair across from the receptionist

listening to her talk to another woman about my situation. They were trying to decide if I could check myself into the hospital because I was only sixteen years old.

They wanted to call someone to get permission to admit me. Mrs. Walker was at the church picnic so I didn't know whom to call because Roy jr. wasn't answering his phone anymore. He lied about picking me up and I had made one last attempt to call him before we left the house, because I didn't want to ride with Mrs. Walker and her friend.

When I was finally wheeled into a room, I was thankful, but I was also afraid.

"You are in the early stages of labor," the nurse said. "You can watch TV and if you need something press this button." All the other women up there had someone with them. I kept hoping that Mrs. Walker would show up to be with me.

I turned on the TV and laughed at the episode of the Flintstones that was showing. Then the pains started getting worse. I cried out and pressed the button for the nurse to come.

"I want to leave," I told her trying to put my clothes back one. "The pains are really bad."

A doctor came in and checked me. "You haven't dilated enough," he said.

The pain was terrible and I wanted to get up.

"You need to stay here", the nurse said pulling me back into the bed. The tears wouldn't stop flowing and neither did the pain. I was afraid.

Every time I felt a pain I hit the button for a nurse and begged her not to leave me because I had no one there. I begged God to take me out of my misery. A woman passed my door and peeked in to see who was in the bed. My eyes were wide open, but all I could do was whimper. I was shaking from fright. The woman was obviously pregnant and wore a hospital gown. How could she get up and walk with so much pain I wondered.

The woman came into my room and stood over me. She

had a big smile on her face, but I could see beads of perspiration on her forehead. She took my hand and held it. I was shaking and the woman tried to keep my hand steady.

"I know you're afraid," she said. "This is my third baby so I guess you can say I'm an old pro." She laughed lightly and kept talking. "My pains started, but they stopped so I am walking around trying to get them started again so I can deliver this baby." I tried to smile at her, but instead I winced in pain.

"You look like you're just a baby yourself, how old are you?"

"Sixteen," I whispered, gripping the woman's hand because of the pain. The nurse came into the room.

"Is this girl here by herself?" She was whispering but I heard her.

"Yes," the nurse answered. My head seemed to spin and I couldn't hear anymore. I felt a tugging. They were checking me again.

"Your pains are five minutes apart and you haven't dilated in the past couple of hours."

The only response she got was a grunt. Over the next hours things got worse and the pain was so intense I couldn't keep silent and cried out loud.

Each nurse that came into the room I held onto until they peeled my hands away. I didn't want to be left alone, but they couldn't stay with me. I cried and cried and it seemed no one was hearing me.

A doctor finally came in and by that time everyone was surrounding me. They all had on green scrubs.

"I think she's ready," I heard someone say.

I grabbed the doctor's arm as they wheeled me into the surgery room.

"You have to let go of my arm," he said to me. I didn't want to let go of him but I did.

The room was cold and the bed they placed me on was

hard and cold. I could feel myself shiver in spite of everything else. I could hear them talking among themselves as if I wasn't even there.

"Is she here all by herself? the doctor asked.

"Where are the parents?"

"The front desk said she was dropped off by her foster mother."

"Well, she got herself into this mess," someone else said.

"That is no excuse for someone to drop a sixteen-year-old child off at the front door of a hospital and leave.

The voices began to fade a little and I paid attention to the persuasive voice that was telling me to push.

"Push, Joyce," I heard the doctor command. I tried to push and push. I was in a lot of pain and was screaming hysterically.

Then I saw something coming down to cover my face.

"Breathe deeply," I heard someone say.

That was the last thing I remembered.

I woke up groggy and tired. A nurse was checking my pulse. I looked up at her.

The pain no longer racked my body, but it was replaced by a soreness I felt in the lower part of my body. My legs felt as if they had been pulled in a vice.

"You had a little boy. He's a perfect five pounds, three ounces."

I wanted a girl badly, but when they brought me my tiny baby boy I fell in love.

"He's a little one," she said, "but he's very healthy. He's only little because he is six weeks early. You had a hard time so we gave you gas as soon as the baby's head was out."

I nodded.

"You're sore because we had to cut you and stitch you back up. This means you will have to soak every day. Would you like to feed your baby?" She asked handing me a bottle.

I put the bottle in his tiny mouth and to my surprise he

drank it all. She showed me how to burp him and when he let it out we both laughed.

I was the youngest patient on the ward so the other women helped me in and out of bed because I was sore. I was angry that Mrs. Walker hadn't even bothered to come see me. I called her every day anyway.

I called Lonnie's house and Marion answered the phone. She told me that she was pregnant and expecting her baby in December. She hung up on me but Lonnie called me later. He was too paranoid to come to the hospital to see the baby and said he would come to Mrs. Walker's house when I got home. I had planned to name my baby after Lonnie, but after I found out about Marion being pregnant I changed my mind and named him Doniel.

The other women in the hospital ward felt sorry for me because I was the only patient that didn't have any visitors. I expected Roy jr. to show up but he never did. The third day I was lying in bed watching TV when I heard someone call my name. I looked over and saw a smiling Joe. I knew Joe would always be there for me. Joe told me he would have been there earlier but he had just found out I was in the hospital. He went by Mrs. Walker's house to see me and she told him. He stayed with me until they made him leave. I spent a week in the hospital and Joe was my only visitor.

The day after I got home Matthew came by. He didn't know I had the baby and scolded me for not calling him. He returned two days later with a couple cases of milk and stacks of diapers. "If you ever need anything, call me," he said.

Mrs. Walker allowed me to move back downstairs with my baby. When Lonnie showed up a few days after I got home from the hospital she was confused. She had never met him and thought Matthew was my boyfriend and the baby's father. I was embarrassed when Mrs. Walker opened the door for Lonnie. She was drunk and walking around in a sheer gown that you could see through. She might as well have been walking around naked. I was embarrassed for her. I had already explained to Lonnie that she had a drinking problem.

"There's a young man here to see you, Joyce," she yelled. Mrs. Walker stood there looking from him to me.

"Who are you?"

"This is the baby's father," I said watching the look on her face change.

"This is the baby's father?" She stared at Lonnie who reached for the baby when I brought him out. He smiled when I handed him the baby. He said he loved us and I believed him. Mrs. Walker was making a lot of remarks to Lonnie who ignored her. Eventually she went into her room and didn't come back out until after he left.

"I like that other young man who comes by to see you. I thought he was your baby's father, especially when he showed up here with cases of milk and diapers for the baby. The one who just left here had the nerve to come see his baby and didn't bring a damn thing."

I felt the anger swelling in me and the more she talked the angrier I got.

"It's none of your damn business about Lonnie and me. I hadn't told Mrs. Walker or the social worker about Lonnie. The social worker was angry because I refused to give her the name of the baby's father. Mrs. Walker and I had so many disagreements about the baby that she moved me back upstairs. I didn't want to go back upstairs but at least Lonnie felt more comfortable coming to visit me when I was upstairs. He could come and leave without Mrs. Walker knowing he was there. He had just started putting a band together. The poster he showed me was magnificent. He reminded me of a young James Brown.

Mrs. Walker was getting worse with her drinking and cussing. She made it clear that she didn't want us living there anymore. The social worker had told me during her last visit that

I had to make some choices about the baby because we had to leave Mrs. Walker's house.

"We will put the baby in one foster home and you in another," she told me.

I knew I had to make the move if I wanted to keep my baby with me. The solution came late one evening when I was feeding my baby. I got Robert's phone number from Stephen and called him from a pay phone the next day. I held my baby close to me and poured my heart out to Robert. I tried not to cry but I couldn't help it. They wanted me to give my baby to strangers and I didn't want to.

"Do what is right for your baby," the social worker had said, hinting about adoption.

"They want to take my baby," I told Robert. "They said that we couldn't stay in Mrs. Walker's foster home any longer. Please let my baby and I come to Denver to live with you."

"You can come," Robert said.

The social worker was apprehensive when I told her about moving back to Denver.

"Weren't you living with him before and it didn't work out?"

"I was only twelve years old then," I told her.

"What if it doesn't work out this time?"

"I am responsible enough to be on my own." I didn't want to tell her that I had been taking care of myself anyway. Mrs. Walker wasn't doing anything for me, not even cooking food.

"We will check your brother out," she said.

The social worker and I flew to Denver in July when Doniel was six weeks old. I found out when I got there that Robert and his wife had separated. He was living in an apartment in East Denver near downtown. I spent a week there, which gave us a chance to catch up on things.

"I will get a two bedroom apartment," Robert told the social worker.

I stopped by to see Beverly who still lived in the same house with her parents. Everyone seemed happy to see me, so that felt good.

Dawna had a daughter who was a couple of years old.

"I'm glad Beverly hasn't had any babies," Mr. Tolliver said to me when he saw my baby. Beverly had already confided in me that she was almost five months pregnant and afraid to tell her parents.

I remember the day I was in the tavern when Ike asked me to come live with him and his wife, Sharon. I was a couple of months pregnant but I hadn't told anyone in my family yet. He had already talked to Joe, Sara and Ralph and they agreed to live with him.

"I rather live in a foster home", I told him. Ike looked at me as if he was angry.

"I am offering you a place to live", he said.

I shook my head. "I already have a place to live".

There was talk that Ike was struggling with his tavern and needed money. I no longer had the desire to live with any relative.

Ralph and Sara left Mrs. Guy's foster home. Sara was over eighteen so her choices were limited. She moved in with Ike and was barely there two weeks when someone from the tavern wondered upstairs to the apartment and tried to rape her. She then moved in with a girlfriend. Sara met Freddie Smith at a social and they got married a short time later. I went to visit her and her baby, who was born the second week of July after I got back from Denver. I met her husband and mother in law. Sara seemed to be happy.

It was September just before school started when the social worker told me that everything had been approved for me to leave. I didn't tell Matthew I was leaving Milwaukee because I didn't want to say goodbye to him. Bernice and Hose were still fighting and I felt sorry for her. I told her that I was leaving town.

In Years To Come

I told Lonnie that I was moving to Denver, but he acted as if he didn't believe me or maybe he did sense I was leaving because he spent the night with me. We slept with the baby between us and talked until we fell asleep. The next morning I told him I would keep in touch with him. He laughed at me and said I wasn't going to leave. I watched him pull away from the curb and burst into tears because I already missed him. I had packed everything and was ready when the social worker came to take me to the airport. Mrs. Walker had been drinking again, but we hugged each other.

Ralph kept in contact with Mr. and Mrs. Williams and attended their church while he was living with Mr. and Mrs. Guy. When he moved in with Ike his whole world changed. He started hanging out with pimps and hustlers. He was gambling, drinking and smoking cigarettes.

Joe moved in with Ike and started stealing radios and eight tracts out of cars. He was in the tavern one day when he got into an altercation with a guy who shot him in the butt. He had a good relationship with Roy jr.'s wife and she wanted him to come live with them. He was only there a few months before Roy jr. told him he had to move.

"I'm going into the military", Joe told me the last time I saw him. He was eighteen years old now. I was glad that Joe was getting out of Milwaukee too.

I called Mrs. Reed and told her about my baby who was three months old. I had planned to take the baby over so she could see him, but I didn't seem to have much time to do anything after he was born.

"I will come back so you can see my baby." I told her.

"Yes, I can't wait to see your baby. Please keep in touch."

The sisters who lived next door were sad to see me leave. They visited me more after the baby was born because Cheryl liked playing with him.

The only other call I made was to Sana.

438

"Make sure you call me," she said in a voice that told me she was crying.

"I'll call and you know I'll be back to visit. I know we were hoping our boys would grow up together, but I can't stay here."

"I understand," Sana said. I hoped she did. Annette had given birth to a little girl.

Finally, I was on the plane to Denver with my baby.

"No one will ever take you away," I whispered in his ear. He was a happy, healthy, baby and I loved and cherished him. In the back of my mind I believed that we were on our way to start a new life in Denver. I wasn't going to look back.

I was looking forward to my new life in Denver. I could see there was a chance that my friendship with Beverly could be renewed. I tried not to think about all the things that had happened to me because I wanted to forget.

The plane took off from Mitchell Field and I held tightly to my baby who was in my lap. After we were in the sky I peeped out the window to get a last glimpse of Milwaukee. I didn't know what it would be like living in Denver again but nothing mattered except that I had my baby with me and we were going to start a new life together.